CARIBBEAN AND
ATLANTIC DIASPORA DANCE

Caribbean and Atlantic Diaspora Dance

Igniting Citizenship

YVONNE DANIEL

UNIVERSITY OF ILLINOIS PRESS

Urbana, Chicago, and Springfield

Acknowledgments for previously published work
appear on pp. xiii–xiv, which constitute an extension
of the copyright page.

Opposite: Katherine Dunham and Yvonne Daniel,
Stanford University, 1989, by H. Douglas Daniel

Cataloging-in-Publication Data available
from the Library of Congress
ISBN 978-0-252-03653-8 (cloth : alk.)
ISBN 978-0-252-07826-2 (paper : alk.)
ISBN 978-0-252-09357-9 (ebook)

For a life dedicated to dance and for her lifelong creative efforts to reveal the beauty and citizenship of African Diaspora dance, this book is dedicated to Katherine Dunham.

CONTENTS

ILLUSTRATIONS

Photographs

Following page 92

Charts

ACKNOWLEDGMENTS

There is never enough space to thank everyone who has contributed to a comprehensive study; however, I want to give proper thanks to the generous co-workers who have supported my research as well as the writing of this book. My apologies for the lengthy list, but first, I thank my collaborator in the Carnival chapter of this volume, Catherine Evleshin—a dancer and researcher who has worked on the Caribbean for years and whose perspectives I share. I am forever grateful to those who read and reread parts of my manuscript: Drs. Sharon Arslanian, Susan Cashion, Julian Gerstin, Alice Horner, all anonymous reviewers, and especially those responsible for funding my research: the Ford Foundation, the Rockefeller Foundation, Smith College, the University of California at Berkeley, Mills College, and the Black Music Research Center in Chicago.

Respectfully, I have relied on the research of fellow Caribbeanists: Drs. Lorna McDaniel, Julian Gerstin, Martha Ellen Davis, Ken Bilby, Dominique Cyrille, Elizabeth McAlister, Gage Averill, Jocelyn Guilbault, Judith Bettleheim, and especially fellow dance specialists: Molly Ahye, Katrina Hazzard-Gordon, Sally Ness, Barbara Browning, and Anita Gonzalez, whom I thank for furthering what we know about the dancing body. Also, I thank those dance specialists who do not often publish their rich knowledge, but simply dance it: Jean Léon Destiné, Nia Love, Gabri Christa, Sonia "La Soso" Marc, Alfredo O'Farrill, Isaura Oliveira, Ana Pérez, Augusto Soledade, and Lourdes Tamayo. I thank the photographers who helped me, and this book, with their Diaspora research: Philippe Bourgade, Umi Vaughan, and Chester Higgins.

A special thanks is extended anthropologist Sheila Walker, who is one of the most learned Diaspora scholars of our time and who has published substantive, little-known findings and answered many questions that others could not in my pursuit of Diaspora understandings. Special thanks also are offered to dance history scholar Brenda Gottschild, whose work has always been central to my analyses.

I was assisted immeasurably by highly skilled librarians whose expertise supported my anthropological fieldwork with historical research, notably for chapter 3: Suzanne Flandreau of CBMR in Chicago, Shirley Lincoln of the Anton Adams Music Research Institute (AMRI) in St. Thomas, Anise Canton of the Humanities Council of St. Thomas, Lianne Leonora of the Curaçao National Library, Caroline Congeley of Trinidad's Heritage Library, Roberto Cassá and Julio Enrique del Campo of the Dominican National Archives, Dean Lizette Carrillo and Jazmin Castillo of the Center for Advanced Studies in Puerto Rico, Guinguan Gwenelle and Gustav Michau-Vige of Médiathéque in Basse Terre, Guadeloupe, and the staff of Shoelcher Library in Fort de France, Martinique.

Additionally, I give public thanks to Awilda Sterling-Duprey, Dr. Noel Allende-Goitía, Mágdalis García Sánchez, Doña Rafaela Brito Vda. Balladares, Jesús Cepeda Brenes, Gilda Hernández San Miguel, María Pérez-Wullert, the late Fredi Moreno—all of Puerto Rico; to Xiomarita Pérez, José Castillo, Nereyda and Senia Rodríguez, Edis Sanchez, Victor Camilo, Adrivel Ruiz, Ida Salusky—all of the Dominican Republic; to Philippe Bourgade, Christian Vallejo, Georges Defrel, and members of Wapa and AM4—all from Martinique; to Marie-Line Dahomay, Jacqui Jaleme, Allen Jean, Jean-José Ambroise, Didier Molza and family—all of Guadeloupe; to Jessel Murray, Mrs. Kate Austin, Janice and Joann McAuley, "Chalkdust," and the late Beryl McBurnie—all of Trinidad. For astute critiques in Curaçao, I thank Roxanne de Leeuw, Richard Doest, Astrid Duran, Jeanne Henríquez, Cesario Jean Louis, Dr. Rene Rosalia, and my driver Ricardo. For the U.S. Virgin Islands, I thank the St. Thomas Heritage dancers, the Mongo Niles Company, the St. Croix dance troupe and consultants Doreen Freeman, Rubina Leonard, Laurel Samuels, and Senator Shawn-Michael Malone.

For Cuba there are so many who have assisted my research that it is impossible to cite them fairly. Suffice it to say—I deeply thank the members of Conjunto Folklórico Nacional, Los Muñequitos de Matanzas, and Afro-Cuba for my foundation in Cuban dance, and I respectfully thank El Centro de la Música in Havana, La Casa del Caribe in Santiago and in Camagüey for unswerving research assistance. I am honored by Havana's Amparito Ramírez and family, Samuel Fernández and family, and the Herrera and Pérez families of Matanzas for my inclusion within their families.

For Haiti, I thank the manager of Castle d'Haiti in 1970, all in Madame's pension, dancers Odette Wilner and Viviane Gauthier, the Vodou communities that permitted my visits, and the Haitian soldier who saved my life in the airport, August 1991. I have been blessed for more than thirty years by the guidance of Katherine Dunham and Lavinia Williams Yarborough.

The Payne and Daniel families have made great sacrifices for me to have had this spectacular, investigative life, and I thank them again for their patience, especially my precious sons: Douglas, Kent, Terry, and Todd Daniel. From across the world, my adopted sisters and brothers: Pearl Lopez, Ilma Bartlow, Dr. Naima Lewis, Marion Girard, Jacqui Hairston, Dr. Gracinha Santana Rodrigué, Nadia Ravales, Dr. Adrianne Andrews, Marlene Li Aling, Dr. Linda Goodrich, Dr. Joan Burroughs, Margot, Jhon, Mamadi Victory, Papo Sterling, Richard Haley, Dr. Chip Maxwell, Van Vandenburg, Edward Murrell, Father Earl Neil, Lou Potter, Q. R. Hand, and Juan Vazquez—they all have made my life more pleasurable than most.

Finally, I thank Joan Catapano and the staff at University of Illinois Press for their continued support in guiding my books toward publication. For this book, especially, and for the wonderful editing experience I have read about and now finally have received, I thank Julie Gay, who made the process smooth and pleasurable.

I am grateful for the permissions granted to quote by the following presses, their Boards of Trustees, and individual authors:

Chapter 1: ABC/CLIO, New York, for "Dance in the African Diaspora: Courageous Performers" In *Encyclopedia of the African Diaspora* (2008), 2:356–66; *Guardian News & Media Ltd.* for "Vanishing Pointe: Where Are All the Great Female Choreographers?" and "Young Choreographers Defining Dance" In *Dance Magazine* (2009).

Chapter 2: Springer Science+Business Media, Dordrecht, The Netherlands, for "Dance and the African Diaspora" in *Encyclopedia of Diasporas: Immigrant and Refugee Cultures Around the World* (2004), 1: 347–56.

Chapter 3: Dr. Orlando Patterson for *Sociology of Slavery* (1969), 37; Cambridge University Press for *Africa and Africans in the Making of the Atlantic World, 1400–1800* (1998/1992), 8, 76, 163; University of New Mexico Press for *National Rhythms, African Roots: The Deep History of Latin American Popular Dance* (2004), 122–23; American Anthropology Association for "A Critical Analysis of Caribbean *Contredanse*," *Transforming Anthropology* 17(2):147–54; University of Illinois Press for "An Ethnographic Comparison of Caribbean Quadrilles," *Black Music Research Journal* 30(1):1–31; Yale University Press for *After Africa: Extracts from British Travel Accounts and Journals of the Seventeenth, Eighteenth, and*

Nineteenth Centuries . . . (1983), 301; and University of the West Indies Press for *Central Africa in the Caribbean: Transcending Time, Transforming Cultures* (2002), 151.

Chapter 4: Indiana University Press for *Rumba: Dance and Social Change in Contemporary Cuba* (1995), 26–44.

Chapter 5: Alfredo O'Farrill for electronic interview; University of Illinois Press for "Rumba Then and Now: *Quindembo*" in *Ballroom, Boogie, Shimmy Sham, Shake: A Social and Popular Dance Reader* (2009), 146–64.

Chapter 6: Yale University Press for *Domination and the Arts of Resistance* (1990), 165; University of California Press for *Rara! Vodou, Power, and Performance in Haiti and Its Diaspora* (2002), 60–1; University of Chicago Press for *A Day for the Hunter, A Day for the Prey* (1997), 154; and Catherine Evleshin for dance descriptions.

Chapter 7: University of Illinois Press for *Dancing Wisdom* (2005), 51–93; University of Florida Press for "*Sa Ka Ta Nou*," 236, and "Dominican Folk Dance," 136–37, in *Caribbean Dance from Abakuá to Zouk*; and Catherine Evleshin for unpublished material.

Chapter 8: *Esquire Magazine* for "*L'Ag'ya* of Martinique" (1939), 12(5):86.

Chapter 9: Tulika Books, New Delhi, India, for "Caribbean Performance and Cultural and Economic Globalization" in *Dance Transcending Borders* (2008), 155–81; *TransAfrica Forum Issue Brief* for "The Impact of Tourism in the Caribbean" (July 2000); Gabri Christa and Sonja Dumas for electronic interviews; and Free Press/Simon and Schuster for *Tyranny of the Majority: Fundamental Fairness in Representative Democracy* (1994), 4, 5, and 7.

PREFACE

Many lovers of the dance are engaged profoundly by African dance, and the aim of this book is to provide a thorough background for those interested in the Caribbean and Afro-Latin contributions to African Diaspora dance. My primary goals are to support teachers and beginning students in their Caribbean dance practice and to dialogue with Diaspora researchers and those audience members who are intensely struck by African Diaspora dance. All forms of dance can be engaging, but each has its special appeal, and viewers of dance profit from specific information for full understanding. My hope is for a solid foundation on which African Diaspora dance genres can be examined as representative culture of related peoples.

I join many American and British anthropologists in the use of "culture" as the determinant for the geographical territories I cover. My perspective is also consistent with recent efforts to reformulate "Africa" and its Diaspora cultures away from geopolitical boundaries. Consequently, I examine dance practices in the many locations that exhibit Diaspora culture, especially in the "Circum-Caribbean culture sphere." That sphere is part of the African Diaspora and includes the Caribbean islands and related mainland territories. At times, this area has included Louisiana, Georgia, Florida, North and South Carolina in the southern United States, coastal segments of Mexico and Central America, and parts of Colombia, Venezuela, and northeastern Brazil. It has consistently included Suriname, Guyana, and French Guiana in South America, and occasionally the sphere has been extended to the Rio Plata region of Uruguay and Argentina. Regardless of location, it is the entanglement of Europe and Africa in the historical practices of plantation economies that has produced a particular mix of peoples and thereby, a particular culture sphere.[1]

With no intent to either diminish constituent peoples or disturb any sense of individual or national identities, this book goes beyond conventional geopolitical boundaries to seek out common dance data. I limit my discussion of Latin America to those territories where the dances and ethnic histories resemble Caribbean dances and people—in other words, select parts of Afro-Latin America. I discuss a few dances from the Atlantic coast and omit many others, in addition to omitting the many related dances of the Pacific coast (for example, Afro-Peru). My main concern is shared dance culture within the reaches of a large but limited Atlantic/Circum-Caribbean cultural sphere.[2]

Accordingly, I expand the examination beyond the hegemony of English-speaking islands. Striving for a more representative view of African Diaspora dance culture, I attempt to move the view *of* the Caribbean from the United States or "the West" to the multilingual, plural perspective *from* the Caribbean and its related mainland sites, where several views must be considered.[3] The scope is huge and the data are not always even for each area. For example, I did no fieldwork in French Guiana, St. Lucia, or Dominica and, therefore, data on these important Circum-Caribbean sites are limited or excluded entirely.

Additionally, I analytically separate dance from music practices. This could be viewed as a violation to Caribbean and Diaspora dance and music, which are most often considered inseparable; however, studies of Caribbean-derived music have been numerous and sometimes misleading when it comes to dance. Caribbean and Diaspora dance studies have only amounted to a few, and these have mainly covered the theme of identity, but Diaspora dance comprises other equally important themes—for example, nationalism, globalism, tourism, agency, coloniality, continuity, resistance, change, etc. Focusing primarily on dance movement for at least this one study can yield intriguing and provocative information.

The result of my concerns and boundaries is an "Afrogenic"[4] investigation of dance genres, a broad but critical review of interrelated dance cultures that I have worked on. Differing from "Afrocentric," the term "Afrogenic" does not insist that African-derived cultures are at the center of concern. Rather, Afrogenic analyses insist on a comparison of Diaspora understandings. My focus on dance and bodily movement across each linguistic segment of the Caribbean and select Afro-Latin cultures balances the available music literature on the same sites with an anthropological and dance specialization perspective.

I began this book as I retired from teaching dance technique, as I completed a research project that surveyed several Caribbean islands, and just after the death of one of my professional foremothers, Katherine Dunham. As I mourned her passing and pondered the activity of my retirement years, I decided to expand some recent articles into a comprehensive text in her honor. My work has always been in the line of Katherine Dunham, a combination of dance and anthropology. Not only did I specialize in Dance Anthropology with her urgings (and those of Robert Thompson), but, more important, I specialized in Dunham dance technique and taught it for more than thirty years. My first fieldwork studies involved Ms. Dunham in Haiti in 1970 and 1974, and I was fortunate enough to have had three additional work periods with her: 1) during her Stanford University residency in 1989 in which I coordinated a symposium for Stanford's Bicentennial celebration of Dunham's contributions to dance and dance research, 2) during a Ford Foundation Fellowship in 1991 at her residence in East St. Louis when she was coming off of her politically-motivated fast for needed attention to Haiti, and 3) during her residency at the Smithsonian Folkways Festival on Maroons societies in 1992. In all cases, I interviewed Dunham privately and publicly, and discussed my research findings. Of course, my work has connected with the work of Ms. Dunham—on Haiti, the Caribbean, political consciousness of the "black experience" and consequently, this book relates frequently to her and her work—beyond its dedication. What have emerged are a testament to the excitement of Diaspora dances and a tribute to the life efforts of Katherine Dunham, the mother of Dance Anthropology and the foremost researcher of Caribbean dance forms.

My book provides only an acquaintance with Caribbean performers; it is more a study of dancing Diaspora cultures. For beginning dance students, each chapter reveals the importance of African-derived roots and their consequences for the entire region. For Diaspora researchers and nonspecialists, each chapter unfolds an interface of history, economics, and politics through dance practices. Chapter 1 seeks to quickly introduce some of the dance artists who have brought Caribbean dance into global view. Thereafter, it underscores the understandings that are closely associated with Diaspora dance forms. Chapter Two reviews the literature that relates to Diaspora dance. In combination, Chapters 1 and 2 provide a base for the study of Caribbean dance and outline the dance commonalities among the Caribbean, Afro-Latin America, Africa, and the Diaspora U.S.

The next four chapters cover the vast arena of social dance. Chapter 3 provides the histories behind all examined dance types, as it also unravels the attachment of African-descended populations to elite European court imitations or *quadrilles*. Chapter 4 examines social dances that display national dance formation and reveals how several dances rise to national status in one country, while other nations identify only one dance for centuries. Chapter 5 looks at popular dances that journey over time and across borders; it follows community *rumba* as it morphed into commercial *rhumba*. Chapter 6 looks at Carnival and other parade dancing that have brought Diaspora people together in festive merrymaking, albeit with pointed political critique.

Chapter 7 shifts the focus from social to sacred dance, a major source of Diaspora dance vocabulary. Unlike my previous writings on sacred dance, this is an overview of each linguistic area's sacred repertoires and it gives an explanation for the spirituality that sometimes erupts in social dance.

Chapter 8 reviews the martial art forms and stick-fighting dances that have peppered Circum-Caribbean history. It traces fighting forms on the African continent and documents Diaspora combat dances that are similar to better-known Brazilian *capoeira* and *maculelê*.

Chapter 9 mediates tourist and concert performance and places a wide lens on all dance genres. Caribbean tourism is central to a review of dance trends in the context of cultural and economic globalization. Suggestions are given for the well-being of Diaspora dance and dance artists, and dance analyses are advocated as an effective vehicle for socio-cultural understanding and socio-political efforts.

The conclusion offers culminating remarks in terms of the transcendence, resilience, and citizenship that reside within so much of Diaspora dance. The entire book casts a large net to gather specifics for Diaspora comparisons. My broad experiences and field research in the Spanish, French/Kreyol, English/Creole, Dutch, former Danish and Portuguese Circum-Caribbean are presented, leaving gaps for future scholars to attend, but hopefully with few important issues escaping through net openings.

CARIBBEAN AND
ATLANTIC DIASPORA DANCE

CHAPTER ONE

DIASPORA DANCE:
COURAGEOUS PERFORMERS

For Emmika of Suriname

Defining Dance, the African Diaspora, and the Caribbean

Throughout the human world, dance is powerful, nonverbal, expressive body communication. Almost everywhere, dance provides festive relaxation and connects movement and music making to things and events beyond entertainment, recreation, or creativity. Even though dance comes from the aesthetic domain of social life, it contains strong links to political, religious, and even economic domains. For example, dance can articulate politics in the spinning and breaking virtuosity of youths as they take charge of urban spaces after being ostracized elsewhere; it can articulate resistance within historically suppressed and marginalized religious rituals; and it can articulate economics at the core of tourist settings where critical financial gains are calculated within aesthetic displays. Dance is play, but not simply play. Across the African continent and in most sectors of its Diaspora, including the Caribbean, dance is that mode of communication often central to social life.[1]

Talented dancers perform and provoke movement responses in others. Participation in a dance event increases as seasoned specialists draw on the relationship between musical sound and bodily movement, and communicate in a multi-channeled manner to other performers and observers alike. As dancing and music making intensifies, so does a sense of group solidarity. It is a temporary condition that is regularly repeated to generate prolonged cohesiveness and to benefit the entire dancing group.

For Diaspora communities like those throughout the Circum-Caribbean culture sphere, the dancing body is almost inseparable from music, and dance and music together are esteemed aesthetic performance that has the capacity to symbolize the full range of human expression. Its after-effects leave a sense of individual centeredness, wholeness, and calm, group connectedness and well-being. As dancing provides physical, psychological, and aesthetic satisfaction, it releases stress and gives energy, spirit, and excitation. For many African descendants, it is a powerful mode of communication and a meaningful emotional resource.

Of course, not only African and Diaspora people are mesmerized by African dance performance. Many viewers of African and Caribbean dance transcend from the ordinary of social life to the extraordinary of unusual, often ecstatic experience. For example, audience members at an African, Diaspora, or Caribbean dance performance are usually transformed by the dance they witness into clapping, shouting, or rhythmically moving participants. As would-be spectators, they become enthralled by the exquisite bodily movement and lush rhythms of African-derived dance. They are stimulated aesthetically and engaged emotionally as performers seduce their attentiveness and stimulate even keener interest. Consequently, so-called spectators become participants as they travel the path of aesthetic transformation. The transcendent potential within Diaspora dance is important and will become clearer in our observations of specific dance types.

Chart 1. Caribbean/Diaspora Dance Typology

1. **Social and Popular Dances**
   A. *Contredanse*-Derived Dances
   B. African-Derived Drum/Dances
   C. Parading Dances
   D. National Dances
   E. Popular and Fad Dances

2. **Sacred Dances**
   A. Native American dance heritage
   B. European dance heritages
   C. African dance heritages
   D. Asian dance heritages

3. **Fighting/Combat Dances**
   A. Unarmed Dances
   B. Armed Dances

4. **Concert and Theatrical Performance**
   (Every type and form in the dance vocabulary of the region)

5. **Tourist Performance**
   (Every type and form in the dance vocabulary of the region)

Defining types of dance is somewhat difficult, since genres change over time.[2] For example, the *waltz* was a popular dance in nineteenth-century Europe and is still "popular" as a twenty-first-century ballroom specialty; however, it is hardly popular in dance halls, cabarets, and nightclubs. Accordingly, social dances are discussed throughout this volume as forms that have the intent to gather people for sociability and dancing. Social dance usually emphasizes couple dancing, but it can also include parading and group forms, which sometimes rise in skill level to professional, exhibition, or theatrical performance, like *tango*, *rumba*, or even *Vodou* dancing.

Popular dance is the prevalent dance of a given social group in a particular period. Both social and popular dance are contained by a time frame; however, Diaspora popular dance relies more on the contemporary choices of the young, and, more than social dance, opposes "high," "fine," and "classical" dance with their associated privileged audiences. Popular dance can engage local communities and spread across borders to become international phenomena like *salsa* and *merengue* have done. Popular dance that appears for a relatively short time (from one month to perhaps ten years) and then fades away is discussed here as *fad* dance—the *macarena*, for example. The remaining dance definitions in the skeletal charts are more easily and commonly accepted.

Early Culture Collision and Native Americans

In the Caribbean islands, enslaved Africans replaced native peoples of the region. Enslaved and (later) freed Africans performed what they remembered of African movement traditions in their plantation quarters or in secret, but they also learned and publicly performed the dances of European nations that came to dominate all island groupings. Both African and European forms of movement mingled within New World dance repertoires between the sixteenth to the eighteenth centuries, but by the nineteenth century, distinct dance creations and fresh styles came to identify particular linguistic groupings on the islands. Regardless of differences throughout the islands and related mainland territories, creative improvisation and polyrhythmic textures became characteristic of dance performance. African dance and music understandings survived efforts to destroy or marginalize "things African" within European hegemony.

By the twentieth century, Caribbean dance especially yielded foreign currency and economic profit in addition to aesthetic pleasure, recreation, or spiritual transcendence. Tourism had become the most important economic force in the Caribbean, since it was the only activity that gave the islands

Chart 2. American Colonial Heritages and African Dance

Free and Enslaved Native Americans	
Governing and Indentured European Colonists	
Enslaved and Free Africans	—West African Amalgam Dance Tradition
	—Central African Amalgam Dance Tradition
Free Creoles (European descended)	
Enslaved and Free Creoles (African descended)	
Indentured and Free Asians	

some advantage in competitive international trade and commercialization of dance came with tourism. At times, Caribbean nations were able to present intriguing representations of diverse regional culture, as they also increased much-needed profits from tourist-related industries. More so, however, Caribbean performers were subject to increased contact with black-market industries, prostitution, and crime and were threatened by increased exposure to HIV and AIDS. Additionally, island populations have always had to endure regional health hazards and ecological pressures that have intermittently challenged culture survival: hurricanes, earthquakes, flooding, drought, tropical parasitic infections, etc.

Because of courageous dancers and musicians who defied cultural pressures that would erase African legacies, several types of African movement styles echo across the Diaspora today. Also, because of persistent African-descended artists, African-derived dance practices have been introduced to the mainstream European, Asian, and American dance worlds. Knowledge of African-derived or Diaspora dance has spread by means of concert performances, DVD and CD recordings, both radio and television programming, internet access, and the growth of African American ritual communities; and African-derived dance continues to develop. The Caribbean islands in particular have harbored fascinating dance practices because of their strategic location between either Europe or Africa and the Americas.

Pivotal Performers

Caribbean Performers

Despite serious challenges within colonization and slavery, postcolonial marginalization, and more contemporary sun-sand-and-sex tourism, Caribbean performers have managed to guard African and European heritages, as well as Creole creativity. For Haiti, several distinguished artists have championed African Diaspora dance when most cultural representations were reflecting European models solely. Jean Léon Destiné came to fame in the mid-1940s as Haiti's first professional dancer and founder of the National Folklore Theater (1949). His depictions of Haitian folk characters and jumping over six-foot-high drums are legendary. Although he was trained as a journalist and singer, he has enjoyed a life of stellar dance performance and acclaimed teaching while based in New York.

Lavinia Williams Yarborough, a professional dancer from the United States, went to Haiti to take Destiné's place after his departure. As an acknowledged ballerina and principle dancer in Katherine Dunham's touring company, Yarborough's job was to train National Theater dancers in ballet and Dunham technique. Originally, she was supposed to stay for six months, but her positive influence on Haitian society, especially in guiding young female students toward productive lives, caused the government to request that she remain. For the next forty years, she studied all forms of Haitian dance and shared her command of the Haitian, European, and American dance repertoires with local and international students.

Another great Haitian dancer, Louinès Louinis, was recruited by Jean Léon Destiné for the Haitian National troupe because of his natural dance talents. Louinis danced professionally with Lavinia Yarborough and achieved national distinction before leaving Haiti to perform, choreograph, and teach. He continues to train students in Miami and New York within the distinctive clarity and phenomenal strength of Haitian folkloric dance.

Haitian dancer and choreographer Odette Wilner maintained a well-respected Haitian dance troupe for several decades and presented a variety of Haitian genres in local hotels starting in the 1970s. As well, dancer and teacher Viviane Gauthier trained middle class Haitians not only in ballet and modern dance techniques, but also in Haitian folkloric dance.

The most recognized promoter of Haitian dance, however, was Katherine Dunham, an African American who used what she learned in anthropological research among Haitians, including the Vodou community of the late 1930s, to develop a dance technique. Dunham technique was used to execute her original choreographies on stage and also for training those not born to or familiar with African-based dance.

The dancers named above presented African-derived dance heritage as it evolved in Haiti, the first "black" or African and slave-less Republic in the Americas. These dancers defied societal standards and cultural biases of their times in order to present, preserve, and elaborate African heritage.

Their professional descendants in Haiti and across the Diaspora are numerous: Mona Estimé Amira, Blanche Brown, Joan Burroughs, Elizabeth Chin, Nadia Dieudonné, Colette Eloi, Peniel Guerrier, Julio Jean, Micheline Pierre, Judith Samuels, Serge St. Juste, and literally hundreds more.

Elsewhere in the French/Kreyol-speaking Caribbean, dancers have not been able to hold onto their African heritage as easily as Haitians. For example, Martinique and Guadeloupe are still in a colonial relationship as Departments of the French government and consequently receive immeasurable French cultural input that has historically minimized African legacies in favor of French history and culture. Some Martinicans perform a historical *quadrille* known as *bele* as a symbol of their African and European heritages and some Guadeloupeans perform their traditional drum/dance, called *gwoka* or *lewoz,* to express Afro-Caribbean identity. Many French Caribbeans look to the directors of *bele* and *gwoka* organizations, such as Martinican La Soso, for artistic as well as sociopolitical leadership, leadership that they believe conserves African culture linkages. Others, like Josiane Antourel and Josy Michalon on Martinique, and Léna Blou on Guadeloupe, use African heritage as seminal material for choreographic, concert, and technique development.

African style persists in the Spanish Caribbean through choreographies of well-respected Cuban, Puerto Rican, and Dominican dance specialists. Ramiro Guerra was the leader of a revolutionary dance movement in the 1950s that initiated the study of the Cuban body and resulted in *danza cubana,* a modern dance technique that adds the African roots of Cuban culture to Martha Graham and José Limón techniques. Guerra continues in the fore of Cuban dance with published and performed explorations of voluptuousness, sexuality, and gender through dance.[3]

Two U.S. Americans influenced Cuban dance during Guerra's early period: Elfrida Mahler and Lorna Burdsall, who specialized in Doris Humphrey, José Limón, and Graham techniques. Burdsall was part of Guerra's pivotal group in the development of *danza,* and many other choreographers have followed in the Cuban choreographic tradition, notably Eduardo Rivera, Teresa Gonzalez, Manolo Micler, Juan de Dios, to name a few. Each in his or her way (through folkloric dance, ballet, modern dance, or combinations of these) has brought to light the distinct Cuban-ness that resides in Cuban forms.

The late Sylvia del Villard almost single-handedly fostered the recognition of African dance in Puerto Rico, when it was more popular to identify with Spanish heritage only. She and two families who are noted for the dance *bomba,* the Ayalas and the Cepedas, have boosted Afro–Puerto Rican heritage into the

Caribbean dance repertoire, as well as into public discourse. More recently, Puerto Rican transnational identity and migration experiences have brought forward the crucial role that Puerto Ricans have played in the formation of *salsa,* a dance with Cuban roots that has gone global as "world dance."

In the Dominican Republic, the inevitable forces of change have caused African heritage to emerge after centuries of severe anti-African and anti-Haitian perspectives. Neyreda Rodrigues, like Sylvia del Villard in Puerto Rico, has used a Dunham-like model that validates African and Diaspora dance in segregated or prejudicial environments. These dancers have developed dance schools in addition to their companies, which are dedicated to the development of African-descended youths. Rodrigues' daughter, Senia, like other young twenty-first-century dance artists, works with impoverished communities in cooperative artistic productions that provide purpose and productivity for Dominican youths.

In the English/Creole Caribbean or the West Indies, few Caribbean dancers have been as articulate about African dance legacies and Diaspora elaborations as the late Rex Nettleford, former Minister of Culture and founder of the National Dance Theater of Jamaica. Nettleford's company continues to maintain island history, as well as present the issues of "black liberation" and social justice through staged choreographies and professional dance training programs. His company has made alliances throughout the Caribbean that have promoted a dance education program and strengthened positive images of Caribbean life on stage. For example, the company repeatedly engaged Eduardo Rivera of Cuba to mount his work on Jamaican performers, and before her death, the company routinely employed Lavinia Yarborough from Haiti to lead intensive dance workshops.

On Trinidad and Tobago, Beryl McBurnie, J. D. Elder, and Molly Ahye have formed the backbone of both professional dance performance and documented dance research for their two-island nation; however, Trinidad-born Geoffrey Holder and his wife, Carmen de Lavallade, have perhaps made a more global impact as Caribbean dance artists. Holder came to Broadway's attention in "House of Flowers" in 1963 with a distinctive bass voice, incredible dance technique, and success as a painter and art collector (which made him known in New York's art world as a "Caribbean Renaissance man"). De Lavallade has been acknowledged as a prima ballerina, having danced with the New York Metropolitan Opera Company, John Butler's Company, and in association with Alvin Ailey for several years. Additionally, she danced Caribbean forms in several of her husband's choreographies. Her exquisite dancing and striking beauty made her name stellar on the dance concert stage.

On Trinidad proper and working against strong British influence up through the mid-twentieth century, an influence which negated "things African," Beryl McBurnie's artistic leadership promoted local history and culture through "the Carib Theater." She and her professional disciples provided development models for the spread of African-based heritage. They supplied solid, creative legacies for generations of choreographers and teachers such as Cyril St. Lewis, Astor Johnson, Robert Johnson, Wilfred Mark, Hazel Franco, Sonja Dumas, and others.

In the Dutch islands, Diaspora dance and music still prevail despite colonial and postcolonial antagonisms. On Curaçao, for example, the struggle of Protestant antidance, antidrum, and anti-"black" biases has reopened public examination of *tambú* dance practice and its related religion. *Tambú* has become a resource for Curaçaoan poets, drummers, storytellers, as well as for dancers and martial art experts.

Among the former Danish islands—the U.S. Virgin Islands today—Diaspora dances energize cultural performance and historical investigation through African-derived social dance forms. Legendary *bamboula* specialist Ms. Clara in effect guarded and revealed African dance history through an array of drum/dance opportunities. Additionally, *quadrille* dance troupe leaders Bradley Christian, Carlos Woods, and Edwin Davis joined in those efforts and preserved *quadrille* repertories so that today, elders and children practice square, line, and circle dances and maintain differentiated styles that signal community dedication and individual pride over centuries. Conserving what is known, remembered, or imagined of African cultures has become important in the process of promoting Caribbean and other Diaspora cultures.

Thus, noted dance performers across the islands are not always theatrical or concert professionals, but are also identified specialists from varying dance genres. Many islands promote local performers in traditional dance practices and stage these regularly for community entertainment and as tourist attractions.

Mainland Circum-Caribbean Performers

Recognized promoters of African dance heritage in related mainland territories of the Caribbean are most prominently from Brazil: Marlene Silva in Rio (choreographer of 1958 film, *Orfeo Negro,* or "Black Orpheus"); "King" Raimundo dos Santos and his disciples Augusto Omolú, Luiz Badaró, and Rosangela Sylvestre in Bahia; with José Lorenzo and, more recently, Isaura Oliveira and Augusto Soledade as transnational Brazilians in the United States. Modern dancer Clyde Morgan is a U.S. American Brazilianist located in New York; another, Linda Yudin, heads *Viver Brazil* with Luiz Badaró (noted previously) in the most sought-after Brazilian dance company based in the States. These dancers are uniquely responsible for promoting Brazilian forms; they use Afro-Brazilian and modern concert dance techniques on the concert, community, and education stages to make Brazilian dance spectacle. Most aforementioned dancers were tutored in ballet and/ or modern dance, but they embraced the styles and movement vocabulary of Afro-Brazil to present under-represented Brazilian history and exciting New World/American culture through dance performance.

Also, *capoeira* masters (for example, Mestre Jojo Grande, Mestre Jojo Pequeno, Mestre Cobrinha, Mestre Acordeon, Jelon Veira, and others) have introduced thousands of students to the Afro-Brazilian martial art / dance / game with its inherent African-derived philosophies and cultural values. They too have influenced not only Brazilian and other Diaspora performance but also many international dance scenes, as they acknowledge, preserve, and promote African-based heritage.

Very often in the large nation states of the Circum-Caribbean and Afro–Latin America, the artistic community assumes family and governmental responsibilities when the government and the official Church (usually Roman Catholic) are not able to fulfill community needs. Many Brazilian dance groups—for example, the modern dance Grupo Corpo in Belo Horizonte and Balé Folclórico in Bahia—align themselves with sociopolitical projects. Similarly, dance artists in Columbia, Venezuela, Belize, and Uruguay specialize in and promote related Afro–Latin heritage in specific nonartistic productions. For example, Uruguayan dance artist Tomás Oliveira Chirimini and others work simultaneously in concert performances and community enrichment projects. Some are in the business of building homes for low-income families, assisting treatment programs for drug and alcohol addiction, and educating the impoverished about HIV and AIDS and other health issues—primarily through dance projects; others work with children in nutrition and enrichment programs. Again, the persistence and courage of African-descended artists have resulted in the acknowledgment of African dance legacies and the promotion of African-derived styles.

Continental African Performers in the Diaspora

With the independence of African nation-states after 1957, many African musicians, dancers, and scholars crossed the Atlantic Ocean to teach and perform in Diaspora schools, studios, and theaters. African dancers/musicians did not have to fight automatically for preservation of their heritages; they were received respectfully and have benefited from a more current interest in "things African."[4] For example, the Ladzepko brothers from Ghana and Zak Diouf from Senegal influenced California dance performance by their presence on tours, in teaching, and in extended family networks that still organize dance and music camps for intensive African dance training.

Similarly, Marie Basse-Wales, Ibrahim Camara, Hasan Kounta, and the late griot Djimo Kouyate brought dance and music expertise from ancient Mali Empire traditions (contemporary Senegal and Mali) to New York City and Washington, D.C. Additionally, Ladji Camara, Famadou Konate, and Sekou Sylla have concentrated on Guinean legacies in New York and across New England, and Sule Diop from the Gambia influenced New York and later the Atlanta area. The late Malonga Casquelourds from the Republic of the Congo became established in California and was honored across the United States as a formidable artistic director and performer, but also as one of the highest ranking and most influential dance teachers to impact the Diaspora U.S. Also, the late Nigerian music master Babatunde Olatunji was a major African voice who educated the Diaspora community and the international public about African music. Through his "world beat" emphases, he and many Diaspora musicians assisted the mélange of modern and traditional African music materials (along with John Coltrane, Yusef Lateef, Chief Bey, Nana Yao Dinizulu, and many others). To my knowledge, African dance masters have not stayed in contact with Caribbean dance teachers beyond occasional performance tours to the islands.

Today, dancers are relinking historical connections across Diaspora communities to the African continent. A unique generation of African choreographers is moving beyond the idea of "traditional Africa." Germaine Acogny Cree of Benin, Salia Sanou and Seydou Boro from Burkina Faso, Youssouf Kambassa from Guinea, Nii Yarty of Ghana, and Nora Chipaumare from Zimbabwe, just to name a few, are outspoken, creative artists who have shaped daring inter-Diaspora performance and have shown both the U.S. and Caribbean influence on African artists. The interplay of African and Diaspora dance materials is the result of more frequent engagement with the commonalities and distinctions that exist among African and Diaspora cultures. Contrasts and fusions are taking place on stage, across airwaves, and online—everywhere in the expanding world of technologically connected nations. A vast array of African and Diaspora dance aesthetics has been percolating during the first decade of the twenty-first century.

For all its successes, African-derived dance is threatened by two issues: the extent of interest in science, telecommunication, and microtechnologies, which are mesmerizing younger African generations who may not carry historical traditions forward, and a lingering bias against "things African," even on the continent. The latter is more acute and a consequence of worldwide European colonialism and postcolonial coloniality, the inferior/superior assumptions that are placed into cultural interactions and the residue of colonial exploitation. Opposition to and marginalization of African-derived cultures filter mainstream cultures, such that a worldwide racist potential or unequal reality has required persistence on the part of committed Diaspora artists. Promoters of African-derived dance in its own right have had to be strong and resilient.

Performers in the Diaspora U.S.

Similarly over time, African descendants in the United States have perceived African and Diaspora dance as either a reservoir of cultural pride and historic legacy or as a source of embarrassment and erasure. African dance elements, such as call-and-response form, flexed-and-readied body orientation, interdependency of movement and music-making, etc., have produced a great deal of African American creativity, which has influenced both "black" and "white" America.

Dancer Asadata Dafora, originally from Sierra Leone, is often cited as the first successful African dancer/choreographer on the U.S. American concert stage. After Dafora's huge success in 1934, however, segregated theaters in the United States did not include African dance or promote African dance masters. Improvements did not come until the 1960s, and then only because of enforced integrationist policies for the public domain, including theaters and schools. Enforcement of civil rights laws coincided with significant immigration from newly independent African nations, particularly musicians and dancers. However, expressed racism has affected and continues to affect performance opportunities for African and Diaspora dancers because the United States has never fully relinquished its Puritan views concerning the human body and the dancing body,[5] nor has it completely released latent biases against African styles of dance movement.

For centuries, rigid restrictions on dancing and music making in Judeo-Christian locales across the United States have inhibited the dancing body, curtailed remembrances of African dances, and negated African performance styles. Disregarding immense cultural pressures over time, some African Americans were able to release their bodies in dance and music in order to manifest spirit—on plantations, in rural praise-houses, and later in storefront urban churches. By the nineteenth century, U.S. African Americans had to protect their dance repertoire from extremists and critics through segregated performance spaces in family homes, within community performances, and through vaudeville and "chitlin' circuit" theaters for African American audiences only.[6]

In addition, U.S. African American dancers maintained their own dance training centers. "Black performance" prevailed in dance studios and community centers during the twentieth century. In fact, in 1998 Philadanco's Joan Myers Brown, Dayton Contemporary Dance Company's (DCDC) Jeraldyne Blunden, Dallas Black Dance Theater's Ann Williams, Denver's Cleo Parker Robinson, and Los Angeles's Lula Washington—all African American dancers/directors/teachers—were feted nationally for training and jointly contributing more than one thousand African American dance artists to national and international dance companies. And there are many others, such as Ruth Beckford and Deborah Vaughan in Oakland, California; Mary Lois Hudson Sweatt in Dallas; R'wanda Lewis in Los Angeles; and Elma Lewis and De Ama Battle in Boston, all of whom kept African and Diaspora dance in the fore of community activity for more than five decades. The dance companies and schools—and dance itself, by extension—supported local African-descended communities by keeping adults in honest and regular employment, children off the streets, and youths out of prison.[7]

Most senior Diaspora U.S. dance teachers and artists can trace their professional heritage to either of two African American dancers/researchers/community educators. Katherine Dunham was mentioned previously in terms of her contribution to Haiti, but in the United States, she was one of the most acknowledged choreographers for stage and film in the 1930s and 1940s. The other choreographer, Pearl Primus, literally jumped onto the American concert stage in the 1950s as a brilliant soloist. Like Dunham, Primus encouraged learning about African heritage when people in the United States were even more mis-educated about the African continent than they are now. Both Dunham and Primus infused the then-new modern dance with images from a segregated United States. They paved the way for thousands of talented African American dancers and choreographers, like Talley Beatty, Janet Collins, Chuck Davis, Bill T. Jones, Donald McKayle, Charles Moore, Eleo Palmare, and hundreds more.[8]

In an unsolicited fashion, Joe Nash, a Katherine Dunham dancer who became a dance historian, kept track of African American dancers and their ephemeral art form for decades. Nash took stock of early-twentieth-century performances by African Americans in a personal archive at a time when established dance critics routinely neglected African American performance. African American griot Dianne McIntyre and Dayton Contemporary Dance Company's Jeraldyne Blunden worked similarly by archiving and performing the repertoires of African American choreographers. Eventually, the

Dance Division of the New York Public Library catalogued the informative historical collections of Joe Nash and others, collated the records of performers and performances, and inserted the documented achievements of African-descended dancers and choreographers within the largest collection of dance and dance-related materials in the world. It was choreographer Alvin Ailey, however, whose successes in the 1960s exploded worldwide and made African American dance the dance emblem of the United States. Through Ailey's exquisite choreographies and phenomenal company of dancers, dance enthusiasts around the globe came to believe that the best dance in the United States looked liked what the Ailey Company performed, which was Diaspora dance or modern concert dance infused with African Diaspora movement values and stylistic choices.

Particularly since the 1970s, Diaspora dance has skyrocketed across the world via public dance clubs, television, and more recently the Internet, often combining body movements and musical rhythms from the United States and the Caribbean. Computerized technology has permitted international youths to jam to rap songs and spoken word, and to assume Diaspora body gestures in *hip-hop* and other dance-related culture. These elements have come to define a major portion of popular culture—from dance and music to fashion and language. Tap dance in the United States has been entwined with modern concert dance; break dance has been on stage with ballet and was a television mainstay in the late twentieth century; Caribbean and African traditional materials are being fused to European and North American as well as Diaspora concert dance; and a Diaspora movement vocabulary dominates mainstream dance on videos, films, and dance floors.

Such a penetration of culture is viewed by many Caribbean specialists as the "transculturation" of Diaspora forms and forces authenticity, appropriation, and globalization to loom large as provocative issues.[9] Thus, dancers and musicians, not only from each Caribbean island, but also from across the mainland territories on both sides of the Atlantic Ocean, are responsible for the continuity of African-based dance. These specialists make virtuoso displays that encourage African dance heritages. The persistence of such courageous performers has made possible the rich array of dances found throughout the Diaspora (listed in chart 1).

Primary Understandings within Diaspora Dance

Beyond actual movement, there are important assumptions that accompany dance performance. For example, in African-derived communities, there is substantial reliance on what happens within the dancing body as it performs, and there is overt response to emotive messages that the body relays during performance. Additionally, there is respect for musicians and their interdependence with dancers; consequently, live joint performance is a standard, and regard is given to both musical and danced detail. Also, there is relative agreement about what "fine form" is, how dance develops appropriately, and what, for example, is considered "sacred" in performance.

Dance in Diaspora cultures is kinesthetic, but also visual, aural, oral, physical, and cognitive. Knowledge of African-derived dance and music has been stored in the ancient archives of the dancing body and only recently in articles, books, and visual materials. Musicians and dancers have been the major archivists of Diaspora dance and (as I have coined elsewhere) these "experiential librarians" have guarded sound and movement traditions across the Diaspora. African-derived communities have relied on the "body knowledge" within "living libraries" for centuries, in order to maintain values and transmit customary dance and music practices. Dancers have been able to "get into" or bodily examine Diaspora dance practices and then match in repeated performance what they have found within music making and spirited dancing. Dance and music provide continuous learning and are a resource for many kinds of knowing. Accordingly, dancers and musicians have conserved a literal body of African Diaspora knowledge.[10]

Several scholars have posited definitions of African-derived dance. Historian of African art Robert Thompson recognized the influence of dance movement on the many peoples and vast geography he surveyed for visual art on the continent in *African Art in Motion*. Dance Artist/Scholar Kariamu Welsh-Asante augmented this definition with similar content but distinct vocabulary in "Commonalities in African Dance: A Foundation for African Dance."[11] Later, dance artist and dance historian Brenda Gottschild used Thompson's classification of dance elements to make comparisons within theatrical practices of the United States in her book, *Digging the Africanist Presence in American Performance: Dance and Other Contexts*. The perspectives and terms of Thompson, Welsh-Asante, and Gottschild are immediately applicable across the Diaspora.

Despite the extreme expanse of more than fifty countries on the continent, the twenty-eight habitable Caribbean islands, and the more than one dozen Latin American Atlantic countries, very similar movement preferences and tendencies (reflecting specific areas from which the majority of the Diaspora enslaved came) have coalesced into identifiable qualities within Diaspora performance. For example, Diaspora performers repeatedly rely most on soft or flexed knees, a gentle, forward-tilted back, polyrhythmic body-part articulation, and a cool or controlled approach within an extensive range of dynamics. They highlight movement that has an intimate relationship with music, visual art, history, and cosmology. A preponderance of such characteristic movement stabilizes dance patterns and music formations in the Caribbean and other Diaspora locales—from Canada to Uruguay, Argentina, and Chile, from Barbados to Hawaii.

Observation of dance practices across the Atlantic Diaspora has yielded similarity in dance structures. Similar preferences are demonstrated in: 1) circular group forms that involve alternating solo performers or duos who dance rhythmically in the center to percussion and vocal accompaniment; 2) linear set-group forms in which groups and/or groups of couples dance patterns to percussion, string, and wind instruments; 3) groups of couples in primarily closed (but also alternating open and closed) partner positions that feature torso division and body-part isolation while performing to percussion, string, wind, and brass instrumentation; and 4) couple dancing in closed, almost "pasted together" position. When grossly summarizing dance history over centuries, the data show that most often males and females dance separately in African and Diaspora dance practices, and where couple dancing is the requisite form, most often African-descended couples do not dance in consistently closed position. Rather, they dance together but intermittently apart. "Approach closely, retreat, and approach again" is the pervasive social dance pattern that echoes within each configuration, whether circle, square, line, or couple dancing. "Plastered" or "grinding" couple dancing has appeared as a common alternate pattern since the twentieth century.

On the continent and in the Diaspora, dance structure is contingent on rhythm or an order of repeated rhythms with supra-rhythmic display—in other words, established patterns with superimposed improvisation. Rhythm is not always restricted to music and can be found additionally within multiple body parts that, when examined carefully, yield simultaneous layered polyrhythms. Body part isolations in syncopated or accented rhythms are repeated extensively, making repetition a paramount characteristic also.

Repetition in African-derived performance intensifies bodily statements. Repeated dance sequences are contrasted with improvised movements, alternate timing, or development sections. Repeated sequences are esteemed by performers and community members, as well as by intrigued and knowing non-natives, for their anticipated qualitative resolution or the innovative change that results from captivating, incredulous, repetitive polyrhythms.

Explaining the spectacular movements—the polyrhythmic and accented body isolations, the continuously divided, pulsing or gyrating torso, and especially the connected purposes of nonverbal body communication—has always been a daunting task. African values about the body itself, about the inherent connections between the dancing body and very different arenas of interest, are distinct from other body values and dance definitions, such that cultural preferences and basic tendencies need to be made clear. For example, the opposition of secular and nonsecular dance performance is not as absolute as it is in European and North American cultures. In Caribbean and other Diaspora traditions, the same dance can be social in one event and sacred in another; the category of any group of dance steps is ambiguous until the context is scrutinized and determined.

What is of constant concern is the relationship between dance movement and African-based philosophies. Dance can relate to anything and everything as part of the totality of African-derived social life, but it also maintains a special relationship with spiritual practices. African Diaspora cultures use dance and music to pray; dance becomes a connection to "the Creator," the ancestors, or a pantheon of cosmic entities.[12] Thus, the entire context of Diaspora dances needs to be examined carefully before presuming that a given dance is either sacred or secular.

A sizeable portion of Diaspora dance involves the supra-human body since, historically, African dance and music spring from religious belief systems. The supra-human body is a human body that has been transformed by a spiritual incorporation. A common occurrence or thread across the Diaspora is for particular gestures, special rhythms, and vocal or percussive music to align the social community with the spiritual world. Throughout continental Africa and across the Caribbean, many religions involve dancing divinities that are masked or entranced worshipers who dance as divine beings. Similarly in the Diaspora U.S., Africanized versions of Protestant practice involve worshipers who pray and receive the Holy Spirit by congregational swaying, call and response singing, and spiritual "jumping for joy." In fact, much dancing in Diaspora cultures reveals legacies from hundreds of uprooted African ethnic groups that express belief in the corporeal inhabitance of spirit. African legacies presume that dancing and music making give relief from the sufferings inherent within social realities; African dance rituals provide energy, endurance, perseverance, and agency in the splendor of expressive body movement.

Consequences of Diaspora Performance

Caribbean and other Diaspora performers have followed the ground-breaking paths of the renowned dance leaders mentioned earlier and ancient others who have performed, taught, and thereby revealed the physical, psychological, creative, and political consequences of African and Diaspora dance. First, dancing sustains good physical health and psychological balance—important attributes to those in historical bondage or in economic impoverishment. Dancing also initiates vitality and expresses well-being—important attributes for human contentment or satisfaction. Such consequences of dance performance underscore the centrality of dance in African and Diaspora communities and the attraction of so many enthusiasts to African-derived dance.

Not only are there consequences of dance performance for dancers, but also for the dance practices. For example, *tap, rumba, reggae, samba, tango, bomba, zouk, salsa,* and *hip-hop* have affected the world beyond their African-descended creators and international performers. Most often, African and Diaspora dances have accomplished this through riveting excitation and creative participatory response. Also, African and Diaspora dances have been core to many non-African creative enterprises, producing fusions of all sorts.

Fusion is not unique to the African Diaspora or to dance practices. Katherine Dunham's technique and choreographies of the 1930s–1950s are fusions—most often of local Haitian and other Caribbean dances to U.S. modern concert dance. Also, Cuba's national concert dance company has presented fusion worldwide through *danza cubana,* a modern dance and Afro-Cuban dance aesthetic. Another dance fusion occurred at the international level in the 1970s when Puerto Rican contributions to both Cuban *son* dancing and U.S. Afro-Latin *jazz* music developed into and popularized *salsa.* For twenty-first century contemporary artists, however, fusion is emblematic of theoretical issues: identity formation, authenticity, hybridity, transculturation, appropriation, transnationalism, and globalization. Many young Diaspora dance artists are presenting concert work in the United States and abroad that fuses two "home bases." They examine transnational identities artistically and, in the process, forge fresh dance fusions.[13]

Some Diaspora performers, like the continental artists mentioned earlier, are not satisfied with the multicultural mixture of African and mainstream North American or European dance materials. They are involved in intra-Caribbean and inter-Diaspora combinations and possible fusions. Popular dancers especially have experimented by mixing U.S. *soul* and Trinidadian *calypso,* producing *soca* music and dance; Haitian *kadans* and Trinidadian *calypso* have become *cadence-lypso* in Dominica. Some of the most profound fusions to appear on stage have come from concert dance and jazz music; for example, saxophonist Antoine Roney and dancer Nia Love have united African and Diaspora music in refreshing proximity, but also continental and Diaspora dance, resulting in creative, hybrid dance formations.[14]

Beyond the positive physical, psychological, and creative consequences, Diaspora performances exhibit some unfortunate political realities. The Diaspora is still permeated with patriarchy, gender bias, and arts-industry politics. Local "old-boy" and even "old-girl" networks harness power and control the gates to presentations of Diaspora dance. Feminism, gender, and queer studies have only begun to raise consciousness against these biases within public understanding and among those who fund dance performance.[15] It often seems that female dance artists, while more numerous than and as prolific as male dance artists, still "pay the price" to a male-dominated international arts industry, with regard to Ron K. Brown, Bill T. Jones, Ralph Lemon, Mark Morris, Doug Verone, for example.[16] Writing in the U.K. *Guardian,* Judith Mackrell states: "Recent research in the U.S. showed that only 10 out of the top 59 dance companies were run by women. In 2000, a list of 18 grants awarded to modern choreographers by the National Endowment of the Arts featured just five women. Worse, the average size of each award amounted to $10,000 for men and just $5,000 for women."

Perhaps because there are generally fewer males than females in dance, male choreographers are encouraged or solicited and receive more support. For whatever reason, they are often disproportionately accorded the serious financial support that on the one hand comes as a result of public recognition of artistic excellence, but on the other hand is the foundation on which development of public recognition and deemed excellence are based. Regardless, women choreographers, but Diaspora women especially, need more support.

Most Diaspora dance performers struggle constantly to engage in dance as life work, and there are too many dance artists whose journeys and challenges have proven to be overwhelming.[17] In New York City, the heart of world performance, dance space is expensive and scarce, and Diaspora dancers have only a few spaces to develop technique, choreography, and artistry beyond the Alvin Ailey School and Dance Theatre of Harlem's conservatory-like spaces—the New Dance Group, Djoniba's, Boys' Harbor, and a few more private studios come to mind. Brilliant choreographies like Alvin Ailey's "Revelations," Garth Fagan's "Lion King," Jawole Zolar's "Praise House" or "Hair," Marlies Yearby's "Rent," or even stellar mélanges of dance, music, and theater in Les Ballets Africains of Guinea, Les Ballets Senegalais, or Folklórico Nacional de Cuba have all earned tremendous acclaim; however, these are the phenomenal exceptions of well-funded and successful African and Diaspora dance projects.

Regardless of the obstacles that patriarchy, sexism, and racism insert into Diaspora social life, African heritage continues. African-descended communities survive and African-descended performers thrive. As courageous and persistent Diaspora performers keep communities dancing, they endure marginalization and overcome erasures due to racism, religious biases, or fear of the body itself. They celebrate in dance and music making as their ancestors have done for centuries across world geography and multiple generations. Their fierce efforts fortify dance practices across the Diaspora as resilient and joyful body communication.

This chapter has explored the foundation of Diaspora dance and its relationship to African dance and music in anticipation of a comparison among related but distinct dance practices throughout the Circum-Caribbean culture sphere. Definitions and analyses of particular ways of moving and preferences for certain dance formations have been discussed within a brief introduction to exemplary Diaspora dancers. The next chapter continues to build foundational understanding of Diaspora dance culture with a shift from the dancer's perspective to a dance studies perspective.[18]

CHAPTER TWO

DIASPORA DANCE IN THE
HISTORY OF DANCE STUDIES

This chapter offers a substantive review of the research findings that have constituted a growing literature on African Diaspora dance and provides annotation of the many references discussed and cited in following chapters. It emphasizes a thorough grounding in Caribbean dance by reviewing the major Caribbean, Afro-Latin, Diaspora U.S., and African dance studies and acknowledges the beginnings of Diaspora dance studies with Katherine Dunham's publications on Caribbean dance.

Founders of Dance Anthropology
and Diaspora Dance Study

African Diaspora dance research began with three dancers who forged a specialization within the field of anthropology. That field examines the cultural contexts of dance performance and has been called dance anthropology, dance ethnology, choreology, and human movement studies, and it is included in performance studies. By any of these names, the approach has been the serious consideration of dance practices, not simply as universal human behaviors or as the exotic movements of a given society's members, but as a focus on body aesthetic displays whose analyses yield data from the social, political, religious, historical, and/or economic spheres. Beyond written studies, dance research includes films and videos, which have substantially augmented knowledge of continental and Diaspora dance.

Native American dance studies by anthropologist Franz Boas and his students at the turn of the twentieth century were probably the first formal dance studies of the Americas; however, their studies were integrated within the survey of many other culture items, as were those of anthropologist Zora

Neale Hurston. Two studies that focused solely on dance were published in 1928 by E. E. Evans-Pritchard and Margaret Mead and initiated documented dance case studies.[1] British anthropologist Evans-Pritchard analyzed an Azande beer dance from Central Africa in which the obvious instrumental and vocal music, as well as the gendered organization of a dance event, were linked significantly to social, religious, and economic concerns. On the surface, the social context of the Azande beer dance included festive dancing, music making, and the distribution of beer, but at deeper levels of analysis, Evans-Pritchard connected the dance to traditional religious beliefs and economic pursuits. The Azande believed in ancestral funeral pyres, and a labor force was needed to construct them. The festive atmosphere of a beer party guaranteed numbers of Azande relatives in attendance and thereby congenial moods for the ultimate demand of cooperative labor in making the pyres.[2]

American anthropologist Margaret Mead dedicated an entire chapter of her monograph on Samoan society to dance practices that influenced the social expectations of boys and girls and symbolized the distinctly gendered Samoan education system. During informal and nonceremonial dance events, young Samoan children were not treated with the rigorous subordination that they endured within ordinary life. Rather, they enjoyed family and village praise and received attentive support during dance performances. Children were either encouraged or coerced to dance publicly and thereby displayed their personalities during performance, either fearlessly or with substantial fear. Mead postulated that given the severe restrictions accorded Samoan children generally, improvised dancing permitted spontaneity and individual relief or produced tension and continued demands. Dance was a seminal tool for Samoan education.[3]

Evans-Pritchard's and Mead's studies were the first anthropological studies to suggest that beyond aesthetic descriptions and artistic critique, the study of dance was a fruitful sociological undertaking. In addition, Mead's film, *Trance and Dance in Bali* (filmed in the 1930s and released in 1952), examined dance performance and the trance state, as well as the dance symbols of good and evil, life and death.

(From here on, I recount the evolving American dance literature that influenced the Circum-Caribbean culture sphere. Generally, British dance literature focused on African countries more than on Diaspora sites, with the major exception being the British West Indies.)

Shortly following those contributions and working independently in the United States, Gertrude Kurath and Katherine Dunham became profoundly intrigued with dance research. They were both drawn to forms of African-related dance. Dunham examined Caribbean dance starting around 1934 or 1935 and Kurath began to examine African American dance in 1956 after extensive investigation of Native American dance starting just before 1946.[4] Most important, and unlike the case studies of Evans-Pritchard and Mead, Dunham and Kurath envisioned a broad field of cultural study that employed dance analysis. Dunham named the new perspective "Dance Anthropology" in correspondence with her advisor, renowned anthropologist Melville Herskovits,[5] as she prepared for fieldwork in 1936. Kurath proposed a similar view, called "Choreology," in *Cultural Anthropology,* "Panorama of Dance Ethnology," published in 1960.

Although neither received a terminal degree (PhD or MFA) in her special interest, both were trained researchers. Dunham studied anthropology at University of Chicago with Robert Redfield and at Northwestern University with Herskovits. Kurath studied art history and music at Bryn Mawr with Ernst Diez and theater at Yale University. Their ongoing research interests echoed the major themes of early anthropology/sociology. Their long lives reflected the successes, rigors, biases, and constraints of their early academic efforts. Kurath died in 1992 at age eighty-six and Dunham died in 2006 just before her ninety-seventh birthday.[6]

Kurath has been acknowledged in a volume that celebrates her more than fifty years of dance investigation.[7] She became dedicated to dance research and publishing as a result of her abiding interest in performance and also due in part to her personal life circumstances. As a performer and choreographer, Kurath was engulfed by Isadora Duncan dance techniques and the Dalcroze method in music, which were most influential in her day. She organized a successful dance company and performed in it from 1932–46. Ultimately, she had to disband the company when, after her marriage, she followed her husband to Ann Arbor, where he was a professor at the University of Michigan. In those days, university statutes denied work to married couples at the same institution, and her husband had the official appointment.

Kurath was thereby placed in a research environment of libraries, college-wide lectures, and critical analyses at a time when she was thwarted in the further pursuit of artistic work. She spent her time feeding her ravenous intellectual curiosity by doing research while also carrying out her responsibilities of wife and mother. Of course, her multiple roles were bound by the restrictions on women in the early twentieth century, particularly on women in academe. It is amazing, therefore, that she produced the number and quality of articles and books that she did. It appears, however, that she had to rely on male co-authorship to get some of her findings published.[8]

Kurath first examined the contemporary concert dance of her time, but by 1946, she had become interested in the dance of other Americans. She was eager to carry out ethnographic research on eastern, plains, and Mexican Indians, and to publish her findings in academic journals. She was also practical and focused on the cultures that were nearest and most intriguing to her, turning to "Negro Dance" in Ann Arbor in 1952.[9] She operated primarily as a sociologically interested art historian, but equally in the vein of then-current cultural anthropologists.

Kurath's mind was ever alert. She read constantly over her lifetime and stayed in contact with other dance researchers like Joann Kealiinohomoku, Adrienne Kaeppler, Judith Hanna, Drid Williams, and Anya Royce. This contact kept her abreast of current trends and findings within the maturing subdiscipline. As time went on, she became the model dance researcher who gave presentations on dance studies and published in refereed journals.

Dunham, on the other hand, had other opportunities and other constraints.[10] She published *The Dance in Haiti,* her master's thesis, in 1947, ten years after the original fieldwork in Jamaica, Trinidad and Tobago, Martinique, and Haiti (1936–37). Her thesis may not have been emphasized in the training of later dance researchers because it was originally published in a Spanish journal, and she placed her early research into the technical training of the body and the development of dance curricula that included language and cultural studies. She utilized her research most prominently within studio offerings, professional theaters, films, and on the concert stage. These spaces were acknowledged entertainment sites, but they were also extraordinary classrooms that educated lay audiences about Caribbean and other Diaspora cultures. Literature scholar Veve Clark asserted that Dunham's performance methods constituted research on stage.[11]

The United States government publicly recognized Dunham's national and international successes at the Kennedy Center, Washington, D.C., in 1988, but her system of dance technique and her influence on cultural studies were marginalized and generally overlooked in dance education until the 1970s. Dunham developed a dance technique that was comparative to the techniques of Martha Graham, Doris Humphrey, and José Limon.[12] Due to the marginalization of African American creativity and the resulting erasure of originating authorship, her technique was rarely acknowledged as a bona fide foundational technique in mainstream dance histories; yet, it was as defined as other techniques that were forming in the same decades. Her technique has always been acknowledged in the oral tradition by the African American dance community and among her professional disciples, including Vannoy Aikens, Tommy Gomez, Syvilla Fort, Eartha Kitt, Julie Belafonte, Ann Smith, Ruth Beckford, Naima Lewis, Deborah Vaughan, Elendar Barnes, Shirley Brown, Linda Goodrich, Albirda Rose, Mary Lois Hudson Sweatte, Elma Lewis, De Ama Battle, Joan Burroughs, myself, and hundreds, if not thousands, more.

Dunham technique runs parallel to or at the base of jazz technique in "isolation" sequences, which are taught in much variation today. In an interview at Stanford University in 1989, Dunham talked to me about her "isolation sequence," and she told Albirda Rose, director of the Dunham Teacher Certification program, that much of her material was "borrowed or stolen."[13] Isolation sequences developed either in Dunham's technique evolution after her first Caribbean fieldwork in 1936–37,[14] within her first studio classes from 1931–36, or with Jack Cole in studio and films. U.S. American dance specialist Annette McDonald presents Cole as a jazz original and conceivably a major contributor to "isolations" found in jazz warm-up sequences.[15] Dance historian Constance Hill believes that Cole's technique was grounded in his long-term study of East Indian classical dance.[16] Jazz practitioner Sue Samuels emphasizes the diversity of backgrounds that early jazz teachers came from: modern dance of the era, Asian, African, as well as classical ballet.[17] Probably most jazz instructors since the 1950s did not know where the isolation sequences came from, but they were an early staple in Dunham technique.

Dunham did not have the academic resources that Kurath had, but her success as an entertainer publicized her research interests. During her years of performing and directing a world-renowned company, she authored three books, several other book manuscripts, and numerous articles in academic journals, trade magazines, and newspapers.[18] The way in which she programmed dance performance—in other words, her paradigm for a cross-cultural audience experience—literally circled the globe, in Asia, Africa, Europe, Latin America, and throughout the United States. Her self-produced company toured internationally for thirty years and served as a model for future dance companies in Ghana, Guinea, Senegal, Mali, and the Diaspora. The structure of Dunham's concerts was replicated within the presentation of African, Caribbean, and other national dance cultures, as independence was celebrated across the African continent, but more so as many nations introduced their cultures to nonnative dance audiences. A vivid example is Les Ballets Africains of the Republic of Guinea in its presentation to the United Nations and the world in 1967.[19]

Although Dunham named the field and received over fifteen honorary doctorates, she has still not been acknowledged by the academic leadership of dance anthropology as a founder or major contributor to dance studies. Her work began in the same years of Kurath's work and, unlike Kurath, she was determined early on about the anthropological objectives within her research. Apparently, her reflexive writing style was not appreciated as much as the objective style of Kurath; her published narratives and prolific presentations were minimized by Kurath's academic output in conferences, juried journals, and published proceedings. Dunham's approach has prevailed despite her personal academic marginalization and at present is comfortably nested within the recent literary canons of ethnography and performance studies.[20]

In the late 1940s and early 1950s, a decade after Kurath's or Dunham's beginnings, noted dancer/choreographer/educator Pearl Primus made two artistic bridges by means of dance performance: one between modern concert dance and Diaspora dance, and the other between Africa and the Diaspora community. Primus was serious about comparative studies and trained accordingly to advance dance studies. As an education specialist, she was one of the first known African or American researchers to examine dance on the African continent, and she was one of the early artists to encourage investigations on all that is encompassed within "black" or African and Diaspora dance. She performed and traveled throughout the Diaspora, encouraging respectful regard for African and Diaspora cultures, as well as demonstrating the power of dance through performance, choreography, and dance education.

In step with American anthropology of the era, this Trinidad-born researcher documented the place of dance in West and Central Africa and completed a study in 1968 on the influence of dance in British and American education systems. Primus's research in Africa, resulting from a Rosenwald grant in 1959 and a Harkness Foundation Grant in 1969, paved the way for her doctoral training at New York University. Due to a dispute in which she insisted that one of her doctoral qualification languages was "dance," a nonverbal communication system, her anthropology degree was not conferred until 1977. While her publishing was limited due to her distinguished performing career, she wrote articles on African dance and was the subject for numerous journals, magazines, and newspapers.[21]

The three "founding foremothers," as opposed to the later "pioneers" of anthropology's sub-discipline, noted here as dance anthropology, were not evaluated as bona fide anthropologists, and secure academic posts evaded them most of their lives. Dunham and Primus were the victims of triple discrimination—first against dance as an intellectual enterprise, then against creative women intellectuals, and also against anything that was African-derived (research or personnel). They were forced to live their last years in economically vulnerable and politically impotent situations, despite their national prominence, international recognition, and significant contributions to Diaspora dance. Much of what is recognized as the anthropological examination of dance today began with the research and publications of these three women: Dunham in anthropology, emphasizing dance; Kurath in ethnomusicology, emphasizing dance; and Primus in anthropology, emphasizing dance education. Historical records indicate that these three maintained the anthropological approach and methods, regardless of what name the field was called or to what extent their work was acknowledged.

Pioneers and Pioneering Literature of Dance Anthropology

Research from an anthropological perspective traced the beginnings of dance anthropology but omitted much discussion of Primus and Dunham, even in comprehensive bibliographies. This was particularly unfortunate, since the pioneers of dance anthropology reviewed the historical literature so impressively otherwise. They did not omit African or African-based dance, however.[22]

The decades of the 1960s and 1970s ultimately institutionalized dance research within mainstream education in the United States and Europe with the completion of several PhD dissertations on cultural dance forms, including research on African dance.[23] Several faculty posts at major universities generated student interest in dance research and the gradual growth of the subdiscipline. The institutions that supported dance research significantly were Indiana University, Northwestern University, University of Chicago, Columbia University, University of California at Los Angeles, University of Wisconsin, University of Hawaii, Texas Women's College, New York University, and University of California at Berkeley. Unfortunately, Caribbean institutions have yet to position dance analysis within terminal degree university programming.

Dancer and anthropologist Joann Kealiinohomoku made a serious impact on Diaspora dance studies when she produced a master's thesis that compared African and African American motor behaviors, including dance, with those of European performers. It was published in *Dance Research Journal,* the juried publication of the Committee on Research in Dance (CORD). Following Dunham, Kealiinohomoku studied under Herskovits and, accordingly, generated what interest she could in Diaspora dance; she was thwarted throughout her career by the severe biases that still existed against the legitimate study of dance. Probably her most important contribution to the scholarly community was her article, "An Anthropologist Looks at Ballet as an Ethnic Dance," which thrust the anthropological perspective onto the dance and dance education worlds.[24]

Also, Ghanaian musicologist J. H. K. Nketia was the major reference to any discussion of African or African-derived dance in the 1960s. Nketia published on Ghanaian music and dance and his careful analyses brought the commonalities among African and Diasporic dances into full view.[25] Shortly thereafter, the very useful comparative analyses of African American composer and musicologist Olly Wilson came into the dance literature.[26] Both Nketia and Wilson focused specifically on dance within their musical analyses. Thereafter in the 1970s, dance scholar Odette Blum expanded Nketia's work through her dance specialization and seemed to point the way toward separate national dance studies for the African continent. Unfortunately, these did not develop systematically.[27]

Accurate African dance studies for the many countries of the continent are important because many in the Americas indiscriminately "lump" diverse African and related Caribbean cultural forms together. Up through the 1960s especially, clear distinctions among African cultures were missing from comprehensive understandings in dance education and Diaspora dance studio communities. Since then, there has been a gradual mushrooming of defining articles and books. Some of the richest dance descriptions and clearest analyses of world dance forms are found within four respected journals: *Dance Research Journal, Society of Dance History Journal, Ethnomusicology*, and *Yearbook for Traditional Music*. There is equivalent excellence in the holdings from the Dance Collection of the New York Public Library. Also, the Schomburg Library in New York City and the Center for Black Music Research in Chicago have important African and Diaspora dance-related materials.

Those who write about dance attempt to reveal its multilayered significance. Authors point to powerful, textured body communication from several approaches, and there is a tremendous array of African and Diaspora genres and styles to investigate. The array of dances is just as complex and exquisite as the published analyses on African-descended communities. The following sections review the remaining literature by geographical area.

Caribbean Island Analyses

Some of the earliest Caribbean dance literature describes not only the dancing of arriving Africans but also the dancing of Europeans and mixed groups
in the seventeenth and eighteenth centuries. Father Jean-Baptiste Labat
lived on Martinique and Guadeloupe and traveled extensively among many
islands from 1696–1705. Using his scientific knowledge of botany and engineering, he published an eight-volume opus in the 1720s on indigenous
life, plants and animals in the islands, sickness, attacks and other events,
as well as prevailing colonial habits and customs, including the dance and
musical instruments of enslaved Africans.[28] Also, Governor Médéric Louis
Elie Moreau de Saint-Méry of Martinique was fascinated by the dance
performances he witnessed among the enslaved and free communities.[29] His
published descriptions of specific African dances detailed the existence and
continuity of African practices, as well as the transplanting of European set
dancing onto African bodies.

Several Caribbean dancers developed dance typologies during the 1950s,
although they did not always recount the contexts of named dances. Beryl
McBurnie, considered the "Mother of Caribbean Dance" in the English/
Creole Caribbean, published *Dance Trinidad Dance.* Lavinia Williams Yar-
borough published *Haiti Dance,* and in the 1980s, Rex Nettleford published
Dance Jamaica. Later, McBurnie's professional descendant, Trinidadian
Molly Ahye, published a more fully fleshed overview of Trinidadian and
Tobagonian dance, as well as the life story and contributions of McBurnie
to Caribbean dance.[30]

Two anthologies have culled scattered information on Caribbean dance
into one source. *Nation Dance: Religion, Identity, and Cultural Difference
in the Caribbean,* edited by Caribbean religion specialist Patrick Taylor,
centers on the English/Creole Caribbean; *Caribbean Dance from Abakuá
to Zouk: How Movement Shapes Identity,* edited by dance writer Susanna
Sloat, sweeps across English, Spanish, Dutch, and French Caribbean dance
studies. Both volumes offer considerable expertise on the pertinent distinctions among Caribbean dance types and on the intersection between dance
and social identity.

Additional studies on Caribbean dance have appeared recently. Ethnomusicologist Peter Manuel's *Creolizing Contradance in the Caribbean* is
a collection of five area studies on the evolving forms of English country
dancing and French *contredanse.* The authors are musicologists who present
riveting, fully documented analyses on dance forms. Sloat has presented a

second reader, *Making Caribbean Dance,* a collection of twenty-one brief essays on dance within ten Caribbean islands that is fortuitously written by dance specialists (mainly). The volume updates two previously published dance articles, translates two major Caribbean dance voices, as well as highlights less-documented islands, like Barbados and Dominica.

Spanish Caribbean Dance Studies

Cuban ethnologist Fernando Ortiz studied Afro-Cuban dance traditions from the 1920s to the 1950s and published formidable documentation.[31] While Ortiz is known for the concept of "transculturation" (the fluid way in which African and European cultures operated while in colonial and postcolonial contact), his studies on dance and theater gave clear renderings of four distinct African-derived dance and music traditions and indicated African continuity and Creole creativity. His work on Yoruba drumming and chants was translated into English during the 1960s by Ifa practitioners in California and thereafter distributed among percussionists and investigators.[32]

Over time, Cuba developed an extensive dance and music literature. Cuban dance historians Graciela Chao Carbonero and Sara Lamerán provided teaching manuals that identified and categorized the African and Spanish heritages of Cuban dance.[33] Latin American dance scholar Susan Cashion contributed a study on dance training that was the result of arts education in Revolutionary Cuba.[34] U.S. American dancer Suki John examined *la técnica cubana,* which showed how Cuban dancers dealt with political and social isolation of the twentieth century in the creation of a modern concert form.[35] Also, historian John Chasteen dissected nineteenth-century social and political events through the strong connections between dance and the rise of nationalism in Cuba, Brazil, and Argentina.[36] Additionally, I presented an anthropological study of Cuban *rumba,* and in the process found persistent African heritage in Cuba sixty years after Ortiz' findings. My research unfolded the relevance of dance in domestic and international politics, as well as in tourist settings. My later study, *Dancing Wisdom,* highlighted the reliance on an interrelationship of dance, music, religion, and sacred ritual.[37]

In 1986, Puerto Rican sociologist Ángel Quintero Rivera published a seminal article on the relationship of dance to national culture, entitled "Ponce, the Danza, and the National Question: Notes toward a Sociology of Puerto Rican Music." He also spurred growth in Puerto Rican dance studies with his 1998 study, *Salsa, sabor y control.* For example, sociologist/cultural theorist Juan Flores contributed an analysis of Puerto Rican identity

Chart 3. Spanish Caribbean Dance Typology

Dance Forms	Cuba	Puerto Rico	Dominican Republic
SOCIAL			
Contredanse-Derived or -Related			
	Contradanza	Los Seises (Chorreao, Masón, Yubá, Belén, Bambulé, Bombeao)	Contradanza
	Tumba francesa/Tajona (Masón, Yubá Frenté)		Jacana (Sarandunga)
	Tejido de las cintas (maypole)		Carabiné
			Yuca
			Tumba
			Mangulina
African-Derived Drum/Dances			
	Yuka	Paracumbé, Guineo,	Calenda
	Makuta	Gumbé, Zarambeque	Bamboulá
	Chica	Portorrico	Djouba
		Bomba	Chica
Popular			
	Son	Danza	Merengue
	Rumba	Plena	Bachata
	Danza	Salsa	Salsa*
	Danzón		
	Mambo		
	Chachachá		
	Mozambique		
	Casino/Salsa/Timba		
Parading			
	Processions and Patron Saints		
	Dia de los reyes	*Dia de los reyes*	*Dia de los reyes*
	Carnavales (Tumba francesa, Tajona)	Carnavales	Carnavales
	Gagá		Gagá
	Congas/Comparsas (Santiaguera, Regla) (Chancleta)		
SACRED			
	Palo (Bantú/Congó)	(Palo)*	Bailes de Palo
	Arará	(Vodú)*	Vodú/Gagá
	Carabalí/Abakuá	(Yoruba)*	Sarandunga (Morano, Capitana, Bomba, Jacana)
	Yoruba		
	Vodú/Gagá		
FIGHTING/COMBAT			
	Juego de Maní	Bomba calinda	
CONCERT AND TOURIST PERFORMANCE			
	Ballet; Danza contemporánea; Folklórico; Cabaret/Espectáculo		

*Transported form, not indigenous

through a critique of dance forms in *From Bomba to Hip-Hop,* and in "The Challenges of Puerto Rican Bomba," anthropologist Hal Barton focused on the historical development of Puerto Rican *bomba* and contrasted its history with contemporary practices on the island and within its transnational communities. Also, Frances Aparicio, and Cándida Jáquez (with María Elena Cepeda), discussed transnationalism and hybridity primarily in the Caribbean through *Musical Migrations.*[38] In *Situating Salsa,* Lise Waxer presented *salsa* studies, starting with the squabble between Puerto Rico and Cuba about origins, to *salsa* studies from around the world; she included understandings from percussionists, horn players, singers, and composers. Quintero Rivera's latest work meticulously examines "*las músicas mulatas*" and suggests that the Afro-Caribbean dancing body and creolized Latin dance music have continuously challenged mainstream North American and European cultures with the latter's tremendous penchant for mind/ body and culture/body separations.

Dance in the Dominican Republic came into recent prominence with the investigations of ethnomusicologists Deborah Pacini, Paul Austerlitz, and Dario Tejeda. Dominican dance had been studied from the view of folklore by Dominican ethnologists Edna Garrido de Boggs and Fradique Lizardo; however, ethnomusicologist Martha Ellen Davis went beyond Dominican prejudices to concentrate on African-descended Dominicans and their dances.[39]

(Caribbean dance charts, in this chapter especially, aim for graphic condensing of recognized dance genres and for clarity among abundant and potentially confusing information.)

French/Kreyol Caribbean Dance Studies

For the Haitian dance literature, ethnologist Lamartinière Honorat and U.S. American dancer Lavinia Williams Yarborough published overviews of Haitian dance in the 1950s; later, Emmanuel Paul provided another. All are reliable accounts of Haitian dance from the colonial period through the early twentieth century.[40] Katherine Dunham's two major works, *The Dances of Haiti* (1947) and *Island Possessed* (1960), provide significant information also. Subsequent research by dance anthropologist Joan Burroughs has tracked the journey of Vodou dances from ceremonial spaces to the concert stage. Ethnomusicologist Lois Wilckens has reviewed that same journey from the music perspective. Additionally, years ago I analyzed Petro/Petwo dance from Haitian Vodou, which has been updated in my comparative study on Diaspora religions.[41]

Chart 4. French/Kreyol Caribbean Dance Typology

Dance Forms	Haiti	Martinique	Guadeloupe
SOCIAL			
Contredanse-Derived			
	Contredanse	Haut-taille	Kadril au commandement
	Affranchi (Mazoun congo)	Pastourelle (Vals, Mazouk, Polka, Pastourelle, Polka-la-poule)	French Kadril (Pantelón, Été, Poule, Pastourelle, Biguine)
		Lakadri/Kadril	Lancers
		Réjane	
African-Derived			
	Calenda	Calenda ticano	Calenda
	Djouba/Matinik	Bele Linò (Bele, bélia, pitche, bidjin/dous, gwanbèlè)	Gwoka/Lewoz (Tumblak, Lewoz, Kaladja, Graj, Kadjenbel, Woulé, Menndé)
	Bamboula	Bele Lisid/du sud (Bele, Gwanbèlè)	
	Chica	Lalinklè (Woulé, Mango, Bénézuel, Kanigwé, Ting bang, Mabélo)	
Popular			
	Carabinier	Vals Creole	Vals Creole
	Méringue/Mereng	Mazouk	Mazouk
	Mazouk	Biguine	Biguine
	Kadans	Kadans/Konpa*	Kadans/Konpa*
	Konpa	Mereng*	Mereng*
	Salsa*	Salsa/Casino*	Salsa/Casino*
	Zouk*	Zouk (love, béton)	Zouk (love, béton)
		Reggae/Ragga*	
Parading			
	Rara (Majò-jon dances)	Carnaval (*diable* dances)	Carnaval
	Kanaval		
	Koudyay		
SACRED			
	Rada/Vodou		
	Congo/Vodou		
	Petwo/Vodou		
FIGHTING/COMBAT			
	Calinda	Danmyé/Ladja	Mayoleur/Calinda
	Mousonai		Kaladja
			Konvalen/Calinda
CONCERT AND TOURIST PERFORMANCE			
	Ballet; Danse moderne; Folklorique; Cabaret/Spectaculaire		

*Transported form, not indigenous

The dance literature of Martinique and Guadeloupe in the French Caribbean has been examined mainly by ethnomusicologists. Julian Gerstin has analyzed the interrelationship of drummers and dancers in Martinican *bele* and has presented a study of *bele* dance and music and their positions within island and French politics. These two studies apparently generated a third, an examination of early colonial dances. Additionally, musicologist Dominique Cyrille has overviewed Martinican and Guadeloupean dance types, as well as specific *contredanse*-derived forms. I, too, have presented findings on Caribbean *contredanse*-derived forms, but from an anthropological perspective.[42]

English/Creole Caribbean Dance Studies

In the 1960s, the world of dance scholarship produced one of its most articulate spokespersons on Diaspora dance traditions. The late Rex Nettleford, founder and director of the Jamaican National Dance Company, used his sociological training and artistic genius to herald an impressive Jamaican identity through dance performance. His published work chronicled the effort to release ingrained colonial attitudes, the public recognition of distinct African heritages for Jamaica and other Caribbean sites, as well as the artistic creativity of Jamaicans.[43] More recently, artist/scholar Deborah Thomas has added provocative contributions on the effects of colonialism through analyses of Jamaican dance culture.[44]

On smaller English/Creole islands, like Carriacou in the Grenadine islands, Caribbean people have begun to acknowledge more publicly and formally (in schools and in print) the sometimes-demeaned dance practices of African ancestors. U.S. American dance researcher Annette Macdonald has updated her 1978 article on the *Nation Dances* of these tiny but important African legacy islands. Carriacouan dance educator Christine David has published her findings also. More recently and more thoroughly, musicologist Lorna McDaniel has examined Carriacou's dances.[45]

Dutch Caribbean Dance Studies

The Dutch Caribbean literature is fascinating, but it is just beginning to percolate in terms of dance. Since I have not completed exhaustive fieldwork (only Suriname and Curaçao), I chart the limited list of dances with which I am acquainted.

Chart 5. English/Creole Caribbean Dance Typology (Former British, French, and Danish Caribbean)

Dance Forms	Trinidad & Tobago	Jamaica	Grenadines (Carriacou)	U.S. Virgin Islands (former Danish)
SOCIAL				
Contredanse-Derived				
Quadrille	Quadrille (ballroom, camp; mento)	Cadrille	German Kwadril
	Belair/Bele	Maypole	Belair/Bele	French Quadrille
	Lancers			Lancers
	Jig			
African-Derived Drum/Dances				
	Bamboula	Bamboula	Bamboula	Bamboula
	Djouba	Djouba	Djouba/Juba	Djouba
	Calenda	Shay-shay	Old Kalenda	Kalenda
	Bele	Adowa	Woman Kalenda	
			Bele	
Popular				
	Calypso	Mento		Waltz
	Soca	Ska		Polka
	Salsa*	Reggae		Shottische
	Merengue*	Dancehall		
Parading				
	Carnival (Jouvé *djab-djab* or *djab molassie*; *Mardi Gras*; *Canboulay*)	Carnival	Carnival	Carnival
	Lavway/Leggo	Jonkanoo		
	Road March	Roots Junkanoo		
		Maroon Day		
SACRED				
	Spiritual Baptists	Kumina	Nation Dance (Creole-belair, Old Kalenda, Juba, Quelbe)	
	Shango	Etu/Nago	Nation Dance	
	Vodou	Maroon (Kromanti play, Myal)		
	Nation Dance	Nine Night		
	Reel dance	Pocomania/Rivival		
		Tambu/Makumbe		
		Nyabingi/Rasta		
FIGHTING/COMBAT				
	Kalinda	Old Kalenda		Cited
CONCERT AND TOURIST PERFORMANCE				
	Ballet; Contemporary Dance Theater; Folkloric; Cabaret/Spectacle			

*Transported form, not indigenous

Chart 6. Dutch Caribbean Dance Typology

Dance Forms	Netherland Antilles (Curaçao, Aruba, Bonair)	Suriname
SOCIAL		
Contredanse-Derived		
	Quadrilla	
	Bailia de lei	
African-Derived Drum/Dances		
	Chica	Saramaka-Adunke
	Tambú	Saramaka–Djombo Seketi
		Saramaka-Bandammba
		Ndjuka-Awasa
		Aluku (Boni)–Awasa
		Paramaka-Awasa
Popular		
	Tumba	Kaseko
	Salsa*	Matawai-Banya
	Merengue*	Loketo
		Reggae*
		Dance Hall*
Parading		
	Curaçao–Carnival di tumba	
	Aruba–Calypso (no tumba)	
	Curaçao-Seu	
SACRED		
	Chica	Winti/Pee
	Tambú	Saramaka-Bandammba Tjeke seketi
		Ndjuka-Awasa
		Aluku (Boni)-Awasa
		Kwinti
		Paramaka
		Matawai
FIGHTING/COMBAT		
	Kokomakaku/Tambú	Alesingo
CONCERT AND TOURIST PERFORMANCE		
	Ballet; Modern; Folklore; Cabaret/Spectacle	

*Transported form, not indigenous

Dance Studies of Afro-Latin Territories

Brazilian controversies about 'race' aside, the largest African population outside of the African continent imprints its African heritage and identity on Brazil's national dances. From *samba* and *carnaval* to *capoeira* and Candomblé (Brazilian religious forms), African customs and performance values reign; however, Brazilian dance documentation is relatively scarce.[46]

The most relevant areas are in the states of Salvador da Bahia and Rio de Janeiro, but Maranhão, Minas Gerais, Pernambuco, and other states have important African heritage also.

Brazilian scholar Edison Carneiros wrote about the sacred Candomblé dances, giving the literature glimpses of what religious dances looked like in the 1930s and 1940s.[47] More recently Brazilian dance archives have been activated by both *samba* studies (Brazil's national dance music) and *carnaval* studies (Brazil's national and international holiday dancing). Alma Guillermoprieto and Barbara Browning have written penetrating accounts of the implications within Afro-Brazilian dance for the entire country.[48] Performance critic Anna Scott's investigation of *"blocos"* or neighborhood Carnival groups takes previous understandings further and unfolds the local and global effects of popular dance in contemporary Brazilian society.[49]

Other fascinating Brazilian rituals include its martial art/dance form *capoeira,* a stick-fighting form called *maculelê,* and the full range of religious dances from the *Jeje, Angola,* and *Caboclo* nations/religions, as well as the *Candomblé* religion. Mestre Bira Almeida, historian John Lewis, and anthropologist/*capoeirista* Julio Cesar de Tavares give instructive accounts of the development of *capoeira* as its dance movements have spread from Brazil across the Diaspora and beyond;[50] de Tavares has also compared the rhythmic moves of *capoeira's ginga* to the "cool" walk of African Americans in Harlem.[51] In fact, dance and dance-like movement are so important among Afro-Brazilians that anthropologist Sheila Walker framed her overview of the *Candomblé* religion in terms of "A Choreography of the Universe."[52]

Although Central and South America are vast and noted for their Native American dance heritages, these areas have also received the indelible influence of African dance. African-derived dance formations have survived and are ongoing in African niches—from Maroon encampments (African settlements deep in mountainous or densely forested regions) of San Basilio in Colombia and Yanga/San Lorenzo de los Negros in Mexico, to northern Surinamese nations, to western Pacific coastal communities in Peru, Ecuador, and Colombia and southeastern Afro-Latin communities in the Rio Plata of Uruguay and Argentina, and even Chile.[53] Most often, however, African legacies were erased from Central and South American histories through an emphasis on the Native American and European mixtures or *mestisaje,* which undoubtedly occurred regularly.[54] Yet most South American countries have at least one named African dance, and even *mestisaje* observers give credit to the resilience of "things African" when they note particular movements, instrumentation, and languages in the songs and dances of Latin America. Two examples would be the relaxed hip punctuation over *zapateo* (foot-stamping) steps and the percussive playing of the harp, both in Veracruz, Mexico.[55]

Also across the Diaspora today, thousands of mixed Native American and African descendants organize annually around music making and dance—for example, in Belize, where the Garifuna gather for *punta* dancing and sociopolitical agendas, and in St. Vincent and Dominica, where Carib descendants also celebrate in dancing.[56]

To date, the northern section of South America has publicly recognized African heritage more often than the southern section. Latinos from Colombia, Venezuela, Peru, Ecuador, Guyana, French Guiana, and Suriname have exhibited African characteristics in their local and national dance music forms over centuries, but by the 1950s many of these data were only available in short passages as inferences within historical writings, suggesting either erasure or marginalization of Afro-Latin aesthetic production. One stellar exception stands out in the 1946 investigations of Gonzalo Aguirre Beltrán (another student of Melville Herskovits) with his identification of the "black" population of Mexico. The late Lise Waxer is another who documented the crucial influence of African descendants on Latin American dance; she cited *chombos* (in this case Caribbean sailors) who brought and circulated the early *salsa* recordings that established Colombia and Venezuela as *salsa* centers.[57]

In the southern cone of South America, both Argentine *tango* and Uruguayan *candombe* have been transposed to the new key of twenty-first century African roots, as researchers are now documenting the influence of African dance across North, Central, and South America. Thus, English, Spanish, and French literatures, with limited Dutch and Danish literatures, have provided descriptions and analyses of African dance heritage in the Diaspora.[58]

Brief View of African Dance Studies

African dance data that are most accessible in the Americas have historically emphasized Ghanaian and Nigerian dance, although in more recent years the dances of Senegal, Mali, and Guinea have actually dominated the appetites of Diaspora studio performers and dance educators. South African dances have also enjoyed great popularity; however, the written documentation of the vast quantities of African dance is still impoverished. One important resource is the collection by British anthropologist Paul Spencer,[59] who includes studies by John Middleton on the Lugbara of Uganda, John Blacking on the Venda of South Africa, and his own work on the Samburu of

Kenya.[60] Other anthropologists, education specialists, and dance scholars have contributed to the African dance literature, including U.S. Americans Drid Williams, Judith Hanna, Doris Green, and African Felix Begho, who have worked on varied West African practices. Musicologist Gerhard Kubik is a rare resource with contributions on Central African dance and music found in Brazil, as is dance scholar Kariamu Welsh-Asante, who has published on Shona practices in Zimbabwe.[61]

The works of performance theorist Margaret Thompson Drewal, African art specialist Henry Drewal, and theater analyst Omofolabo Ajayi join those of several formidable ethnomusicologists (John Miller Chernoff, John Blacking, and Charles Waterman) who have also concentrated on West Africa.[62] The two Drewals and Ajayi pointedly examine the movement materials of differing Yoruba village festivals. Margaret Drewal's early descriptions of Anago Yoruba dance ritual gave students precise descriptions of how the dance appeared before video images became standard. Her written images and those painted later by Ajayi give detailed accounts that show Yoruba elaboration in dance ritual. Yoruba dance on the continent is still tied to local shrines and often involves spectacular communal masking traditions.

Overview of Diaspora U.S. Dance Studies

Studies of African-based dance were stymied in the Diaspora U.S. because of segregationist and racist educational policies until 1972, when dancers and researchers received one of the first important accesses to African-derived dance history. Choreographer/scholar Lynne Emery provided a detailed account of significant African dance legacies in American contexts and contributed to the understanding of evolving African American dance traditions in *Black Dance from 1610 to 1970*. Later, other critical analyses took shape with *Jookin': The Rise of Social Dance Formations in African American Culture* (1990), by sociologist Katrina Hazzard-Gordon, and *Digging the Africanist Presence in American Performance* (1996), by dance historian/critic Brenda Gottschild.

Hazzard-Gordon focused on those dance forms that emerged as African Americans migrated from the emancipated rural South to the industrialized North in the United States. Her study of vernacular dance was important not only for its solid analysis but also for its affirmation of research equity among dance types; she modeled the rewards of studying popular dance as well as concert or fine art types. Gottschild scrutinized the influence of African American dance styles within the esteemed dance genres of the concert stage. Using almost ten years of public bashing from mainstream dance critics to her advantage, Gottschild's published work documented what many others up to the 1990s found so hard to believe. She argued for the significant influence of African and African American dance legacies on presumed European and European American dance forms. In an analysis of 'race' within ballet and modern dance, Gottschild unveiled the erasure and unacknowledged import of African-derived culture in the United States, which then stimulated questions about erasures in other American dance contexts. Another outstanding study that points out the deep place of "race" in U.S. dance is dance historian Sharon Arslanian's "History of Tap Dance in Education: 1920–1950" (unpublished dissertation, Temple University).

A more recent inquiry on African roots in the dance repertoires of the United States was compiled by choreographer and dance historian Thomas De Frantz. In *Dancing Many Drums: Excavations in African American Dance* (2002), De Franz and others have provided learned studies on the impact of powerful choreographers whose dance work has illuminated Diaspora issues.[63] The chapters on Pearl Primus and Katherine Dunham are particularly insightful with regard to the present survey of Diaspora dance literature; all chapters recount the incredible achievements of Diaspora dancers in the face of postemancipation injustice.[64] I look forward to published findings from a recent symposium on "Embodied Knowledge" at Harvard University (March 25–27, 2011), which not only confronted some of the dilemmas and opportunities within Diaspora dance studies and offered young dance artists/scholars solid support and validity in performing, documenting, and analyzing the import of Diaspora dance, but also balanced the North American hegemonic interest among Diaspora dance studies with Circum-Caribbean and West African studies.

Visual Studies and Visceral Analyses

There is an immense African and Diaspora dance literature that now exists on video and film. A few basics that concentrate on the Circum-Caribbean culture sphere are: *Black Orpheus, Divine Horsemen, To Serve the Gods, Dance in America, Great Performances: Katherine Dunham, JVC Anthology of World Music and Dance, JVC/Smithsonian Video Anthology of the Americas, Bahia: Africa in the Americas, Rumba, A Glimpse of Cuba through Dance* (Insight Media, New York), the PBS specials (8 vols.) *Dancing, Free to Dance,* and many more. Here, my main point is that visual examinations of dance formations permit a visceral understanding of Diaspora dance. Visceral knowledge surfaces swiftly when dance images are combined with the written investigations of the identified dance scholars discussed in this chapter.

With this sweeping overview of dance studies and the previous chapter's review of representative dancers and guiding premises on the relationship between African and Diaspora dance formations, a preliminary grounding in African, Diaspora, and especially Caribbean dance is complete. The next chapters focus on particular types of Diaspora dance and the aim from here on is for deeper understanding of the nexus between dance and social meaning.

CHAPTER THREE

CONTREDANSE AND CARIBBEAN BODIES

Introduction

The category of social dance comprises drum/dances, set dances, parading dances, national dances, popular dances, and fad dances,[1] which are the subjects of the next four chapters. All chapters relay the varied meanings of social dance. They address differences—among several types of social dance and among several meanings for Diaspora peoples. They presume a historical, ongoing flow of dance exchange over time, between the folk and nobility, peasants and aristocracy, and rural and urban dwellers.[2]

In this chapter, I concentrate on *contredanse*-derived practices in representative Caribbean sites that I surveyed during fieldwork 2005–06. My

Chart 7. Carribean/Diaspora Social Dances

A. *Contredanse*-Derived Dances

  bele, belair, haut-taille, bele linò, bele lisid, kadril, kwadril, quadrilla, cuadrilla, sarandunga, German and French quadrille, tumba francesa, affranchi, Curaçaoan danza, candombe, etc.

B. African-Derived Drum/Dances

  yuka, makuta, paracumbé, guineo, calenda, gumbé, zarambeque, bamboulá, djouba, chica, Portorrico, bomba, gwoka/lewoz, lalinklè, tambú, etc.

C. Parading Dances

  Carnivals, Saints Day Processions, Jonkannu, *Rara, Gagá, Koudyay, sambas de carnavales, llamadas,* etc.

D. National Dances

  danzón, mereng/merengue, danza puertorriqueña, gwoka/lewoz, calypso, reggae, etc.

E. Popular Dances

  mambo, chachacha, plena, salsa, merengue, dancehall, soca, regetón, zouk, timba, etc.

---

findings suggest that historical *contredanse* forms represent pivotal values that have influenced past and present performers. Such values have made striking marks on Diaspora thought and behavior in terms of social identity, dance performance, ancestor reverence, and the colonial experience. Royal pageantry, drum/dances, and dance categorization have also surfaced as related issues, but ultimately the analyses reveal camouflaged agency and overt coloniality over time. Also, during the seventeenth and early eighteenth century, an imbalanced dance exchange existed between the dominant and dominated classes who shared Caribbean space. Despite limited and dispersed dance descriptions for this era and changed meanings over time, I attempt to explicate the cultural values that informed varied but related dances.[3]

Since there are many types of *contredanse*-related practices, I analyze each linguistic sector of the Caribbean region separately. The summaries that precede dance analyses form the historical background not only for widespread *contredanse*-related practices, but also for most Caribbean dance types. While each linguistic area has historical distinctiveness, each also shares many of the characteristics that are discussed within any one sector. What distinguishes *contredanse*-related practices is their pervasiveness throughout the region over time and their national importance despite emancipation and decolonization.

Contredanse-related dances have been performed in the region from the late seventeenth to the twenty-first century—among the Spanish, English/Creole, French/Kreyol, Dutch, and former Danish islands.[4] European dances are significantly represented among descendants of enslaved and free Africans, not just in the French or English/Creole Caribbean as a predominantly French dance might suggest, but throughout the islands and related territories. Today, elder populations in organized social "societies," children in school classrooms and village recitals, and professional dancers in troupes and tourist settings highlight *contredanse*-derived practices in their repertoires.[5]

Contredanse form is derived from French court dancing that spread throughout Europe during the sixteenth and seventeenth centuries. It followed very formal couple dances that were performed by the aristocracy, who danced in hierarchical order as theatrical entertainment during balls. Elegant group *contredanses* followed, which involved couples dancing in lines, facing each other (*contre,* against, contrary to), and a series of elaborate dance patterns or figures. Before the 1780s in France, line dances were called *contredanses*; after the 1790s, those dances whose lines formed a square were first called *cotillions* (which had been one of the earlier *contredanse* sets) and later called *quadrilles*.[6]

Dance sets or movement sections evolved from instrumental music suites (including the *pavanne, galliard, minuet, courante, passepied, sarabande, gavotte, gigue,* etc.) and focused keenly on manners, sociability, and courting practices that were taught by expert dance masters. Dancing was the primary instrument for educating the young and was the model for proper social behavior of the time. Partners touched only occasionally as they danced, and the complex figures projected differentiated statuses. Those who could perform the figures were upper class and those who could not were considered to be lacking class. Like the *minuet* (a highly elaborated couple dance from the 1650s-1750s), the *English country dance* (called *contredanse francaise* with its arrival at Louis XIV's court around 1710 as a lively square formation) became one of the most favored dances in the French or European *contredanse*.[7]

Generally, the French model of *contredanse* was performed in lines called *contredanses* or in squares called *quadrilles.* The dances were performed in sequential sets, often but not always with alternating tempi and dynamics. In all of the sets, males and females bowed and curtsied, approached each other and bowed again. They turned around each other with one arm raised high and fingers gently touching and reversed similarly in the opposite direction. Thereafter any number of floor patterns or "figures" could be employed, such that (generally) the line of women would dance with different male partners and vice versa. Couples would promenade, cross the room several times and end by bowing and curtsying to their original partners.

Actual descriptions of early Caribbean *contredanse* practices are scarce, and dance names were indiscriminately alternated or changed over time; still, some generalizations seem to have taken place. As in French stylization, Caribbean versions were organized toward five or more sets, most often called *le pantalon* (trousers), *l'été* (summer), *la poule* (hen), *la pastourelle* (shepherdess), and *finale* after earlier European set developments. Common steps or figures were: back-to-back step (*do-si-do*), *balancé* (step down, step up, step down, alternate), chain, reel, wheel, star, heel and toe, and promenade, which yielded sequences of advance and retreat, crossing, circling, and honoring floor patterns. Some figures did not require abundant dance skill, so both elites in ballrooms and nonelites in the countryside enjoyed group dancing.

Caribbean couples danced together, but not in closed partner or face-to-face position for an entire dance. Couples only danced in closed position, if at all, during the fifth or last set, primarily after mid-nineteenth century when the *waltz* and the *polka* were in colonial practice. Thus, face-to-face, independent partnering for an entire dance was a severe change for the dancing body and became an important boundary for dance categorization.[8]

Several very different names replaced the term *contredanse* in the Caribbean: *quadrille, bele, kuadria, kadril, haut-taille, affranchi, tumba francesa,* etc.[9] Most terms included circle, square, and line formations; however, the more general forms were either a double line or a square and are referred to here as Caribbean *quadrilles,* set dances, or *contredanse*-derived performance. African-descended performers, who became the overwhelming Caribbean population over time, were generally prohibited from dancing their dances of origin in public except on special occasions, like *Dias de los reyes* (January 6) in the Spanish islands and at times at the Feast of Corpus Christi (a varied date according to the Christian calendar) on other islands. At other times, "dancers of all colors"—Europeans, Europeans born in the Americas, or Creoles, as well as mixed descent persons—participated in dance lessons with dance masters, as in the case of Martinique, which was observed by Moreau de Saint Méry in 1789.[10] Dance instruction was in preparation for invitational balls, special performances after Mass, and for less formal, home entertainments, and some instructors were of African descent.[11]

Dancing among enslaved Africans was noticed by colonists and missionaries,[12] and the *courante* and *passepied* (running, jumping, kicking dances) especially were taught to discourage African-style performance.[13] Domestic servants and freed African descendents were able to dance more elegant dances and utilize the dance training that they observed within colonial families and among dance masters.[14] Over time, the African dances that were abhorred by Europeans were replaced by imitations, parodies, and extensions of the *contredanse*-derived performances that African descendants could observe and practice. They taught the dances to younger generations, appropriating a revered symbol of their oppressors by means of a physical assertion or a finessed affront. Despite repeated colonial assessments of bad form or awkwardness, New World Africans took great care to learn, remember, adapt, and pass on European dance structure, style, and patterns, and these can be seen across the Caribbean today.

Historical Dance Patterns

Both West and Central African dance practices share characteristics that dancers refer to in terms of how the body moves.[15] Dance historian and cultural critic Brenda Gottschild, following historian of African art Robert Thompson and hundreds of community dance instructors from Katherine Dunham and Beryl McBurnie forward, has identified the "grounded," low, or readied stances and body-part isolations that are emphasized in African-derived movement. In addition, the manner in which the torso divides and often initiates movement, the frequent polyrhythms in the movement as well as in the music, the regular intimacy between musical sound and danced movement, the percussion that usually accompanies the dance, and the cool luminosity and spiritual connection that are often attached to movement sequences are all listed among identifiable "African" dance characteristics.[16] Artist/scholar Kariamu Welsh-Asante has also examined African dance comparatively and provided additional identification of Africanness in movement: polyrhythm (layered independent rhythmic patterns), polycentrism (many overlapping points of interest/authority/power), curvilinearity (characterized by curved lines), multidimensionality (many aspects), epic memory (extended narrative of the past), repetition (intentional, purposeful reproduction), and holism (integrated unification of parts).[17] These movement qualities and associations have guided determinations of what is (and thereby what is not) African-derived within comparisons among Caribbean *quadrilles*.

Based on Thompson's, Gottschild's, and Welsh-Asante's lists of characteristics, solo and duet dancing in front of the drums or drum/dances routinely cited for the colonial Caribbean such as *bamboula, chica, djouba, kalenda* or *calenda*, etc., were set apart in my analyses as African-Creole dance practices, not *contredanse* material, but differentiated precursors to *contredanse* influence. Parading and procession dancing are ubiquitous among human groups, but when these were found to accompany set dances, they were assessed as related *contredanse* material. King and Queen pageantry was consistently linked to Caribbean set dancing, which left set figure dancing and King and Queen pageantry as the primary dance foci for analyses. Chart 8 unites all data gathered for *contredanse*-derived practices, with dances now arranged farther or closer to a Creole center.[18]

Over all, Caribbean set dances exhibited French/European structure because the dances were originally European, because of the control Europeans had over enslaved Africans across the islands, and because of the constraint on behaviors of most free African descendants in the colonial period. Legacies of and attachments to European *contredanse* were found during my fieldwork within the Puerto Rican *seis*, Dominican *sarandunga*, Trinidadian and Tobagonian *bele/belair*, U.S. Virgin Island *quadrilles*, Curaçaoan *quadrilla/kuadria*, St. Lucian *kwadril*, Martinican *bele* and *haut-taille*, Guadeloupean *kadril*, Cuban *tumba francesa*, and Haitian *affranchi*. Such a wide diffusion among distinct representatives makes a strong case for finding them on other Caribbean islands as well. All *quadrille* or *contredanse*-derived types demonstrated bona fide French court-related form: processions,

Chart 8. Revised Circum-Caribbean *Quadrille* Continuum

African Forms	Creole Forms	European Forms
African Style of Movement		**European Style of Movement**
Flexed posture		Erect posture
All body parts in isolation		Emphasized extremities
Divided torso		Undivided torso
Serial solo & couple dancing in front of drums		Partnered ballroom dancing

* * *

African-Creole Forms		**European-Creole Forms**
bamboula		Caribbean country/long dance
djouba		Caribbean *contredanse*
kalenda, calenda		Caribbean *contradanza*
chica		Circum-Caribbean *contradança*

* * *

Puerto Rican *bomba sicá*		*Chica*
Dominican *sarandunga,* [*tumba, yuca*]		*Los seises*
Cuban *rumba*		
Guadeloupean *gwoka/lewoz*		
Carriacouan *Nation dances*		
Trinidadian *Nation dances,* Queen's *bele2*		

* * *

Caribbean *Quadrille* Variations
(Primarily set dancing with royal pageantry)

Trinidadian Queen's *bele/belair2*		
Martinican *bele linó*		
		Cuban *contradanza, tumba francesa*
		Puerto Rican *contradanza*
		Dominican *contradanza, carabiné, jacana* (*sarandunga*)
		Haitian *affranchi* [*minuet-congo*]
		Martinican *haut-taille*
		Guadeloupean *kadril*
		St. Lucian *kwadril*
		Cruzan *French quadrille*
		St. Thomian *German quadrille, lancers*
		Trinidadian *bele/belair1, piqué*
		Curaçaoan *quadrilla/kuadria*
		(Uruguayan *candombe*)

Curaçaoan danza

* * *

***Contredanse*-Related, Face to Face Creole Dances**

Cuba: *danza, danzón, danzonete, danzonchá*
Puerto Rico: *danza, plena*
Dominican Republic: *carabiné, mangulina, danza/merengue del Cibao*
Haiti: *carabinier, méringue/mereng*
Martinique: *vals, mazouk, polka, biguine*
Guadeloupe: *vals, mazouk, polka, biguine*
St. Croix: *vals, mazurka, polka*
St. Thomas: *vals, mazurka, polka, schottish*
Dominica: *danza*
Trinidad: *leggo*
Jamaica: *mento*

parades or promenades, followed by a series of alternating slow and fast sets of repeating dance figures, and a final parade and/or curtsy. Colonists in each linguistic area of the region attempted to terminate African dance practices and encouraged French dance style and form. As well, different island performances were European at their core because of similar European and Roman Catholic influence on the lifestyle and mores of the colonies from the fifteenth century forward, and like French *contredanse,* Caribbean *contredanse* practices suggested differentiated identities: between Europeans and Europeans, between Europeans and non-Europeans, and between free and enslaved African descendants. Performances on all representative islands usually aimed for elegance, propriety, and fun. *Contredanse*-derived practices within religious services were only observed once (in Afro-Latin Uruguay), and they were never mentioned by Caribbean collaborators during my *quadrille* fieldwork on four trips and across seven islands. I would assume that where *contredanse*-related practices were associated with religious services, they aimed for elegance, propriety, and spiritual functioning.[19]

Recent publications have traced the significance of Martinican *quadrilles* for the French Caribbean in terms of a performed dialogue among Europeans, Africans, and their descendants or in terms of modern sociopolitical demonstrations.[20] Other research emphasizes processes of ongoing creolization of both music and movement.[21] My comparative research for the region is dance oriented and shows *contredanse*-derived practices over time and across geography that unfold coloniality and camouflaged agency.[22]

Summarized Sixteenth- to Eighteenth-Century Caribbean History

Spanish Influence

Music and dance specialist Emilio Rodriguez Demorizi cites the earliest dancing on Santo Domingo in 1509 at the Corte de María Toledo and in 1510 in La Vega at important celebratory Masses.[23] He describes masked dances, comedies, and dramas inside the church that caused alarm among the clergy. Music historian Noel Allende-Goitía and historian of Latin America John Chasteen also paint vivid pictures of sixteenth- to eighteenth-century Spanish colonial environments in which Europeans and Africans routinely danced and made merry together.[24] Allende-Goitía suggests a "colonization of daily life" in the Spanish colonies that permitted Africans to influence culture in a way that parallels contemporary global popular culture, which is heavily laden with African-derived styles despite the fact of a low population percentage for African descendants in the United States, for example. Both Allende-Goitía's and Chasteen's research reiterate first-hand testimonies by the Spanish clergy and match reports of traveling Europeans in the late 1600s and 1700s.

For example, Fray Iñigo Abbad y Lasierra relates the tremendous importance of dance for early islanders on Puerto Rico:

> The most enjoyable diversion for these islanders is dancing; they dance with no more reason than to pass the time away. . . .
> . . . When a contredanse ends, another begins and thus they alternate night and day, making . . . (relatively long) trips, without any other objective than to dance. . . . No one misses this diversion: from young girls . . . [t]o men and women of all ages and classes.[25]

Spanish Caribbean history also documents the fact that performers were African as well as European. Botanist André Pierre Ledru, traveling through Puerto Rico in 1797, reports specifically about ethnicity and class:

> During my stay in the house of Don Benito, I myself went to a dance given by the mayor of the estate to celebrate the birth of his first son. The gathering included forty or fifty Creole neighbors of both sexes. Some had come from . . . (far distances) because these men of ordinary lazy or indolent character are passionate for dancing. The gathering of *whites, mulattos, and free blacks* [emphasis added] was quite an original grouping: the men in cotton (Indian) pants and shirts, the women with white dresses and large golden necklaces, all with their heads covered by colorful handkerchiefs with a huge round hat. They performed African and Creole dances one after another to the sound of the guitar and the tambourine, called in their vernacular language, *bomba*.[26]

Varied *carnavales* began prior to the Lenten period of the 1520s on Hispaniola and spread gradually with Spanish settlement throughout the Catholic colonial world. Spanish settlement did not involve huge numbers of Africans until the eighteenth and nineteenth centuries, but from Allende-Goitía's and Chasteen's documentations African and African-Creole inhabitants participated with Europeans in patron saints' festivities as towns and cities developed. Dance performance had been part of sacred and civil ceremony in Spain from the seventh century, and in the Spanish colonies processions, parades, and promenades were common both outside church walls and also within the Church in front of the altar by mid- to late seventeenth century.[27] Solemn processions often gave way to more frivolous activities resembling fairs. For example, profane comedies, cockfighting, bullfighting, horsemanship displays, juggling, storytelling, games, music, and dancing were described on both Santo Domingo and Puerto Rico inside the atrium of cathedrals or in the unmanicured grounds around haciendas on several Spanish islands.[28]

French Influence

The entire Caribbean region contains the influence of colonial France, irrespective of how long the French occupied any particular island. French culture (from the courts of Louis XIII in the 1650s and Louis XIV in the 1680s especially) enveloped not only Europe but all European colonies. For the French and their followers, dancing was not simply a recreational activity but a sign, a means of education, an indication of social class and proper upbringing, and the major vehicle for courtship and eventual marriage. These values culminated in the Americas through the model of eighteenth-century French *contredanse*. In fact, the French model persisted on Haiti even after the demise of most Europeans on that island.

Both Martinique and Guadeloupe were purchased from Spain in 1635 and ultimately served as active sugar plantation and refinery sites. They became successful outposts for French exploration and expansion of the slave trade. The French arrived as sailors, army officers, and recruits, along with other European indentured workers and took possession of the largest, most easterly of the small Antillean islands. These were intended as bases for French conquest of other islands and French bases for wars with the Spanish and the English.[29]

The French were quite indignant about the earlier division of the known world by the Catholic Papal Bull of 1494 that gave the Spanish all new territories in the Americas and the Portuguese all new territories on the African continent. The French established their own sociopolitical goals for territories around the equator or "Equinoxiale," which specifically promised a transfer of French culture to the New World. The French are also associated with the illegal trade in Africans between islands. On the French possession of St. Christophe in 1635, French *corsaires* (pirates) arranged for the sale of Africans to the Dutch, marking the beginning of an interisland slave trade. The French generally received African captives from West Africa, but the interisland slave trade that followed from the event on St. Christophe brought enslaved peoples from Central African ports also, first to St. Christophe and then to Guadeloupe.[30] Later, the British reclaimed St. Christophe (calling it St. Kitts), but a consistent trade between the French on Guadeloupe and the Dutch on Curaçao made Guadeloupe a major French depot for enslaved Africans after 1680.

The French had control of about fourteen islands in 1642, but by the 1730s they had been forced to relinquish most of them. The English, Dutch, and Spanish took over the French possessions as the French became embroiled in domestic turmoil; however, colonial dances show the indelible cultural norms of the French across the Caribbean.

British/English/Creole Influence

Several of the twenty-eight habitable islands of the Caribbean make up the English/Creole-speaking Caribbean. Jamaica and Barbados are the English-speaking islands; most, like Trinidad and Tobago, St. Lucia, Dominica, St. Vincent, and the Grenadines, etc., have been English and French Creole-speaking. Even though the Spaniards landed first, for example on Trinidad and Tobago in 1577, English buccaneers were among the first Europeans to settle these islands. They stationed themselves to fight against the Spanish or the French for the next one hundred years.[31]

By the 1780s, the French and Irish were recruited for Trinidadian settlement, and the French, Dutch, British, and Scots emigrated to Tobago. In 1797, after almost two centuries of French rule, the British recovered the islands, forcibly implanted British culture, imported Chinese workers from Macao, and in 1834 added Portuguese immigrants from Madeira. Thus, a French-influenced cluster of islands with unusually diverse populations became characteristic of the English/Creole Caribbean.

The main developer of Trinidad, the largest of the Lesser Antilles, was Philippe Saint Laurent, a Frenchman who, like other French colonists, saw possible French resources and a peaceful home for himself outside of France.[32] In 1777 he began recruiting government interest in the resettlement of French society throughout the Antilles and particularly on Trinidad. In 1783 a Cedula of Population was drawn up that gave benefits to established Catholics (for example, waivers on tithing and taxes), gave land grants to some Africans, Asians, and Europeans, and permitted limited guarantees of trade in Europe for colonial products, all in return for help in defending the island for France. It was Saint Laurent who wrote a revised Code Noir that was considerably lenient in terms of recognizing the legal rights of the enslaved. He was ignored because of this leniency, and in 1789 another more rigid set of rules was approved by the British, who were then in control.

Sugar and cocoa plantations were the mainstay of British colonial interest after many dismal attempts to populate the islands with British, Scottish, Welsh, and Irish peoples between 1655 and 1700. Africans entering the British islands were both Central and West Africans, and they outnumbered Europeans three to one.[33] Sociologist Orlando Patterson has detailed very sharp divisions and horrific conditions that marked Jamaican social life.[34]

Jamaica differed from other English/Creole islands because of its ample land mass, which held significant numbers of enslaved Africans on plantations, and its mountainous and dense forested terrain, which protected Maroon "runaways" who escaped either from arriving boats as they reached

American shores or from plantation slavery and forged African settlements.[35] Escape from plantations was regularly attempted, and Maroons maintained permanent, hidden encampments. Success in *marronnage* led to Maroon wars, which marked Jamaican history from 1734 through 1795. As Jamaica, St. Lucia, Dominica, St. Vincent, the Grenadines, Barbados, Bermuda, St. Kitts, Antigua, Montserrat, Nevis, and other areas prospered, colonists who made fortunes returned to England as absentee landlords. Patterson points out that "approximately 1.7 percent of the entire master population owned over one-sixth of all the slaves, and the majority of the slaves . . . were owned by approximately 8 percent of the masters . . . [and further,] nine-tenths of all the land under cultivation in the island before emancipation was owned by absentees."[36]

Complacency and lack of education within the European population led to incompetence, irresponsibility, and a lack of morality, noticeably in the English clergy, which acted no better than the dredges of secular society. Such chaotic conditions gave African descendants openings for undetected actions. The economic ineffectiveness of British plantations, compared to other areas of the Caribbean, eventually weakened the British plantation system and assisted political efforts to deconstruct the institution of slavery and establish emancipation earlier than other colonies (1834–48).[37]

The Roman Catholicism that usually accompanied French cultural hegemony was confronted in the English/Creole islands by the force of Anglican Protestantism, and later by competing Moravian, Methodist, Baptist, and other Protestant missionaries.[38] Many missionaries preached abolition of slavery beginning around 1754, and several antimissionary revolts punctuated the history of the English/Creole Caribbean during the early 1800s.[39]

Danish Influence

The Danes were also involved in Caribbean colonization, slavery, and long-term exploitation. For example, the U.S. Virgin Islands were controlled by the Danes from 1655 to 1917. The three islands had different resources and thereby produced distinct histories. St. Thomas has an incredibly deep harbor, which made shipping, transport, and distribution its major interests. St. Croix is flat, which afforded choice cultivation land for sugar cane; thus, plantations and refineries were its legacies. St. John was used as a site for sugar also, but due to its smaller size, it was not as prosperous as St. Croix; however, the Danes were industrious in each setting.[40]

Plans to colonize St. Thomas began in 1665, and several Danish colonists and indentured servants attempted settlement. The Dutch and English war broke out in Europe; English pirates plundered early Danish posts, and clashes with the French deterred meaningful occupation until 1680. In 1685 the Danes entered into a treaty with the Dutch for thirty years in order to establish commerce in the slave trade. The Danish West Indies Company helped to populate the islands substantially with enslaved and free Africans, but also with Danes, English, Irish, Scots, Dutch, German, Spanish, French, and Jews.[41]

The enslaved were prohibited from gathering for feasts, holding drum/ dances, carrying knives or clubs, and being outside after sunset. On the other hand, free African descendants enjoyed a high degree of mobility. Many were on St. Thomas as artisans, crafts persons, and skilled laborers because of its cosmopolitan setting and bustling commercial enterprises. Plantations on St. Croix and St. John necessitated manual laborers, and consequently enslaved workers predominated on these islands; however, many Africans bought their freedom after years of service or were manumitted according to the death wishes of colonial masters. Free Africans adopted the manners and ways of Europeans to such an extent that the Danes made laws to curb their accomplishments. For example, in 1786, free Creoles or "coloreds" were forbidden to wear silk stockings, gold, silver, or lace, since such items were "too extravagant" for non-Europeans.[42]

Dutch Influence

What is different about the Dutch Caribbean is its military, administrative, and commercial character, and its late settlement patterns. Accordingly, the early historical records do not provide the descriptive evidence of European and African social encounters that were more typical of Spanish settlement in the sixteenth century and French, British, and Danish settlement in the seventeenth century. What they do indicate, however, is the significance of Dutch slave trafficking patterns in the Caribbean, emanating from Dutch forts on the African continent and affecting Caribbean trade in Africans and, ultimately, New World African performance practices.[43]

When the Portuguese were subdued under the Spanish crown in 1580, the Dutch became commercial leaders. They hoped to block the Portuguese from Brazil and dominate the lucrative trade in salt and sugar for Europe and enslaved Africans for the Americas. They could sell to the Spanish, who, under the Papal bull, would never have forts on the African continent and would always have to buy enslaved Africans from other European traders. The Dutch became pivotal for Central African trafficking after taking control of two Portuguese posts on the African coast: Argyn or Elmina (or São Jorge), in 1637 and then Ndongo or Angola, in 1641. Also, because Curaçao was not suited for plantation agriculture, its desert conditions served as a major slave depot for the Dutch from 1634 to about 1749, facilitating the transport of thousands of enslaved Africans across Caribbean territories for more than a hundred years. This brought many Africans, particularly Central Africans, to Dutch ports of Curaçao and New Amsterdam (New York) starting in the early seventeenth century.[44] Curaçao continued as an important way station for recuperating Africans after the Middle Passage.[45] By 1778, the natural increase of the enslaved population made slave trafficking almost unnecessary; noticeably, however, abolition did not come to Dutch territories until late in 1865.[46]

As Spain left island territories unprotected and uninhabited for mainland interests in Mexico and South America, there was constant flux among Europeans in the Caribbean. Dutch leaders looked to Curaçao as their strategic economic center for enslaved merchandise, but they lost their early sources in Angola and were defeated by the Portuguese by the mid-seventeenth century. Also, as Britain became increasingly powerful on the seas and the Portuguese were freed from Spanish rule, they both became competition for the Dutch, on sea as well as land. Additionally, the French challenged the Dutch as the squeeze for territories and profit narrowed.

European settlement on Curaçao does not appear until the entry of Jewish families in the late seventeenth century.[47] They were the largest colonial group on the island for the next hundred years, influencing all matters because they controlled trade. My Curaçaoan consultants often reported that Dutch Sephardic Jews coming from Brazil brought the secret of sugar refining to Tobago, not Curaçao, which is often cited. Curaçao, they explained, was too dry for sugarcane production.[48] Also, the Catholic Franciscan order sent clergy to educate, aid, and evangelize African captives. Catholic brotherhoods must have played a role in African-derived performance of European-derived dances, since they encouraged European as well as Christian behaviors and sought to prohibit African practices.[49]

Dutch colonial history suggests that dance- and music-making events, such as those described for other parts of the Caribbean, were minimal, which reflects the puritanical blinders of many Dutch colonial Protestants. One can infer from Dutch history that whatever dancing took place among Europeans and Africans probably did not occur routinely until the last decades of the eighteenth century and the beginning of the nineteenth century. Thus, most Dutch Caribbean dance practices were influenced either by a slow development or by later European dance practices than those that initiated *contredanse*-related performance elsewhere in the Caribbean.[50]

Caribbean Set Dancing

Cuban *contradanza* and *tumba francesa*

Although Spanish culture in Spain and its colonies had been heavily influenced by the French court, additional French culture came to Spanish islands with a wave of French immigration between 1790 and 1820. Anticipating the Haitian Revolution, French and Creole colonists brought both their French-Haitian and enslaved or "black" French-Haitian families to Cuba, Puerto Rico, Alabama, and Louisiana.[51] French-Haitian colonists quickly filled an economic niche in coffee production throughout the eastern provinces of Cuba, where land was cheap and coffee grew well. The new immigrants were welcomed most, however, as musicologist Olavo Alén reports, because of fears concerning the mounting "black" majority. Spanish colonists thought that French immigrants could balance, as well as *blanquear,* or "whiten," the enlarging African population of the Spanish colonies at the end of the eighteenth century.[52]

French *contredanse,* which had come to Cuba originally with both aristocrats and workers, now became the rage among the entire European population—Spanish *peninsulares,* Spanish *criollos,* and "white" French-Haitians. Colonists danced sets of "the minuet, rigadons, lanciers and Contradanzas in the large salons" at the invitation of *bastoneros,* those who directed group dancing, who "called" the figures, and who also set partners for each dance.[53] Historian John Chasteen reports:

> Closed-couple choreography entered the most strait-laced balls only gradually. It was never danced, for example, by Queen Victoria, at whose court quadrilles predominated through the nineteenth century. . . . Between 1800 and 1850, . . . the social dance repertoire of Rio, Havana, and Buenos Aires derived from three distinct overlapping waves. Open couple dances were fading but still danced. One, the minuet, with its many little ceremonies and hierarchy-conscious courtesies, remained the standard first number at dances with any pretensions of social gravity. . . . The first couples were followed by others in strict descending order of social prestige. Interdependent-couple dances—contradance, quadrille, cotillion, and local variations—normally followed the minuet. Waltzing began later, when the dancers were warmed up, the minuet dancers had said goodnight, and everybody else had made a few trips to the punch bowl. . . . The waltz retained its slightly risqué air . . . well into the middle of the nineteenth century.[54]

Accordingly, the mixed heritage of Creole or mulatto musicians who played *contradanzas* and other salon music, as well as instrumental music for ensemble entertainment, operas, theater, and military bands, fueled the controversy around dancing.[55] Dancing was influenced by the distinct styles and rhythms that gradually entered salons from the plantation barracks by means of *mulato* musicians, who comprised military bands and played for most social events since dance musician was not an accepted role for Europeans. Also, European men attended *mulata* (women of color) balls, learned sequences, felt alternate rhythms, and returned to perform in and influence "proper" society. Dance academies were popular and simultaneously scandalous, but the dances flourished. As the century wore on, set dancing was influenced by the freer style of independent couple dancing in the last set.[56]

What colonists danced and called *"contradanza"* in the Spanish Caribbean was influenced by African-derived French-Haitian musicians who played for colonists but also for their own versions of set dancing. Africans arriving from Haiti differentiated themselves from other African-descended peoples first by speaking and singing in the Creole (Kreyol) language that had developed on Haiti for almost two centuries, and second by dancing their set dances to drum accompaniment and call-and-response singing. Their *tumba francesa* included *cinquillo* (*quintolet*) or a syncopated, repetitive, five-note/beat rhythmic motif—among other rhythms.[57] *Tumba francesa* set dancing (*masón, yubá,* and *frenté*) maintained an undivided torso and straight back in accordance with both the lines and configured designs of European court style and the imitative style of Creole Europeans in both Haiti and Cuba. At the ending section, however, the African-descended King or leader danced with two or more women, turning them alternately. He then proceeded to a solo section of virtuoso footwork in syncopated rhythms and (in contemporary versions) employed gymnastic splits and lunges (see photos 3 and 4).[58]

While *contradanza* among the new French immigrants was energetic as well as beautiful, it did not reach the degree of improvisation or scale of torso-generated and, later, gymnastic movement that were included in *tumba francesa. Contradanza* served as group set dancing with increasing interest in the last set of closed-couple, rhythmic dancing; additionally for Cuba, *contradanza* was part of the classical instrumental music repertoire.[59] In their dance and music development, *contradanzas* were discussed as a diabolical plot perpetrated by the French on the Spanish or as an assault on Christianity. Thus, two distinct *contredanse*-derived practices engaged the Cuban population, and both displayed courtly, aristocratic, or regal qualities. Cuban *contradanza* underwent significant change in the last two decades of the eighteenth century and registered as a completely new *danza* or the *danzón* complex, which today serves a national, historical function.[60] *Tumba francesa* continues in practice within intimate social functions of remaining French-Haitian societies and within Cuban cultural and tourist displays.[61]

Puerto Rican *contradanza, los seises* and the Influence of *la bomba*

One of Puerto Rico's earliest dance practices existed inside Catholic churches and was derived from *los seises* performance in Spain. There, *seises* were a series of changing figures with upright body orientation danced by six (*seis*) young altar boys during the Catholic Mass[62]; they were linked to the dance of six young mulatto girls in the colonies who danced to guitar music in front of the altar after Mass.[63] Both dances featured *contredanse*-related materials—sets, intricate figures, and a repeated *balancé* step. As dancing inside churches was criticized and curtailed over time, the sacred *seises* influenced the secular dancing that was permitted and performed by rural farmworkers outside churches.

Historian Manuel Alonso described *seis* dance patterns, noting the similarity between early *seises* and later *contradanzas*.[64] Folkloric dance specialist Mágdalis García Sánchez also emphasizes the structural linkages between *seis* and *contradanza* practices as she relates their survival in the center of the island as historical/folkloric forms. Her data suggest that both French-Haitian and African-French-Haitian migrations influenced Puerto Rican *contradanza* in the late eighteenth century, particularly on the western coast of Puerto Rico from Aguadilla to Ponce.[65] As in Cuba, *contradanzas* in Puerto Rico were "figure" dances directed by a *bastonero,* who controlled both the dance patterns and who danced with whom. The dances were performed outdoors as well as indoors and, despite some restrictions, all levels of society occasionally danced together in public.[66] Line choreographies were influenced by Afro-Puerto Rican military bands that regularly accompanied social dances. Dances were also influenced by both French/Haitian and Venezuelan migrations to Puerto Rico.[67] *Contradanza* became (*contredanse*-related) face-to-face *danza* and, later, *plena*.

Both *danza* and *plena* are distinct Creole dance creations of nineteenth- and early-twentieth-century Puerto Rico. Both emphasized closed-couple position throughout most of the dance; therefore, Puerto Rican *danzas* overtook *contradanza* form with the rejection of established line and square configurations, just as the Cuban *danzón* did in Cuba.[68] *Los seises,* on the other hand, retained its close relationship to *contradanzas* and also to *bomba,* Puerto Rico's signature traditional dance.[69]

A series of alternating and contrasting sets reflected the European base of *los seises,* which meshed with African solo and duet improvisations in front of drums to form Creole *bomba* (see Ledru, quote above). Dance researcher García Sánchez reports that in the sixth figure of the *seis,* which is the fastest and most virtuoso set (called *el seis bombeao),* the *seis* dancers shout *"bomba"* when the music stops at the end of a couplet refrain. Jesús Cepeda Brenes (of Grupo Folklórico Nacional Hermanos Cepeda), a musician from one of several renowned *bomba* families, corroborated García Sánchez from the music perspective and offered another connection among *seises, contradanzas,* and *bombas.* He referred to the series of seven drum rhythms in the *sicá* section of *bomba: lero, belén, yubá, yubá cuembe, yubá mason, yubá corrido,* and *colbé,* in which *bomba* drumming structure parallels the set dance structure of five (or more) succeeding parts and displays French-Haitian influence on Puerto Rican dance.[70]

Bomba sicá terminology also placed *bomba* in close relationship to *contradanza. Lero* is a Spanish rendering of the French *la rose,* which was a figure in the French *contredanse* set called *lanciers.* Also, Spanish *belén* references French *bele* or *"belle air"* (beautiful melody) and becomes yet another potential linguistic link to Puerto Rican *contradanza* practices.[71] Beyond linguistic semblances, however, *belén* recalls *contradanza* in actual dance descriptions by folklorists de Figueroa Berríos and López Cruz y Ríos: " [O]ne interprets a group in line formation; each couple dances in front of the musicians and then performs its part passing afterward to the end of the line so that couples dance in succession until everyone has had his/her turn, and that ends the dance."[72]

In terms of *bomba* movements and for the *sicá* rhythms especially, the dance today features reminiscences of French court deportment. There is a salutation and the men hold only the tips of the women's fingers as they dance certain sections. Both performers' backs are held upright and straight, as opposed to the main dancing that follows, which involves a forward inclined back in front of the drums. Another dance specialist, Gilda Hernández San Miguel, also emphasized the courtly French influence of *contradanza* within *bomba'*s salutation section when she related oral culture that has emphasized similar postural stylizations as a result of the French-Haitian migration to Puerto Rico after the Haitian Revolution.[73] Dance and music experts alike emphasize the stately and regal deportment of (contemporary) western Puerto Rican *bomba* performers[74]; however, the dance perspective turns most often to the connections between *los seises* and *contradanzas.*[75]

A similar development of European *contredanses* and *quadrilles* to American *contradanza* set dancing evolved in Puerto Rico; however, the surge to couple dancing usurped set form and lingered until the mid-twentieth century in Puerto Rico.[76] After 1840, invitational salon parties began to include the closed-partnered circling of the *waltz* and later, the face-to-face coupling of the *polka; bastoneros* were gradually eliminated, which freed the dancing couple and musicians as well; accordingly, *contradanza* morphed toward *danza puertorriqueña.*

Dominican *sarandunga* vs. *carabiné* and *mangulina*

Ethnomusicologist Martha Ellen Davis has focused on Afro-Dominican dance and music practices within the Dominican dance taxonomies provided by ethnologists Edna Garrido de Boggs and Fradique Lizardo.[77] More recent study of Dominican dance has focused on popular dance from the music and social history perspective—for example, *bachata* and *merengue.*[78] In these sources, authors posit *contredanse* as the elegant French influence within eighteenth- and nineteenth-century Dominican dance history. Several dance types emerged in the seventeenth and early eighteenth centuries: *tumba, yucca, carabiné, mangulina, chenché,* and others. All began as set dances, but most evolved into specific local dances with face-to-face, independent couple dancing.[79]

Contradanza was *tumba* in the Dominican Republic, line dancing with couple figures and repeating and then alternating sets (similar to neighboring Haitian *tumba francesa*). It employed four couples in concentric circles or double lines of dancers with little intimacy between dancers, and it was distinguished from a two-couple *contradanza* that came independently from Spain.[80] *Tumba* was replaced first by *quadrilles* or square formations, which became the rage after 1750 but disappeared after 1840.

Among the districts of Villa Mella, Baní, and Samaná (the small Dominican communities known for their African heritage and Haitian influence), however, Martha Davis introduced me to Dominican *sarandunga*[81] in Baní. Led by family elders with hierarchically related titles, dancers perform two dances—first, *la capitana* and *la bomba* (not Puerto Rican *bomba*). In contrast with the first two sets of *sarandunga* as well as with described versions of *la mangulina* and *la carabiné,* I found contemporary remnants of *contredanse* in the figures of *jacana.*

The entire *sarandunga* performance begins explicitly with a parade or procession, called *el morano,* which conforms to *contredanse* form. It proceeds to *la capitana,* a set dance that involves a circling chase of a seemingly shy female dancer by a male dancer in restrained pursuit (reminiscent of *calenda* couple dancing in front of the drums). The Dominican *bomba* set did not vary from *capitana* in terms of movement; rather, different songs indicated the new set. New songs and rhythms announced *jacana* also, but these signaled quite different steps, body positioning, and movement sequences. Each couple dropped the pseudo-chase and danced a greeting and honoring sequence in repeated formality: the pattern of advance, retreat, counterclockwise circling, followed by clockwise circling—all typical features of French *contredanse* form and style. Performance echoed court dance imitation with noticeably straight backs and only scant hip movement, but there was the added accompaniment of a small percussion ensemble with lead singer and chorus (see photo 5). While *jacana* is the only set within *sarandunga* form that achieves *contradanza*-like patterns, there could be other dances that contain *contredanse* linkages elsewhere in the island nation, possibly with differing names.[82]

From the dance perspective, Dominican *contredanse*-related forms were influenced more by incessant island struggles with France and Spain and the impetus toward independence, both in society and in dance form. With sentiments that encompassed Europe and the Americas just preceding the French (1789) and the Haitian (1791) Revolutions, Dominican forms of *contradanza* were replaced by *danza dominicana* (like the entire *danzón* complex of Cuba and *danza* and *plena* in Puerto Rico). Dominican Director of Folkloric Dance at the Autónoma University of Santo Domingo José Castillo, as well as Director of National Folklore Xiomarita Perez, point to *la carabiné, la mangulina,* and *la yuca* as the closest Dominican forms to historical French *contredanse* practices. As demonstrated by them, the dance steps resemble the *waltz* and an alternating quick walk. The walk uses a petite double step in which the female accents small hip shifts to both sides. Both the *waltz* and the quick step accommodate many spatial designs; however, Dominican couples used a face-to-face dancing position for most of their historic salon dances, indicating Dominican tastes, but also the move toward *danza* or couple dancing rather than ensemble *contredanse*-derived figures.[83]

Chart 9. Revised *Sarandunga* Form

A. *El morano*	(a procession)
B. *La capitana*	(a set, "*kalenda*-like" chase)
C. *La bomba*	(a set, "*kalenda*-like" chase)
D. *Jacana*	(a set, *quadrille*-like)

Haitian Affranchi Dances

Haiti is historically unique as the first African-derived republic of the Americas and the first slaveless society of the New World; therefore, its case differs from other French-influenced islands. Since the Haitian Revolution (1791–1804), the island nation has been marked by African heritage and tremendous foreign intervention from Europe, the Middle East, Canada, and the United States; however, non-African heritages on the island have not made significant contributions to Haitian dance.[84] Haiti's history of African-descended liberators produced an African-derived dance history with a group of colonial dances called *affranchis,* the *contredanse*s and *quadrilles* of the European and Affranchi (African/European or Creole) class.[85]

Haitian dance master Jean Léon Destiné describes *affranchi* as the entertainment that Europeans delighted in on Saint Domingue/Haiti. The dance name was taken from the European men and African-descended women who lived *placé* (common-law marriage) and whose descendants formed a separate, privileged class (Affranchi, in Kreyol *mulat*). Both Europeans and Affranchis performed the varied line and square configurations and often insisted that the enslaved community perform the dances as entertainment for colonial guests. Less stylized versions are practiced in the countryside at *fet chanpet* (country festivals), occasionally apart from, but also during Vodou services, and more manicured versions are presented in tourist programming.[86]

Ethnomusicologist Michel Largey has summarized the ambiguous early history of Haitian *contredanse* and emphasized the influence of *mulato* military band musicians in the formation and decline of *contredanse* figures, as they also played for *bals* on plantations, rendering influences within and between their repertoires of *marches,* drills, *quadrilles, waltzes,* and *polkas.* Largey notes the sponsorship of dance parties and balls by women of color, in Saint-Marc and Jérémie especially.[87] He identifies *carabinier* dance (from "rifleman") as a set within *contredanse* figures that mushroomed into a couple dance with distinct rhythmic interest (*cinquillo, quintolet, habanera*[88]), which eventually influenced the entire Caribbean.

Similar to Cuban *tumba francesa* form, *affranchi* involved a series of straight-backed, held-torso, French-styled figures and then, African-styled improvisation in a final set.[89] Destiné accentuated the historical shift from *minuets* and *kadrils* to *congo minuet* and *carabinier,* when, as artistic director for the National Troupe of Haiti, he revived the dances in the 1950s. He used a series of alternating set dances, slow and fast, with squares of four couples dancing to the instructions of the *commandeur/komande/met dans,* who called the figures. This was contrasted with a fast or up-tempo, improvisational set with virtuoso acrobatics and ample "*picads*" or pelvic thrusts, revealing torso division and hip isolations or African movement characteristics. *Contredanse* and *affranchi* practices permeated the island, accompanied by African-descended Kings and Queens. It was this highly esteemed performance style and regal association that were taken to Cuba, Puerto Rico, and the Diaspora U.S. in the late eighteenth century.[90]

Martinican *Bele* and *Haut-Taille*

On Martinique, the terms *belle air, belair,* or *bele* came into use as one of four types of *quadrille* practice: *lakadri* or *pastourelle, haut-taille, lancers,* and *bele*.[91] The French *"belle air"* is often reported as "lovely song," but linguists indicate its alternate, *bele,* can refer to "a dance that features hip movement."[92] Among my field consultants, there was yet another understanding of *bele* that pointed to dance, but also to a cleared, usually flat, space of earth where one can build something. A beautiful space or ambiance coincides with the Lingala (Bantu/Central African) term, *mabele,* which means "earth, land, ground, or floor." It is on such types of clearings, inside thick banana groves for example, that *gwanbele* and *bele swarés,* the big *bele* collectives, are still conducted.[93]

Despite an obvious association with European court forms, Martinicans dance their versions of colonial square dance—specifically *bele linó*—in bare feet, just as Dominican women dance *sarandunga* and Puerto Rican women dance some forms of *los seises.* Today, women wear long or short, wide or narrow skirts with white petticoats showing or not; but most important, they wrap a scarf around or under their hips to accent lower torso and hip movements. Men dance in pants or jeans, shirts, and sometimes carry a scarf in one hand. The dance sets are strict in form, but improvisational in content within a recognized dance vocabulary of rhythmic movements, suspensions, and accents.[94]

Ethnomusicologist Julian Gerstin has described the revival of Martinican *bele* that has permeated the island for the past few decades as a sign of island identity among different classes and across different levels of political consciousness.[95] The first circling in a counterclockwise direction and the clockwise circling at the end are, in fact, short processions—just like the beginning of Cuban *tumba francesa,* Dominican *sarandunga* and Curaçaoan *kuadria* (discussed below), but here the procession proceeds in a circle. The procession does not initiate face-to-face partnered dancing (as it did in Puerto Rico and the Dominican Republic). Rather, the circles proceed quickly to square formation and *quadrille* continues with side-by-side couple dancing in opposing lines that form the sides of the square.

Four couples dance in a series of exchanges between male and female partners and partner opposites, at each side of the square formation. In the next section, each couple dances alone and, after rhythmic flirtation in dance, advances toward the drum to mark three culminating accents that acknowledge both the drummer and each performer's expertise in dance. After each of the four couples has completed this salutation to the drum, everyone resumes the circle procession to finish the set.

Bele is filled with ingenious body articulation and rhythmic figures. Its formal structure features a divided torso, virtuosity, and rhythmically distinct body part isolation. Innovative frolic between partners, between opposing partners, and between dancer and lead drummer are constant (see photos 1 and 2). It is absolute fun when the form and vocabulary are mastered and spontaneous creativity rules.[96]

Following the French Code Noir stipulations, rigid laws prohibited African-inspired dancing and outlawed the drums; however, Martinicans responded by using one drum played by two drummers: one with sticks on the side of the drum, the other with bare hands and a distinct heel-lifting technique that changes the tones of the drumhead (transverse drumming). The drummer who plays on the side keeps a steady, repetitive rhythm (*ostinato*), while the main drummer fills out the accompaniment as he also leads and responds to performing dancers.[97] The solo drum contrasts with other Caribbean *quadrille* musical groupings of three to five (or more) instruments and lighter musical textures. The seeming visual imbalance is not heard; the solo drum does not produce a shallow sound; in fact, its emphatic syncopation aids dancers in the process of inserting their improvised rhythms as foot movements, hand, arm, or hip gestures, and short dance sequences.

Martinican *bele* contrasts with Martinican *haut-taille,* where couples also dance sets in square formation, but with more restrained movement. Ethnomusicologist Esther Eloidin has concentrated on this type of Caribbean *quadrille,* which only remains in François District today, and reports the general pattern: all dancers formally bow and curtsy, change places adroitly, and execute distinctive foot patterns.[98] Rather than indulge in the extensive improvisational body play of *bele linó, haut-taille* retains the stately quality of court practices, but with *en aire* movements (little jumps, hops, and kicks performed by men) that characterize most elaboration.

Both Martinican *haut-taille* and *bele* continue set-dance structure; however, *haut-taille* has very few representatives. Conversely, *bele* performance is encouraged and taught through cultural organizations, such as AM4, in an effort to preserve African-derived creativity and to avoid clashes over differing regional styles.[99] Interpretations of Martinican *bele* and *haut-taille* range from purposely ridiculing European performance style, to transposing

Africanist body orientation and practices onto French structural form, to approximating stately ballroom dance and/or creating French Caribbean community through group dancing. Historically, *haut-tailles* were performed inside residences or salons, while *beles* were performed outdoors in the countryside; however, both are rural forms today. Within my entire comparison of Caribbean *contredanse*-derived forms, Martinican *bele linó* proved to be unique as the most genuinely original or truly Creole *quadrille* creation.

Guadeloupean *Kadril, Lewoz,* and *Bele*

From a movement perspective, Guadeloupean *kadril (lakadri)* parallels the French-influenced forms discussed earlier: *belén/sicá* rhythms of *bomba,* the sixth figure of *los seises puertorriqueños,* Cuban *tumba francesa,* Dominican *sarandunga,* and Martinican *haut-taille.* Four couples or groups of four couples first dance a *vals creole* set and then, proceed to four other sets: *la pantelon, l'été, la poule,* and *la pastourelle.* Couples dance in the face-to-face formation of nineteenth-century salon dances after the five sets—for example, *mazouk (mazurka), biguine,* or *la boulangé.* According to a local consultant, *la boulangé* was created in the municipal district of Abyme and is now used after the four traditional French sets; however, *la boulangère* was the name of a French *contredanse* or line *(cotillion)* dance that became part of nineteenth-century French *quadrille* and was subsequently adopted by *quadrille* dancers in Guadeloupe and Martinique.[100] *Biguine,* with its face-to-face couple positioning and distinct rhythm, became a preferred French Caribbean salon or ballroom dance.

Despite contrasts, Martinique and Guadeloupe yield three enduring *contredanse*-derived variations, two of which signal stately, restrained posture, an undivided torso, and little body part isolation throughout a series of set dances.[101] Neither the literature nor fieldwork to date has sufficiently explained the absence of *lewoz* inside Guadeloupean *kadril. Lewoz* surfaces in Guadeloupean *gwoka* rather than in *kadril,* where it might be expected. This placement suggests a European element *(lewoz)* within *gwoka,* but that would mean accepting a legacy from European *contredanse,* which Guadeloupeans do not accept thus far. In that case also, *gwoka* would be a *contredanse*-derived creation in the way that Martinican *bele linó* and Trinidadian *bele2* are, on the African-Creole side of a Caribbean *contredanse*-derived continuum.

The word *lewoz,* which is important to set dancing generally, is additionally perplexing on Guadeloupe since it relates to the French "*la rose*" and to French sets of the *contredanse,* where *la rose* was the second set dance. So far, however, that is not recognized in the districts under observation or among the practitioners who were interviewed. Also, *lewoz* connects to the Spanish "*lero*" of Puerto Rican *bomba sicá* variations; however, Guadeloupeans see *lewoz* as a multivocalic or multiple channel term for: 1) a social gathering with food, drinks, music and dancing, 2) one of seven drum rhythms in *gwoka*, and 3) one of the dances in *gwoka*. Like other Caribbean creations, Guadeloupean *lewoz* is an event, a rhythm, and a drum/dance, but not a *contredanse*-derived performance. Also, Guadeloupeans do not include *bele* as a dance; their sung *bele* connects to wakes and funerals (as danced *bele* does in Puerto Rico, Trinidad, and other islands).[102]

Trinidadian *Bele* and *Piqué*

On Trinidad and Tobago, Dominica, St. Lucia, and Carriacou, the Caribbean *quadrille* is called *bele, belair,* or *kwadril,* and there are other names and related dances among the small islands—like *piqué* in Trinidad, a related flirtatious solo derivative.[103] Contemporary practices of English/Creole islands accentuate women's dance movement in French court-inspired costuming. The skirt in madras or flowered prints is distinctive with a split at the front that allows cut-lace or lace-decorated white petticoats to show.[104] Women wear intriguingly wrapped head-ties and sometimes carry a *mouchoir,* or fan, while men accent their shirt and pants, waistcoats, or tails with a *foulard,* or neck-scarf. Head-ties are abundantly varied.[105]

Trinidadian *bele1* (ensemble form) has predetermined figures or patterned steps, as opposed to improvisation; it generally includes a caller who directs the dancers, as well as a Queen, *la reine,* underscoring again the association of royalty roles.[106] *Contredanse*-derived dances are performed by both men and women to musical ensembles consisting of: a) a mixture of percussion, strings, and woodwinds, b) strings and woodwinds only, or c) total percussion (in Queen's *bele2,* which I discuss below).

St. Lucian *Kwadril*

Ethnomusicologist Jocelyne Guilbault has grounded the striking St. Lucian video example that was collected during my field research with her ethnography of La Rose and La Marguerite "societies," two rival social divisions (*moeties*) that comprise St. Lucia.[107] Both societies have a list of officers and roles, including a King, Queen, Prince, and Princess. The La Rose society was known for its free form, inventiveness, oral vs. literate approach to performance, and the inclusion of dancing, which the competing La Marguerite society did not have as characteristic behavior. La Rose members dance the *kwadril* among three other types of dances. St. Lucian *kwadril* performance during a regional festival on St. Thomas is exquisite with attention to publicly articulated manners, control of the body in exacting and repeating figures,

and elegant carriage for both men and women. St. Lucian performance became an exemplary model of Caribbean *contredanse* variations.[108]

Jamaican *Contredanse* Legacies

In spite of the historical and religious differences between the English and
English/Creole areas, Jamaica's dance record is relatively consistent with
other English/Creole islands.[109] Jamaica's *quadrille*-related dance history
features *quadrilles* and *lancers,* followed by a meshing of European and
African dancing called *mento.* Lingering Maroon heritage is related and
unique; its dances have been heavily affected by centuries of British folk-
dance influence.[110] Anthropologists Roger Abrahams and John Szwed report
on African "country dancing" in Jamaica:

> A sort of subscription balls [*sic*] are set on foot, and parties of both sexes as-
> semble and dance country dances to the music of a violin, tambarine, &c. But
> this improvement of taste [over African ring dancing] is in a great measure
> confined to those who are, or have been, domestics about the houses of the
> whites, and have in consequence imbibed a fondness for their amusements, and
> some skill in the performance. They affect, too, the language, manners, and
> conversation of the whites: those who have it in their power have at times their
> convivial parties, when they will endeavour to mimic their masters . . . and it is
> laughable to see with what awkward minuteness they aim at such imitations.[111]

Dance researchers Katherine Dunham and Catherine Evleshin have documented Maroon practices of *do si do* figures, reeling, and "turned out" feet
and toes, which are figures and body positions associated with European
folk and French court practices.[112] Additionally, anthropologist Ken Bilby
references the introduction of *mento* as the fifth or sixth "round" couple
figure of Jamaican *quadrille* heritage.[113] *Mento* was the couple dance that
first augmented Jamaican *kwadril* in early-nineteenth-century sets and anticipated sustained face-to-face couple dancing (like the *waltz, danza* and
biguine had done in the Spanish and French/Creole Caribbean). According to
Jamaican dancer/researcher Cheryl Ryman, *mento* evolved into a twentieth-
century popular dance with sensuous hip circling.[114]

Due to insistent distrust of dancing that permeated Protestant religious
thought generally, which was promoted by the Church of England and many
Protestant sects, the set dancing that has remained in the English/Creole
islands is strict in form and restrained in style. When it stimulates spirit
manifestation (as Bilby and Neely report for Monserrat and Tobago[115]),
it would seem to reflect the severe prohibitions on dancing and enslaved
worshipers who were in conflict with deeply ingrained associations between
dance and spirituality, no matter what movement style was performed, and
point to resignification or the new meanings for old forms over time.[116]

English/Creole *quadrilles* are still linked to the Spanish and French Caribbean islands by the performance of *contredanse*-derived set form, figure dances, and by an associated hierarchy of royal personages.

Danish Development of German and French *Quadrille* Styles

Free Africans who were numerous on the former Danish/U.S. Virgin Islands imitated and adapted the *contredanse* practices of the many types of Europeans on the islands, such that two distinct styles unfolded. A German style on St. Thomas is robust with flat-foot stepping. A French style on St. Croix is considered more decorative, with fancy steps on the ball of the foot. The contemporary order of dances varies, but *contredanse* and *lancers* are favored among the *seven-step, heel-and-toe, mazurka,* and *polka-mazurka* sets. The vast majority of *contredanse* in the Virgin Islands is performed in lines or squares as men and women dance patterned figures in a familiar order of formal bows and curtsies between a series of crossings, passes, circling, and promenading. A caller directs the figures, called "figure 1," "figure 2," "figure 3," and "figure 4," with regular calls of "balancey," "tourney," and "promenade," etc.

Contemporary Virgin Islanders who claim *quadrille* as their specialty trace their expertise through apprenticeships with "old heads" (Mongo Niles, Lucille Roberts, or Adam Peterson, among others). Bradley Christian (from St. Croix) and Carlos Woods (from St. Thomas) apprenticed by observing when elders called and danced *quadrilles*. Consultants verified that while some danced with *bamboula* and drum/dance specialist Ms. Clara, they routinely practiced *quadrille* and helped to establish several groups. All were concerned with island identity, ancestor heritage, and social dance that involved community and individual fun.[117]

Virgin Island performing groups continue the tradition of royalty roles with responsibilities for the presentation of dances and public recognition of organizations. Elegance, propriety, and gracefulness in the dancing are rarely abandoned; proper style is best exemplified in *lancers* performance.[118] Thus, the former Danish Caribbean augments the pervasiveness of Caribbean *quadrilles* across the region, as it displays similar longevity in *contredanse*-derived practices and commonalities in structure and royalty roles to those of Spanish, French/Kreyol, and English/Creole islands.

Dutch *Kuadria/Quadrilla* and *Curaçaoan Danza*

Field consultants report that *kuadria* or *quadrilla* involves a caller and a procession or parade of many dancers and musicians, called *bailia de lei*. This is a direct parallel to Dominican *sarandunga,* which involved the *morano* parade, Martinican *bele linó* with its parade-like circling at the beginning and the end, as well as the formal parading that begins St. Lucian *kwadril,* Cuban *tumba francesa,* Haitian *affranchi,* and Virgin Island *quadrilles.* Curaçaoan couples parade with hands held high or with interlocked elbows and they often carry candles or lights.[119] The parading ensemble stops in front of the house or building with the dance space, enters formally, and then proceeds to the first of a five-part set dance or *kuadria* performance: *la rose, la victoire, le moulinet, la visite,* and *les lancers* or *lancero.*[120] At the close of the directed sets today, the next dance is a *waltz* followed by the *mazurka, polka,* and other face-to-face couple dances.[121]

Curaçaoans perform a unique *danza,* which connects them to Spanish heritage on Dutch Caribbean shores and simultaneously distinguishes them from Puerto Rican, Dominican, and Cuban *danza* performers. *Curaçaoan danza* is danced in *contredanse* style: a square with a series of set figures, in side-by-side couple dancing—not in continuous face-to-face style. Couples dance in *danza* rhythm, which is preceded and interrupted at times by promenading, parading, and a series of salutations or bows in a distinct *march* rhythm. The dance ends with an additional bow, and couples exit in a returning *danza* rhythm.

Curaçaoan danza marks the transition from *contradanza* to *danza;* it shows what *contradanza* might have looked like as figure and couple dancing alternated. Since its Dutch performers arrived later than other Europeans and the *contradanza* was in a late stage of Caribbean development, it appears as a unique ("arrested") variation of *contredanse* practice. In my survey, it falls on the European stylistic end of a Caribbean *quadrille* continuum, in opposition to Martinican *bele linó,* but in a more genuine Creole space toward the center of the chart, where face-to-face (*contredanse*-related) *danza* forms are placed. *Curaçaoan danza* alternates between set and couple dancing and retains square formation for both arrangements; it does not include independent spatial paths and thereby shares *contredanse*-derived and *contredanse*-related practices from each area in the region.[122]

Deciphering Dance Movement and Dance Categories: Creations or Variations?

With the addition of Dutch *contredanse*-derived performances to Spanish, French/Kreyol, English/Creole, and former Danish versions, this chapter has secured the longevity and pervasiveness of *contredanse*-related practices across the Caribbean. This produces a continuum of colonial dances that emphasize upright, straight, and restrained body orientation, as in St. Lucian and St. Thomian *quadrilles* on one side, and a divided torso and abundant body part isolation as in Martinican *bele linó* on the other side. The survey references related African-Creole drum/dance creations that are listed separately due to their flexed and constantly articulating bodies in solo and duet dancing in front of the drums (as in Guadeloupean *gwoka* and Puerto Rican *bomba*), which contrast sharply with set dancing of the same era. It also references European-Creole creations, which are technically *contredanse* legacies also, but those that feature continuous face-to-face couple dancing and, consequently, are listed at the center where Creole creations converge. From a dance perspective, most Caribbean *quadrilles* are French court dance imitations and extensions, performed by African-descended performers according to European dance values; they are "Africanized European" dances or *contredanse* variations.

African imitations of European/American imitations of elite French court dance practices have formed a major dance category throughout the Caribbean. Ultimately, the dance practices are evidence of an indelible creolization, transculturation, or hybridization process, but this particular category does not routinely comprise "new" dance creations, which are generally recognized as veritable Creole dances. Unless musical elements are considered, the dances cannot be deemed "Creole."[123]

Myriad Creole dances have formed in the Caribbean, some as drum/dances (*rumba, bomba, gwoka,* etc.) and others as independent couple or solo dancing (*son, mambo, chachacha, merengue, konpa, bachata, danza, salsa, reggae, calypso, zouk*). Regardless of type, the dances just named are neither African nor European, but instead they are Caribbean Creole creations that combine both European and African movement heritages. Among the *quadrilles* I surveyed, Martinique's *bele linó* reigns as a veritable Creole creation with roots of rather equal African and European proportions. *Curaçaoan danza* is also Creole and displays the transition from variation to Creole creativity. It still demands *contredanse* criteria, like set dance figures and square form, but it also employs *danza* criteria, like couple dancing and some torso division and hip isolation, i.e., both European and African movement characteristics.

While Cuban *tumba francesa*, St. Lucian *kwadril* and Curaçaoan *kuadria* contain essential elements of *contredanse* form, they do not include what most dance researchers take for granted as prime African dance characteristics. A divided torso with isolated hip movement, a forward tilted back with flexed knees (or a "grounded" stance), polyrhythms, and multidimensionality are the strongest and most common indicators of African-derived dance among other characteristics, but in the dances just named, as well as in Dominican *jacana*, Martinican *haut-taille*, St. Thomas' German *quadrille*, and St. Croix's French *quadrille*, these critical characteristics are essentially absent or minimized. Thus, dancing in most Caribbean *quadrilles* does not display African or Creole dance practice, and the question of African descendants adopting European dance values across the Caribbean over centuries is underscored.

Caribbean *quadrilles* are most often performed in terms of European movement values due to the historical popularity of French *contredanse* and the commanding impositions of European colonists, Catholic priests, and later Protestant missionaries who forbade the drums and were horrified by African performance practices. Only Martinican *bele linó* among the representative *contredanse*-derived Caribbean dances I surveyed contains an obvious regard for African movement or style.[124] In fact, French/European dance structure and movement stylization continued within African-derived populations even after abolition of slavery and independence from colonial rule.

African-ness is not entirely lost within Caribbean *quadrilles*, however. First, African-descended bodies perform the *quadrilles*. Percussion often dominates the musical ensemble (as in Cuban *tumba francesa*), even though violins, flutes, and accordions carry the song line or assist the vocal lead (as in St. Lucian *kwadril* and Guadeloupean *kadril*). There is musical polyrhythm, call-and-response song form, and interplay of music and movement—all basic elements of African performance. Therefore, the music ensembles for Caribbean *quadrilles* exhibit strong evidence of creolization, while key dance movements (other than Martinican *bele linó*) are not characteristically African-derived. From the movement perspective, face-to-face *danzas* are genuine Creole creations while most Caribbean *quadrilles* are not; they are variations of European form and style. In addition to non-African body orientation, there is little polyrhythm, curvilinearity, or multidimensionality in the majority of Caribbean set dances. Because of their distinct dance movements and consistent presence over geography and time, however, Caribbean *quadrilles* warrant the separate dance category that chart 8 outlines.

Deciphering King and Queen Pageantry

As noted in each regional description of *contredanse*-derived dance above, King and Queen pageantry characteristically accompanies *quadrille* practices. The collected dance data confirm that regal roles were emblematic of most Caribbean *quadrille* organizations. For example, Olavo Alén reports on Kings and Queens, *presidentes y presidentas,* in Cuba's *tumba francesa*; Jocelyn Guilbault describes the structural hierarchy within St. Lucian *kwadril*, from King to Princess positions; and Virgin Island *quadrille* ensembles that I danced with display King, Queen, Master of Ceremonies, Floor Master, and Honoree roles, and royalty deference was profuse. The practice continues beyond *contredanse*-related dances: for example, Elizabeth McAlister has listed twenty-four titled posts for Rara organizations from presidents, *koronèls*, and *majò jons* (baton majors), in addition to Kings and Queens, Secretary, and Rear Guard, and contemporary Jamaican dancehall has Kings and Queens also.[125]

African leadership roles surfaced most often within *cabildo* and *cofradía* organizations (the mutual-aid associations of African descendants) for processions during *Dia de los reyes*, *Corpus Christi*, and patron saints celebrations. Deference to African Kings and Queens within enslaved populations was noticed by Caribbean colonists and was documented.[126] More important, however, were the elegant parading, extravagant virtuosity, and regal pageantry associated with seventeenth- and eighteenth-century Church calendars. These made King and Queen pageantry almost routine for both Europeans and Africans. A display of both European nobility and African royalty was possible whenever Africans were permitted to celebrate with Europeans in events sponsored by the Catholic Church. New World Africans could re-enact the royal pageantry of former and ongoing hierarchical roles within African communities. Historian John Thornton makes the point: "On the whole, the evidence supports the idea that at least some [enslaved Africans], *and probably a significant number, in all parts of the Atlantic world* possessed sufficient freedom of movement and social interaction to participate actively in the cultural life of the region. . . . Sixteenth- and seventeenth-century European observers were fully aware that African societies were both politically and economically inegalitarian and that these inequalities were represented in social and legal structures."[127]

Additionally, art historian Judith Bettelheim first identified the imitation of European nobility as the source for such pageantry in the English/Creole Caribbean, but reflecting later on contemporary Cuban royalty performances, she noted the genuine and fictive legacies of African royal lineages: "[R]oyal authority is still respected. Rank and authority were not being 'imitated' . . . but rather self-authority was being publicly displayed."[128]

To these data and to the prominence of the Congo kingdom in history,[129] dance investigation adds the omnipresence of dancing African Kings and Queens in the Diaspora, which results in long-surviving royalty references.[130] Central African enslavement accounted for about 40 percent of the entire slave trade over time,[131] and among the many groupings within colonial "Angola"—covering what are now northern Angola, southern Democratic Republic of the Congo, much of the Republic of the Congo and some of Gabon—the Congo kingdom was the major political entity in the region.[132] It was a huge entity of related but differing groups and kingdoms, and many Africans were named and referred to as "Congos" (the northern kingdoms) or "Angolas" (the southern kingdoms, also the Portuguese reference) because of the multiple African subgroups within the Congo kingdom, because of the few Central African ports through which they were funneled into slavery, or because other ethnic names "lost their specificity."[133] Except where I am referencing other authors who use different names and spelling for the same cultural area and ethnic groups, I will hereafter refer to this huge geographic region and massive cultural condensation as Congo/Angola territory and heritage.

References to and drawings, illustrations, and photographs of Kings and Queens are interspersed within colonial histories and Caribbean dance histories (e.g., Cuban and Antiguan royalty, Haitian *Rara* Kings and Queens, Trinidadian Carnival Kings and Queens, *bele/belair* Queens and Kings/Princes of Trinidad and Tobago and Carriacou, staged aristocracy characterizations in Jamaica with Maroon leader Nanny and Kumina Kings and Queens, and Congo Kings in Brazil, etc.).[134] The illustrations and dance examples over centuries suggest that in Caribbean performance settings, Kings and Queens were routinely present and expressed African leadership, hierarchy, a display of male and/or female gender, individual prowess, and virtuosity, most often through superbly managed physical feats. Additionally, specific Central African dance elements emerge: 1) abundant hip-circling movement, 2) an approach and retreat couple dance pattern, and 3) elegant parading in the context of Congo-descended royalty practices.[135] While these data parallel accounts of West African Kings and Queens as well, the related dance data point to more consistent Central African connections.

Deciphering Queen Performance

The survey of *contredanse*-derived dance practices had to take notice of one solo performance (Trinidadian Queen's *bele2*) because its name referenced *quadrille* practices. This dance did *not* conform to *quadrille* movement characteristics, although it contained the essence of royalty performance.[136] In order to place the solo Queen anomaly in proper perspective, a brief review follows of solo and duet practices, as opposed to ensemble set dancing.

In most Afro-Caribbean solo and duet dancing before the eighteenth centuries (in other words, drum/dances like *kalendas, djoubas, bamboulas,* and *chicas*), performance did *not* reference nobility status or indicate regal pageantry. Performances occurred during festive collectives, and dance movements were sequences toward or improvisations with the drums. Researchers have found virtuosity, competition, sensuality/sexuality, and intense communication among dancing soloists or couples and between dancers and drummers, but not royalty references.[137] "King performance" has been pronounced at times, perhaps as a display of male virtuosity in a trio or duet, as in Cuban *tumba francesa,* but more often the King was simply a protector of the Queen who escorted her into and out of the dance space.[138] On the other hand, "Queen performance" has resonated frequently and has been highlighted across the Caribbean as a solo or at least as an organizing central figure within a performance event. Unlike King and Queen practices within ensemble *quadrilles,* the Queen's solo of Trinidad or *bele2* includes African-based torso-division, hip circling, rhythmic intricacies of the feet, and upper-body-part rhythmic isolation. This is movement vocabulary found in descriptions of *kalenda, djouba, bamboula,* and *chica* performances, even though the latter group of dances customarily retained virtuoso display as their objective.

Given the Queen's grand costuming, a reference to African royalty as well as to seventeenth- and eighteenth-century colonial history, and the social deference within a solo, her movement display could have been an explicit imitation of French set dancing or *contredanse*-derived performance only. Conversely however, her performance on Trinidad and Tobago was decidedly Creole. She wore skirts that referenced European fashion and camouflaged African understandings; overskirts above multiple petticoats outwardly imitated European conventions, but when opened they alluded to escaping enslavement, "flying away to Africa," as multiple tales, song lyrics, and McDaniel's Carriacouan research have established.[139] The Queen was leader of a dancing community and thereby free to dance her choice of style—at least in some settings. In this second form of *bele,* she was an African-descended Queen, dressed in imitation of both European finery and African royalty who elected to dialogue with drummers in African rhythmic/body communication.

Therefore, despite its seeming dissonance with the French-influenced ensemble movement of other Caribbean *quadrilles, bele2* is placed in two positions on the Quadrille Continuum: under African solos and duets and between African-Creole forms and Caribbean *quadrille* forms. (Trinidadian *bele1* remains among ensemble set dancing.) In its first position, Trinidad's *bele2* is an African-based drum/dance that contrasts with Caribbean set dancing. In its second position, it is a condensation of the royal pageantry that exists within ensemble set dancing—this time, in one regal set that symbolizes the enslaved community's opposition; this time, as performed agency through intermittent African movement in front of drums. Linguist and cultural interpreter Maureen Warner-Lewis records a description of that solo written by renowned dancer Beryl McBurnie in 1958:

> Certainly this swaying of the skirt-hems is a hallmark of the *bele* of the Eastern Caribbean, where it is an exclusive female performance. Dressed in the *dwiyet* . . . , an ankle-length frilled skirt with an overskirt opened down the front, the dancer takes
>
>> "the hem of her dress in both hands, and held straight out at the sides, she shuffles and glides, alternating with *mincing steps of heel and toe* . . . Then she swings the hem up front, which forms a long loop from the fingers to the waist, with arms full stretched. . . . Now her rhythmic feet are doing a slow three beat *counter to the time set*. . . . In a split second, she throws the hem of her douillette over both arms. . . . *Spreading her right foot in a wide circle,* she quickly follows it with her left, and puts her right foot in place again. The pattern is repeated on the left side."[140] "Now ready for her 'grand gesture,' she moves with the stalking grace of a peacock. Then with great speed, she *swings around the dance space* like a tropical bird in flight. Frilly petticoats, like soft down flurrying in the wind, a setting for her plumes of rich plaid. There is an uproar in the crowd; running commentary on her brilliant performance. The audience is hers. She *gracefully moves her hips,* which she controls with her hands in her hem bulked behind."[141]

Very much like the final *contredanse* sets in the Cuban and Haitian ensemble examples that explode with African movement qualities after a full display of dance figures in French style, the Queen's *bele2* stands out as the moment when a limited few African-descended women regularly performed a particularly expressive African-Creole dance. When McBurnie states that the Queen spreads her feet wide and "gracefully moves her hips," her dance is no longer a "mincing" European imitation, but a challenge, named after other appropriated dances—*bele*.[142]

Drawing on both a special case and more common *contredanse*-derived practices, the cross-cultural dance data imply that the assimilation of European-styled movements and the appropriation of elite French form early in Caribbean colonial histories, and then, over time, ultimately constituted bodily challenges to European power in each Caribbean linguistic area. In the process, African dances were lost and in their places a dance category of Caribbean set dances developed that facilitated the reenactment of Congo/Angola royalty heritage.

Deciphering African Values and Coloniality

Several cultural values interact within Caribbean *quadrille* performances. Most apparent is a sense of coloniality or neocolonialism that frames most set dancing and establishes strong echoes of French court values.[143] Through European body orientation and dance figures, a sense of proper behavior and elite status is communicated. Performance elements project the neocolonialism that persists after colonization and decolonization, which contrasts with African values of contestation and agency that are camouflaged, but projected also.

As historian Gabriel Entioppe, musicologist Dominique Cyrille, anthropologist Bill Mauer, and others have shown, dance of all sorts by African-descended performers could be viewed as a form of resistance in the period of enslavement and beyond.[144] Instead of "resistance," I use the definition favored by Richard D. E. Burton and Umi Vaughan that employs "contestation" or "opposition" for the kind of resistance dance practices are.[145] It is "opposition" or "contestation" when the means of resistance are found *within* a given system, as opposed to weapons and other resources or tools from *outside* a system. As described in firsthand accounts, Africans and their descendants rushed to dance in their own spaces even after prolonged hours of horrendous work.[146] Only in their own quarters was there temporary liberation from the plantation or, as historian Gabriel Entioppe concludes, "a *marronnage* of the mind"; however, dance in the presence of colonial masters had to be calculated performance, camouflaged opposition, or concealed agency.[147]

In the seventeenth and eighteenth centuries, pervasive African values about the centrality of dance in society coincided with overwhelming European values pertaining to dance.[148] Like European dancing, African dancing was routinely used for more than recreation; like European dancing, African dancing regularly communicated social and cultural values within society; and like European dancing, African dancing repeatedly communicated differentiated identities and statuses between Europeans and Africans and between free and enslaved classes. *Quadrille* performances suggested a raised status for those who could execute the exacting figures and retain the required body comportment; thereby, an undercurrent of the "cool" permeated *contredanse* performance.

"Coolness" was among several important African dance characteristics that were delineated by Robert Thompson and Brenda Gottschild earlier. It signified calm composure and required poise, calculating, knowing, smooth, "slick," deliberate, quiet, and purposeful behaviors.[149] For many African descendants, the practice of European set dancing was an entertainment, but it was also a deliberate performance of what was officially expected, a performance of endurance with a submerged purpose concerning humane identity. The subtexts of the dances necessitated coolness.

In addition, another African value permeated surface coloniality: the guarding of what the ancestors did, said, and valued, or ancestor reverence. Thompson discusses the important reliance on an ancestral past as "the ability to incarnate the past" or "ancestorism," and Gottschild discusses it as "collective/communal trust."[150] While ancestor reverence was invisible within *contredanse*-derived practices, it was indelibly understood across the seven representative Caribbean islands of this survey. Most *contredanse* performers viewed their performance as a repetition of what their ancestors had danced before. When performers were asked why they continued *quadrille* performance, they repeated what one St. Thomian consultant stated most clearly: "Because so many of my ancestors did also."[151] For African-descended performers, *quadrilles* were no longer European dances, but resignified dances of their African-descended New World ancestors. *Quadrilles* reflected old understandings in new ways.

African ancestors passed the dances on as responsible behaviors displayed bodily and dictated nonverbally within the horrific circumstances of enslavement and colonization. Their descendants resisted European values that would destroy esteemed African values and appropriated what would otherwise be an aversion—imitation of French court dancing. In either imitative or creative styles (e.g., Guadeloupean *kadril* and Martinican *bele* respectively), *contredanse* performers expressed the African value of ancestor respect covertly within overt coloniality; simultaneously, they expressed agency through French dance figures performed in cool control.

Dances of Authority

Long after colonists, Catholic priests, and Protestant missionaries insisted on European dance movement, Caribbean performers held on to *contredanse*-derived practices as they executed the graceful and exacting steps of *quadrilles*, skillfully played appropriate instruments, and taught the declarative dance style to their children. Persistent set dancing today suggests neocolonial attachment to European culture at the movement level of analysis but also suggests camouflaged agency, indelible contestation, and persistent opposition to elite subjugation at the cultural level of analysis.

As contemporary performers dance social genres of the past for entertainment and informative recreation, they also underscore the shift from

European to Caribbean authority. Contemporary island nations struggle to stand on equal footing with other national powers, and identity and status are repeatedly performed, especially on protocol occasions, to articulate equality and contest notions of superiority and dominance. Caribbean bodies dance sovereignty in front of world powers, some of whom represent former colonial masters; they affirm island and regional integrity in the nonverbal communication of dance performance.

Caribbean *quadrille* dancers continue to express their yearnings for full citizenship, even within the realities of national independence that they have achieved already. Contemporary *quadrille* practices represent the status quo of Caribbean identity, both its sovereignty and its inequality, within a twenty-first-century global community. The need for performed freedom, dignified independence, and a genuine sense of belonging has continued over centuries.

CHAPTER FOUR

CREOLE DANCES IN
NATIONAL RHYTHMS

Creole dance creations have become synonymous with island identity: Cuban *danzón* or *rumba*, Jamaican *reggae*, Trinidadian *calypso*, Dominican *merengue*, and French Caribbean *zouk* are some examples. These and other social dances have come to light first as popular community dances and often thereafter as endeared folk or ballroom forms that have permeated the region and sometimes the world. In their sites of origin, the dances became popular because of their capacity to generate contagious pleasure and their close alignment with both local conditions and island values.[1] This chapter focuses first on several Caribbean national dances and then examines national dance formation through the Cuban case, since Cuba has a unique but representative dance history.

Mereng/Merengue, Danza/Bomba,
Gwoka/Biguine, Calypso, and *Reggae*

While historian John Chasteen cites the first closed-couple dancing with the earliest of European and African mixing off the coast of Africa on

Chart 10. Caribbean National Dances

Cuba:	*danzón* [*son, rumba, conga/comparsa, salsa/casino*]
Puerto Rico:	*danza* [*bomba, plena, salsa*]
Dominican Republic:	*merengue* [*bachata*]
Haiti:	*mereng* [*konpa*]
Martinique:	*bele, biguine*
Guadeloupe:	*gwoka/lewoz, biguine*
Trinidad:	*calypso*
Jamaica:	*reggae* [*dancehall*]
Circum-Caribbean Brazil:	*samba*

[unofficial national dances are in square brackets]

Portuguese São Tomé and Cape Verde in the 1500s,[2] it is closed-couple form that delineates social dance types after the 1840s in the Caribbean. *Mereng/Merengue* origins are ambiguous in Haiti, the Dominican Republic, and Puerto Rico (along with related Venezuela and Colombia), but their style is characteristically lively and historically sensual. Haitian *mereng* and Dominican *merengue* have reiterated the same form and have embodied the values of one island with two distinct nations since the end of the eighteenth century. When Saint Domingue became Haiti at the end of the Haitian Revolution, *méringue/mereng* had already emerged as a musical rhythm from within popular *contredanse* sets and as a popular social dance first called *carabinier* ("rifleman dance").[3] Music historian Jean Fouchard proposed that from the merging of African drum/dances (like *chica* and *calenda*) and European salon or ballroom *contredanse* imitations (like *congo minuet* and *quadrille*), *carabinier* emerged as a new dance in Haiti. He asserted that Haitians were so touched by the Creole rendering of a Mozambican song and dance called "*mouringue*" that they appropriated the name and attached it to Haitian *carabinier* as "*méringue*" (French, later spelled *mereng* in Kreyol).[4] Regardless of origins, with the island's division into Haiti and the Dominican Republic after 1844, *mereng* and *merengue* developed certain distinctions, received their Kreyol and Spanish biases, and became sources of bitter rivalry.

The longevity of the dances as national phenomena is connected to values and social circumstances that remain: foremost, a desired detachment from European centers and colonial ways, and later from U.S. American dominance, which was first imposed by the United States' Marine occupation of Haiti from 1915–34 and of the Dominican Republic from 1916–24. An engaging, independent couple form first distinguished its style by favoring duple-metered, free-directional *danza* form over triple-metered, circling *waltz* form. As a result of sustained colonization and occupation, some of the African elements within *mereng/merengue* were minimized and some prejudice was suspended or submerged in order to promote national identity and distinct Caribbean performance in the presence of foreign domination. Even the most elite-oriented of Haitians and Dominicans eventually embraced a fully creolized dance.[5]

By the mid-twentieth century, *mereng* in Haiti was a moderate-tempo dance that featured hip isolation with an accent on one of two alternating steps (either *RIGHT, L, RL, RL,* or *RLEFT, RL, RL,* etc.). Couples spontaneously crisscrossed the dance space or danced steadily in place with this two-step pattern. In the Dominican Republic, a more accelerated tempo was attached to *merengue,* which accentuated side-to-side alternation of hip thrusts and favored an extremely close body-to-body position. Both nations displayed the very basic foot pattern of a "danced walk," mostly to *tambora* or bass drum, gourd shaker or scrapper, and *acordeón* sounds.

Mereng/Merengue necessitates only the most common denominator of dancing—movement accessibility—and perhaps that makes it one of the most contagious dance forms, since almost all community participants are able to perform it. At times, couples dance pasted together (*kole kole*), hips moving in figure-eight patterns (*vole mabouye* or "shine the belt buckle"/ *klere bouk sentiwon*). At other times, they dance locked in highly suggestive sexual motion (*ploge*).[6]

In Puerto Rico, a different set of concerns produced another national dance. Sylvia del Villard, the "Mother of Afro–Puerto Rican dance," contended that Puerto Rico's *danza* and *plena* (salon dances) had more African heritage in their music than in their movements, so she taught *bomba* as Puerto Rico's Creole heritage.[7] *Danza* is Puerto Rico's nineteenth-century national dance, which began with a promenade or *paseo* section in a counterclockwise direction, and then couples formed closed position and danced a *merengue* section that was substantially longer and emphasized hip accents to syncopated rhythms.[8] *Plena* came into prominence in the late nineteenth and early twentieth centuries as a rhythm[9]; *plena* was *contradanza*-derived dancing that was originally performed with a tambourine drum, or *pandereta*, and string instruments. From the dance perspective, *danza, plena,* and even *salsa* have shared a "European" dance tendency toward upright posture and have added continuous passing and improvised turning to a linear or straight-spine orientation. (Unlike *danza* and *plena, salsa* occasionally employs sacred African references in its songs, rhythms, and instrumentation, which then can inject African dance vocabulary within performance.)

Bomba, on the other hand, has been traced to an Ashanti court dance during the seventeenth century by ethnologist Hector Vega-Drouet; anthropologist Hal Barton cites both its African and European characteristics, pointing out *bomba's* European linkage, particularly in the upper body's flamenco-like lift and African linkage in a mostly separated dancing couple or a series of solo improvisers.[10] Each succeeding couple or soloist dances simultaneously with a partner and the lead drummer, emphasizing improvisation, polyrhythms, curvilinear form, and body-part isolation—especially hips over exacting footwork. Eventually, each performer either challenges or receives a challenge from the lead drummer; instantaneously consonant dance, music, and play result.

Puerto Rican *bomba* is Creole dance that echoes both African couple and solo competitive dance in front of drums and European set structure with straight- and tilted-back alternation or linear orientation. It resembles *rumba* in Cuba, *rumba columbia* especially where a series of males compete corporally and rhythmically, but also with the highest pitched *quinto* drum. *Bomba* recalls sections of Martinican *bele* where individual couples break square/*quadrille* form and proceed toward the drums in rhythmic and stylistic challenge. These characteristics suggest Congo/Angola heritage where the dance practice is festive, often competitive and flirtatious, not firmly separated into binary categories of secular or sacred, and where dancing corresponds mainly to barrel-shaped drums and hand-on-animal-skin drumming.[11] What is curious, however, is that although *bomba* is definitely important to core ideas about Puerto Rico and Caribbean dance, it is not reported as a national dance.

Because of its early association with "black" and lower-class communities, *bomba* would need a high level thrust and persistent marketing, like Cuban *rumba* has had, to situate it near *danza puertoriqueña*, the acclaimed Puerto Rican national dance. *Bomba* is loaded with the primacy of its African heritage, and unlike Dominican *merengue*, it does not have agreement about its primacy in the national character, even though it is clearly at the center of island identity and notions of historical pride. Puerto Rico's selection of *danza* has to do with nineteenth-century demands for island independence from Spain and overriding challenges across the island, which eventually favored a European-Creole salon form that represented both rural and urban centers away from the colonial center over an African-Creole drum/dance that recalled African enslavement to those in power.[12] *Danza puertoriqueña* usurped set figure dancing early and flaunted a Pan-Caribbean excitement with independent couple form and distinct Creole rhythms; its popularity challenged opposing laws and its prohibition failed. The people danced it back as "*upa cubana*" and reestablished it as *danza puertoriqueña*.[13]

The opposite result seems to have occurred in the case of Guadeloupe. *Biguine,* Guadeloupe's late-nineteenth-century salon dance, which derived from combinations of *bele, mazurka, polka,* and early jazz legacies, apparently did not succeed in usurping an African-Creole drum/dance. *Gwoka* is Guadeloupe's signature dance and music; alternately called *lewoz, gwoka* is a series of rhythmic challenges that are performed by a series of soloists in front of one drum with two drummers, a lead singer, and chorus. As in *bomba* and *rumba,* male and female dancers are inspired to elaborate spontaneously to codified drum rhythms. *Gwoka* retains strong political and cultural identification with African history in the face of French cultural dominance; it connects to youths and social activists on both Martinique and Guadeloupe. Thus, *gwoka* competes for sustained island predominance with its historic African connections and virtuoso improvisational moves against a series of popular dances, as is the case with *zouk*, a twentieth-century Pan-Caribbean mixture that promotes Creole identity within informal couple or dance-party style.[14]

In the English/Creole-speaking islands, a basic "danced walk" is characteristic for its couple forms (*leggo, calypso, mento, reggae,* etc.); however, the English/Creole islands vibrate with the melodic sounds of guitars and eventually steel "pans" in place of Spanish and French Caribbean drum and accordion sounds or ballroom orchestrations. Body movement consists of either an alternating, unaccented, two-step foot pattern (RL, RL) with side-to-side hip motion, or an almost stationary alternation of weight with circular hip motion. The walking foot pattern is *chippin'* in Trinidad and Tobago, and the gyrating hips from high to low to high level is *winin'* in Jamaica.

As in *mereng/merengue,* the English/Creole national dances use a moderate to fast walking tempo, but they vary in steps and style. For example, Trinidadian *calypso* shifts the foot pattern to: step R touch L, step L touch R (still a two-step pattern); and Jamaican *reggae* shifts to double vertical bounces over each slowly alternating RLRL foot pattern, rather than side-to-side accented hips. The accessibility of the movement and the "heartbeat" rhythms generate comfort, ease, and a contagious connectedness within groups of couples or dancing individuals; both accessibility and connectedness encourage a national dance pattern, but synchrony with local values is paramount.

In the Dutch and former Danish islands, the historical proximity to and mixture of European and African movement over time has caused similar couple orientation and significant hip isolation as that of other islands. Curaçao, Aruba, St. Thomas, St. Croix, and St. Johns were historically in intermittent economic and social contact with Spanish Caribbean culture.[15] Sailors, merchants, and elite and bourgeois visitors spread the European *waltz* and *polka* to Caribbean ports throughout the late eighteenth and early nineteenth centuries; however, the nineteenth century was marked more by local stylization and intra-Caribbean exchange with *danzas, danzas criollas,* or *danzas nacionales*. Spanish musical tastes influenced dancing through a repeated rhythm (*ostinato*) that instigated a syncopated rather than an even foot pattern, which spread across the Caribbean. An elaborated three-step sequence (either RLR hold, LRL hold, or R hold LR, L hold RL) matched the *cinquillo* and related *habanera* rhythms found in popular music of the day.[16] For example, Spanish-influenced *danzas holandesas* were popular in salons, ballrooms, and dance halls because they captured daring political values of independence and equal rights that were pushing social mores within exciting dance movements. Whether *danzas cubanas, puertoriqueñas,* or *holandesas,* the new dances featured spontaneous use of space and were fully distinguished from the formality and designed restrictions of precursor *contradanzas.*

Obviously, the development of Caribbean national dances goes beyond foot patterns and involves a range of influences, from "race," ethnicity, history, and economics to politics. With an unveiling of such issues through the Cuban example, a glimpse of the delicate considerations within processes of national dance formation can be seen. Already, however, reigning power is seen at the core of national dance selection.[17]

The Cuban Example

Cuba is pivotal to understanding Caribbean (and Latino) social dance since its dance rhythms and musical approaches have affected the region, Latin America, and Caribbean niches in the United States, Europe, Africa, Japan, Denmark, Norway, Australia, and other areas of the world. Sociologist Ángel Quintero Rivera and others argue that Puerto Rico is equally important in the development of dance music because Puerto Rico was one of the earliest sites of Caribbean (and Latino) dance music and has been increasingly influential as such; however, the Cuban dance matrix is large and inclusive and, thereby, representative of the entire Caribbean for the present study.[18]

Cuba has profound dance and music legacies, first in the *fandangos* and *seguidillas* of Spain, the fifteenth-to-eighteenth-century couple and trio dances, out of which *zapateo* or rhythmic footwork developed.[19] British occupation from 1762–63 brought English *country dance* input and, as chapter 3 has reported, French *contredanses* and *quadrilles* infiltrated Cuba's dance history also. Additionally, there are more types of African dance in Cuba than elsewhere. Nowhere in the Caribbean—or anywhere in the Americas, in fact—were African descendants able to maintain, reconfigure, or transpose as many stylistic roots of African dance and musics as in Cuba.

The tremendously deep and wide port of Havana was critical also: it made Havana the colonial hub of intercontinental trade and thereby a major site of interchange among Europeans, Africans, and Americans.[20] Twice each year, Spanish *flotas* consisting of seventy-five to one hundred ships brought supplies and materials in exchange for cattle products, sugar, tobacco, and coffee. Celebrations on those occasions facilitated the exchange and creation of dances and musics. As Cuban ethnologist Fernando Ortiz noted: "Songs, wild dancing, and music came and went, i.e., flowed between Andalusia, the Americas, and Africa, and Havana was the center where the rainbow's hottest and most polychromatic hues blended."[21] Consequently, Cuba's dance matrix contains an inherently large dance vocabulary, and its geographical and political influence over time have made Cuba relevant to any discussion of dance music development in the Americas and a solid case of germinating national dance.

Cuban Dance Matrix

A dance matrix percolates over time and becomes that collection of historical segments and group preferences that fits together, resonates (almost) unilaterally, and gradually shapes a sense of national identity in movement and music. In Cuba, the cultural segments came from the new lands of the Americas, southern Spain, the west coast of Africa, and the island of Saint Domingue/Haiti. Cultural preferences and tendencies meshed and combined or dissolved and disappeared over three centuries to form a distinct island identity, one that characterized significant (although not complete) unity within the diversity of arriving groups.

Native American Dance

The first segment of the Cuban dance matrix, Native American, needs clarification; however, its consequences for Cuban national dance are almost nil. Most Caribbean islands were inhabited by indigenous peoples whose dances were described by European colonists as they entered the Americas. Native Americans did not survive past the first fifty years of contact on Cuba and were decimated on most other islands within one hundred years.[22] Dominica and St. Vincent in the English/Creole area were exceptions where Caribs (and previously Taino/Arawak) lived and gathered to hide in the wake of military wars, colonial enslavement, and/or ruinous diseases from the late fifteenth century onward.[23] Indigenous culture quickly disappeared; thus far, no identifiable Native American elements are found within Cuban dance.

European Segment: Spanish Dance

Europeans dominated Caribbean culture formation—whether Spanish, French, British, Dutch, or Danish—and established a long-lasting segment within the dance matrix. The Spanish crown offered land grants to influential military men and church officials, as well as to ambitious landless workers and sailors, who settled Hispaniola as early as 1501, then Puerto Rico in 1508, and Cuba in 1511.[24] Spanish rulers had learned that people do not easily give up lands that are destined to become their own. They consequently associated conquest and settlement as a means to create physical and emotional barriers against threats of invasion from either Native Americans or other exploring Europeans. After serving their indentured years, however, many Spanish settlers left the islands for the prospect of mainland gold. Some stayed to raise cattle, learned to plant tobacco, and grew citrus fruits, peppers, and various staples in the lush and productive soil.[25]

Cuban settlements were significantly different from early English, French, Dutch, and Danish encampments, where colonists arrived for exploration and exploitation, paying little attention to long-term residence, at least for many years. From the fifteenth to the eighteenth century, Cuba was developed as *latifundios* and *estancias,* large and small cattle ranges. Lands allocated and divided in this way created a foundation for both large- and small-scale proprietors and, later, for an emerging nation.

With the introduction of sugarcane between 1590 and 1600, a demographic shift between Europeans and Africans began across the Caribbean.[26] In Cuba, sugar development was exceedingly slow, and as a result Cuba maintained a large European population well into the twentieth century. Elsewhere in the Caribbean, sugar production created an early African-descended majority; however, Cuba's Spanish population included African heritage from Muslim/Arab/North African domination of Spain for eight hundred years. Spanish Africans, or *Ladinos,* entered Cuba and other islands from Spain; thus, African influence in the Americas came from Spain as well as from Africa.[27]

Between the sixteenth and eighteenth centuries, Spain gave less attention to island territories than to the gold-filled mainland of Mexico, and Central and South America; thereby, the Spanish Caribbean experienced economic isolation and an increase in the free colored or mulatto sector. Before the nineteenth century, slave codes facilitated a large free population (children from mixed marriages and unions of free coloreds), and Africans could sometimes work off their indebtedness or be manumitted at the death of a plantation master.[28] As Cuban sugar production increased in the nineteenth century, the need for workers grew, and the enslaved population mushroomed in massive portions, as was the case previously on other islands.[29]

The plantation environment and the Roman Catholic Church set boundaries of structure and form for Cuban dance. Public dancing occurred on secular festive days, for marriages of the elite, military victories, notices of royal births in Spain, or baptisms and confirmations in the colonies and other such events.[30] Dancing to Christmas carols within farces and comedies was authorized by the church until the middle of the seventeenth century, sometimes with dancing inside the church.[31] On saints' days in Havana's Plaza de las Armas, people celebrated in processions; each *cofradía,* or guild (trade guild, church fraternity—Spanish or *Ladino,* or local patron saint organization), would advance toward the church and dance.

Dances were related to Spanish folk dances and European court forms, such as *chaconas, pavannes,* and *zarabandas.*[32] For example, the *fandango* was originally a courtship dance that featured a couple who locked eyes, passed and circled one another in exhaustive footwork, but never touched. Another was the *seguidilla,* which also involved a passing and turning couple (or couples) in close eye contact. Both dances could be performed with castanets and were known for their liveliness. *Fandango,* especially, became the name for any colonial festive dancing or merrymaking.

Caribbean variations remained significantly close to their European dance origins: *zapateo* is one example.[33] Historical accounts document the development of rhythmic footwork, which became integral to dance practices both in Spain and her colonies. *Zapateo* (which refers to the rhythmic sound of shoes beating against a wooden floor, exemplified most notably in modern theatrical *flamenco* dancing) was performed by indentured workers and elite colonists from Andalusia. It included rhythmic steps with heel, toe, and flat foot stamping. *Zapateo* continued as a rural or *campesino* dance in Cuba; today, it is primarily performed and preserved by dance organizations and cultural institutions to commemorate Cuba's Spanish origins.

African Dance Segment

Africans had a continuous influence on Cuba after 1518, but particularly between 1700 and 1886.[34] During these years, massive numbers of new arrivals kept a persistent force on emerging national culture. African influence flourished despite dominant Spanish authority and overwhelming restrictions. New World plantation owners did not have the resources or, eventually, the inclination to comply with Old World directives. Consequently, African dance culture survived in the nooks and crannies of daily life.

Cuban plantation owners tried to "deculturate" the enslaved population, to strip it of identity, cohesion, and dignity, so as to secure a workforce that was totally dependent on the European planter class.[35] Owners organized the enslaved in competing ethnic groups from differing regions of Africa, called *cabildos* in Cuba, in order to deflect the organization of slave rebellions; colonial authorities thought that factionalism among *cabildo* groups would diminish the danger to outnumbered Europeans. Additionally, organization into groups tended to maximize production, and in turn, increase colonial profit. In the end, however, separate African heritages proved helpful to enslaved groups by guarding subordinated culture from European hegemony.[36]

Cuban *cabildos* comprised amalgams of relatively homogeneous African ethnic groups, which were permitted to congregate regularly and, like *cofradias* in Spain, operated as semi-autonomous, mutual-aid societies.[37]

They conserved ritual practices, dances, songs and chants, instruments and instrument-making techniques, and several African ritual languages.[38] They contributed to the crystallization of certain Diaspora dance and music concepts, namely (1) that dance and music are not simply entertainment forms, (2) that dance and music are most often interdependent; (3) that their structure utilizes both set and improvisational elements; (4) that complexity and depth in dance and music are built by the layering and interfacing of small, simple, diverse units; and (5) that the dancing human body is paramount.

Though some dances, such as *ziripi*[39] (a dance referencing enslaved peoples in chains) and *juego de mani*[40] (a martial dance/art), did *not* survive the centuries of oppression that Africans experienced, four branches of African influence continued: Congo/Angola, Arará, Carabalí, and Yoruba.[41] Despite the fact that most branches contained sacred and secret-society dance vocabularies, Africans and their descendants contributed to and decidedly influenced several Cuban dances.

Haitian Dance Segment

French/Haitian immigrants brought the last elements from Saint Domingue to the simmering matrix. The newcomers arrived at the end of the eighteenth century, just as the sense of Cuban nationhood was coming into view. As chapter 3 has detailed, elite French families brought *contredanse* and African-French-Haitian families brought *tumba francesa*. Consequently, Cuba's dance mixture was both European court and folk dances and African sacred and social dances. Chart 11 shows distinct dances that provided the important germinal layer or matrix, as well as an array of dances that grew from that matrix as Cuban creations. This process was replicated across the Caribbean.[42]

National Dance Development

During the nineteenth century, a defined culture emerged in Cuba and in many parts of the Caribbean (as did cultures in Europe also). Something new sprang from particular environmental conditions, political circumstances, and economic interests of the region. In the midst of a cattle-breeding and cash-crop economy, a developing sugarcane industry, and emerging tobacco and coffee industries, local Cuban colonists gradually gained a singular political voice to battle the pressures of overseas interests. In terms of a creolizing dance process, different cultural elements within Cuba formed definite affinities and repositioned themselves in relation to one another. Ethnic elements crystallized to form a "Cuban" expression, and new dances

Chart 11. Cuban National Dance Formation

The Dance Matrix (Antecedent Dances)	
Native American	*areítos*
European	1) Patron Saint processions
	2) Spanish folk forms: *fandango, seguidilla, zapateo, flamenco*, etc.
	3) French court forms: *pavanne, galliard, minuet, courante, chaconne, allemande, sarabande, gigue*, etc.
	4) *contradanza*
African	1) *Kongo-Angola* Complex: *yuka, makuta*, etc.
	2) *Palo* Complex: *Sarabanda, Madre de Agua*, etc.
	3) *Arará* Complex: *Gebioso, Afrekete*, etc.
	4) *Carabalí* Complex: *Abakuá, Bríkamo*, etc.
	5) *Yoruba* Complex: *Yemayá, Ochún, Changó, Ogún*, etc.
	6) Other Central and West African Dance Practices: Royalty processions, Social dances, Combat practices
Haitian	*contredanse*
	tumba francesa (masón, yubá, frente, etc.)
National Dances (Cuban Creole Creations)	
Compesino Complex	Zapateo Cubano: *Chancleta*, etc.
	Congas/Comparsas
Son Complex	*Son*
	Montuno
	Guaracha
	Changüí
	Sucu-Sucu
	Mambo
	Mozambique
	Casino
	Timba
Rumba Complex	*Rumbas del tiempo de España: Yambú, Mama'buela, Papalote, Muñeca, Gavilán, Karinga*
	Tahona
	Guaguancó
	Columbia
	Mañunga
	Giribilla
	Batarumba
	Guarapachangueo
Danzón Complex	*Danza*
	Danzón
	Danzonete
	Danzonchá
	Chachachá
Other Critical Dance Influences	
Russian	*Ballet* (Vaganova/Cecchetti School) > *Ballet cubano:*
	La Escuela de Ballet Pro-Arte Musical: Alberto and Fernando Alonso, Alicia Alonso
	Ballet de Alicia Alonso
	Agrupación La Silva—Alberto Alonso
	Ballet Nacional de Cuba de Habana (Alicia Alonso)
	Ballet Nacional de Cuba de Camagüey (Fernando Alonso)
Haitian	*Gagá* > Haitian/Cuban traditions
	Vodú Complex: *Yenvalú, Nago, Petwo, Gedé*, etc. > Haitian/Cuban traditions
North American	*Modern Dance:* Martha Graham Technique, José Limón Technique > *danza contemporanea cubana*
	Relaxation and Contact Techniques > Guerra Voluptuous Dance, etc.

were fashioned with distinct styles. These were neither African, Spanish, Haitian, nor indigenous American, but national, Creole, and Cuban.

Political stances yielded aesthetic stances. For example, Spain's administrative rules and laws were deemed unmanageable, as were the set dance figures that were practiced in dance schools and halls and which required regimented steps and memorized formulas. These movement requirements were rejected in favor of the new *danzas,* which permitted independent couples to hold each other throughout the entire dance, encouraged them to travel freely throughout the dance space, and allowed their lower bodies to fashion sensual movement to repeated, syncopated rhythms. The dances fit the time and favored a break with convention; they expressed individual freedom, corporeal and rhythmic exploration, as well as national independence.[43]

Official National Dance of Cuba:
Nineteenth-Century *Danzón*

Danza became tremendously popular throughout the Spanish Caribbean, but it was first called *contradanza* in Cuba; it was *merengue* in Puerto Rico and the Dominican Republic, and, later, *danzas puertorriqueñas,* and *merengues dominicanas.* Yet, a more unique creation developed in *danza*'s wake in Cuba. *El danzón* (a huge *danza*/dance) appeared in the last decades of nineteenth-century Cuba and ushered not simply a new set of rhythms as *danza* had done before, but a new dance structure and style as well. The new form alternated a "resting" sequence with a danced sequence every eight measures. The resting sequence (*el primero* or *paseo*) was for dancers to promenade casually, socialize, and periodically adjust to the heat and humidity while dancing in a tropical climate; the danced sequence (*el segundo* or *merengue*) was the new type of *danza,* independent couple dancing. Tempos in *danzón* were even more important because they permitted emphasis on an innovative gliding or sliding step, which was placed on the second half of the musical pattern. Danced "counter rhythm" with intentional hip accentuation made *danzón* absolutely original, more "Cuban" than the Pan-Caribbean *danzas* had been, and it was proclaimed Cuba's nineteenth-century national dance in 1960 by the Castro government.[44]

The alterations to Pan-Caribbean *danza* within *danzón* demonstrated Cuban tastes and preferences, and blended select choices: European instruments and couple face-to-face form, and African body-part isolations and accented polyrhythms. *Danzón* added subtlety and sensuality in movement, as its *paseo* allowed time for sexual tensions, aroused by close partnering in the *merengue* section, to subside. Contemporary Cuban instructors say that couples danced no more than four inches apart, purportedly within the space of one tile on a fully tiled floor.[45] In Puerto Rico, *danza* acquired three sections: *paseo* (promenade), *merengue* (main couple dancing), and *jaleo* (joyous elaboration). In the Dominican Republic, *danza* developed in regional distinctions—for example, *merengue/merengue dominicana, merengue Cibao, merengue típico,* etc.

In their beginnings, both *danza* and *danzón* generated prejudice against African-descended Cubans and their dance practices. A controversy ensued over the immorality of the movements. Critics remarked, "For some time . . . we have been reading your pretended defense of *la danza* and *el danzón,* dances which you and others call Cuban, when they are really a degeneration of the African *tango. . . ,*" and also, "Mothers who have daughters, inspire in them an aversion for dance. Make war against all sensual dances. Ask for the *lancer,* the *rigodon,* the *quadrille,* and the *cotillion,* but never *danza* nor the inferno of feelings which are called *danzón.*"[46]

Danzón was elevated to national status in retrospect because it best symbolized Cuba's nineteenth-century spirit. Despite its early associations with African-descended sectors of the population, *danzón*'s polished smoothness emerged as more relevant (than *rumba* or *son*) to leaders within Cuban mainstream society. *Danzón*'s slower tempo and countering polyrhythms eventually resonated with both "black" and "white" Cubans. As in music, literature, and theater of the period also, the dance, through *danzón,* symbolized the emergence of independent Cuban thought, separation from colonial domination, and, thereby, national distinctiveness.[47]

The *danzón* complex, however, which includes *danza, danzón, danzonete, danzonchá* (and later, *chachacha*), is a group of related couple dances that began with musicians of African descent, since "musician" was not an acceptable role for people of European descent in the colonial era. As the composers and accompanists in orchestras, military bands, and the smaller ensembles of salons and dance halls, mulatto musicians interspersed African rhythmic motifs, percussion instruments, and improvisation as seminal structure within then-present European performance practices they also performed. African influences on European music and dance forms changed the feeling and types of Cuban dance. Over time, the Cuban public accepted *danzón* with a sense of affinity, and the previously ruffled feathers of society leaders subsided.[48]

Unofficial National Dances: Cuban *Son* and *Rumba*

Other dance expressions usurped the official declaration of "national dance" by means of their persistence, mass popularity, and apparent relevance over time. For example, twentieth-century Cubans looked to *son* and its derivatives as the most pervasive and popular of Cuban dance complexes. They claimed that more Cubans danced *son* and its variations than any other dance, and that *son* dancing was the epitome of Cuba.

Cuban *son* had its origins in open-air, collective occasions among the rural, cattle-farming families of sixteenth- to nineteenth-century Cuba, where a minimum of performers and participants were involved (originally a few couples or even a man with his guitar). *Sones* grew in the intermittent re-unions and celebrations among agricultural families who participated in song, instrumental music, and dance as periodic recreation. Gradually, the graceful, lilting movement style and sensuous close partnering from urban salons were combined with the zest and fervor of Cuban rural workers when they relaxed. The blending of European and African dance and music formulated the essential Creole or "*mulata*" dance music of the Americas. *Son* was mixed-heritage and became as tantalizing and feminine as the *macho* gaze could imagine (see photo 6).[49]

In mid-twentieth century form, *son* opened the closed partnering of previ-ous salon style and allowed individual *mambo* couples to alternate between closed-couple position and independent but related solo and couple posi-tions. When the thick-textured polyrhythms and embroidered improvisa-tional playing of standardized bands and orchestras were added, Cuban *son/mambo* became the essential skeleton of Latin American popular dance music. Today what is called *salsa* finds its antecedents in the *son* complex of Cuba and the creative elaborations of Puerto Rican musicians. *Mambo, Mozambique,* and *casino* are twentieth-century *son* types, and *timba* has breached the twenty-first century as another.[50] Movements in these ex-amples are *son*-derived or modern applications of *son*. Today, *son* is not limited to any segment of the population or region of Cuba; in fact, it has crossed many borders. Still, it epitomizes Cuban and other Latin prefer-ences in social dance: pleasure in the dancing body, sensual display within independent couple form, marked gender presentation and interplay, and intergenerational dancing.

Cuba produced yet another unofficial, national dance. In contrast to the *son* of haciendas and salons, *rumba* emerged as the dance of lower-class Cubans who congregated primarily in rural plantations and the shared patios of *solares*, the barrios of nineteenth-century urban ports. Like many social dances, *rumba* began with a despised reputation, but it was favored generation after generation among those of identifiable African descent. Its flirtatious movements are deceivingly demanding, and its songs include political commentary on the life conditions of enslaved and free persons, both poor "black" and "white" workers.[51]

Rumba became a twentieth-century national dance, in effect, when Fidel Castro's Ministry of Culture officially recognized its contribution to national history and scheduled weekly performances in every province of Cuba for more than four decades. Traditional *rumba* dancers and musicians traveled internationally as representatives of Cuba, and *rumba* groups proliferated in Cuba as a result. *Rumba* dancing was reintroduced to the United States, Europe, Japan, and elsewhere, after a decline from its international heyday (1930s and 1940s). Cuban *rumba* was sought by international performers who defied the U.S. blockade against trade with Cuba (1959–present) as they crossed geopolitical borders for contact with one of Cuba's national treasures.[52] The national dialogue had to include *rumba*.

And another contender for Cuban national dance, called *conga* or *comparsa*, has enjoyed remarkable popularity among the Cuban masses for centuries. Like Haitian/Dominican *mereng/merengue*, Trinidadian *calypso*, and Jamaican *reggae*, *conga*'s parading (danced walk) movements and basic execution are exceedingly simple. To date, however, *conga/comparsa* has not been included in discussions of national dance among officials or scholars; only Cuban dancers and the lay public comment in ways that elevate *conga* to a national position (see photo 8). This suggests that accessibility and popularity, while essential, are not sufficient qualities for confirmed national status. The social conditions and power relations that are associated with a dance form play critical roles in determining "national dance."[53]

Historical Conditions and the National Imagination

Looking from the twenty-first century beyond *danzón, son, rumba,* and the ubiquitous parading form *conga/comparsa*, other dance genres have achieved national acclaim and could also be relegated (if they are not already) to national status—for example, *danza cubana* (Cuban modern dance) or *ballet cubano* (Cuban-style ballet). These are certainly unique Cuban expressions that have gained national and international praise. However, the Cuban case teaches that "national dance" depends on relevance to historical conditions, which class/group is in power, and the pertinent cultural values that are encapsulated within dance movement—in other words, what the dance expresses and/or symbolizes. New forms in the nineteenth century signaled several Cuban realities through dance movement, but only one reality was promoted as representative of island history and then-present conditions. As the Cuban public assessed national dances in twentieth-century discussions, they favored *son* and rejected the elite position of *danzón* as a salon or ballroom dance of the privileged. They sometimes rejected *rumba* as well, because they knew that despite its current prestige, culture officials often made courtesy appearances only during *rumba* events and other Cubans mumbled rudely and passed by Rumba Saturday activities. They knew neither *danzón* nor *rumba* generated full acceptance for the twentieth century, so their choice was between *son* and *conga*. Perhaps their evaluations were also a way of registering their upset over not having a voice in the selection process.

Cuba's dance history suggests how other Caribbean dances surface toward the national level, match national concerns, and become attached to the national imagination. Cataloguing the many choices there are within a given nation reveals the dynamics of selection and underscores the critical importance of power relations.[54] Certain dance formations in the Spanish, French/Kreyol, English/Creole, Dutch, and former Danish Caribbean have maintained national statuses through accessible movement, the dynamics of partnered, sensuous dancing, and the contagious rhythmic play that these elements generate. Performance elements seem to be broadly based, agreed-upon, and shifting choices within the dancing public, but the question remains: Are national dances those that have enjoyed popularity or national affinity across most local communities?

Each Caribbean island has had its own national dance pyramid, and performers on all islands access the myriad rhythms of national dances, elaborate them bodily, and embody a sense of community, national, or regional belonging. Those without economic or political power have continually strived to articulate the connectedness they feel within the dance; dancers promote notions of belonging and desired citizenship through the aesthetic and artistic power they feel while dancing. Nevertheless, the data show that mass choices have not always been recognized. National dances reveal most what those in power choose as representative dance culture—in other words, what those in power think of themselves. The challenge is to facilitate entry of the views and estimations of the powerless within the preferences of even well-intentioned leaders.

1. *Bele* in Sainte Marie, Martinique, 2003, by Philippe Bourgade

2. *Bele linó*, Martinique, 2000, by Philippe Bourgade

3. (Above) *Tumba francesa* #1,
Guantanamo, Cuba, 2003,
by Umi Vaughan

4. (Right) *Tumba francesa* #2,
Guantanamo, Cuba, 2003, by
Umi Vaughan

5. *Jacana/sarandunga,*
Museo del hombre,
Dominican Republic,
2009, by Martha Davis

6. *Son santiaguero,* Cuba, 2003, by Umi Vaughan

7. *Timba/tembleque* in Havana, Cuba, 2003, by Umi Vaughan

8. (Left) *Conga santiaguera,*
Cuba, 2003, by Umi Vaughan

9. (Below) Carnival Girl,
Santiago de Cuba, 2003, by
Umi Vaughan

10. *Vodou congo,* Sucrie Danash, Haiti, 1991, by Yvonne Daniel

11. *Vodou ecstasy,* Sucrie Danash, Haiti, 1991, by Yvonne Daniel

12. *Danmyé* #1, Martinique, 2002, by Philippe Bourgade

13. *Danmyé* #2, Martinique, 2002, by Philippe Bourgade

CHAPTER FIVE

CARIBBEAN POPULAR DANCE TRANSFORMATIONS

Caribbean Creativity

Popular dance in the Caribbean is distinguished by Creole innovation and intra-Caribbean music mixtures. The previous chapter tracked the development of a few Creole innovations from the mid-nineteenth and early twentieth centuries, the result of two or more *distinctly different* parent sources (*danzón* and *bomba*, for example). This chapter dwells on intra-Caribbean dances and their dance music mixtures, the result of *distinctly similar* parent sources or second-generation Caribbean Creole. For example, Haitian *rasin* is a combination of Haitian religious and folkloric music with social and commercial genres like Haitian *mereng/konpa* and Cuban *casino/salsa*. Other intra-Caribbean mixtures include: the blend of Cuban *son* and Jamaican *reggae* to make *regetón*; the mix of Cuban *rumba, salsa,* and *Oricha* dances that becomes *batarumba* or *batarumbasón*; and earlier (in chapter 1) I noted that the mix of Haitian *kadans* and Trinidadian *calypso* became *cadence-lypso* ; that Trinidadian *calypso* and U.S. *soul music* meshing in the 1970s made *soca*; and that Jamaican *reggae* and Brazilian *samba* combinations made *sambareggae*. In the 1980s, the "grand combination" of Martinique and Guadeloupe yielded *zouk*, which has elements of French Caribbean *gwoka, mazouk,* and *biguine*, Cuban/Puerto Rican *salsa*, and Haitian/Dominican *merengue*. Intra-Caribbean mixtures have spread across the islands as popular dance.[1]

At first, Caribbean dance mixtures were simply fad dance crazes, but when their unique combinations spread to Caribbean niches elsewhere (or vice versa), they joined the many popular dances that recall the histories and circumstances of related island peoples. Serving the important function that social visiting, sailors, and brothels performed in spreading Caribbean

Chart 12. Caribbean Popular Dances

Cuba	*casino, rumba, regetón, hip-hop, timba*
Puerto Rico	*salsa, bomba, hip-hop, merengue*
Dominican Republic	*merengue, bachata, salsa, hip-hop*
Haiti	*mereng, konpa, rasin, salsa, hip-hop*
Martinique	*zouk, salsa, raga, konpa, cadanse, mereng, hiphop*
Guadeloupe	*zouk, gwoka/lewoz, salsa, konpa, cadanse, hiphop*
Trinidad and Tobago	*calypso, soca, reggae, salsa, hip-hop*
Jamaica	*reggae, dancehall, salsa, merengue*
Dominica	*cadanse-lypso, salsa, merengue*
Curaçao	*tumba, salsa, merengue*
Circum-Caribbean Brazil	*sambareggae, samba do pe, salsa, merengue, hip-hop*

rhythms among nineteenth-century ports,[2] twentieth- and twenty-first-century performances, recordings, television, and internet displays have spread Pan-Caribbean dance musics to New York, Paris, London, Dakar, Caracas, Cali, Miami, and Montreal, the major dance capitals of the world. *Zouk* and *timba* are prime examples.

Zouk is a 1980s intricate musical mixture for either couple-embrace dancing or individual dance rapture.[3] Its basic dance patterns, two-step (RL) and three-step (RLR hold, alternate), resonated comfortably with both Caribbean and non-Caribbean dancers, who were able to innovate bodily above the foot patterns. Through combined rhythms and Creole lyrics, *zouk* updated *lewoz, mazouk,* and *biguine,* promoted Caribbean dance music throughout the world, and in the process projected nostalgia for a Caribbean home among the many Caribbean immigrants across the globe. *Zouk's* main connections to its performers were sociopolitical, first with its lyrics that communicated directly in a Creole understood by Caribbeans, Africans, Canadians, and Europeans. Then, *zouk's* rise in popularity across the globe gave a rise in status for Martinicans, Guadeloupeans, and other Creole-speaking islanders. Martinicans and Guadeloupeans especially enjoyed an identity apart from dependent department connections to France.[4]

Timba, an evolved form of *son* dancing from historic plazas to contemporary nightclubs, was the rage in Cuba during the 1990s—a provocative style performed by working-class dancers and sophisticated yet street-smart musicians.[5] Cuban musical geniuses led a persistent "black" youth culture to perform specific identities, to stand up in politically conscious ways, relishing in self displays that were unheard of decades before. The main leader, José Luís Cortés, and his band, NG La Banda, were censored repeatedly for blasting conventional boundaries publicly.

While the government emphasized frugality, the nation, and socialism, *timba* projected consumerism, individualism, and the brashness of youth.[6] Despite the costs of dressing up, paying entrance fees, and being hassled by police in Cuban/international music spaces, young dancers of all colors defied official mandates to reject the "West," commercialism, and rules concerning fraternization with tourists. Instead, they danced provocatively in tourist establishments and bawdily in open community spaces to captivating music and brazen lyrics; they brashly mimicked the knowingly impolite words and gestured crude honesty from lower-class *barrio* behaviors. *Timba* dancing presented what had been stringently camouflaged in performances during enslavement by positioning Afro-Cubans visibly at the center of Cuban society and permitting their bodies to speak implied demands.[7]

Timba started with closed-couple dancing that became aggressive as it contradicted conventional ideas, shifted proxemics, and emphasized edgy fashion. It dared to favor dancing couples in both standard couple position and tight, suggestive, "cupped" partnering: both partners facing the same direction with hips and thighs, backs and torsos touching. This body rubbing and grinding came from historical mass *conga/comparsa* dancing in Cuba, *winin'* in Jamaica and Trinidad, *groyad* in Haiti and the French Caribbean, called *tembleque* in *timba* (see photos 7 and 8).

Body movement followed melody, rhythm, but especially lyrics, which were stubborn (long) and raw (vulgar) in terms of energy, dynamics, and meaning. *Timba* dancing was explicit and irreverent for twenty-first-century eyes, "rougher" dancing than the smooth *son* or slick *salsa* of the past. Today, it is in process of fading or remaining at a less popular level as the Afro-Cuban youth at its center either age, defect, or emigrate.

Replicating the repeated situation of social/popular dance, *timba* began with morality charges, but it will eventually receive the acceptance accorded to *danzón* or *rumba*. *Timba* confronted struggles and hypocrisies within the status quo of Cuba; its dance placed a spotlight on African culture at Cuba's core and on Afro-Cuban performers who led its innovations and mass followings, but who still did not have the equality and privilege that other Cubans had and have. Similar to *zouk, reggae, dancehall, konpa,* and other Caribbean popular dances, *timba* was a contagious dance sensation that was keenly associated with *"negros"* or dark-skinned dancers and musicians, and like many popular dances of the past, it was avoided, tolerated, or loved by varied sectors of the population.

Both *timba* and *zouk* have been powerful dance crazes, powerful sociopolitical stances, or both, for Caribbean natives, Caribbean immigrants abroad, and international dancers. Dancers divide their torsos incredibly and explore rhythmic creativity or the kinesthetic pull of gyrating hips and enticing partners. The dances are not likely to fade as "museum pieces," but they will probably shift slightly in appearance and change their names within the Caribbean popular dance scene. They challenge mainstream dances in the United States, Europe, Asia, the Middle East, and Africa as viable, every-night dance choices.[8]

Perhaps the journey of an older dance can better illustrate how popular dance changes shape and identities and travels across old and new borders.

Cuban *Rumba* Example

Nineteenth-century *rumba* left its origin site in Cuba and traveled to other popular dance destinations during the twentieth and twenty-first centuries. Like so many other Caribbean social/popular dances, *rumba* had to change with the times.[9] Its performance has been refined, but, most important, traditional *rumberos* have been teaching proper form to their children, neighbors, and friends over centuries. Witness the film *Dame la mano* on traditional *rumba,* which was enthusiastically documented in New Jersey in 2003, the innovative rumba *guarapachangueo* in Cuba, 2010[10], and the tremendously enthusiastic welcome of Los Muñequitos on tour from Seattle and San Francisco to New York and Miami, with many cities in between during 2011.

Names for popular dances change frequently over time, and this fact leads the public to think that there are different dances or major changes in the steps. Sometimes this is true, but often it is not. It might be helpful to have specificity within the naming of popular and fad dances, some of which are intimately related. Unfortunately, it is not we—the researchers—but all of us, the community, who names both those social dances that arise as popular dance and those that fade as fad dance.

Rumba's Domestic Journey

Musicologist Isabelle Leymarie links the song *"El Yambú,"* which surfaced around 1850, to the beginnings of *rumba.* Musicologist Olavo Alén Rodrí-guez states that the beginnings of *rumba* follow the abolition of slavery in 1886, when formerly enslaved peoples clustered in ports and urban spaces.[11] My dance data suggest that not only free but also enslaved Africans were part of the formation process of *rumba,* especially *rumba Columbia.* They suggest parallel *rumba* growth with that of the African population starting in mid-century. They also take into account earlier traces and precursors before the full blossoming of any aesthetic creation. Thus, *rumba* was probably percolating among the enslaved and free Cubans from around 1840 through the end of the nineteenth century. Its music eventually traveled to Spain, parts of Africa, Mexico, across the Caribbean, and to the United States and European centers. Its original dance stayed in the urban and rural homes, communal patios, and public squares of mainly "black" Cuban neighborhoods. By the end of the twentieth century, a group of "dance-pretenders"[12] had traveled from Cuba to flashy cabarets, intimate theaters, and other international performance settings; in the process, original *rumba* accumulated varied dance patterns, numerous stylizations, and alternate names.

Early *rumba* was mimetic, often telling stories about rag dolls, flying kites, harvesting and preparing rice, and wayward boys with grandmothers who had caught them *rumbancheando*. That *rumba* was graceful, delicately alluring, and included an approach and retreat pattern of a dancing couple (for example, from *yuka* and *makuta* heritage, the lingering Congo/Angola dances of Cuba). Additionally, traditional *rumba* made use of ample hip isolations, rib shifts, and rhythmic improvisation within the body. These elements (duets with approach/retreat form, body-part isolation, and rhythmic improvisation) were at creative variance with layered, syncopated percussion: three drums, a stick-playing *cata* or bamboo box, a shaker or *güiro*—all in sync with the *claves* (sticks, rhythms) of satirical and/or romantic songs.

Graceful mimetic *rumba*s, called *rumba yambú* or *rumba de cajón* (box *rumba*—because they used boxes that carried codfish and candles across the Atlantic instead of outlawed drums), were identified with *el tiempo de España,* the colonial and enslavement period. They were among the first Creole creations of the new environment, which took structure from remembered African movement and form, and layered these with fresh European and American stylistic content. *Rumba* came forth with the customs, mannerisms, gestures, clothing, language, and new understandings of the Americas. In its urban beginnings, *rumba* was performed near ports, in common patio areas of tenement homes (*solares*), and among a variety of peoples—granted, mostly among free Africans, the enslaved, and indentured others. It claimed a resistant motif on the Cuban soul despite the prestige, popularity, and simultaneous development of Cuban *son*.[13]

Son predates *rumba,* beginning among sixteenth-century Spanish immigrants who came with *Ladino* or "Moorish" bloodlines from Muslim/ Arab/North African–influenced Spain of the eighth to fifteenth centuries. Isolated Spaniards settled the ranchlands and waited for limited, occasional sociability. They had guitar-like instruments (*guitarras, laúdes, tiples,* and *bandurrias*) and *decima*-stanza songs for entertainment. They enjoyed intermittent parties and dancing, which came with sparse local visiting, routine celebrations of the Roman Catholic Church, and the arrival of ships with new supplies of people, instruments, trends, and fashions.

With extended colonial settlement and the trappings of European court values, the rancher's solo alternated with couples in group dancing, and European *contredanse* became American *contradanza*. As soon as the set dances shifted to permit dancing couples in what historian John Chasteen calls "the dance of two," *danza* and *danzón* became the staple dances of Cuban salons and dance halls and within rural hacienda society.[14] *Son* developed also—gradually tying rural songs to urban dancehall couple dancing and to decidedly Afro-Cuban rhythms, percussion, and brass (over wind instruments) by the twentieth century.[15]

Rumba developed "on the other side of the tracks," away from colonial elites and primarily among Africans and their descendants. The dance included a full range of percussion; human voices in responsorial patterns laced with satiric, comedic, and provocative subjects; and a wide spectrum of playful movement.[16] *Yambú, guaguancó,* and *columbia* were differentiated as *rumba* types by the end of the nineteenth century because they depended on specific social conditions—the critical male to female ratio, for example.

Both *rumba yambú* and *rumba guaguancó* (still the most popular *rumba* type) required the *pareja,* the partnered man and woman, the resulting sensuous movement, and double entendre lyrics. It was in the urban areas where a close ratio of males and females prevailed that the earlier graceful *rumba yambú* began to alternate with what became *rumba guaguancó.* As *rumba* acquired a quicker tempo and a chase rather than polite flirtation, it also acquired specific gestures: for the man, the *vacunao,* a pelvic thrust (his gesture of possessing the women), and for the woman, a deflecting *botao.* When the dance form included the chase and suggestive gestures, it acquired the name *guaguancó.*

Another kind of gender ratio produced yet another *rumba* type. The huge imbalance in the male to female ratio within the African-descended population was predicated on sugar refinery development and not just sugar cultivation. Refineries came to Cuba in the 1860s to the 1880s and demanded more enslaved Africans than cultivation alone required. African men were used more often than women, and they were settled on plantation lands away from urban ports. In rural areas of Matanzas Province near the refineries (people say especially in Cárdenas), huge numbers of laboring men were placed together in anticipation of the *zafra,* or sugar harvest. When not working, men danced together in challenge performance, and the third "classic" type emerged, *rumba columbia.*

Rumba carried the same misleading reputation as many social dances did (for example, *English country dance, danza, danzón*). They were all "trashed" by gossip among elites and newspapers but enjoyed by other classes. Dance chronicler Moreau de St. Méry said in essence that they were risqué.[17] *Rumba* also shared in the estimation of African dances as "lewd and lascivious."

There was an abandon and sense of freedom that characterized African style in any dance, theirs or those of their colonial masters. Such movements were considered improper because the African-descended dancer would divide the torso while dancing, accent hip and other body part actions, and sometimes lower the entire body toward the floor, all of which was considered very "uncivilized" and "barbaric" for those who loved to dance elongated at the back and elevated on the balls of their feet. Despite its magnetism, African dance was initially rejected because of its extremes in flexibility and sensuality. Torso division allowed the lower pelvis area and the upper abdomen and chest area to move forward and backward, side to side, and around in clockwise or counterclockwise directions. The dancing torso could be smooth and sensuous in sustained energy or aggressive in percussive bursts of energy, revealing a range of emotional dynamics. It could swing, vibrate, and nuance a wide range of expressiveness, and *rumba* used all of the dancing torso's potential. Overt sensuality and uninhibited proximity of dancing bodies proved to be core elements of the African contribution to *mulata*, Creole, or New World performance.[18]

Despite nineteenth-century outcries against racial mixing as well as against specific dances, the sensuality of African-derived performance attracted Europeans. European men had more opportunities to dance with African-descended women than European women with African-descended men.[19] Their hopes surrounded fantasies of seduction and rape and permitted physical contact with the socially and religiously forbidden "black" or *mulata* woman. Through her dance, they experienced the exotic world of the African dancing body, African torso flexibility, and Creole rhythmic hypnosis. Over time, the entire Spanish-descended population included portions of African performance style within their dance preferences.

There were two tracks of *rumba* development, one inside and the other outside of Cuba. Ethnologist Fernando Ortiz commented on how *rumba* had "degenerated" by the mid-twentieth century.[20] He referred to traditional *guaguancó* that contained risqué elements within a mimetic story line (reminiscent of *rumbas del tiempo de España*). Two popular scenarios placed the woman on her hands and knees (on "all fours")—in one, washing the floor, and in the other, shoeing a mule (*herrar la mula*). In the now infamous *rumba* song, "Lola (or Lala) no sabe na," a *rumbera* mimes washing clothes, hanging them out to dry, ironing, sweeping and mopping the floors, washing dishes, and sewing—all in front of her dancing partner and within her traditional *rumba* step. She responds to the instructive lyrics of the lead singer and gyrates within her partner's stealthy gaze. He usually waits for her complete array of suggestive gestures before he attempts his *vacunao*.

For Ortiz and other mainstream Cubans in the 1920s to 1950s, this *rumba* was too explicit, as historian Louis Pérez states: "For respectable Cuban society, bourgeois and middle class alike, the notion that the *son* or the *rumba* symbolized Cuba was as inconceivable as it was inadmissible."[21] With its risqué scenarios, *rumba* was *baja cultura* (low culture) in a society that officially preferred late-nineteenth-century ballroom dance, like *danzón*. Despite this, Cubans eventually offered *rumba* performance to both a domestic commercial market as well as an international tourist market.[22]

In aesthetically rendering a playful dance of flirtation, the *rumba* couple reinforced the seductive *mulata* and the cool *macho* as profound etchings on the Cuban mind—at once etchings of Cuban-ness in dance, but also etchings of racism and sexism.[23] For the first performances, light-skinned or "white" performers were preferred over dark-skinned performers. The tawny or olive-skinned and dark-skinned *mulatas* were seen as "easily laid" Cuban women, and gradually they were highlighted in theaters and cabarets.[24]

The first "white" performers were from the middle and upper classes with conservatory training and concert aspirations before they became involved with popular theater dance (Carmita Ortiz and Julio [Pons] Richards, for example). They drew their stylization from cultural values of the time that degraded "things African" and yet peppered execution with what audiences wanted, including *mulata* sensuality and *macho* bravura. Their references were from blackface musical theater of the day and from vague and imagined notions of original *rumba*. It was in this vein that the renowned *mulata* entertainer Rita Moliner began to emphasize and develop Afro-Cuban elements within her performances.[25] With theatrical and commercial performance, *rumba* began a metamorphosis.

Slowly, *rumba* moved toward Santiago, and the *son* moved toward Havana, as musicians and dancers crossed both ends of the island.[26] Many Cubans who had difficulty finding jobs in rural areas moved to urban centers and became part of the *septeto* musical development of the 1930s. Cubans outside of Havana and Matanzas were less familiar with traditional *rumba*—for example, the *rumba tahona* form, which was played on bread crates in and around Havana. Some were familiar with *rumba chancleta,* a Santiaguera/eastern form that featured *zapateo*-influenced clicking sandals within *rumba* performance. Dark-skinned workers found employment in theaters as *rumberos,* even though some of them were just as ignorant of traditional *rumba* as the first light-skinned performers had been.

Original *rumba* continued also as the *rumba* gathering (sometimes called *rumbón* or huge *rumba*), which was a festive affair in which elaborate attire, sumptuous foods and drinks, all sorts of fad dances, as well as skilled and virtuoso *rumba* performance, were included. *Rumba* gatherings were always *quindembo*—huge mixtures of dances.[27]

Although some Cubans might say that *rumba* "died out" by the middle of the twentieth century, other observers of daily life among "black" Cubans point to the two- and three-year-olds who can still differentiate between *rumba* and *Oricha* rhythms, little four-year-old girls who know how to demonstrate a *botao* in response to a *vacunao* before they can read or write, and numerous precocious five- to eight-year-old drummers, who today in twenty-first-century Cuba still display their genius through improvisational *rumba* drumming. The insistent desire for Cuban "home-style" performance and its deep communal interactions have kept a constant *rumba clave* and a sufficient communal sense so that traditional *rumba* has thrived inside Cuba along with its variants for more than a century and a half.

Since the Revolution of 1959, government support of the three classic types of *rumba* has established regular presentations and historical explanations of traditional *rumba* across Cuba. Simultaneously, the Cuban National Folkloric Dance Companies in Havana and Santiago de Cuba have instituted *Rumba* Saturdays and Sundays. Currently, new forms have been emerging—*guarapachangueo*, for example, the improvisational sounds and specific highlighting of heavy *cajon* playing beneath rippling elaboration and above implied clave.[28] Despite its appropriation from lower-class locales and commercialization for theaters, cabarets, and tourist interests, *rumba* continues both as a Cuban treasure and as a persistent popular (folkloric) dance.[29]

Rhumba's International Journey

Rumba was also appropriated outside of Cuba—this time as *rhumba,* an international communalized popular dance. *Rhumba,* as *rumba* was most often called in its international heyday, was also *quindembo*—a mixture of different dances that were all called *rhumba*.[30] This powerfully suggestive name—"*rhumba*" or "*rumba*"—became a couple-dance phenomenon.[31]

Ethnomusicologist Robin Moore details how those who moved *rumba* from community performance to cabaret and theaters also took *rhumba* outside of Cuba to the international stage.[32] The Cuban theater scene modeled a staged *rhumba* for the international tourist scene abroad. As dark-skinned

Cubans became more involved in the tourist trade inside Cuba and as the cabaret format of *rhumba* was featured outside of Cuba, traditional *rumba* became "staged *rumba*" inside Cuba and "*rhumba*" outside of Cuba, and the *rhumba* craze of the 1930s was in full force.

From its first international trips to Paris in 1927, Berlin in 1931, and Chicago in 1933, *rhumba* performance mixed traditional *rumba* elements with its "lighter-skinned sister," the Cuban *son*, making *son rumba*'s "pretender."[33] This was not particularly difficult because they both had the same mother/African and father/European dance heritages. Cuban musicologists Argeliers León, María Teresa Linares, and Olavo Alén Rodríguez have discussed the Creole or mixed essence of both *rumba* and *son*[34] and agree with music historian John Storm Roberts when he writes about *son* as "certainly the classic Afro-Cuban form, an almost perfect balance of African and Hispanic elements."[35] Additionally, nineteenth-century understanding held that *son* was basically an African-derived style of dancing.[36] Thus, the facile *quindembo* of sister dances (cousins, if you like), one *mulata/rumba* and the other *trigueña/son,* assisted the public craze for an enticing but "crude and forbidden" *rumba.*

Rumba traveled from a segregated and elitist society to a racist international environment.[37] The place of Cuba in the international community, during the 1920s to 1950s particularly, was centered in adventure, gambling, and sexual fantasy, with music and dance steering the activity among North American and European tourists and elite Cuban society. Within what was called *rhumba,* traditional *rumba* could *not* be seen; it was only referenced through its name and rhythms. *Son* dance style substituted for *rumba* during this era.

At the 1933 World's Fair in Chicago, Cuban performers danced the altered version of *rumba* in endless rows of ruffles and without its native curvilinear frame. Theatrical costuming looked like roosters' feathers standing on edge or like peacocks' elongated plumed tails—accentuating a Spanish rather than a genuine Afro-Cuban flare. The dance team that has been documented repeatedly and that caused a stir in its demonstration of *rumba* and other Cuban dances at the fair was Afro-Cuban: René Rivero Guillén and Ramona Ajón (*la pareja de baile* René and Estela).[38] They were from Matanzas in western Cuba, an origin site of *rumba,* and perhaps knew traditional *rumba* style; however, their performance at the World's Fair was supposedly the first time *rumba* was danced "without embarrassment."[39]

More than *conga, bolero, tango, samba,* the U.S. *fox-trot,* or other popular dances of the time (which were all called *rhumbas* outside of Cuba), *son* body orientation matched the image that stage, movie, and theatrical performers thought was appropriate for public performance of *rumba*. Away from its native *solar* ambiance, traditional *rumba* did not keep its traditional orientation or sequences. It had been a dance of both men and women with flexed knees and backs tilted at the forward diagonal. As the dancing couple circled each other in small steps, they used an abundance of hip swaying, chest shifting, and shoulder shimmying. *Rumba*'s distinct foot pattern, whether actualized exactly or syncopated and varied, is flat-footed, gentle stamps (Right, R, Left, L or RRLL, RRLL, etc.). In comparison, *rhumba* dancing involved men holding women face to face in an upright position, above a repetitive and alternating right and left three-step foot pattern (RLR-hold, LRL-hold, etc.). The dancing couple travels through space with rhythmic elegance and accentuated hip movement (as in photo 6). Thus, in body orientation, foot patterns, proxemics, and touching, the dance called "international" or "commercial *rhumba*" was closer to Cuban *son* than it was to its namesake, even in spite of the intermittent risqué theatrics described earlier in "Lola no sabe na" and "Herrar la mula."

Other means of *quindembo* ensured the pretender's success. Performers danced to *rumba* rhythms, but with extensive musical instrumentation beyond percussion and voice. There were elaborate orchestrations of brass and woodwinds that meshed with *son*'s visual image and spatial configurations. Popular music ensembles had produced a commercial version for Cuban locales, and again, these assisted the international tourist market. Additionally, music companies published medleys of Cuban/Caribbean and Latin American songs, much of which was categorized as *rhumbas* because of their "Latin" or rhythmic feel. Even some Cuban compositions, such as Emilio Grenet's *tango-conga* "Ay Mama Inés," Moisés Simons' *son* "Con picante y sin picante," and the Chiquita Banana jingle were lumped into the *rhumba* category. Leymarie reports: "From 1913 to 1915, the American record companies Victor and then Columbia . . . spread the *danzón*, the *son*, the *guaracha*, and the *bolero* abroad, labeling almost everything '*rumba*' or '*rhumba*.'"[40] As well, the movie industry did not make distinctions among Cuban dance creations, but indiscriminately named movies and played music in movies that had little or no relationship to genuine or classic *rumba* dance types (for example, George Raft's movies *Rumba* in 1935 and *Bolero* in 1934).[41]

From the beginning, in attempts to make Afro-Cuban *rumba* less "crude" and more acceptable to both upper-class Cubans and international audiences, *rumba* was robbed of much of its essence in the name of sophistication. Performers and producers tried to make *rumba* "fit" a new public. Cuban dance soloist, now dance educator, Alfredo O'Farrill states: "What happened to the *rumba* when it began to be called 'cabaret' was fundamentally the result of advertising the Cuban woman's body as cheap merchandise, just like toasting sex and liquor. . . . So they created a type of ballroom dance in their own image . . . which was sold as an elaborate product, one that was cleansed of its 'black' element."[42]

The need to bring *rumba* up from *baja cultura* permeated the *rhumba* craze. *Rumba* blended with *son, bolero, and conga,* and then *quindembo* resulted. Cuban music researcher Ned Sublette concludes that rumba "seeped into [many types of] Cuban music in profound ways."[43] *Rhumba* outside of Cuba and its staged version inside Cuba were mixed. *Rhumba* on stage had some traditional *rumba* elements—the chase of the woman, fancy footwork of the man in pursuit, sensuous and accentuated hip movements, and body part isolation (like vibrating shoulders)—but again, these *rhumbas* were danced in a *son* key.[44]

Mambo, Son, and *Rumba*

Similar mixing and (con)fusion among Cuban popular dances occurred in the 1950s with the popularization of Cuban *mambo,* a descendant of *son.* Taking its name and essence from the repeated riff section of *son* musical form over which improvisation takes place, a modernized version of *son* dancing appeared, called *mambo. Mambo* music arrived and sported fresh energy; however, *mambo* dance inside Cuba evolved into a series of choreographed movements. In part, this was a response to jazz music and the *lindy hop* of the 1940s in Diaspora U.S.

In tropical Cuba, there were few occasions suitable for the *lindy*'s acrobatics; rather, Cuban *mambo* was a bouncy toe-step pattern on alternating feet that combined hip flexion from front to back in double time under ribcage shifts. It had little jumps that shoved parallel knees twice on either side of a dancing partner. Next, a repetitive step, step, step, kick-R, step, step, step, kick-L pattern had a variation with couples changing sides in three counts and making the big kick facing each other on count four.[45] With calculated steps like these, *mambo* in Cuba did not enjoy the popularity it gained elsewhere in the 1950s; it became too disciplined. Most of the creative juice that made the dance a craze elsewhere was because of added improvisations from Puerto Rican musicians and Puerto Rican, African American, Italian, and Jewish dancers in New York City.[46]

The intensification and elaboration of basic *son* outside of Cuba yielded a determined, driven (hot) dance; *mambo* became *son*'s pretender, and *quindembo* reigned again. *Mambo* symbolized the improvised "insurrection spirit" of nineteenth-century *mambises* or guerilla independence fighters inside the improvisational music display of the *mambo* section. When *mambo* recordings of Arsenio Rodriguez, Machito's Afro-Cubans, or Perez Prado played in the 1950s, the dancing *pareja* went wild, moving in *son*'s alternating foot pattern (RLR hold, LRL hold); however, the partners did not hold each other in the closed partner position of *son*. The "dance-of-two" had become boring, constricting, and in need of liberation. Even though *mambo* partners started in an upright *son* position, their *rumba* heritage ultimately separated and settled them in a slight forward tilt over bent knees, "ready for anything" positioning. The *mambo pareja* utilized its antecedent African approach/retreat pattern, which simulated traditional *rumba* dance movement over *son* foot patterns. Men and women improvised independently over a repetitive rhythm, sometimes turning together, sometimes in opposition to one another. Without touching between the dancing-two, there was room for play, flirtation, and competition. *Mambo,* a daughter of *son,* drew upon her "Aunt *Rumba*'s" characteristics and Congo/Angola grandmother's *mambisa* temperament! She set these not to *rumba* percussion but instead to *son*'s orchestrated brass trumpets, trombones, and saxophones contrasted with piano, bass, and full percussion.

The dance description above would not be familiar among competitive ballroom dancers outside of Cuba. For them, the *son* foot pattern, *son* proxemics, and certainly *son* body orientation are more in keeping with competition *mambo*. In the United States and Britain, *mambo* is taught as an alternating step: quick, quick, slow, or slow, quick, quick repeatedly in a varied direction pattern. Competitive *rhumba* is danced to a variety of musics, some modernized *son,* but also to music unrelated to Cuban *rumba* or *son. Quindembo* yet again!

Quindembo and Liberation in Popular Dance Contexts

There should be little surprise regarding the substitution of *son*-like performance for genuine *rumba* in the 1930s and 1940s, the substitution of *rumba*-like performance for *son*-derived *mambo* in the 1950s, and the substitution of *son*-like performance for both *rumba* and *mambo* at least since the 1950s in international ballroom *rhumba*. This is the course of popular dance, whether considered "folk," "vernacular," "salon," or "ballroom" types. Popular dance is always borrowing, returning, imitating, shifting, reversing, inverting, improvising, camouflaging, subverting, elaborating, and in the process shaping yet another named creation for the current day. That creation is then susceptible to other manipulations of old and new gestures, as well as different orders of emphases and standardizations. Sometimes, the original comes back into public popularity, but in a new era and often with a new name.

At home during family gatherings or abroad during parties, Caribbeans have rarely discounted their native popular dances. They have simultaneously danced international dance crazes as well as their own local favorites. With migration away from the islands in the 1980s, melancholy, homesickness, and struggle have supported innovations within intra-island and Pan-Caribbean genres, and *zouk* has vibrated internationally. The 1990s added *timba* to the list of Caribbean mass dance expressions, and, again, the lower-class public, usually "black," instigated its dance on the streets, patios, and waterfronts, and in nightclubs and theaters. The insistent ache of poverty and struggle was dulled in the moments of popular dance. Feelings of aliveness and kinship or desires for local and national belonging became consonant with the joy of the dance.

The social and political tensions that are interwoven within social life are minimized in the dance. Dancers can strike out in opposition to any obstacle symbolically. For the marginalized masses, the popular dance experience is like Entioppe's "*marronnage* of the mind."[47] For the middle and upper classes, however, popular dances are at once contagious, fascinating, and pleasurable, but also disastrous, embarrassing, and irritating.

Most Caribbeans dance regularly, and there is always *quindembo* in popular dance—a mixture of dance movement vocabulary that keeps refreshing itself with new trends. Although not all popular dances cross local borders to international destinations, like Cuban/Puerto Rican *salsa*, Haitian/Dominican *merengue,* Jamaican *reggae,* or French Caribbean *zouk,* popular dance is in step with local sociopolitical conditions, often striking out against present conventions for future change. It is influenced by every linguistic, technological, and other cultural shift that comes into the environment. Dance *quindembo* takes from all the bits and pieces of social life and weaves a particular kaleidoscope of gestures and foot patterns that thrill, energize, and ultimately relax performers. What the Caribbean public feels comes out in popular dance, and differentiated classes generate stylistic distinctions that display the characteristics, confines, contradictions, and celebrations of their life pursuits.

Within Caribbean popular dance, liberation is personal; it is felt, experienced, stored, and remembered bodily. Dancers become intensely involved, active participants who give and receive from a community of participating dancers and musicians. Their daily struggles are muted temporarily and replaced by body freedom and rhythmic connectedness. Within the combination of movements, rhythms, and lyrics, dancers let go of physical and emotional tension; they are engrossed in kinesthetic and aural overtones, as sensual movements allude to spontaneity, freedom, and pleasure. Dancers relax into limitless body expression, including sexual play, and popular dance reveals its magic, fun, and eroticism. After hours of dancing in tropical heat or humidity, sweaty bodies wind down on buses or sea breeze-filled streets, and the dance has served its purpose: to gather lovers of the dance together, compel them to dig deep into music with their bodies, and express something new, remembered, and real. Profound delight in the dance experience lingers day after day, gnawing at the body repeatedly thereafter.

The local to transnational journey I have mapped here for *rumba* can be reiterated similarly for other popular dances. Caribbean popular dances challenge mainstream European and North American dances for the spotlight, and frequently they become the global attraction.

CHAPTER SIX

PARADING THE CARNIVALESQUE: MASKING CIRCUM-CARIBBEAN DEMANDS

With Catherine Evleshin

> One cannot know the entirety of a rhythm without knowing
> and experiencing its dance at the same time, because with the
> dance moves, additional rhythms are generated.
> —Elizabeth McAlister, *Rara! Vodou, Power, and
> Performance in Haiti and Its Diaspora*

The Carnivalesque

Imagine that you have just made the journey to the Caribbean or Circum-Caribbean Brazil to experience Carnival. You step into the anarchy of the streets; out of the crowd a ruffian appears in face paint, dreadlocks adorned with mismatched feathers and other suspicious-looking items, and a t-shirt adorned with a phrase ending in an exclamation point. The youth shouts threats in a language quite removed from your high school French or Portuguese, or your native English or Spanish. He dances about until you hand him a five-dollar bill. If you look genuinely baffled and give him nothing, he flashes a smile and throws a handful of harmless red powder over you, and then darts away in search of another victim. You remember to breathe and head down the street in search of an organized parade of pretty women in scant clothing.

This is the essential Carnivalesque experience, the metaphoric challenge to quotidian rules, the mocking or satirical challenge to authority and to traditional social order. In your imagined state of ignorance, you may have escaped the *aguinaldo,* the expected largesse from the privileged, the reciprocity and/or inversion that is intimated during Carnival and other parading dance events. Serious business, this Carnivalesque, along with a deliberate component of shock value. This chapter examines the Carnival dancing that is sprinkled within many Caribbean cultural calendars.

Chart 13. Circum-Caribbean Parading

Caribbean	Saints Day Processions, *Dia de los Reyes*
Cuba	*Carnaval, Congas/Comparsas, Gagá*
Puerto Rico	*Carnaval*
Dominican Republic	*Canavales regionales, Gagá*
Haiti	*Kanaval, Rara, Koudyay*
Martinique	*Carnaval*
Guadeloupe	*Carnaval*
Trinidad and Tobago	Carnival (*Jouvé, Mardi Gras*)
Jamaica	Jonkonnu, Carnival
Circum-Caribbean Brazil	*Carnaval (Batucaje, Blocos, Afroxés), Maracatú*

Carnival Characteristics

Parading and processional forms were exceedingly important for the entertainment of early Caribbean travelers and settlers. In both European and African history, periodic processions marked the year and the ritual calendar. Pageantry, dance, and annual cleansing rituals included sacred offerings to insure fertility, fermented beverages that preserved food through late-winter scarcity, the sacrifice of a goat or fatted calf, and merrymaking before the semi-starvation of early spring. In the Caribbean, the drudgery and horror of plantation life for Africans, the loneliness and gender imbalance for both Africans and Europeans, the endless colonial and class conflicts—all these things necessitated the suspension of rules periodically. For a day or a week, small farm and large plantation populations were permitted to celebrate in outlandish attire with sumptuous foods and drinks and airs of suspect freedom. Carnival participants mocked fun at one another, and a celebration of disorder, role reversals, or inversion of power punctuated the season. Defiance of authority encouraged a "shape-changing" character for carnivalesque festivities, which were centered on lavish costuming, sexualized debauchery, boisterous disorder or anger, opposition, and maliciousness.

While Carnival dancing is not part of Church ritual or religious in actual character, it socially marks the beginning of sacred time, so it has a religious function. The wild parading, masking, and dancing herald Catholic and Protestant celebrations of Lent and serve as the preamble to the holiest of Christian seasons—Easter. The dates of most festivals are or once were connected to this holiday. The unquestioned religious purpose and regularity of Church calendar festivals provided routine opportunities for the display and interfacing of European and African dance practices. Carnival and processional dancing may have been among the few possible vehicles for acknowledgment of African heritage that the African-descended community had. Costumed reenactments of hierarchy and theatrical play could have transposed African customs to American behaviors.

Often, the only actions available to the powerless or denigrated were transgressions in words or behaviors against sexual and gender codes. Historically, gender rules were rigid in both Catholic- and Protestant-dominated societies (apart from covert colonial sex practices). Exaggerated machismo, hyperfemininity, cross-dressing and gender bending became more and more the rule as Caribbean Carnivals incorporated the carnivalesque. Defying rules regarding gender roles, conventional dress, and sexual behavior would be expected when the world was "turned upside down" at Carnival time, and indeed, this rule breaking still occurs in almost every pre-Lenten celebration or equivalent carnivalesque festival.[1]

A related Carnival characteristic is *malcriado,* or "bad child" or "impolite, crude behavior," which is rampant. The Spanish and Portuguese translations mean not only an ill-mannered child, but also a protester, rebel, or rude trickster. It is *malcriado* that manifests in Jamaican Carnival costumes and Trinidadian floats and appears as Zarenyen, the Haitian trickster spider, who uses his wit to prevail over presidents, military men, and other Goliaths. *Malcriado* in Circum-Caribbean Brazil is the black, one-legged forest spirit (Saci Perere), who is reminiscent of a slave who was mutilated for attempting to escape. He (or she, more rarely) can be viewed as a positive or negative force, but *malcriado* references are enmeshed within Carnivals and the carnivalesque.[2]

Devils (selfish, cunning, malicious, and uneven-tempered) are also important elements of Carnival and parading festivals in the region. Although the performing devils tend to be African, Native American, and non-Christian, the concept of the Devil is Christian/European, and in Christianity, a nonbeliever was and is believed today to be subject to the Devil's influence.

Spanish and Portuguese conquerors came to the Americas during the Inquisition, when they had regained control of the Iberian Peninsula after eight centuries of Islamic/African rule. A new dance appeared at the same time—*morisca (morisco, morisque* or *moresque* in France, *morris dance* in England)—which employed *contredanse* figures and line and circle configurations to depict a battle between the Moors and Christians, sometimes with sticks or swords. The dance included varying picaresque characters: a pregnant woman, a jester, a devil, etc. At the end of the dance, the warriors turn on the Devil to symbolize the triumph of Christianity over evil. In some cases, the *morris dance* was (and still is) performed in "blackface" or masked blackface. Inevitably, Africans were cast in the roles of the enemy or the Devil.[3]

The conquest of the Americas became an endless *morisca,* both a theatrical and genuine effort to conquer the unconverted and subdue evil. In the Dominican Republic, *diablo cojuelo* ("limping devil" or many-horned *papier maché* mask) pretends he is lame to get near and strike children and young women on their backsides.[4] In Loiza Aldea, an Afro–Puerto Rican village, *el vejigante,* the mask of evil, is carved from a coconut husk and resembles a ghost figure or an unusual clown as it parades with old men and Spanish knight characters and eventually fights good against evil, Moors against Christians, or life against death. In Martinique, Carnival is devoted to red devils, *les diables rouges,* who wear elaborate masks that feature horns and mirrors. On Ash Wednesday, when the rest of the Catholic world is nursing a hangover and going to church to repent Carnival behaviors, Martinican revelers dressed in black and white still dance in the streets; at sunset, they witness King Vaval burned in effigy. Vaval is the spirit of Carnival ("va" diminutive and "Carna-val.") Originally, the burning of a powerful Carnival figure was a European tradition, but beyond Martinique's unique King example, it is usually a Judas figure that is burned on Easter Sunday in Haiti and Cuba.

Masking existed on both the European and African continents before the conquest of the Americas; "The Devil" was beaten down on the Feast of Corpus Christi in southern Europe, and "evil" was driven out of Nigeria and other African spaces through danced rituals in white masks. The Devil, *malcriado,* and "challenge to order" choreographies were in place and the characters already cast when the cultures of two continents took over the Americas. Accordingly, similar and new practices evolved in the Caribbean. Following are brief descriptions and comparisons of major masking and parade dance traditions in Trinidad and Tobago, Jamaica, Cuba, Haiti, and Brazil. Some parading and processional forms continue to be relaxing entertainment, but many are simultaneously seeking genuine political reform.

Carnival in Trinidad

Probably the oldest celebrated Carnival in the Americas is the riotous pre-Lenten parading festival in English/Creole Trinidad and Tobago. In synchrony with Catholic and Protestant calendars, colonists and their captives repeated three-day European rituals that emphasized revelry and gluttony in preparation for the following forty days of fasting, cleansing, and purification of Lent. Later, *canboulay,* or "the burning of the cane field," was grafted onto Trinidadian Carnival. This was a stick-fighting and dance ritual on the

Sunday night before Ash Wednesday, which commemorated emancipation from slavery.[5]

Trinidadian Carnival devotes an entire day to perhaps the most carnivalesque of all events: *"djab"* or *"djab-djab,"* from the French *diable* (devil), and full community participation is encouraged. Beginning in the wee hours of *Jouvé* (*Jour Ouvert,* Opening Day, the Monday before Ash Wednesday), thousands of locals, tourists, and "Trinis" from abroad take to the streets *chippin'*—the flat-footed, hip-jerking walk that permits packed crowds to parade for hours, stopping only to drink beer, rum, or scotch (ideally with coconut water). The nearly nude *djab molassie* ("molasses devils") smear one or more of the following: molasses, motor oil (toxic!), blue or red paint, or just plain mud over their entire bodies. Trinidad-born anthropologist Patricia Alleyne-Dettmers describes *Jouvé*: "Caked only in mud, we no longer recognize ourselves. We return to the belly of the ancestors, to Mama La Terre (Mother Earth), bearing witness to the gift of life even after the horrific traumas of slavery and colonization."[6]

In the first years after the abolition of slavery, Europeans attempted to curtail the license that newly liberated Africans were exercising during the three days before Ash Wednesday. Police tried to stop Carnival that year and then gave up, letting Afro-Trinidadians "do their thing."[7] The original challenge was probably a one-time event, but it became the stuff of legend, reenacted each year. Neighborhood gangs with "Pierrot" (costumed leaders) as well as stick fighters in *neg jardin* or bloused shirts fought and marked Carnival competitions of the past[8]; however, fights and fight-dancing had the potential to erupt into real rebellion. Consequently, contemporary contests for the "most talented" and/or the "most beautiful" were substituted, ending with the crowning of a Carnival King and Queen.

Mardi Gras, or "Fat Tuesday," before Ash Wednesday, became the most celebrated day and the apex of Trinidadian Carnival. On this day in the nineteenth century, the European, African, and Creole populations followed parading bands that traveled from estate to estate to observe masked theatricals.[9] Dance ethnologist Molly Ahye has described the masked revelers' dance: a close sliding of both feet or "chipping" (also described, imprecisely, as "shuffling"[10]) with accompanying hip action that displayed an African-derived style. The exaggerated "hip-walking-to-the-music" was first expressed as "leggo" or "let go" movement and was performed to string and bamboo instruments at countryside festivities.[11] *Lavway* or *leggo* street-traveling band music accompanied revelers until the introduction of steel drums or "pans," which were later augmented or replaced by amplified combinations of *calypso, soca,* and what was called *road march* music.[12]

In the twentieth and twenty-first centuries, Trinidadians have paraded across Port-of-Spain's central savannah dressed in colonial attire, sailors' uniforms, African-like loincloths, but also in sequins, huge plumes, and skimpy as well as skin-tight costumes. Both the ruling class and the enslaved in historical time and all social classes in modern times have participated in boisterous merrymaking throughout the long weekend.

Politics and Trinidadian Celebrations

Costumed masking and parade dancing have generated the sociopolitical havoc that is associated with Carnival. For example, in the genius of European-descended Trinidadian costume designer Peter Minshall, contemporary Carnival has had a profound effect on Trinidadian politics and aesthetics. Minshall's use of lightweight fiberglass revolutionized Carnival costuming. His incredible engineering wonders presented legendary warriors and monsters as gigantic costumed puppets weighing up to one hundred pounds that reached twenty feet or more into the air. In 2006, Minshall's gigantic condom float uprooted conventional attitudes within the English/Creole Caribbean and urged an aggressive campaign against the increase of HIV and AIDS across the islands. Just before and during Carnival activities, radios and televisions blasted throughout residential areas with pros and cons regarding not simply Minshall's daring float, but also the value of condom use. Minshall's political Carnival artworks have included commentary on war, industrialization, and ecological outrage. Examples include floats called "Madame Hiroshima," "ManCrab," "Sounds of Earth," "Papillon," etc.[13]

Similar celebrations of the controversial have traditionally occurred in Trinidadian Carnival. Challenging insults, as well as the ritualized boasting and oratory of early Carnival, influenced the formation of *calypso* song form and, simultaneously, *calypso* dancing. Calypsonians, the masters of licentious metaphor, performed from estate to estate among visiting neighbors and over time developed their verbal and rhyming prowess, particularly in tent shows.[14] These singing poets tattled on everyday tricksters—cheating spouses, men who submit to other men, promiscuous women, crooked politicians, and schemers of every stripe. Misogyny? Homophobia? Of course! Otherwise, it would not be the carnivalesque.

Carnavales of Cuba

On Three Kings Day (*Día de los reyes*), Epiphany on the Roman Catholic calendar (January 6), the Church and Spanish civil authorities permitted Europeans of all classes and both free and enslaved Africans to celebrate collectively with music, dance, and masking in the streets. Processional displays were presented to governing captains, their entourages, and church officials in return for gifts to African captives. The annual festivity was a substitute for the earlier celebration of Festival of Corpus Christi (May), which was deemed too serious an ecclesiastic event to permit African participation.[15] Historic artwork and texts reveal African ethnic groups, dressed in peacock feathers, tutus, silk hats, face paints, sailor uniforms, raffia skirts, etc., parading and dancing with their Kings and Queens.

Beyond *Día de los reyes* parading, similar Carnival parading developed and continues on proclaimed Carnival days for all thirteen Cuban provinces, often on patron saints' days. During other non-Carnival events—for example, at the opening or closing of conferences or at New Year's celebrations—parading and carnivalesque dancing sometimes flow out of homes and theaters into nearby streets and plazas. Also, neighborhood collectives, work groups, student organizations, and other associations organize Cuban dance performances with parading bands that march toward a centrally located plaza or in front of a raised stand of onlookers. Sometimes at the climax of these true spectator events, prizes are awarded to the best music and dance groups, and, economy permitting, there are floats. Cuban *Carnavales* are a public yet controlled "free-for-all" with dancing, parading, beer in great quantities, and raucous or bitter laughter.[16]

Also through the years, Cubans have featured festive and symbolic clothing to highlight their allegiance to neighborhood collectives.[17] "Red and blue bands" have paraded, performed staged battles, and competed with friendly and not-so-friendly attitudes.[18] Remnants of such competition are found in *rumba* groups of Matanzas around New Year's Day, dressed in red and blue coordinated outfits.

Legend has it that a *conga* dance was invented on slave ships when African captives were brought on deck to exercise. "Conga line" is English for a serpentine form that is actualized by people dancing with their hands on the hips of the person in front of them (far removed from its Congo/Angola approach/retreat antecedents). The traditional *conga* pattern in *Carnaval cubano* consists of three steps to alternating diagonal sides, followed by a syncopated jerk, lurch, or catch step, said to symbolize coming to the end of the chains that bound the legs of enslaved Africans. This simple dance allows for large or small, fast or slow, walking or running steps with torso isolations that are dictated by gender or the Carnival character being portrayed; hence, there are a dozen or more elaborations of the *conga* parading step.

In Cuba, the largest of the Caribbean islands, even the event date takes on a carnivalesque quality, jumping around the calendar in response to the vicissitudes of history. Before the Revolution, Cubans who identified as Spanish European celebrated a pre-Lenten *Carnaval* in February or March, sometimes called "white Carnival," now all but forgotten. On January 1, the descendants of Ekpe and Efik ethnic groups from the Calabar region of Nigeria, called Carabalí, Abakuá, or (more derogatively) Ñañigo in Cuba, parade with other *cabildo* organizations in the streets as well as in *plantes* (meeting houses) of Havana and Matanzas provinces.[19] In Abakuá rites, an *íreme* or masked spirit of the dead with huge eyes, believed blind yet all-seeing, is called from the grave to identify evil and restore positive balance in the community.[20]

This fearsome character also appears in July *Carnavales*, where he is manifested by mature, initiated men, yet he is called a *"diablito,"* or little Devil. The diminutive in Spanish does little to dilute the awe of masked figures cavorting and darting in counterpoint, miming a stalking leopard in a mesmerizing dance of stillness and bravado. Two years before the abolition of slavery in 1886, *cabildos* were outlawed as centers of protest,[21] and *Carnaval* became the domain of neighborhood parading organizations, generally called *comparsas* in Havana and *congas* in Santiago de Cuba. Each *comparsa/conga* rehearsed its finest dance arrangements, which were measured by the force and unity of musical instruments, striking costumes, unified dancing, and original songs.[22]

In Santiago de Cuba, the second largest city of Cuba, Saint James' Day (July 26) became the day for parading and revelry. The Catholic Church had established patron saints for each town and city, and indeed for every New World site where its representatives claimed dominance. Each saint had her or his own site, calendar day, and celebration. Thus, eastern Cuba officially celebrates *Carnaval* on July 26 and 27, while western Cuba celebrates on July 25 and 26; in reality, *Carnaval cubano* uses both weekends surrounding July 26.

When Frenchmen in Haiti and their enslaved were caught in the upheaval of independence from France in 1804, some fled to eastern Saint Domingue away from Haitian control, where they continued *Carnaval* celebrations. Others settled in Mobile, Alabama (the first capital of French territories in the United States) and New Orleans, Louisiana. Both sites developed *Carnival* and *Mardi Gras* as pre-Lenten parading of the carnivalesque and, until the late twentieth century, they remained the only Carnivals in the Protestant-dominated United States.[23] Still other Haitians made a mass exodus from Haiti to Cuba and, once there, combined existing parading to make *conga santiaguera* (see photos 8 and 9).

A signature rhythm, *la conga,* was and still is played on drums and other percussion for Carnivals; however, *Carnaval santiaguero* features the

Chart 14. Conga Rhythm

trompeta china, a double-reed horn peculiar to the eastern provinces and a salute to the Chinese indentured workers who built Cuban railroads in the late nineteenth century. *Chancleta,* a dance in which flat wooden sandals are stomped in rhythmic patterns, is often danced to the *conga* rhythm and integrated into *conga santiaguera.*

The Haitians of eastern Cuba also brought their relentless parading dance, *gagá. Gagá* in Cuba is equivalent to *Rara* in Haiti and is performed intermittently throughout the Lenten season and constantly during Easter Week. The dance movements involve "danced-walking" with pronounced hip gyrations from high to low levels, which make it a dance of endurance and strength but also of brazen politics and bold sexuality.[24] *Gagá* is now an integrated dance practice in both central and eastern Cuba (as well as throughout the Dominican Republic).

Politics and Cuban Celebrations

It took the Revolution of 1959 to unite the Day of Kings parading, the pre-Lenten *Carnaval,* and patron saints' days under one umbrella, and that is its own carnivalesque story. On July 26, 1953, Fidel Castro and his revolutionary guerillas attacked the Moncada Barracks in Santiago, hoping to take advantage of the disorder and drunkenness associated with *Carnaval santiaguero.* The coup failed, but after the revolution succeeded in 1959, Havana and Santiago *Carnavales* were celebrated in an effort to clean up Cuba's previous "sin city" image.

No nudity or cross-dressing was allowed. Cuba's government declared homosexuality a crime, so no extreme behaviors were permitted, with the exception of one African hoop-skirted character, *la culona* (in Malinke, "a wise and educated person"; in colloquial Cuban, "big-ass"). With the scarcity of women in early Cuban enslavement, the dance and the character were appropriated by men, or so the story goes, but originally the dance was performed by women in the Congo/Angola region.[25] In colonial Cuba, "*la culona*" was also called a "*diablito,*" along with *íremes* and other African-derived characters of *Dia de los reyes* festivities.[26] After a few years, the spirit of the revolution and "the carnivalesque" clashed, and *comparsas* no longer assembled in their neighborhoods and paraded miles along the length of the seawall; they became part of a staged spectator event along a short section of the boulevard.[27]

The collapse of the Soviet Union in the early 1990s brought Cuba's biggest economic challenges, and *Carnaval* was cancelled. When it returned in 1999, it was an obvious ploy to draw international tourists to Havana.[28] Today, there is dwindling enthusiasm for the tamed Havana *Carnaval*; in Santiago, where tourism and emigration are minimized, *Carnaval* stands a chance to continue its fascinating development.[29]

Jonkannu and Carnival in Jamaica

After 1655, when British forces drove the Spanish out of Jamaica, Jamaican festivals took an Anglican turn and Carnival celebrations for Lent and Easter were replaced by carnivalesque customs for Christmas. December 26 or "Boxing Day" in England became Jonkannu (Jonkanoo, Junkanoo, or "John Canoe") in Jamaica and other British-controlled islands. Boxing Day was the day when the leftovers from Christmas feasting were "boxed" and given to the poor. It was transformed into a day when the enslaved were free to socialize with plantation owners, many of whom were without their European families.

Jonkannu developed as Roots Jonkannu, an African-derived festival of masking and revelry that was staged as entertainment by 1770, and Fancy Dress Jonkannu, a French-influenced Creole diversion after 1790.[30] African-style masking was the essence of "Roots Jonkannu," with dancing, fighting, and stock characters: Pitchy-Patchy, Devil, Belly-Woman, Whore-Girl, Horse, Cow, Indians, Warriors, etc. The origin of Pitchy-Patchy, an exemplary character, is disputed: in lithographs of the colonial period he is rendered as "Jack-o'-the-Green" of English tradition, and in true shape-shifting character, he also references an escaping slave.[31] Pitchy-Patchy is presumed to be a Jamaican Maroon camouflaged in palm fronds who returns from hidden territories to "steal" family members from the plantation.

After 1790, plantation owners developed "Set Girl" entertainments by providing luxurious, European-style costumes to young African-descended women chosen for their beauty and light skin color. Set Girls added hip and shoulder movements to European "jigs" and "*quadrille balancés*," and Fancy Dress Jonkannu "took off" with the influx of French planters in the region. Specific characters accompanied the Set Girls: "Actor Boy" or "John Canoe" (in the ruffles of a European courtier), and "House," a man who carried the model of a plantation mansion on his head (sometimes merged with "John Canoe"). In response to questions about actual dance steps, Evleshin states:

[I]n a course on Jamaican dance at the Cultural Training Center in Kingston, . . . we learned the movement and "persona" of each of the characters: Set girls prance on the balls of their feet and swing their hips provocatively. Thus they are a caricature of a vain, fine lady. "John Canoe" does jig steps that emphasize the crossing and kicking of legs, with pointed toes and an upright posture and with little torso movement. (The following Jonkannu characters display an earthbound style in contrast to the more aerial style of the set girls and "John Canoe" described above.) "Belly Woman" uses a flat-footed, alternating chug step with legs wide apart, hands on the fake belly, and with lascivious rolling of the hips. Cow lumbers with legs wide, in a lateral rocking motion. Horse leaps forward, then steps backward slightly to get thrust for the next leap (exhausting!). Devils flail arms and jump about, ad libitum. Pitchy-Patchy performs rapid, flat-footed, alternating shrugs with feet placed slightly wider than the hips; this is accompanied by shimmies or vibrations throughout his entire body that set the cloth strips of his costume in motion. The class instruction did not include Warriors, Indians, or "House" dance movements.[32]

Eventually, the two traditions merged, and stick-fighting male dancers competed for the alluring Set Girls; as well, groups of dancing and fighting characters paraded to neighboring plantations and into towns. Their performances showed dramatic skills and individual dance and fighting techniques, but, more important, asserted the prestige of plantation owners.[33]

Today, on January 6 in the self-governing Jamaican Maroon Territories, men of that proud heritage gather in the village of Accompong to celebrate signing of the peace treaty with the British in 1739. They wear foliage on their heads and perform solemn remembrances of their fearless ancestors. After the abolition of British slavery in 1838, Pitchy-Patchy appeared in hundreds of multicolored cloth strips (rags, if you will) that covered him from head to toe, instead of palm fronds. The change in costume is hard to track, since mummers or masked actors in England appeared in similar costumes during that period also.[34] In several parts of West Africa, the same costume is rendered in strips of woven designs, where the figure embodies the spirit of departed ancestral Kings and founders of tradition.[35]

Although virtually extinct today, Pitchy-Patchy shimmied his rags in relentless double-time steps, challenged personal spaces, then twirled and darted away. Jonkannu bands continue, but they perform only for tourists on North Shore Jamaica and for an occasional government-sponsored revival. Bands usually include a European-style red- or black-clad "Devil" with a pitch-fork. Despite the absence of genuine Jonkannu festivals, every Jamaican knows and loves the Pitchy-Patchy character. Both Fancy Dress and Roots Jonkannu dwell in the carnivalesque—the former through satire of the mincing style of European court dance and the latter in the aggressive challenge to authority presented by fearsome masked dancers employing "in-your-face" movements.[36]

Politics and Jonkannu, *Reggae,* and *Kumina*

After emancipation, Jonkannu bands lost the financial support of plantation masters. For the remainder of the nineteenth century, seasonal Roots Jonkannu groups roamed the streets and towns, soliciting funds through their performances. By the twentieth century, the "Back to Africa" movement of Marcus Garvey, the new Rastafarian religion, and rising political consciousness made soliciting money seem degrading to Jonkannu players. Occasional revivals under government and newspaper sponsorship were successful, but in the 1950s, one of these events resulted in serious unrest, and Jonkannu fell back into the shadows of history.[37]

Independence from British rule in 1962 ushered in a new postcolonial Jamaican identity. The singular talent of Bob Marley thrust the small nation and its homegrown Rastafarian religion into the international spotlight. While it would be a stretch to label the sincere expressions and lifestyle of *reggae* as carnivalesque, the fortunes made from the recording industry and the Jamaican Sunsplash music festival obviated the economic and psychological needs for a national festival. The impact was international and enduring, to the extent that *reggae* forever altered popular dance music across the globe.[38] These were Jamaica's golden years, followed by the international financial success of *dancehall* and other popular styles that grew out of a synthesis of *reggae,* North American rap, and *hip-hop* dance.

Reggae was born from the drum rhythms of *Kumina,* a religion of Congo/Angola heritage that emerged in Jamaica.[39] The musical connection between Kumina and *reggae* is easily discerned, since the distinction is primarily in tempo. *Reggae* is about twice as slow, and there is alternation of drums and percussion in Kumina versus guitar and bass in *reggae*; movement connection is hardly recognizable. The basic Kumina step is a small or tight, continuous step in a medium tempo, with one foot slightly ahead of the other, either with both heels in contact with the ground or with one foot flat and the other on the ball of the foot.[40] In contrast, *reggae* dancing involves idiosyncratic, freeform movements, often airborne or with a leaping quality.

Other English/Creole communities, including the Bahamas, Belize, and North Carolina in the Diaspora U.S., have histories of Jonkannu masking and parading. In the Bahamas, Jonkannu comes and goes, perhaps because there, Jonkannu is still identified with the struggle to hammer out a postcolonial identity. In Jamaica, *reggae* and *Rastafari* have usurped a roots identity.[41]

Haitian *Kanaval, Rara,* and *Koudyay*

At Carnival time in Haiti, there used to be few visitors from the United States, since the press had customarily "blacked out" Haiti with all but tragic news of floods, hunger, and disease—before the earthquake of 2010. Canadian and European tourists took advantage of cheap travel, warm winter climate, gracious Haitian hospitality, and sumptuous Haitian cuisine. The elite government provided money for Haitian musicians in New York City and elsewhere to return and play for *Kanaval.* The sounds of *mizik rasin,* Haitian *rap, konpa dirék,* and *zouk* would blare off trucks, while more or less unrestricted crowds comingled with tee-shirted parading groups that carried tin scrapers high above their heads.[42] An occasional float carrying beauty queens in ball gowns was the only nod to European traditions.

The minimal luxury within Haitian *Kanaval* before the devastation of 2010 was more than matched by the maximum power of the music and a populace that never seemed to stop dancing. Politically incendiary song lyrics and sexual gestures, which were only permitted during the pre-Lenten period and *Kanaval,* were signature examples of the carnivalesque. All was essentially suspended in the wake of the 2010 catastrophe.

Usually, however, with the end of *Kanaval* on Ash Wednesday, the season of *Rara* would begin, which the locals describe as "Vodou taken on the road." Communities paraded to lively bamboo horns (*vaksens*) and drum orchestras behind a male religious leader and a group of girls and women. Ethnomusicologist Elizabeth McAlister delineates three performative aspects within *Rara*: play, mystical work, and military movements, which are employed in the petitioning for financial contributions.[43] Parading dances and Vodou dances comprise the dance repertoire. *Vaksen* orchestras provide play, as their *ostinato* pattern is accomplished through "hocketting"; each bamboo plays only one note, but when combined sequentially, melody and rhythm are produced. Women play through responsorial singing with sanctioned Haitian *renns* (or Dominican *mayores*), Queens who lift their skirts, dance erotic movements, and sing sexually charged or dissenting lyrics. *Rara* bands proceed full throttle, stopping only at crossroads, cemeteries, town centers, or the homes of town leaders.

The performative element of mystical work in *Rara* is the hidden core of religious practice. Vodou rites take place as orchestras play and participants dance and sing suggestively.[44] Public acknowledgment of "big men" and their associates within the political hierarchy of male-dominated *Rara* organizations and within town communities is the performative element of the Popular Army. Military titles (such as colonel, general, major) and clothing (Regency satins and breeches, sometimes with cloth strips at the waist or head) convey high status, and officials receive donated money to maintain local village reputations and local leadership status. In this *Rara* component, a contrasting dance style of erect body posture and precise heel-toe movements recalls European military steps.

Some *Rara* bands have continued for decades, and *Rara* is associated with Vodou Petwo rites, which in turn, are credited with the success of the Haitian revolution and are thereby linked to rebellion and adversity.[45] Recently, *Rara* has found a home in Brooklyn, New York, bringing Haitian immigrants together, including many who eschewed this "peasant" expression in their home country. Traveling *Rara* performances are "practice sessions" that help band members build endurance and simultaneously advertise upcoming parades and processions. From Ash Wednesday until Easter, generally throughout the day and often all night, each *Rara* band dances and parades, even if a member dies en route.[46] A *Rara* band is a musical group that gives significant reputation to particular local powerbrokers, but it is also a contract with Haitian spirits, and members must perform at least seven years of service or adversity results.

Politics and Haitian Celebrations

Both *Kanaval* and *Rara* include elements of the carnivalesque along with deadly serious, grassroots political expressions. James C. Scott writes about the arts of political disguise with coded and covert messages of dissent hiding in plain sight: "[T]he dialogue from the public oral traditions of subordinate groups requires a more nuanced and literary reading simply because the hidden transcript has had to costume itself and speak more warily. It succeeds best—and one imagines is most appreciated too—when it dares to preserve as much as possible of the rhetorical force of the hidden transcript while skirting danger."[47]

Politics, religion, and music have been "plaited" in a long historical braid of Haitian affairs.[48] In the Vodou religion, *pwens* (literally "points") are spells or secret combinations of herbs that are used against a person or toward a particular event. When politicians speak publicly, they send verbal *pwens*, which are considered Vodou charms with disguised power, but whose receiver is readily known by listening community members. When *pwens* are sung, *chant pwen*, the messages are usually a means of sociopolitical criticism against the ruling class,[49] and *chant pwen* is well established among the activities of Haitian musicians during *Kanaval* and *Rara* festivities.

McAlister makes the important point that the masses "read" the conspicuous consumption, unforgivable waste, and extreme callousness of elites as utter vulgarity and wanton disrespect. They respond with equivalent crass-ness, vulgarity, and bestiality or sexual innuendo within *Kanaval* and *Rara* songs. In the process, they challenge and assault Catholic morality and of-ficial practices that do not protect or sufficiently provide succor for the poor. The masses agree with the song lyrics that they must address the essential decadence of both political and religious power with absolute obscenity. She writes: "On the most basic level, *betiz*[50] songs perform the cultural work of affirming not only the existence but also the creative life of a people in the face of insecurity and everyday violence. . . . Through the jokes and *betiz*, both Papa Gede [from Vodou] and the Rara bands become free to parody, to question, and to laugh. While this politics is not an engaged political movement, it is a politics of liberation nonetheless."[51]

Ethnomusicologist Gage Averill also describes Haiti's politico-musical-religious relationship where the *Kanaval* and *Rara* song lyrics often go be-yond suggestion to intimidation and speak boldly of the miserable social conditions of Haiti. Additionally, Averill emphasizes the *Koudyay* tradition that is embedded in Haitian carnivalesque practice. As a former colonial military practice that encouraged wholesale public revelry, *Koudyay* was first a show of prestige for visiting guests and celebrated victories.[52] As it evolved, it became a method of control used by a dictatorial leadership to release mass frustration through public delirium and to display financial support for local big men in return for the surrender of political will. For example, Papa Doc Duvalier and his son Baby Doc financially supported street parties for the masses to divert their attention from economic prob-lems and political tensions. Some of the parties were spontaneous *Koudyays* that had no association with actual Carnival, but it was presumed that the populace would feel the President's interest in the people when he provided the carnivalesque: drinks, food, and music for outdoor, overnight dancing and revelry. In fact, however, *Koudyay* performance presented a delicate balance between revelry and rioting, which had to be maintained, should the enthusiasm of street performers not outweigh their concerns over their burdened livelihoods. Averill states: "Carnival is the most important cross-roads of music and power in Haiti. The *koudyay* ambiance of carnival, the tradition of *chant pwen* in carnival songs, the powerful impression made by tens of thousands of lower-class Haitians in control of the streets, and carnivalesque (Gede-esque) exuberance (obscenity, exaggeration, verbal play, parody, excessive consumption, the grotesque, debasement, sexuality, license, transgression, masking, conflict, and Signifying on hierarchies) all contribute to an event that is potentially threatening to the state and to the elite."[53]

In full *Kanaval, Rara,* or *Koudyay* style, there is whistleblowing, conch blowing, and percussion of all sorts, from hitting bottles with spoons or hitting the sides of metal fences along the streets to mass participation in sound or *tenèb*.[54] Generally, both hands of enthusiastic participants are raised into the air; the most frequently used foot pattern is a two-step (danced walk RL, RL) with hips pressed forward and shoulders and head leaning back so as to join the crowd bodily or *apiye pa frape* (leaning, not *lese frappe* or "letting go until you hit or bump another," but most often "going" with the crowd).[55] This pattern sometimes alternates with the kicking of one leg forward with inward rotation for beat one; while same leg is still in the air, it rotates outward for beat 2, rotates inward for beat 3, and then circles outward to step down and permit alternation on the other foot. Body gestures and movements of *Kanaval, Rara,* and *Koudyay* are the same in the midst of uplifted and spirited singing, rendering the dance forms indistinguishable. Their functions are synonymous as well: sponsors of *Kanaval, Rara,* and *Koudyay* believe in public, social release for masses—both the lower class and the small middle class, who both wield powerful symbols for genuine reform through ridicule, satire, and musico-politics. Unlike the restricted Havana *Carnaval* and in the vein of unbridled Trinidadian and Jamaican Carnivals, Haiti's parading involves the dance and the carnivalesque as genuine political maneuvering.

Related Parading Festivals of Brazil

Samba is the dance that is most associated with Brazilian *Carnaval*. Many rhythms and dances have been called *sambas*, the undisputed national dance of Brazil, but not all of them are connected to Brazil's *Carnaval*. Until the late twentieth century, the dances could all be characterized as lightning-fast steps accompanied by specific torso isolations, which would be determined by musical style, gender, and geographical region. Most *samba* is filled with flurries of rapid, virtuosic, "look at me!" movements, followed by a "cut" or an abrupt freeze or hold to indicate an end of a phrase; *samba* emphasizes improvisational skills. An Afro-Brazilian might say he or she is doing *samba* while merely walking with a certain lilt, flexible hips and shoulders, and an open-mouthed smile (the needed "rest step" between energetic flurries).

Rio-style *samba* uses fast alternating triplet steps, hence the term *samba do pé,* or *foot samba.* This type is distinguished by virtuoso dance patterns that turn each foot outward as the heel pivots in place. The hips shift rapidly, accenting each side alternately. In contrast, Bahia-style *samba* combines

Brazilian *samba* and Jamaican *reggae* and becomes *sambareggae,* which is a catch-all term for several ever-changing fad dances.[56] *Sambareggae* focuses on foot patterns that either remain in place as the body bounces vertically over them or that alternate and travel slightly (for example, R, touch L, L, touch R).[57] The hips are not the focus, although they move in original Jamaican *reggae,* but the "gel" between the heartbeat rhythm and the downbeat of the alternating steps is the most important movement in *sambareggae.* The heavy downbeat is most often expressed through a walking step (LRLR), the step-touch in place (noted above), or three side steps and a quick catch-step (change of feet or RLR quickLR; LRL quickRL)—all executed with a small upright contraction on the upbeat and a gentle arch of the upper back on the step. Body posture in the Rio-style *samba* is vertical, with little forward tilt of the back and softly flexed knees, while Bahian *sambareggae* employs deep hip flexion and a variety of slow to moderate foot patterns.

Sambareggae movement includes fad dances (a new one comes out each Carnival season), which are often mimetic of animals, pop-culture icons, current events, and sexual references, with little emphasis on footwork. Movements are small and cramped when dancers are near *barracas,* stores where food and drinks are sold, or amidst crowding thousands. "Afro" movements, which are *Orixá* ritual sequences, are "taken to the streets" with bold flailing arms, wide steps, and deep torso contractions. These are *un*characteristic of both traditional *samba* and genuine *Orixá* rituals, but they form a distinct alternative to *samba* steps for Carnival dancers. Additionally, some performers use fad dance movements from Diaspora U.S. popular dance as *sambareggae* alternatives. *Samba do pé* and *samba de roda* (the older ring/circle drum/dance with the same fast triplet step, but with more subtle hip vibrations)[58] may appear in brief flurries within *sambareggae,* as if the dancers have to "break out" in more rapid and complex movement. Anything goes: *Carnaval* permits Bahians to pull from any movement in their dance repertory, such as "Afro" steps that are taught in dance classes (called *Orixá* movements), *samba de roda* or *samba do pé,* or *maracatú* (another Carnival parading dance from Pernambuco State). Accordingly, it is hard to pin down the dance dimension in Bahia.

In its current form, the lavish Rio *Carnaval* has a shorter history than most parading festivals in the Caribbean. Before 1928, young men marked the pre-Lenten period with drunken and disorderly rampages, throwing *entrudo,* or water-filled (but often urine-filled) balloons. To channel this unruly energy, the government constructed "*samba* schools" in Rio—community centers the size of a city block that offered classes and social services, but, most important, that provided space for neighborhoods to prepare *Carna-*

val presentations. The *Carnaval* support system includes government and private, legal and illegal sponsors, in what Brazilians claim has become "the greatest audiovisual show on earth." Thousands of percussionists, dancers, and singers present set choreographies interspersed with *samba* improvisations to represent Rio's *batucadas, Carnaval* dance and music organizations. For example, the *sambadromo* can be filled by thirteen groups of about three thousand participants each from 9:00 PM to 8:00 AM or so, dancing for about eighty minutes each.

Carnaval themes are varied but usually contain the subtext of praise for Brazilian history and culture. Interestingly, the carnivalesque is what is missing in Rio, just as it is in Havana. The Rio celebration is controlled and manipulated to a fault. Predictably, as a result, street parades of dissent and ridicule have emerged. Even in the last years of Brazil's military dictatorship, a parade of intentionally ragged middle-class artists and poets protested the *samba* schools that exploited unpaid performers from the poorer classes. It is precisely the lack of freedom, the lack of manifesting a carnivalesque spirit, that incites criticism of Rio *Carnaval* and causes thousands of middle-class locals to flee and celebrate in the interior of northeast states, in places like Salvador da Bahia or Pernambuco.

Samba schools never really caught on in Salvador da Bahia, the original national capital, colonial port of entry for slave ships, and the residence of the eighty percent of Bahians who identify as *Afro-Brasileiros.* More grassroots types of *Carnaval* organizations have prevailed wherein an emphasis on extravagant costuming has been substituted by potent political messages within strong dancing and dance music. Thematic examples in Bahian *Carnivals* have resonated as hommages to Zumbi, the leader of Brazilian maroons at Palmares who held off colonial armies for forty years; the emerging independence of India in the 1940s; and the freedom struggles of African nations in the 1960s and 1970s.[59]

Afoxés and *blocos* are two types of Afro-theme groups that are first distinguished by instruments: *Afoxés* use *Candomblé* instruments and *blocos* use *samba* instruments. *Afoxés* are dance and music organizations of Bahian *Carnaval* that are specifically connected to *Candomblé*, the Brazilian religion of African "nations." With the exception of heterosexual male drummers, *ogans* or deacons, and the role concerning animal sacrifice, *Candomblé* is generally dominated by women and gay men, so the hetero men in *Candomblé* families have traditionally belonged to *afoxé* organizations that make public *Carnaval* presentations. The largest and oldest existing *afoxé*, the all-male Filhos de Gandhy (Sons of Gandhi), paraded in 1949 swathed in white cloth trimmed in blue, representing Oxala, the divinity of peace and wisdom, and simultaneously representing Gandhi, the pacifist who led India to freedom the previous year.[60] More than sixty years later, in the midst of the vociferous Bahian *Carnaval,* five thousand Filhos de Gandhy still move through the streets in quiet dignity to the gentle rhythms of Oxala.

There are all-women *afoxés* also, such as Filhas de Gandhy and Filhas de Oxum (the latter features a varied repertoire of *Caboclo* and *Candomblé* dances for the divinity of water and womankind, Oxum). Their expressions remind cajoling *Carnaval* participants of core Afro-Brazilian values surrounding spirituality and community health. Dancer Isaura Oliveira has described the *afoxé* organization of women by Rosangela Guimares, wife of the president of Filhos de Gandhy. She reports Filhos de Oxum now integrates women and men, as well as straight, gay, and transgendered participants; it also feeds community children every Wednesday and ends *Carnaval* with ritual bathing.[61]

The most numerous *Carnaval* organizations are Bahian *blocos* or secular neighborhood dance and music organizations. A dwindling few represent indigenous or other special interest groups, but the most popular are the *blocos afro.* Several *blocos* make recordings and tour outside of Salvador with their best musicians and dancers: Malê Debalê, Timbalada, Ara Ketu, Olodum (which is credited also with solid community work among street children), and Ile-Aye (which also does tremendous community work, but is the only group that restricts membership and participation to those of African descent except on the last day of *Carnaval,* a policy not without controversy in a nation that has made concerted efforts to combat and deny racism).

Olinda, a suburb of Recife (capital of the northeastern state of Pernambuco), is another popular site for *Carnaval,* purportedly with less hassle than in Rio or Bahia. Pernambuco adds important contributions to the Brazilian *Carnaval* dance repertoire: *frevo* and *maracatú. Frevo* is a virtuoso dance with steps that cross the feet, said to be like European sailors' jig dancing. *Maracatú* has two forms. One is a preemancipation festival to honor a Congolese King and Queen, with a solemn parade of masked personages in long-skirted satin and sequined costumes, which are brought out each year. There are striking *naçao* or "nation" banners, a parasol held over the "royalty," and spear carriers flanking the royal personages. A young woman is featured as *Dama de Paço* or the lady-in-waiting of the cortège, who dances graceful steps, turns, and holds the *"calunga,"* a special ritual doll, high above her head. The *calunga* represents the many divinities of African ethnic groups who were brought to this part of Brazil.[62] This first form of *maracatú* is more likely found in the smaller communities of Pernambuco; the other is more athletic and a contemporary version of urban *Carnavales* of Recife and Olinda. Dancers in this more common parading of Pernambuco use bold steps and big opposing arm gestures as they dance fast and in the style of an exuberant *frevo* rather than the slow processional of historic *maracatú*. Compared with other Caribbean Carnivals and while definitely relating to Caribbean parade dancing, the *maracatú* that salutes Congo Kings and Queens is serious performance but lacks the more common carnivalesque atmosphere of Circum-Caribbean parades.

Politics and Brazilian Celebrations

Carnaval in Rio is a huge street phenomenon, despite its rules and regulations. Foreign tourists see it as dangerous because the international press usually emphasizes a rise in crime. Bahian *Carnaval* is more closely aligned with island *Carnavales* through revelry amidst staunch sociopolitical critique; however, it needs no *diablitos* or covert clowns as found in the islands. It is participatory and celebrates African heritage. Bahian *Carnaval* is in the home of the Universidade Federal da Bahia, an intellectual hub that has long been the center of political dissent, and of the Universidade do Estado da Bahia, the intellectual center of many Afro-Brazilian students and communities. In the years of the military dictatorship (1963–85), outspoken Bahians, like musicians Caetano Veloso and Gilberto Gil, were persecuted, jailed, or had to go into exile. Now, cross-dressing and gay pride are managed as two of many sociopolitical realities within Brazil's twenty-first-century democracy.

Not everyone sees *Carnaval* as a stage for political agendas, but the alternative points to the politics of Brazilian racism and the ethnic dimension of *Carnavais brasileiros*. Many "white" *brasileiros* and some foreign tourists prefer the open participation of *trios elétricos*. Dance professor Carla Leite explained that "white" Brazilians preferred dancing to the *trio elétricos* because no torso isolations were required.[63] *Trios* are another type of *bloco*, popularized since the 1950s, which feature the rhythm derived from Pernambuco's *frevo* dance. Afro-Brazilians of Bahia do not dance the *frevo* to the music of the *trio elétricos*, in part because the tempo is too fast, but they jump it instead. The simple beat is used to jump, prance, or jog, with arms thrusting upward or waving in the air. For years, the amplified *trios elétricos* drowned out the acoustic or nonamplified drums of the *blocos* and *afoxés*, and this led to conflict. Later, the Afro-*blocos* added amplified instruments to their drums atop the beds of eighteen-wheel trucks, and the decibels ramped up everywhere.

Contemporary Messages

The carnivalesque is about shock value; it revels in the outlandish and un-expected. It could be argued that every day in contemporary urban society is Carnival, available with the press of a key, button, screen, or the click of a computer mouse. The interactive World Wide Web, blogging, texting, tweeting, etc., encourage public complaining and ridicule with anonymity optional. Perhaps the new freedom of expression and the popularity of African Diaspora cultures signal that a disenfranchised person of African descent has found, or will soon find, venues where she or he is no longer forced to play the fool and hide her or his message in code. The African-derived Creole experience, as it has survived the vicissitudes of Diaspora history, may be the template for future development in societies that yearn to uphold civil rights and social justice. In an increasing number of nations and regions, the *malcriado* or "bad child" is now the truth-speaking man/woman of any color in her or his challenge of the status quo. No longer hidden out of necessity, the messages she or he brings may be even more vivid, forceful, and effective.

CHAPTER SEVEN

RESILIENT DIASPORA RITUALS

Los bailes son maneras de acercarse a lo divino.
—Fernando Ortiz, *Los bailes y el teatro
de los negros en el folklore de Cuba*

In the line of Brenda Gottschild and Katrina Hazzard-Gordon, who documented erasures and neglect of African contributions to dance in the United States, I now draw attention to underexamined histories and the connections between Afro-Latin America and the Caribbean. Following anthropologist Sheila Walker's call in 2001 for Afrogenic analyses (the critical comparison *among* Diaspora cultures [and also in the line of the late Diaspora scholar St. Clair Drake]), I encourage more investigation of Diaspora erasures within Caribbean, Afro-Latin, and Afro-American performance with the following comparison of sacred dance.[1]

Sacred Caribbean Dance Ritual

As a result of interactions within and among dance movement and instrumental and vocal music, the body yields the utmost of aesthetic communication: the wondrous, the spiritual, or the sacred. This is the realm of African-derived dance where aesthetic stimulation mushrooms and lavishly overflows and where transcendent or transformational states of being surface and preside. Even in situations where there is minimal movement or musical sound, heightened states of consciousness can develop within performance. Altered consciousness is triggered, for example, with only flat-foot walking and rhythmic body-part-jerking in the Diaspora U.S. *ring shout*. During minimal movement practices, worshiping congregations reach for religious expression through prayer-filled texts and the interrelationship of dance and music. What they receive in their "reach" are the resultant rhythms of an aesthetic imperative; they become totally engaged, completely involved or "at one" within the dance and music experience.[2]

African-derived rituals approach the sacred constantly, creatively compounding aesthetic stimulation in either prepared designs or improvisational expressions. Dancing worshipers in religious communities give their whole selves to deepened and heightened expression by allowing their selves to be displaced as they assume the human vessel category of a priestly or divine cast. In such circumstances, human performance revels in spiritual purpose; dancers partake of creativity, and, most often, suprahuman performance unfolds. Suprahuman performance in the Caribbean and Afro-Latin America is the result of a transformation from human to spirit and appears with incredible force or subtlety within a determined dance vocabulary. In such states, the body speaks dance in quiet corporeal sequences, expresses emotional states, and communicates ideas in simple or virtuoso displays. Ritual dance or organized sacred performance generates intense interest or belief and demands intense response as the body portrays the sacred.[3]

Selection of Sacred or Secular Lens

Dance reveals and forwards sacred potential. Most Diaspora dance music is a product of the sacred and secular interrelationship. For example, *salsa* dance music often includes New World African religious rhythms and sung chants; R&B musical form in the United States comes out of "black" church music; and a dichotomy is reconciled within Gospel Rap music. An examination of U.S. American *hip-hop,* which became a global hit in the 1990s, can indicate the extent to which Diaspora spirituality has permeated both secular and sacred performance and can set the stage for further analytical details.

From a dance perspective on *hip-hop,* a community gathers in a circle to watch the rhythmic intricacies and virtuoso improvisations of *b-boy* and *b-girl dancing* (*"break dancing,"* as the media call the dance dimension of *hip-hop* culture). Within the center, marvelous wordplay is constantly emerging from one or more competing and supportive rhyme/rhythm artists. Dancing "crews" provide a backdrop and the visual aspect of the music in short, repetitive, often unison dance sequences. Lead rappers brazenly insert "power stances," and a DJ's rhythmic orchestrations inject a contagious stratum onto the performance whole.

With a sacred lens on the same performance, rather than the secular lens just used, the *hip-hop* circle is a twenty-first-century version of *ring shout* structure. It accentuates an implied circular spatial configuration of traditional religious performance found throughout the Diaspora and the alternation of clockwise and counterclockwise dance patterns. *Hip-hop*'s solo and duet segments are standard center-stage virtuosity in many African-derived religious traditions: think of the preacher who ventures away from the lectern and close to parishioners to deliver a dynamic solo; or think of a choir vocalist and a pastor as the duet in the center between the choir and congregation. Call and response and repetition in *hip-hop*'s vocal patterning are also characteristic of sacred Diaspora musics. From time to time, an image flashes from the contemporary corporeal moves of worshiping performers and a familiar message from traditional African-derived religion emerges.

When the rhythms have fully multiplied and the repeating verses or accumulating stories have been fully presented, the *b-boy* and *b-girl dancing* breaks out, and movement takes over. The rapping words and percussive sonic creations that produce a steady and elaborated beat do not suffice, and strong, athletic dancing begins. The sacred lens reads *break-dancing* as spiritual dance/games, like Brazilian *capoeira* and Martinican *danmyé*.[4] At other times, the scene is filled with West and Central African divinities who are embodied in the power stances and brazen self-love of performing youths; modern artists grab their crotches and dance full-out and fiercely. Michael Jackson, M. C. Hammer, Usher, and contemporary others resemble the Cuban spirit-warrior-king Chango, when he puts on his pants and eats his *amala* with exaggerated hip circles; or we can see Omarion and Chris Brown as the Haitian spirit-warrior Ogou suddenly rush downstage bare chested and in the baggy pants and baseball caps of the greatest rappers, slicing through forested areas in ancient traditions, but here overtaking challenging artists with fearless movements.

When the *b-girl dance* occurs (with descendants of classic *In Living Color* b-girls Rosie Perez and Jennifer Lopez), determination and sensual persuasiveness blast forth. Defying the male dominance of *hip-hop* culture and with female spirit-warrior authority from Oya, Yansan, or Ezili Dantor, young women strut, flip, and spin in combative competition. Male and female performance culminates in "free-styling," where anything goes until a dramatic pose or gesture ending, which could be West or Central African-derived "cuts," "*feints*," or breaks. Regardless of which African heritage might be referenced, often the learned viewer can see flashes of sacred African dance movements within secular Diaspora performance.[5]

Transcendence, either into out-of-body states or into the dance movement, is common in Diaspora performance, and a so-called "secular" performance can suggest religious ecstasy, especially with the use of a sacred lens. Compound rhythms, body-part isolations, and intimacy with musical complexity cause the dancer to be enveloped in spontaneous creativity. Those dancers who transcend the ambiguous aesthetic boundaries, those who "give their all," are applauded and critically praised by the community because transformation is highly valued.

Tight knots bind the secular and the sacred in African Diaspora contexts, and consequently, fluidity is maintained between two dimensions of social life. Throughout Diaspora histories, dance uses both dimensions regularly. Examples can be found in several Cuban dances from Congo/Angola heritage, where the same dance steps are performed in both social and sacred settings. In Brazilian and Cuban Yoruba dances and rhythms, consecrated (*atabaque/batá*) drums are used in sacred rituals, but the same dances and rhythms are used in social celebrations given in honor of the spiritual domain, this time with ordinary drums (*aberícula*). Additionally, Haitian Vodou dances are performed as secular entertainment for tourists; however, if a performer transits beyond the aesthetic high of reenactment, the entertainment shifts from a tourist copy to a genuine sacred original. Distinctions between the Diaspora secular and sacred depend on an entire context; viewers and analysts need to alternate between sacred and secular lenses to search for core African values and common Diaspora understandings before determining what the dance means.

Assessment of Common Structures and Shared Values

Similar religious and dance structures have emerged across the Diaspora from common beliefs and social conditions that were shared by thousands of Africans. From a dance perspective, a shared movement vocabulary, belief in contact with a spirit world through dance, music and transcendence, and respect for African ancestors, elders, or the dead were the most important shared values. These coincide with what scholar of religion Diane Stewart has identified as African religious heritage found consistently in Caribbean traditions: communotheistic (as opposed to monotheistic or polytheistic) understanding of the Divine, ancestral veneration, possession trance and mediumship, food offerings and animal sacrifice, divination and herbalism, and an entrenched belief in mystical power.[6] These commonalities, despite other differences, created a foundation for new religious formations based on old understandings.[7]

Anthropologist Alfred Métraux and historian Leslie Desmangles have shown that a Haitian religious organization was forged under the conditions of slavery by the end of the eighteenth century.[8] Similarly, anthropologists William Bascom and George Brandon, as well as Cuban ethnologists Fernando Ortiz, Lydia Cabrera, Natalia Bolívar, and others have traced a common liturgical order and similar religious structures for West and Central African religions in Cuba.[9] Likewise, ethnologist Roger Bastide and historian Rachel Harding have shown parallel developments in Brazil where Africans in the New World persisted in connecting to West and Central African religious teachings.[10] These organizations solidified into umbrella-like religions in Haiti and Brazil, called Vodou and Candomblé, respectively. While there was interaction and sharing in religious amalgams in Cuba also, distinct but related religions emerged: Palo Monte; Arará; Carabalí or Abakuá; and Lukumí, Santería or Ocha.[11]

Enslaved Africans across the Diaspora attempted to pray in the performance terms of their origins; they performed remembered dance practices as strategies for relief, protection, and salvation. They knew the power of dance supported religious beliefs, solidified the group, and expressed spirituality; consequently, they replicated ritual forms that were fundamentally orders of dance and music predicated on "African nations" with local divinities (Fon, Congo, Angola, Mahí, Ibo, Gede, Jeje, Oyo, Iyesa, Ekiti, Ondo, Ijebu, and other Yoruba, plus other ethnic groups).[12] Each nation had a series of dances, rhythms, and songs that were enfolded into one religious order. African religious and cultural groups in Cuba were separated into nominally Catholic associations, or *cabildos*.[13] Separations were less defined in Brazilian brotherhoods and sisterhoods, called *irmandades*; however, a major example was associated with Our Lady of the Rosary of Black Men from Angola (the blue church in Pelourinho, Bahia).[14] Similar religious structures and dances persisted over centuries, even in Protestant English/Creole and Dutch settings where the Church was often more severe in its prohibitions.

Structural similarities have included counterclockwise movement, cardinal-direction emphases, codified step repetition, sequence intensification, and circular patterns. Even within a rectangular space, the participatory circle could be implied, and alternating soloists or duos dance and sometimes compete inside a circle of clapping and/or gesturing worshipers. Most often, the dances are ensemble, unison practices in front of drummers; the congregation comprises those dancers, drummers, and singers who surround an imagined or real center. Dancers perform in either contained spaces or outdoor expanses.

Research, including longitudinal study of Diaspora religions, has pointed toward the importance of shared values within dance movement. Robert Thompson's synesthesia, Brenda Gottschild's premises, and Kariamu Welsh-Asante's foundational principles of African movement emphasize the importance of the spiritual dimension as a prominent characteristic within

African and Diaspora dance practices, called ancestorism, "luminosity," "coolness," and spirituality. Ancestor respect is key because it originally provided access to a position within a dance and music liturgy for each African ethnic group; the resulting order facilitated routine invocation and honor to spiritual guardians. Dance, drumming, and singing combined in the Americas as they could not on the African continent, and new sacred repertoires emerged as Caribbean and Afro-Latin religions. The dance data demand equal emphases on continuity and creativity in the development of New World African religions.[15]

French/Kreyol Sacred Practices

Dances that evolved in Haitian Vodou *ceremònis* were and still are performed for ancestor spirits, the initiated community, and its guests.[16] Songs are sung around a central *potomitan* to invoke particular spirits from remembered and imagined African nations. A choir director or *oungenikon* and a chorus of male and female community members sing in responsorial form. One small bell-like gong and three drums are usually played in a codified musical repertoire.[17] The main dancers are dedicated practitioners who have been trained to lead the congregation in transforming, spirit-giving behaviors (see photo 10). Religious fervor is expressed in dance until worshiping dancers are "mounted" by spiritual riders or *lwas* and then become the "horses" of historic/family *lwas*.[18]

Worshiping dancers start moderately in tempo, build in energy, and augment dynamics in coordination with skilled drummers. Body-part isolation is prominent in dances called by various names: *yenvalu, mayí, zepol, congo,*[19] *Ibo, Petwo, zarenyen, banda,* etc. Shoulders shake and vibrate in *Petwo* but go forward and back in *zepol*; feet slap the ground in *mayí,* while the back and chest undulate continuously in *yenvalu.* Fingers and hands assume a spider or crab-like shape and protrude in the air as a performer hunches close to the floor or runs sporadically in *zarenyen,* the spider dance. And hips circle, sway from side to side, or punch forward and backward in the dance *congo.*

Haitian sacred dance is marked by rhythmic intimacy within the drumming, singing, and heightened and intense (as opposed to restrained, contained, or smooth) dynamics. The movements sometimes imitate representative actions, as in the spider dance, and sometimes they abstract content, as in the dances for Ibo and Congo/Angola ethnic groups—all within established motifs and sequences, but freely performed in space. Transcendence is the ultimate sacred expression (see photo 11). Its first stage displays shuddering, shaking, or bolting as the ancestor/*lwa* tries to make contact with the initiated worshiper. Usually, the dancing believer needs religious instruction to prepare the body for the force of spiritual connection, but whenever it comes, when "the horse is mounted fully," the worshiper goes limp for a moment, collapses or is restrained by a ritual specialist. Then he or she is dressed appropriately as the invoked spirit, indicating the second stage in a process of unfolding religiosity. In the third stage of transformation, the invoked spirit dances with, blesses, and advises the Vodou family. The spirit commands the space and performs repeated, identifiable dance patterns with the congregation.[20]

A shift *within* the context can change analyses, as it does when a genuine Vodou ceremony erupts within a hotel show. As researchers have shown, the transformation of participatory religious practice to controlled secular performances challenges religious and secular boundaries.[21] Still, dancing, drumming and singing are communication vehicles that facilitate a Haitian service of praise, which, in turn, maintains or restores balance between the spirit and human worlds. With an obvious sacred lens on the ritual behaviors described above, a paradigm obtains as a first type of sacred dance practice within an umbrella structure over African nation rites, one that is characterized by transcendence toward ancestor *lwas* (see chart 15).

Many Diaspora sites have suffered such sustained suppression of African practices and religious cleansing—during the colonial period and for centuries afterward—that, at times, African religious expression has gone underground or even disappeared. This seems the case for Martinique and Guadeloupe, whose traditional practices are apparently nonexistent. Musicologist Dominique Cyrille's emic (native) analyses confirm the absence of African religions in this part of the French/Kreyol Caribbean; however, she comments on evidence of Congo/Angola heritage and the similarity—in fact, "identical" features—of Haitian and Martinican dance, and Haitian and Guadeloupean instruments. She states for Martinique's *gwanbele lisid*: "[T]his dance shows influences from Kongo traditions. The dancers perform inside a circle of spectators, either one couple at a time or as a group. The steps in *gwanbèlè lisid* of Martinique resemble those of Trinidad *bele* and Puerto Rican *bomba*. Both the music and the dance are identical to Haitian Kongo dance."[22] Musicologists Alex and Francoise Uri concur with Cyrille's findings for shared Guadeloupean and Haitian instruments (the *boula* and the *make*) and agree that Guadeloupean dance and music are remnants of Kongo secret societies.[23]

In my fieldwork on Congo/Angola heritage in both Haiti and Cuba, festive dance has been core. Whether performers dance alone, as couples, or in processional community parades, the objectives are interaction, playful sociability, and physical discourse. Dancers look at one another or at the lead drummer while dancing, and there is an obvious nonverbal exchange going on. Hip circles that characterize Congo/Angola dance vocabulary are, in effect, presented to someone or the surrounding community. From a dance specialist perspective, Haitian and Cuban dances of this heritage can be festively social and deeply religious simultaneously, while from a lay perspective, these dances might be considered the most "social" and least "religious" in appearance.

Martinican and Guadeloupean consultants answered my incredulousness with verification that no African belief systems exist there; however, they spoke of overflowing "spirituality." Cyrille's insider report is greatly appreciated, therefore, and suggests that while there is no viable traditional African religious paradigm in practice, there are religious vestiges within certain dances. For example, Cyrille notes that particular dances can carry a prayer (as in the dance *bélia*), garner spiritual power (as in the martial dance arts *ladja* and *danmyé*), or occasionally summon spirits (as in the dance *bele*).

In summary for the French/Kreyol Caribbean, Haiti offers a paradigm for Circum-Caribbean religious/aesthetic structure, while it simultaneously exposes contrasts and questions in the absence of any similarities on Martinique and Guadeloupe. As an independent nation, Haiti had enormous possibilities over related but dominated territories to develop African-derived practices; consequently, its case points to African agency in determining a sacred Diaspora practice that has continued for more than five centuries. The French Department islands point out what sustained prohibition can do; however, if Congo/Angola heritage has predominated there, it suggests that African Christianity is the overriding heritage and abundant religious practice of Guadeloupe and Martinique. From the fifteenth century forward, Christianity was the religious orientation of the Congo kingdom, which had the widest political influence also. Despite the varied forms of sixteenth- and seventeenth-century African Christianity, the Congo/Angola region had enduring contact with European Christianity and this might account for the absence of African tradition-based religions among Central African descendants.[24]

English/Creole Sacred Practices

The Caribbean is known for its mélange of cultures; however, the English/ Creole Caribbean is particularly noted for British, Spanish, Danish, Dutch, and French colonial input. Overall, there is huge French influence despite

British domination for centuries. Additionally, after abolition in British territories between 1834 and 1838 and in related Creole territories in 1848, East Indian and other Asian cultures became significant elements in English/Creole culture.[25] The feature that differentiates Trinidad and Tobago, Jamaica, the Grenadines, and other English/Creole islands from the rest of the Caribbean, however, is that they are sites where Africa and Europe may have intermingled, but where there were more precise divides than elsewhere. Protestantism clashed with African religious/aesthetic expression, as did Catholicism, but rigid dance perspectives affected English/Creole practices in terms of Orisha and Rada rites, *reel* dancing, *Nation Dances,* wake dancing, *reggae,* Maroon dances, and the Kumina religion.

Yoruba- and Fon-based worship of Orisha/Shango and Rada are important African-derived religions of Trinidad and Tobago, and these correspond to a paradigm most closely identified with Cuba (discussed below). Both religions have been influenced dramatically by Anglican heritage, and Biblical texts guide religious practice in conjunction with African religious philosophies. Worship focuses "ecumenically," as dancer/scholar Molly Ahye describes transcendent African divinities who are aligned with Catholic and Anglican Saints, Protestant biblical verses, or both.[26]

The Tobago *reel* dance of Congo/Angola derivation is another sacred performance that is enacted by colorfully dressed male and female dancers just before weddings or at wakes to invoke ancestor manifestation. Couples dance *quadrille*-like patterns, trace circles on the floor, and cross each other's paths only to "reel" or turn away sharply and repeat advancing, passing, turning, and reeling. As the reeling increases, performers enter an altered state of consciousness, and the ancestors are deemed near. *Reel* dancing straddles secular festivities and sacred goals, and it is an example of the resignification that Bilby and Neely speak of for European dances that enter African performance practices.[27] When the enslaved were prohibited from practicing their religious beliefs or sacred dances, they apparently used whatever sustained movement sequences that were available in order to transcend difficulties and maintain spirit contact. Secular performance of *quadrilles,* despite other meanings, became targeted opportunities to "let go" or "fly away" in remembered transcendence.[28]

Generally, Protestant practices prohibited or avoided dancing; however, transcendent bodily actions are associated with many worship services, especially fundamentalist practices today. Both Protestant and Roman Catholic churches frowned on the insistent dancing of "black" populations, even though there is evidence of dancing inside New World Catholic churches since the sixteenth century.[29] Bishops and brothers wrote to European monarchs and the Pope for official regulation of dance practices. For most Protestants in the English-speaking islands, associations with the body, particularly the female body and especially the dancing body, have been historically attributed to evil, the Devil, or Satanic worship. Additionally, Protestant sects do not always define "dance" as others do. They accept "receiving the Holy Sprit," which is rhythmic body movement with uncrossed legs, as wholesome religious expression, and they reject "dance," which, for them, is rhythmic body movement with crossed legs.[30]

The English/Creole case changes slightly in the Grenadines (Grenada, Carriacou, and Petit Martinique) with *Nation Dances* and provides a second, unique religious/aesthetic paradigm (#2 in chart 15). Despite a similar history of Spanish Roman Catholic, French elite, and eventual British Protestant dominance in contact with African beliefs, a Diaspora ritual developed that, surprisingly for dance criteria, excluded transcendence, the outward sign and goal of human and spiritual world connection. The influence of Protestant colonialism is most responsible for such an official omission within the Big Drum of Carriacou and for the narrow range of bodily movement within its *Nation Dances*. Minimalist movement is in contrast with the wide range of motion within Haitian Vodou, Trinidadian Shango, and other "dancing religions"; however, African heritage in Big Drum rituals persists in the solemn recognition of African ancestors—through drum rhythms, songs, and dances of African nations as created in the Diaspora: Cromanti (Gold Coast in Africa), Arada (Bight of Benin), Chamba (Bight of Biafra), Manding (Senegambia, Mali), Congo (Congo/Angola), Banda (Gold Coast or Congo/Angola), Igbo (Bight of Biafra), Temne (Sierra Leone), Moko (Bight of Biafra). Nine nations are honored at weddings, dedications of new homes, boat launchings, children's first hair cutting, Maroon sacrifices for spiritual goodwill, political events, tourist cultural presentations, but particularly at tombstone feasts for burials and memorials of death. These are public displays of ancestor reverence.[31]

Ethnomusicologist Lorna McDaniel characterizes *Nation Dances* as earthbound or lowered body orientation with distinguishing hand gestures for different African nations. Usually, mature female soloists dance in counterclockwise circles in front of three drummers. The lead drummer mirrors and interacts with a soloist's foot patterns in sounded improvisations. Soloists alternate by means of a "wheel pattern": a soloist contacts another dancer around the waist and the two travel counterclockwise and then clockwise before the drummer signals a break. The first dancer retreats and the second dialogues with drummers in limited dance.[32]

Big Drum rituals involve *Nation*, Creole, and Frivolous dances, which have sacred and secular themes. Generally, male and female dancers focus on outstretched or "winged" skirt manipulations of females who wind in small hip circles repeatedly (winin').[33] All dances are integrated into a ritual order and worshipers view their performance as religious and spiritual; however, their serious facial expressions are in sharp contrast with the sexual calls and humorous expressions from the surrounding congregation in the Creole and Frivolous dancing.

In my Caribbean field experience, sex is first understood as a sacred means of human continuity, and male and female couples dance together to signal social life, courting, mating, and continuity, but they do not usually touch. This represents a reconciliation of aesthetic behaviors (dance) that crosscut differing life dimensions (social) or the mediation of potential opposites.[34] Dance mediates not only life and death, sacrifice and offering, material world and spiritual world, but also sex and the sacred. All are temporary stages of an ongoing incorporation of life principles. In *Nation* dances of the English/Creole Caribbean, couples dance apart in an ambiance of sexual calls expressing comfort in the sacred and the sexual simultaneously.

Molly Ahye describes widespread dancing at wakes in the English/Creole Caribbean, unveiling other reconciliations of dance aesthetics as it crosscuts social life and the incorporation of seeming opposites. These wakes and other Diaspora examples (Spanish, French/Kreyol, and Dutch/Suriname Maroons) incorporate the ancestors into a different plane of existence rather than concentrate on human death or loss per se. For example, Tobago community members gather to comfort grieving families with hymns and the *bongo* dance, which amicably and respectfully "sends off" the departed. In *bongo,* men compete in strenuous virtuoso foot patterns, and there is constant crossing of feet to upbeat tempos. While the dancing is a social diversion with competition, it is also a spiritual offering, a "prestation" or gift to the ancestors. Inside the homes of grieving family members and within what would otherwise appear as nonreligious dance, *bongo* dancing accomplishes a sacred funeral task through inversion and supports a transition from the human world to the mirrored world of ancestor spirits.[35] The festive and otherwise social dancing celebrates the life on earth of a new ancestor and joyfully facilitates a smooth sacred journey to the hereafter. Thus, dance rituals, which might otherwise be categorized as social and secular in terms of movement and ambiance, at times become sacred due to the incorporation function of ancestor rites (at wakes, funerals, tombstone feasts, and weddings, for example).

For the English-speaking islands, sacred dance is closely related to Yoruba heritage (in Jamaica called Etu and Nago) and other Africanist religions, like Obeah, Myalism, and Pocomania, with their dance practices. These religions have been infused with Christian theology, and many Protestant forms abound—from Anglican Episcopalian to Pentecostal, Convince, and Zionist congregations. There is also reported evidence of Curaçaoan *Tambú* religion in Jamaica, but the square *Goombeh* drum is present across the island, suggesting other possible sacred drum rituals. Of course, Nyabingi or Rastafarian beliefs, surfacing in the early twentieth century with admiration and adoption of Ethiopian and other spiritual practices, involves dance as well.

Jamaica reveals variations and fragments of each of the three structural paradigms offered in this chapter, but it is hegemonic British colonialism and Protestant conservatism that have shaped Jamaican sacred dance. With the exception of Etu/Nago, most Jamaican religions have an emphasis on foot patterns, an undivided torso, and a comparatively small range of bodily movement. While dancing is energetic and the sexually suggestive winin' movements are highlighted (as in Big Drum rituals), the sacred is achieved without expansive movement.[36]

Recently, a few reports have surfaced on sacred dance among Jamaican Maroons. Katherine Dunham was the first to report on Maroon dancing in 1936, and her research matches research completed fifty-eight years later by dance researcher Catherine Evleshin. Both reports confirm the devastating influences of colonialism and Protestantism on Maroon dance, where, ironically, rituals among the most African descendants on the island have lost much of their Africanity. Compare the following:

> The introduction seemed to be a disjointed walking around a Circle. . . . Then Henry Rowe and I are facing each other doing a step which could easily be compared to an Irish reel. Hands on hips, we hop from one foot to the other, feet turned out at right angles to the body or well 'turned out' in ballet vernacular. . . . We turned our backs and walked away, then turned suddenly again and hopped together. . . . Some of the men wave sticks in the air, and the women tear off their handkerchiefs and wave them on high as they dance . . . ; a moment later we are 'bush fightin', crouching down and advancing in line to attack an imaginary enemy with many feints, swerves, and much pantomime."[37]

> They [Maroons] presented several short pieces . . . arranged themselves in a circle and the floor patterns involved European features such as couples spinning with same arms joined at the elbows, circling holding hands, and back-to-back *do-si-do*s. . . . No sign of spirit possession, real or staged, was evident in any of the dances. . . . All [the dances] involved an almost continuous high hopping and vigorous running steps, reminiscent of a hornpipe from the British Isles."[38]

Interestingly, dancer and cultural studies scholar Cheryl Ryman includes Maroon dance within assessments of Kumina, Bongo, and Convince groups that practice ancestor spirit manifestation with "jumps and contortions," suggesting expansive movement and possible change.[39]

In contrast with Maroon practices, other Jamaicans have identified with Congo/Angola roots in Kumina dance rituals.[40] Ryman describes Kumina dance as constant hip shifts over bent knees, inching flat feet with uneven weight, and a relaxed to straight back. Musicologist Olive Lewin describes dancers circling around drummers, who are at the center with an altar or a table of candles nearby. Ancestral spirits (*nkuyu*) are invited to dance and give advice.

To conclude, dance has accompanied divination, ancestral veneration, trance, mediumship, food offerings, and animal sacrifice in the English/ Creole Caribbean, generating religious intensity through contained and restricted movement or, less frequently, through expansive and explosive movement. Respect for the ancestors is fundamental as a highly esteemed value, but the most intriguing contributions from the English/Creole Caribbean are its explanatory examples of the spiritual function of social dance at wakes and the thin boundaries among the sacred, secular, and sexual.

Spanish Caribbean Sacred Practices

While Cuba provides substantial data on African religious/aesthetic expressions, Puerto Rico and the Dominican Republic contrast with few, if any, indigenous sacred practices. Anthropologist George Brandon points out that *cofradias* and *cabildos* were variants of Catholic associations for lay Christians, including Africans, that responded to the needs of the poor and acted as mutual-aid societies. In *cofradia* formations of the Dominican Republic, most African religious dance expression was curtailed, whereas in Cuba, similar *cabildo* organizations were greatly responsible for sacred dance survival.[41] Puerto Rico has few, if any, sacred dances in its dance taxonomy, and the Dominican Republic's sacred practices are fundamentally Haitian or Cuban. These contradictory data call for attention, since sacred dance usually responds to change slowly and retains root legacies more than transient secular dances. An applied Afrogenic perspective on Spanish Caribbean data challenges the analysis again to explain missing dance examples.

Like conclusions for the French Caribbean, some Spanish sacred dance takes the form of African Catholicism, which would be Congo/Angola legacies that continued or Catholicism that developed in the Diaspora. Where there is strong sacred "traditional," non-Christian or non-Moslem, African dance practice, a nation-oriented, ancestor-derived construction of Caribbean religions is usually present.[42] For example, in Cuba, Palo or Palo Monte arose from Congo/Angola legacies. Arará, Lukumí (Santería), and Abakuá (Carabalí)[43] arose from Fon, Ewe, Oyo, Ijesa, Egba, Nago, Efik, Ejagham,

Bangyam, and other groups, but mainly ethnic amalgams from the Bight of Benin, Bight of Biafra, and the Calabar River areas of Cameroon and Nigeria. Each distinct religion is structurally similar to the Haitian and Carriacouan paradigms described above; however, Cuba provides a third paradigm that thus far, has little "umbrella" structure (#3 in chart 15). Relatively separated groups of African nations practice sacred choreographies, drum rhythms, and chants, both for the ancestors and cosmic divinities, and additionally maintain the practice of transcendence.

In Cuban Lukumí/Santería, the drum rhythms are essential to dance and song, but the primary initiators of ritual are the lead singers who guide performance and accompany priests/priestesses as they lead religious services to completion. Responsorial singing with the congregation assists drummers in gradually accelerating and intensifying a series of sacred rhythms. Drummers and the lead singer watch the dancing worshipers carefully for overt signs that a guardian spirit is near.

Similar to the Haitian and Trinidadian examples, the first bodily signs of transcendence in Cuba are heightened intensity and accelerating dynamics in movement, demonstrating profound interpenetration of drum rhythm, chant, and dance movement. Sometimes dancers "freeze" and then tremble or vibrate; others flail and shake the entire body about the sacred space (sometimes with eyes drawing upward and disoriented facial expression). When any of these physical actions appear, the lead drummer "musically escorts" the dancing worshiper across the threshold between the human and spiritual worlds. Thus, the singer and chants initiate sacred performance, but drummers and rhythms, working with dancing worshipers and the entire community's bodily movement, all facilitate the climax into transcendence. Ensemble human movement in accelerating dynamics again characterizes the dancing and ultimately produces solo virtuoso or suprahuman performance. When the congregation's foot patterns and arm gestures connect with exciting rhythms, dynamic energy floods the entire group, and individual transcendence can generate collective transformations.[44]

Almost the same structure is shared among the four belief systems of Cuba, but in stylistically different ways. For example in Yoruba dancing, the elbows push forward and back most often, and codified arm movements reference a given divinity. In Arará dancing, attention goes first to worshipers' shoulders, which keep a continuous rhythmic pulse (up and back) while the arms change gestures, depending on which divinity is being invoked. In Palo dancing, forceful, traveling foot patterns and aggressive fist and lower-arm gestures characterize the Congo/Angola spirit family. In Abakuá/Carabalí dance, masked spirits alternately stride through the space and survey all participants, then lunge to present fluttering hands and stroking gestures.[45]

Abakuá is differentiated from *cabildo* religions not only by its movement style but also by its organizational precepts. Abakuá is a male society that developed from secret societies in present-day Nigeria and Cameroon,[46] but it could also have connections to male martial arts societies that were organized on nonkinship bases in colonial Angola.[47] Militaristic societies on the African continent often held ideological beliefs at their core and initiated males for martial art training. Cuban Abakuá societies in Havana and Matanzas provinces were ultimately responsible for justice inside plantation quarters. Intermittent initiation meetings, judicial "happenings" at night, and regular calendar rites comprised their rituals. Thus, each separate organization in Cuba varies stylistically, but not from its core ancestral heritage. Like Haiti in the French/Kreyol Caribbean and Carriacou in the English/Creole Caribbean, Cuba yields another Caribbean religious/aesthetic paradigm.

Catholic heritage in Puerto Rico produced saints' day processions, *misas*, and wakes (*velatorios*) that did not emphasize African dance characteristics. Despite a history of enslaved Africans who cultivated coffee, tobacco, and sugar, Puerto Rico had a negative sacred dance result. Perhaps because of the strength of Spanish Catholicism and because a different ratio of Europeans to Africans influenced the amount of African dance that developed as sacred performance,[48] Puerto Rico has shared Cuban and Haitian sacred dances and created few, if any, of its own. African-derived dances that remain are not easily considered sacred: *bomba*, *danza*, *plena*, and *salsa*.

While *bomba* and other Caribbean social dances have no strict religious function, the data do not allow quick dismissal. Historian Lydia Milagros González states: "[T]he [*bomba*] dancer mounts his dance until his entire body is shaking, very much in the same way dancers tremble when possessed by a spirit in ritual ceremonies."[49] I have written elsewhere about Cuban *rumba*, that it can exhibit "almost possessed or totally concentrated states."[50] Additionally, as far back as Moreau de St. Méry, observers have repeatedly reported intense solos and couple dancing among African descendants, as if the social dance practices were religious, ecstatic, or transcendent.[51] When data such as these put the secular context in question, the analyst needs to alternate secular and spiritual lenses on whatever performance is under investigation.

Bomba's revered apex is found in the interrelationship of dancer and lead drummer, within their internal aesthetic processes of intensification, interconnection, and creativity. *Bomba* performance morphs from secular entertainment with aesthetic expression to spiritual expression with heightened aesthetics when performers access the edges, the highest or farthest borders of the aesthetic realm and reveal a connection between "the aesthetic" and "the sacred."[52]

With a social lens, *bomba* performances display a continuum from amusing display, to engaged play and heightened aesthetic expression. With a sacred lens, *bomba* remains on the social and expressive end of a secular/spiritual continuum until—and only if—the dance and the drumming become an exceedingly extraordinary performance. Then the dance dwells in the moment when aesthetic expression coincides with the spiritual—when "the social" registers as "sacred." Within some of the most acclaimed Caribbean secular dances (*reggae, zouk, bomba, rumba, biguine,* and perhaps even *lewoz* and *bele*), performers can enter the sacred realm. These cases reveal the commonalities within religious and aesthetic experiences that philosopher/psychologist/arts educator John Dewey argued for long ago. His claim was that both religious and aesthetic experiences erupt as very similar behaviors, where they are, in his words, "different aspects of the same reality . . . , each with the potential to develop its fund of inchoate meaning and value in the direction of the divine, the beautiful, or both."[53] Examination of more social dances might lead to other examples of the secular registered as the sacred.

Puerto Rico eventually became the site of powerful deterrents to sacred dance beyond its colonial distancing from "things African." In the nineteenth century, Kardecian Spiritualism spread from Europe to the Caribbean, and fundamentalist Protestantism began to infiltrate Catholic strongholds. United States political control in the twentieth and twenty-first centuries added new layers of elitist and racist thinking, and the African religious past was further marginalized. Both Catholic and Protestant influence continuously restricted sacred dance practices, such that Santería and Vodú have been practiced clandestinely in Puerto Rico.[54]

Dominican history is replete with anti-African and anti-Haitian attitudes, initiated in colonial times and harshly advocated during the (President Rafael) Trujillo era, 1930–61. In the Dominican Republic, sacred African dance was mainly the shared roots of Haitian Vodou among both Haitian and Dominican descendants living on the eastern side of the island. Dominican Vodú, which contains African-derived instruments, a vocal literature, and dances that reflect "sister," if not "twin" forms to Haitian Vodou, continues today despite Catholic omnipresence. Dominican Vodú dancing replicates what has already been described as sacred Haitian dance, and, therefore, its structure corresponds to the Haitian paradigm (#1).

Another important sacred practice is Dominican *Gaga,* which is performed on weekends during Lent and continuously during Holy Week. *Gaga* is almost identical to Haitian *Rara,* as a simultaneously public Vodú celebration and a nominal Christian celebration. These celebrations are associated with fertility, life, and transformation as well as with Easter, rebirth, and reincarnation or African/Catholic syncretism.[55]

Apart from heavily influenced Haitian-derived practices, the Dominican Republic has Catholic brotherhoods or *cofradias* that reflect a particular African heritage. Catholic conversion in the histories of enslaved Congo/Angola worshipers and implied linkages between traditional African religions and Christianity may be responsible for the strong ties to African-Catholic practices on the eastern side of the island.[56] Again, the Congo kingdom was huge, powerful, and Catholic before the Atlantic slave trade mushroomed and many African captives who came from this region were Catholic and were dispersed throughout the Diaspora. With development of powerful drumming traditions and emphases on ancestor reverence and funeral rites, Dominican sacred behaviors suggest a long legacy of African heritage, but this time localized in Christianity. Unlike Cuban *cabildos,* Dominican brotherhoods did not preserve non-Christian religious thought or African dance style. They gave attention to the saints and the dead beyond official Catholic teachings, and they followed the orthodox Catholic structural paradigm (not one of the Caribbean religion paradigms referenced here).

Afro-Dominican *cofradias* perform organized dance and drumming activities on Catholic saints days. Their religious practice has produced pilgrimages, chromolithographs of the saints, *velaciones* (a performance in payment for a vow to a saint), rosary rites, and funeral events for members. *Cofradia* drumming is definitely African derived, but the dancing is enigmatic in terms of the African dance canon referenced earlier by Gottschild, Thompson, and Welsh-Asante, and also in terms of the limited African dance studies that are available for comparison. *Cofradia* dancing provides contrast among Spanish Caribbean cases. For example, in describing Dominican *baile de palo* for *velaciones,* specialist in Afro-Dominican culture Martha Ellen Davis states:

> To generalize, it [*baile de palo*] is a couples' dance traditionally performed *suelto* (un-embraced) as a *baile de respeto* (dance of respect) due to its sacred contexts of performance at saints' festivals and death rituals. Reflecting European influence, it is a dance of much foot movement, little movement of the arms, and practically no hip movement. The dancers maintain a formal, rigid torso, although with the non-European feature of keeping the knees and waist slightly bent. This posture and the lack of physical contact between the male and female dancers—except an occasional guiding hand on the woman's shoulder or waist

by the man in pursuit—differentiates this dance of respect from Dominican social dance, which is described as *baile de regocijo* (a dance of enjoyment) and is often danced *agarrado* (embraced) and may use more hip movement."[57]

Davis's photographs show the extent of contradiction to African dance form that exists—from facial expression while dancing, sense of community participation, and, most influential, dancing to drum music, all of which would predict African-derived movement, but there is very little, as she states directly. From the dance perspective, *baile de palo* dancing seems influenced most by Europe and colonial attitudes toward dancing. While the music is decidedly African-derived, the dance seems Creole with African body orientation wedged into European movement patterns and style.[58] On the other hand, Dominican popular dance is replete with Africanisms, often cast as "indigenous" or "Caribbean" elements.

In summation for the Spanish Caribbean, the Cuban case reflects the African heritages of specific ethnic groups, the extent of agency that was possible within Catholic domination, and perhaps the differences in island histories and population ratios over time. The Dominican and Puerto Rican cases reveal how non-Christian African dance was replaced by Christian forms and European stylization; how African dance style was suppressed by Catholic (and later, Protestant) values; and how African-derived dances subtly released their strong tendency toward transcendence within social dance forms. Parallel to French/Kreyol and English/Creole findings, the contrasts within Spanish Caribbean sacred practices offer examples of African agency in guarding sacred dance legacies and also African creativity in shaping dominating spiritual traditions.

Dutch Caribbean Sacred Practices

African-derived dance and music have served as potent reminders of African heritage in Aruba, Bonaire, Curaçao, St. Martens, Saba, and St. Eustatius, the former Netherland Antilles. There, only vestiges of ritual paradigms appear, but they prove the force of African spirituality. For example, despite the demise of *Tambú* religious practice in Curaçao, *tambú* remains as dance music and is also remembered as the lost African religion of the Dutch Caribbean.[59] The Dutch and Portuguese slave trades, colonialism and Roman Catholicism, and Protestant Dutch administration all waged a horrific battle to destroy African-derived performance and indeed succeeded in curtailing Dutch Caribbean religious ritual; however, related social practices have kept African memories alive.

Tambú as a dance practice features incredible speed in movement and a drum by the same name. Tiny steps carry both women and men in circular paths in front of drums with outstretched, uplifted arms above the head and hip-circling as fast as you can imagine. When couples dance *tambú* and another man wishes to "cut in" or ask permission to dance from a present male partner, the two men usually practice *trankamentu,* meaning they push or shove before relinquishing the lady.[60] Contemporary performers still dance to songs that can last for an hour each, as *tambú* dance music allows islanders to connect to a measure of African heritage. Despite strong social prohibitions, the drum/dance lingers today.[61] Curaçaoan migrants have taken *tambú* dance to Bonaire, Jamaica, Puerto Rico, Cuba, and to nearby Venezuela, where it has influenced the development of other dance practices.

Tambú, the Dutch Caribbean's solitary reference to a sacred African past, underscores the strength of African ancestor values as it also underscores sustained European domination over centuries. The pivotal importance of an African ancestral heritage resurfaces in long-lived dance performance, which even in the absence of religious ritual continues to reference sacred African legacies.[62]

Intermediate Assessment

Thus far, I can confirm that the Caribbean islands—French/Kreyol, English/Creole, Spanish, and former Danish—have ongoing displays and creative elaborations of African-derived sacred dance practices. Where little or no evidence of sacred performance remains, it appears that social dance has periodically achieved sacred conditions and displayed the importance of spirituality among Diaspora performers. At this point, discussion continues with more evidence for Diaspora comparisons from related territories that share Caribbean culture. Even though many historical accounts deny the presence of African peoples in the region (for example, in Argentina, Uruguay, Paraguay, Bolivia, and Chile) and minimize Caribbean-like practices so far away from the islands, Diaspora research has connected Caribbean and Afro-Latin culture.[63] Accordingly, I turn "south of the border" and additionally north to the Diaspora U.S. for sacred examples and conclusions.

Atlantic Afro-Latin Sacred Practices

Brazil

The Lusophone, or Portuguese-speaking, part of the Circum-Caribbean culture sphere contains the largest African population outside of continental

Africa. Any Diaspora study would be remiss without an investigation of an African-related region so close to the Caribbean and one that shares a similar, although distinct, history. Brazil is a major part of the African Diaspora, especially in Salvador da Bahia, Rio de Janeiro, Maranhão, Minas Gerais, and Pernambuco. In these states, flourishing religious structures and dance performances resemble those in the Caribbean. Despite differentiating cultural input from Native Americans throughout Brazil, Afro-Brazilian culture permeates the fabric of Brazilian society, especially in these states.

Candomblé, the main African religion of Brazil, is a near replica of Caribbean island religious form. It shares the umbrella structure of Haitian Vodou and the stylistic movement and drumming practices of Cuban vocabularies (Palo, Arará, and Yoruba).[64] Candomblé practices, called Ketu or Nago/Ketu nation rites, are conspicuously Yoruba-derived, but the umbrella name, Candomblé, is Congo/Angola heritage. Within and surrounding the Yoruba content, there are heavy layers of Central African practice, called Angola, as well as unmistakable sections of Fon-based culture, called Jêjê. Native American rites, called Caboclo, are also associated with Candomblé; sometimes these are separated out and sometimes they are included under the Candomblé umbrella.[65] Additionally, Candomblé is connected to Catholic brotherhoods and sisterhoods, or *irmandades*.

In research on historical contact between Africa and Brazil, anthropologist J. Lorand Matory documents how a Yoruba "nation" was constructed through the influence of freed Africans or "returnees" in both African continental and Diaspora communities.[66] After emancipation throughout the Americas, some Oyos, Egbes, Iyesas, and other related groups who had been enslaved during the eighteenth and early nineteenth centuries were able to return to urban centers of what are now Sierra Leone, Liberia, Benin, and Nigeria. Many took positions as teachers, administrators, and especially as translators for British missionaries. These entrepreneurial and genuinely related peoples asserted a new identity among European authority groups in Africa, who also promoted the new "Yoruba" identity. Over time the related West African Yoruba groups became associated as one group—a learned, hierarchical, religious, and artistic "Yoruba" people. Some returned again to Brazil and Cuba, where their input shaped African-descended religious practice.

The differences between Brazilian Yoruba dances and those of Cuban Yoruba worshipers do not constitute extreme contrasts with what has been previously summarized above for Cuba. For example, in Cuban Yoruba dance, Chango requires an alternating kick, step, step, step as a four-beat pattern with arms alternating also and reaching diagonally high to low. In Brazilian Candomblé, the parallel divinity, Xango, has a pattern that alternately thrusts each foot forward (or kicks) for two counts in a four-beat pattern with both arms raised high for two beats and then low for two beats. Many of the same songs are sung in Brazil and Cuba in archaic ritual language to slightly different drum rhythms. The inclusion of Caboclo movement and stylization differentiates Candomblé in Brazil from Lukumí/Santería in Cuba; however, these additions do not hamper the very apparent relationship between the two dance practices. What is most important about the Brazilian case is that it contains the same ritual structures, a majority of the codified dance elements, and an overt and overpowering replication of ancestor reverence, all of which define the Caribbean sacred. For dance purposes, Candomblé fits comfortably among Caribbean religions.[67]

Suriname

Some of the "purest" African cultures and dance practices in the Americas are found in northern South America among the Ndjuka, Saramaka, Matawai, Aluku (Boni), Paramaka, and Kwinti nations. These are quasi-independent "upriver" nations within Suriname.[68] Since the coastal territories of Suriname contain densely forested areas leading toward the Amazon River, they did not appeal as fully welcoming areas for settlement in the sixteenth, seventeenth, and eighteenth centuries. Maroons escaped from the colonial domination of Suriname's coastal plantations to live in secret encampments, hidden villages, and protected outposts within area rainforests. There, they recreated African communities with some influence from Native Americans in the region, but with only minimal European influence until the last decades of the twentieth century.

The isolated sovereign nations within Suriname's borders contain distinct African practices and also African religious amalgams that are parallel in structure to Caribbean religious/aesthetic paradigms. Surinamese Maroons were able to conserve African religious practices from the seventeenth century and have comparatively little of the Christian influence that exists in the Caribbean or among Jamaican Maroons. Foundational practices of these "upriver" nations involve nature, ancestor, and spirit rites of the Akan and their West African neighbors. Common performance characteristics include drums and other percussion, call-and-response singing, dancing with routine handclapping and elaborate hand gestures, and spirit manifestation or transcendence. Among the Eastern Maroon groups (Ndjuka, Aluku (Boni), and Paramaka), both male and female performers use ankle bracelets made from dried seed pods. Dancers' rhythms are highlighted as soloists emerge from group dancing and display very short virtuoso performance in front of the drums.[69]

"Winti" is a Surinamese sacred practice that is shared by the Maroons and the African Creoles who live "downriver" on former plantation lands near the coast, though significant stylistic variation is evident depending on a group's location and ethnic ties. Particularly among the Creoles, Winti dances are closely related to Caribbean religious paradigms. The Creole sacred performance, or "pee," involves boldly colored body wraps of cloth, a liturgical order of dance and music, and transcendence, during which the incorporated body is often covered or designed with white *pemba* clay. Worshipers dance in a counterclockwise circular path in front of the drums and the ceremonies follow strikingly similar patterns of Haitian Vodou and Cuban Lukumí/Santería paradigms.[70]

Style is the distinguishing characteristic among upriver (Maroon), downriver (Surinamese Creole), and Caribbean dance. Upriver performance features Maroon males in extremely low squatting positions on their toes. Maroon female dancing is upright with the back either tilted forward gently or in a sharp forty-five-degree angle. Downriver and Caribbean practices do not keep the body as low to the ground and, in comparison, are more upright, although flexed at the hips and knees. Upriver performance is a series of brief solos in demanding ranges for all body parts, while downriver and Caribbean solos are longer and more often within the normal to wide range of body motion.[71]

Uruguay

African heritage is also found deep in Uruguay and nearby territories where Africans may have been written out of official histories but where they were not totally decimated nor had their African ways entirely obliterated. As in the Dutch Caribbean, the southern cone of South America lacks fully organized African-derived religions except contemporary borrowings from Afro-Brazilian practices; however, the findings of dance ethnographer Tomás Olivera Chirimini and others have raised questions about the assumed erasure of African ways.[72] Olivera Chirimini has documented the African roots of Uruguayan *candombe* (vs. Brazilian Candomblé), which is the dance that is currently promoted as national culture in the Rio Plata region of Uruguay and Argentina. The word *ka-ndombe* (*ndombe* meaning "black" and "*ka*" being a diminutive in Congo/Angola or Bantu-based languages) is said to mean "*cosas de negros*" in Rio Plata as I also say, "things African." The term exists in Paraguay, Argentina, and Brazil for music/dance forms. In Uruguay, *candombe* is a slice of colonial history and a consummate example of Caribbean and Afro-Latin connections.

Candombe displays the Catholic hegemony, European colonialism, and

African heritage that influence Caribbean sacred practices. For example, historically at Christmas through January 6 (or Three Kings Day), and also at Carnival time just before Lent, *candombe* performers paraded in Catholic patron saint processions and danced European dance sets. Their saints, however, were "black"—Saint Benedict the Moor and Saint Balthasar from the Three Kings—and performers paraded behind carved wooden statues in African-descended entourages. Olivera Chirimini's data indicate that performers alternated parading with *contradanza,* intricate eighteenth-century figure dancing.[73]

Today, African-descended and other Uruguayans reenact the series of contrasting sets with elegant carriage and fastidious manners. Women wear aristocratic-looking lace gowns, lavish headwraps, quantities of cloth, and they carry parasols; men wear tight, white leggings with waistcoats—all of which illustrate the African imitation of American colonists' imitation of European court practices in the eighteenth century. The last set is an improvisational dance in which the entire ensemble "drops" European movement and performs in African style to the heightened volume and thick texture of twenty to one hundred or so drums. The previous elegance and glamour of royal costumes, elite postures, and diverse set figures are juxtaposed with exquisite torso-generated movement, fantastic body-part isolation, and accented syncopation. Rhythmically complex drumming, animated call-and-response singing, and strenuous freeform dancing fill the dance space.

Afro-Uruguayans also perform solos and duets to *candombe* rhythms and feature character dancing within a tradition of *llamadas,* mass drumming batteries that "call" people to the streets to celebrate weddings, visitors, holy days, and now soccer games. The characters, *personas típicas,* represent prominent African roles of the colonial era. For example, a mammy, an herbal doctor (or *gramillero)*, and a sweeper (or *escobero*) dance regal solos and playful duets to *candombe* rhythms. Their performance could be a reflection of European understandings, perhaps from European pagan rituals. The mammy could be the symbolic midwife who assists the doctor in birthing rites, among other things. The sweeper could be sweeping away death or evil spirits before the rebirth of the seasons, or he could announce important news or rules by hitting his staff on the earth or stamping his broom on the floor. Interpretation through the roles of enslaved Africans, however, finds the *gramillero* (herbal doctor), who leads the spectacular parading entrance and departure, as a prominent authority figure over the religious congregation. The mammy, in this perspective, is the housemaid who plays and dances humorously with the houseman or sweeper.

When I witnessed *candombe* and *llamada* character dancing for the first time, I thought the entire Uruguayan scene could have been a Haitian *affranchi* dance or an elite transposition of a peasant *Rara* performance, Dominican *Gaga,* or vintage Trinidadian Carnival parading. The mammy's appearance, gestures, and movement sequences prominently referenced African-derived spiritual entities from the Caribbean, perhaps Cuba's Ochun or Haiti's Ezili. The herbal doctor's high hat and cane not only reflected his high status, but also a mischievous but authoritative Elegba from Cuban Lukumí/Santería and/or a powerful Baron Sanmdi from Haitian Vodou. The *escobero's* broom or baton, like Elegba's *garabato* in Lukumí or Baron Sanmdi's walking cane in Vodou, pointed to Fon and Yoruba heritage in the Caribbean.

In *llamadas,* African-descended bodies spoke loudly, not only in terms of identity and skin color, but also in terms of contextual echoes from an African past, as do similar Caribbean religious practices. In *candombe*'s European dance repertory, which in the Caribbean is mainly secular, sacred African-derived culture was reiterated over time and retained in memory through those dance practices that were permitted. If all such familiarity and symbols prove to be invalid for connections between the Caribbean and Afro-Latin countries (which I sincerely doubt), the last dance set of *candombe* confirms European/African syncretism and cannot be ignored as a strong link to Caribbean dance form.

The compared data indicate that enslaved African descendants and free people of color danced Uruguayan and other South American colonial forms when permitted to participate in religious processionals; they also employed African dance vocabularies intermittently. Just as Diaspora musicians and dancers interspersed African concepts of music making and dance practice into European performance, so contemporary *candombe* practices suggest that African-derived sacred-dance vocabulary was interspersed within European sacred and parading dance forms in Afro-Latin America.

It is safe to summarize that *candombe* is a recreation of Catholic rituals and a regal display that are reenacted for the remembrance of colonial and Afro-Latin history. From an Afrogenic perspective that compares the Atlantic and Circum-Caribbean regions, *candombe* restates colonial class relationships in a dance practice of the powerful with a finale that is free-form contestation of those relationships. *Llamada* character dances transpose mammies and street sweepers into dancing African divinities, and they display camouflage and agency at work in the public domain. Beyond a festival and a challenge, *candombe* is a sacred dance in honor of African heritage. Ancestor reverence is embedded within such practices, and the dancing—the type, style, and vocabulary—embodies submerged agency of

African descendants.[74] In sum, there are intriguing connections to Caribbean sacred practices within Atlantic Afro-Latin sacred performance.

Diaspora U.S. Sacred Practices

While the United States is now the most powerful and central nation of the world in terms of politics and economics, here the perspective is not from the United States but rather from the Caribbean center, making the United States part of the periphery or the Diaspora U.S. It contains many Diaspora communities, Caribbean as well as African American, and each is marked by either the continuity or the diminution of African-derived dance practice. Due to Protestant perceptions of the body as a site of evil or the world of "Satanic flesh," the dancing body in the United States has historically caused upset. Yet this is nothing compared to the disturbance created by the African-descended dancing body.[75]

There were attempts to bar African-derived dancing from all proper religious practice, as well as from social life, but African movement and musical qualities persisted in the whole of U.S. American culture. In fact, according to dance historian Brenda Gottschild, Africanisms became ingrained as *the* identifying characteristic of U.S. "American" culture.[76] Dance forms, types, and styles that have differentiated U.S. American forms from like European forms—ballet, musical theater, etc.—have displayed African bodily and musical expressions despite engulfing Protestant constraints.

Colonial history shows that Africans and their descendants were first coerced to be baptized as Christians; they later joined Christian churches and fashioned their own style of Judeo-Christian worship in the United States. Most African-descended communities were encouraged to limit their dancing.[77] Northern and Southern colonists (some of Pilgrim heritage) knew the fervor of exalted religious expression well and were also well acquainted with the African custom of dancing toward transcendence.[78] American colonists discussed African-derived dances like the *kalenda/calenda, chica, bamboula,* and *juba,* which continuously surfaced from Boston, Charleston, and New Orleans to Havana, Port-au-Prince, Salvador da Bahia, Buenos Aires, and Montevideo.[79] Despite colonial disgust with African-derived dancing, the African-descended dancing body was simultaneously admired for the power, flexibility, and expressiveness it exuded. It was exoticized for the perverse sexual attraction it generated toward enslaved, dark-hued beings, and it was feared because of hostile undercurrents that were exposed repeatedly in ordinary plantation life and later in urban industrial life.

One measure of African dancing stubbornly permeated African American life in the nineteenth and early twentieth centuries. The African circle of social and spiritual life was reconfirmed in the *ring shout* of the United States.[80] It traced the ongoing reality of and necessity for life as deeply improvisational "danced walking." A description of sacred dance from within the United States shows how forceful its minimalist movements could become:

> Very likely more than half the population of the plantation is gathered together. . . . benches are pushed back to the wall when the formal meeting is over, and old and young, men and women . . . all stand up in the middle of the floor, and, when the "sperichil" is struck up, begin first walking and by-and-by shuffling round, one after the other, in a ring. The foot is hardly taken from the floor, and the progression is mainly due to a jerking, hitching motion, which agitates the entire shouter and soon brings out streams of perspiration. Sometimes they dance silently, sometimes as they shuffle, as they sing the chorus of the spiritual, and sometimes the song itself is also sung by the dancers. But more frequently a band, composed of some of the best singers and of tired shouters, stand at the side of the room to "base" the others, singing the body of the song and clapping their hands together or on the knees. Song and dance are alike extremely energetic, and often, . . . the monotonous thud . . . of the feet prevents sleep within half a mile of the praise-house.[81]

Free, openly expressive body movement such as that found in Caribbean sacred performance was rarely described in U.S. African American sacred settings. By the nineteenth century, limited, restricted, European-influenced movement was the norm for many religious settings and African dance vocabulary was relegated to secular, segregated entertainment.[82] As in the Protestant areas of the Caribbean where religious dance, African dance, and dancing itself were curtailed or prohibited, sacred dance in the United States was almost "squeezed dry" by restrictive Protestant rules that reinterpreted the definition of dance. For example, rhythmic jumping with raised or waving hands to drum, fiddle, and string bass were part of Protestant practices, but these were not considered "dance." In the Diaspora U.S., these and other dance-like movements (for example, running patterns back and forth, and transcendent flailing, leaning, or "falling out" on fellow worshipers) were considered religious "shouting" or "receiving the Holy Ghost." African-derived movement in sacred contexts in the United States was thereby abbreviated—but not abandoned.

Later in the twentieth century, economic and political migration from the Circum-Caribbean and continental Africa influenced Diaspora U.S. sacred performance. Differing Africans brought several variants of African worship to urban centers, including Islam, Akan, and Orisa religions, which require sacred gestures, postures, and sequences. Haitians also brought Vodou performance; Cubans and Brazilians brought Santería, Candomblé, Palo, and Angola dance rituals; and Jamaicans and Trinidadians brought remnants of Nyabingi, Big Drum *Nation dances,* and Spiritual Baptist praise dance—to say nothing of Native, Asian, and European sacred practices that shared the same space with Diaspora religious practices over time.

Since the ecumenical councils of the 1960s, liturgical dance specialists have led sections of the Catholic Mass and Protestant services to amplify conventional religious practice in the United States and to gently break through lingering cultural rules against dance performance and the dancing body.[83] Tendencies and customs of European-derived Judeo-Christian congregations have met the spontaneous responsorial chanting, preaching style, percussive accompaniment, and gestured performance of African-derived Christians in sermons, spirituals, and gospel music. Together, ricocheting from European-influenced to African-influenced styles, contemporary religious practices in the United States have grown. In rectangular church, synagogue, and temple spaces where the circle can still be implied, contemporary congregations have begun to move rhythmically, even if only rocking in praise while seated.

Additionally, transpositions of African and Caribbean sacred practices have crisscrossed the United States. Twenty-first century Christians in the south have begun to reference African religions and spiritual beings and to align themselves as "sister churches or parishes" with African churches. Some trace African-descended saints and direct services solely through African-Catholic, African-Episcopalian, and African-Baptist perspectives; others use African movement, as in dancing while processing through the nave of the church. Most do *not* integrate Lukumí/Santería and Vodou practices, but "black" Christian churches publicly recognize African religions more often than historically (for example, the interdenominational services at Hillside Chapel and Truth Center in Atlanta). In New England, Puerto Rican and Brazilian communities hold Lukumí/Santería and Candomblé ceremonies often and more publicly (in Springfield and Boston, Massachusetts). Out west, traditional drums serve spiritual communities of California, Washington, and Oregon in sacred Circum-Caribbean drum/dance. Thus, the United States comprises the African legacies of its own history in plantation slavery, as well as new deposits of sacred African, Circum-Caribbean, and Afro-Latin practices, all of which have facilitated growth of bodily expression in U.S. American religious practices over time.

Chart 15. Sacred Diaspora Ritual Forms

Umbrella religious structure with rites	OR	Distinct religious structures
Judeo-Christian orientation	OR	African Nation orientation
African/Christian syncretism	OR	Intra-African syncretism
Minimum body movement	OR	Maximum body involvement
Contained, restrained energy	OR	Expansive, explosive energy
No or little transcendence	OR	Transcendence

French/Kreyol Caribbean

Haitian Vodou (***Paradigm #1) — Umbrella religious structure; African nation orientation (Rada and Petwo rites); intra-African syncretism, maximum body involvement, expansive, explosive energy; transcendence (toward family ancestors/*Lwas* and cosmic divinities)

Martinique — No known African sacred structures or dances (some recent transport of Cuban and Haitian religions)

Guadeloupe — No known African sacred structures or dances

English/Creole Caribbean

Trinidad & Tobago Shango — Distinct religious structures; African nation orientation; African/Christian syncretism; maximum body involvement, expansive, explosive movement; transcendence

Carriacou Big Drum/Nation Dance (***Paradigm #2) — Umbrella structure; African nation orientation (ancestor, Creole, and Frivolous rites); minimum body movement, contained, restrained movement; no transcendence

Jamaican Rasta/Kumina/Pocomania — Distinct structures; Judeo-Christian orientation and African/Christian orientation; moderate-minimum body movement

Spanish Caribbean

Cuban Santería/Arará/Palo/Carabalí (***Paradigm #3) — Distinct religious structures; African nation orientation; maximum body involvement, expansive, explosive movement; transcendence toward ancestor and cosmic divinities

Puerto Rico — same as Cuban Santería

Dominican Republic — same as Haitian Vodou (Vodú)

Portuguese Circum-Caribbean

Brazilian Candomblé/Jeje/ Angola/Caboclo — Umbrella religious structures; African nation orientation; African/Native American syncretism; maximum body involvement, expansive, explosive movement; transcendence toward ancestor, cosmic, Native American divinities, and *eres*

Dutch Circum-Caribbean

Surinamese Winti — Distinct religious structures; African nation orientation; moderate to maximum body involvement, expansive movement; transcendence

Diaspora U.S.

Judeo-Christian, Islamic, Fundamentalist, Santería, Vodou, etc. — Distinct religious structures; Christian orientation mainly; African nation orientation; minimal, restrained to maximum body involvement; transcendence (in Fundamentalist, Santería, and Vodou practices)

Afrogenic Comparisons

In the sacred dance performances that have been surveyed throughout this chapter, Diaspora performers have repeatedly highlighted the aesthetic system and dance as the crosscutting domain of the whole of social life, including the sacred dimension. During religious rituals, dancing worshipers have relied on African-derived dance movement characteristics, employed African concepts of music making, and illuminated African cultural values over centuries. Sacred dance performance has commemorated the African value of ancestor reverence in the organizing principle of religious structures, in dance movements, as well as in the ultimate act of spirit transcendence—in other words, bringing the ancestral world to the present.

Sacred dance performance in the Diaspora U.S. has a diminished reliance on the dancing body when compared to the Caribbean islands and some mainland Afro-Latin sites. Historically, worshipers in the United States focus on constrained dancelike movements that they deem are important for spiritual transformation—energetic clapping, swaying, or jumping, for example. For many African descendants in Atlantic Afro-Latin America, sacred dance performance has been a primary vehicle for reattaching contemporary life to historical heritages and reiterating a balance between the spirit and human worlds. In the Caribbean, worshipers dance most often until they are at one with the music, their dancing bodies lost to ordinary experience, dwelling only in suprahuman performance. Dance liturgies present religious beliefs

Chart 16. Continuum of Sacred and Social Dance

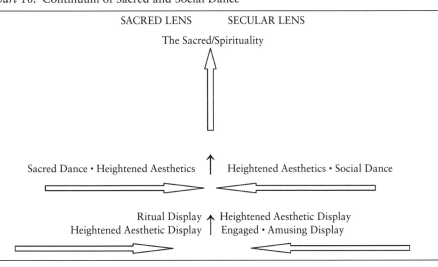

and, despite variations, reach toward ensemble spiritual experiences. Thus, Diaspora dance expresses the sacred aesthetically—and sometimes the social as sacred.

The alternation of analytical lenses on a sacred/spiritual/social dance continuum provides important data. It allows the analyst to determine sacred and social dance contexts and, when there is no apparent evidence of sacred performance, it illuminates whatever information is present. The dynamics of ritual performance are clearly sacred as well as aesthetic, but how social dance, parades, Carnivals, weddings, and wake practices exhibit transcendence becomes evident through analytical alternations of lenses.

In sum, geographically distant—but religiously, aesthetically, and culturally related sacred rituals link the Caribbean to Afro-Latin America and the Diaspora U.S. In each setting, analyses of sacred dance practices have unveiled paradigms that express religious intensity through either contained and restrained or expansive and explosive dance movement. The differences are most apparent in style but also in exhibiting, encouraging, or prohibiting transcendence. Each area displays African-descended resilience, and some version of African sacred practice (traditional or Christianized) is found in four of five linguistically distinct areas. Sacred performance—moving toward an out-of-body experience or being totally at one within the dance performance—involves the social experience of compounding aesthetics or heightened interest, intense response, and their combinations. Its result is most often awe, ecstatic excess, intense interest, religious belief, or engaged spirituality. The continuum in chart 16 indicates how, in effect, transforming ancestral spirits pry open both sacred and secular dance forms to expose hampered Diaspora values, prohibited cultural tendencies or African movement vocabulary and heightened aesthetics reaching toward the spiritual.

CHAPTER EIGHT

FEROCIOUS DANCE

This chapter briefly examines Martinican *ladja/danmyé*, Cuban *juego de maní*, Trinidadian *kalinda*, Curaçaoan *tambú/kokomakaku*, and Brazilian *capoeira/maculelê*, and it advances the inclusion of armed and unarmed combat rituals within Caribbean dance categories. These combat forms are filled with smooth body mechanics, incredible strength, and percussive strikes and blows, but also dance moves, body games, and ample philosophy. As Katherine Dunham said, "The fascination of the real (*Martinican ladja*) lies not in the lust of the combat, but in the finesse of approach and retreat; the tension which becomes almost a hypnosis, then the flash of the two bodies as they leap into the air, fall in a crouch, and whirl at each other in simulated attacks, only to walk nonchalantly away, backs to each other, showing utter indifference before falling again into the rocking motion which rests them physically but excites them emotionally."[1]

African Legacies

African history scholar M. Thomas J. Desch-Obi has found a definitive core of martial arts that were seminal to the societies of colonial Angola and that relate to Caribbean combat dances. While fighting dances appear frequently among human groups, Desch-Obi's findings suggest ways in which martial techniques were transported within enslaved bodies to parts of the African Diaspora, including the Caribbean and its related territories. He concentrates on several wrestling and grappling practices of the Ibo and other West African groups in the Bight of Biafra, but also on kicking, butting, and stone-throwing techniques from Central Africa.

Throughout colonial Angola (which covered both Congos and Angola of today), the martial art traditions combined strength, flexibility, and endurance

training, as well as what we in dance might call body/mind centering, in order
to protect the practitioner from harm and to attack and disable a threatening opponent. By the seventeenth century in southern Angola (particularly
between the city of Benguela and the Kunene River), a mushrooming initiation society of warlords and their military units, called Imbangala, ravaged
many historically agricultural and pastoral lineage groupings and merged
into a combat-ready, warring, interconnected, non-kin organization. Imbangala military bands among Cimbebasian peoples—later called Ovambungala
and Kunene groups—practiced codified and debilitating body kicks, lethal
stick-and-club strikes, and accurate stone-throwing techniques, as opposed
to pugilistic or fistfighting techniques, among other mercenary customs.[2]

Southern Angola striking traditions were known as *engolo*.[3] They were
aligned with the play and fighting of zebras (*ongolo*), which were known
for their speed, strength, agility, and additionally for kicks that could kill.
As well, the zebra trait of sparring with a head stallion for mating privileges
ran parallel to Imbangala initiation rituals that pitted young eligible men in
engolo for eligible young women and the omission of dowry requirements.
Engolo was additionally aligned with the cosmological world of Congo/
Angola ancestors, called *Kalunga*. *Engolo* combative skills were conceived
as a gift from the ancestors, a spiritually laden practice associated with a
mirror reflection of the social world.[4]

Engolo technique involved acrobatic defensive practices, and it was almost
inseparable from music and dance in its ritual or festival (controlled) settings.
In preparatory exercises, which were constant starting from age two to six for
Kunene boys (suggestive of early childhood army-recruitment practices), it
was play-like or game-like competition; its ultimate goal, however, was to be
prepared for deadly battle, to be superior in offensive and defensive skills, to
be able to defend a warlord's cattle or kingdom, a family or a family's herd,
with or without weapons on a moment's notice. From the time practitioners
entered the Imbangala circle to sing rhythmically and thereby announce
their readiness for an opponent, they were prepared for all sorts of violent
bodily warfare. Competitors displayed their preparedness for future battles
in virtuoso performances, some of which also assisted healing rituals.[5]

Martial art practices were also associated with dance performances (*sanga,
n'gola,* and *kipura,* for example).[6] *Sanga* refers collectively to war dances
that tested hand-to-hand combat among many Angola peoples. The *n'gola*
dance is one war dance that marked the passage of young girls to woman-
hood with the martial competition of males in challenging pursuit. *Kipura*
was a "rooster" dance in northern colonial Angola that replicated the swift
defensive and vicious offensive practices of fighting birds. Agile bodies,

capable of contortion and speedy reflexes, were paramount in the practice techniques of the martial arts.

Presumably, at least a few knowledgeable practitioners of Imbangala legacies (in addition to Egyptian, Nubian, Ibo, and other wrestling and grappling legacies) were among the enslaved who arrived in the Circum-Caribbean culture sphere. There, in plantation environments of violence, African martial arts were used and developed as defensive modes and opposition strategies in defense of African-derived communities, their lethal purposes disguised as dance. Desch-Obi makes the case that martial art practices, particularly hand-to-hand combat and the practice of fighting to the death in Angola traditions, assisted the defeat of colonial defenses and the establishment of a new Republic in Haiti.[7] Several traditions appear in historical documents of specific Caribbean islands, and some are still in practice.

Chart 17. Circum-Caribbean Combat Practices

A. Antecedent African Martial Legacies

    Unarmed Practices

        Engolo
        Sanga
        N'gola
        Kipura
        Mgbe, etc.

    Armed Practices

        Kindeka (sticks), etc.

B. Unarmed Caribbean Fighting Dances

    Martinique: *danmyé, l'aguia*
    Cuba: *juego de maní*
    Curaçao: *tambú/trankamentu*
    Circum-Caribbean Brazil: *capoeira*

C. Armed Caribbean Fighting Dances

    Trinidad and Tobago: *kalinda* (sticks)
    Curaçao: *kokomakaku* (sticks)
    Brazil: *maculelê* (sticks, machetes), *capoeira* (razors)
    Cuba: *juego de maní* (wrist bands with nails)

D. Other Cited Fighting Forms

    Puerto Rico: *bomba calindán*
    Guadeloupe: *calinda* or *konvalen, libo*
    Haiti: *mousondi* or *calinda* (sticks, batons)
    Jamaica: *warrick* (sticks)
    Carriacou
    Grenadines
    St. Thomas
    Barbados
    Guyana

Caribbean Combat Dance/Games

Fighting dances engage the Caribbean community today as competitive play, sometimes with body movement only and at other times with sticks. Dance/games provide learning and satisfaction for practitioners, and they give pleasure and excitement to viewers. Fighting dances in the past were part of performance rituals where the enslaved "defined themselves as individuals and united themselves as a cultural community. . . . Thus, public performance became *the* activity through which they asserted and maintained their individuality and self-worth."[8]

Enslaved and freed Africans resisted the status quo when they performed combat dances (or *quadrilles* and parading dances, for that matter) and exercised whatever degree of agency that was possible on behalf of the African community. As Desch-Obi's documentation asserts, combat practices involved honor at their core, even in demeaning and dehumanizing captivity. Body practices taught self-knowledge, understanding of human behavior, and permitted the creation and testing of successful unarmed strategies. Reports show that African women also sought individual and community honor through fierce fighting techniques.[9]

Several types of combat forms are mentioned in the colonial literature, and these are infused with references to dance. Ethnomusicologist Julian Gerstin reports stick-fighting dances performed by men in Trinidad, Grenada, Carriacou, and St. Thomas, and stick fighting called *calinda* or *konvalen* in Guadeloupe; he has found only one stick-fighting *calinda* reference for Martinique.[10] Earlier, Haitian folklore specialist Harold Courlander cited *mousondi* or *calinda* stick fighting for Haiti and *bomba calindán* for Puerto Rico.[11] Dance researcher/choreographer Katherine Dunham's filmed examples show unarmed practices in Jamaica and Martinique in 1936 and 1937.[12] My fieldwork has involved *danmyé* and Brazilian *capoeira* and *maculelê*, but additionally, I have heard of combat dances in Barbados and Guyana; thus, the story of Caribbean fighting forms is filled with differentiated names, diverse practices, and multiple Caribbean locations.

Danmyé and *Ladja* in Martinique

Probably the best-known fighting dance in the Caribbean literature is *ladja* or *danmyé*, and Katherine Dunham helped to bring it to regional and global notice.[13] *L'Ag'ya* (or *Ladja*, 1938), one of Dunham's earliest choreographies, toured in her repertory for decades. Inside Caribbean communities today, the echoes of Congo/Angola dance traditions linger as performers make a circle to observe, evaluate, and support the competitive foot wrapping, smooth leg sweeps, and kick fighting that characterize the practice.[14]

Ladja involves the whole body and a mix of skills (such as hand blows, kicks, head butting).[15] It is formally differentiated from foot fighting only, which is the domain of *danmyé*; but these terms are more often interchangeable. Contenders bend low to the ground and invert themselves slightly to kick at one another; they rarely walk on their hands (as in related Brazilian *capoeira* and Angolan *engolo*). Both elders and young men continue the practice, and from the dance perspective, it seems apparent that some traditions related to southern Angola developed in Martinique (and similarly in Jamaica and Brazil) as combat techniques that relied on a specific knowing or "embodied knowledge" that is gained through the body—the dancing, drumming, combat-dancing body.[16] Exceedingly similar combat practices appeared across the islands and on related mainland territories, and each emphasized martial techniques through dance practices.

Martinican musicologist Dominique Cyrille reports that *ladja* is associated with *achté en pwen,* or "buying a slap," to augment a fighter's chances to win.[17] Martinican fighters are required to use the *pwen* spiritual powers within *ladja* performance or they must strike a tree or an inanimate object and let the power, secret charm, or magical potency dissipate. They believe they will lose the use of an arm or leg if such precautions are not taken.

According to Desch-Obi's historical documentation, the lineage of Martinican *ladja/danmyé* was made possible not solely through the slave trade from Portuguese ports along the coast, but also through African slaving routes from small cities to awaiting French and British traders. He suggests that vast numbers of Angolan ethnic groups and Imbangala warlords who were known for their prowess in *engolo* martial arts were captured and sent into the French slave trade, especially during the period of 1770–90, at the dawn of the Haitian Revolution (1791).[18] Since the French slave trade continued until abolition in 1848, direct knowledge of these martial arts was possible for sixty to eighty years in French-held territories of the Americas.

Contemporary fighting dance in Martinique and Guadeloupe appears to be a consequence of two Angolan capture histories (Portuguese and African), despite demographics of the French Caribbean to the contrary that only show about 20 percent of Angola-derived populations.[19] Something more than demographic preponderance was responsible for the continuity and/or creative development of fighting dance practices (and was perhaps also responsible for salvaging fighting versus sacred dance traditions in French department islands). Desch-Obi states that a tradition can be "spread by a few knowledgeable exponents," and my previous work on sacred dance emphasizes embodied knowledge that was "housed" in the body and perfected in dance.[20] Together these findings suggest that through combat techniques in dance form, influential members of the enslaved were able to creatively develop fighting forms in pockets of the Circum-Caribbean culture sphere and perhaps, also, to effectively protect some behaviors (social dances) to the demise of others (sacred dance repertoires).

Juego de maní in Cuba

According to ethnologist Fernando Ortiz, a fighting dance/game, called *juego* or *baile de maní* (peanut game or dance) was practiced in Cuba among both men and women during the nineteenth century until the 1930s and 1940s.[21] As in Martinique, all participants first danced in a ring; but in Cuba, a group proceeded through a round of eliminations until one remained and thereby became the first to fight everyone in the circle together. Performers fought bare-chested, often with oiled skin to mute or deflect blows. Men defined the ring with interlocked legs, which had to stay planted or they would forfeit the game. Arms were free to swing and punch, according to elaborate rules about fighting with fists only and protecting the liver and stomach areas; but often the men in the circle, as well as the opposing fighter in the center, struck every body part with their hands and heads. At times, they even fought with metal wristbands that had embedded nails, "magic" stones, and other implements. The performer in the center danced and sang improvisations on his bravery, skill, and former conquests. He moved agilely, feinted, jumped, kicked, and surprised each participant, hoping to knock an opponent out of the circle or cause him to fall off balance and move a leg. As the circle of six (or as many as twenty) men was reduced, some fighters received fatal blows; generally however, the dance/game could not stop until there was no one to fight. (Women's rules are not available.)

Cuban musicologist Argeliers León also described the *manicero(a)* or player who evaded the prescribed punches of men/women in a ring.[22] He reported that men and women from the provinces of Matanzas, Havana, and Las Villas (where it was called *mani de bombosá*) were renowned *maniseros(as)*. Drummers marked the punches and strikes with accenting slaps as the dancing fighter evaded severe blows and defended himself or herself from all sides. In the 1950s, Ortiz stated that *juego de mani* was only practiced "'*marcando' los golpes*," meaning as a cultural presentation without horrific consequences.[23]

Kalinda in Trinidad and Tobago

Sticks were treasured as walking canes throughout many regions of Africa, but in cattle-raising areas of colonial Angola or in Imbangala-derived cultures, young Kunene boys had to defend their herds through skilled fighting with two-foot-long sticks. In the New World, evidence of fighting with four- and five-foot sticks or poles has been described in slave quarters and later in the "yards" of free African descendants.[24] Stick-fighting *kalinda* (*kalenda, calenda,* or *calinda*)[25] in the English/Creole islands seems to be connected to the residue of pastoral practices and combat techniques on the continent.

Ethnomusicologist Donald Hill points out that stick fighting on Trinidad and Tobago was associated with Carnival parading dances and after emancipation, with *canboulay* (seasonal burning of cane fields) and its accompanying dance festivities.[26] Local colonial estates competed in stick fighting throughout the eighteenth and nineteenth centuries. Stick fighters carrying long poles and dressed in elaborate stick-fighting costumes (*neg jardin*) appeared in bands throughout city streets. Dueling neighborhood crowds egged on their best fighters, who crouched, leapt, turned swiftly, struck sticks, and fought mercilessly until blood flowed.[27] Blood was placed in a shallow hole in the ground to end the fight. After years of dangerous competitions, *kalinda* was outlawed in 1884 and the techniques were practiced in secret until its legal approval again in 1951. It died down in the 1970s, but this ferocious dance is practiced today in *kalinda* festivals.

Tambú and *Kokomakaku* in Curaçao

Thanks to a growing number of translations from Dutch and Papiamento, the works of legal history and folklore scholar Rene Rosalia, dancer/researcher Gabri Crista Stompf, ethnomusicologist Nannette de Jong, and others have been acknowledged, and Dutch Caribbean dances and martial art traditions are being investigated. These cultural data, in combination with recent historical data (provided by John Thornton, Linda Heywood, James Sweet, M. Thomas J. Desch-Obi, and others), have provided a fuller and more viable category of fighting/combat dances for the Caribbean.

In a 1997 publication in Papiamento, Rene Rosalia traced the persistence of Dutch opposition to the Curaçaoan dance, drum, and fighting rituals of *tambú*.[28] In 2001, Gabri Crista retold the story of *tambú* in English from the dance perspective, which revealed an ongoing practice of the drum/dance tradition.[29] In 2007, Nanette de Jong asserted *tambú*'s relevance within Curaçaoan history by highlighting *kokomakaku,* a stick-fighting practice associated with *tambú* drums.[30] Like Rosalia before her (and anthropologist Elis Juliana[31] in 1983), de Jong pointed to the importance of Angola fighting traditions. Research has repeatedly found a connection between combat techniques and dance and between Angola and Dutch Caribbean cultures. This association is particularly important since the African museum in Curaçao points almost entirely to West African connections and thereby leads not only foreign visitors but also Curaçaoans away from relevant Central African history.

Tambú dance and drums have mainly signaled Afro-Curaçaoan identity, but also they have pointed to opposition and contestation.[32] Rosalia and de Jong document the historical performance of *kokomakaku* as a contest between two stick-wielding contestants who attempt to draw blood as completion of "Blood for the Drum Ritual" (*Sanger pa tambú*).[33] *Kokomakaku* participants sway and clap in a circle with *tambú* drums; they sing in call-and-response form with a song leader, or *pregon,* who handles the blood and initiates all sections of the ritual with vocal signals. Blood is "fed" to the *tambú* drum so that the drum's spirit will be nourished. In declaring a winner, the dance/game/fight promotes pride within the segment of the community or neighborhood that now contains a "Stick Priest."

At other times, the *tambú* drum was played for unarmed competition, as two men danced skillfully atop two poles, five to eight feet tall, held by two men. The first to lose balance and touch the ground was deemed the loser.[34] Also, competition appeared as playful pushing or shoving when a man tried to "cut in" on a dancing couple, called *trankamentu*[35]; however, when the playful game did not resolve with good humor and turned into confrontational fighting, *kokomakaku* was declared and men battled with sticks to draw blood mercilessly.[36]

Over time, the ritual proved to be too dangerous, even in clandestine areas of this desert island. Carrying of walking sticks and canes was prohibited during the late nineteenth century, and, gradually, most Afro-Curaçaoans forgot the fighting skills, the ritual, and its associated religious beliefs. What are known today are the associated drum, songs, and dances.

Christa's work emphasizes the resurgence of *tambú* as "forbidden" dance music among young people. For them, it symbolizes a forgotten, sacred African ritual that was marked particularly by the African Creole class. In bodily contestation against legal restrictions on *tambú* and rigid social conventions, contemporary Curaçaoan dancers protest through their "open" bodies; their hands are stretched high above their heads and their torsos are divided as they rapidly articulate circling hips to ongoing *tambú* rhythms for hours. It appears that *kokomakaku* or stick-fighting performance has ended, but Curaçaoans still sing politically charged *tambú* songs brashly and dance to *tambú* drumming. Beyond identity claims, the performance is filled with overt opposition to the status quo.

Related *Capoeira* and *Maculelê*

By far, the best-known Diaspora combat dance is Brazilian *capoeira*, which has been debated repeatedly as either an African-derived practice or a Creole creation. More important, communication theory specialist Julio Cesar de Tavares suggests that since the body was already treated as a cultural container for work, African descendants learned to develop it as an archive for cultural transmission and as a weapon for cultural defense.[37] Mestre Acordeon says that the game/art/dance is *"con pe,"* a way of walking "forward in life with a conscious determination to become physically strong and healthy, emotionally stable, mentally open, and spiritually wiser."[38] Although no one is sure, it seems that *capoeira* developed through male play and skills learned in the hostile environment of *kilombos* or Brazilian encampment villages of escaped Maroons where inner strength was just as important as physical strength. Others speculate that it was developed by means of men in chains or with manacled hands in order to escape captivity and flee to the surrounding wilderness of Brazilian *fazendas* and *plantaçaos* (ranches and plantation houses). Today, *capoeira* is often seen onstage, sometimes with a stick dance, *maculelê*, which is another fight/dance from Bahia that uses *grimas* (sticks or machetes from Brazilian plantation history) and their rhythms to fight with and dance to.

Capoeira employs a strategy, a series of standing and inverted postures that free the feet and legs to become weapons—sometimes, literally, with razors held between the toes. Performers make a circle in front of the musicians and, two by two, demonstrate their expertise in making swift blows that just miss hurting an opponent and in evading strikes from sweeping legs and kicking feet. Fighting also occurs in *maculelê*, which is now a staged performance for groups of men or women with two-foot sticks, knives, or machetes. Stick wielders dance to specific rhythms and strike their opponent's blades or the ground in choreographed sequences; they alternately jump with splits in the air, fall to their knees, or spin rapidly, only to rise and strike the stick or knife of their opponent with rhythmic precision. Contemporary practice involves *capoeira* flexibility and *maculelê* strikes.

Both *capoeira* and *maculelê* are taught in thousands of *capoeira* schools throughout Bahia, Rio de Janeiro, Pernambuco and São Paolo States, and also throughout the Diaspora. The main division of instruction is between *capoeira Angola* and *capoeira regional* styles; the former strives to keep moves and strength techniques at ground level, presuming traditional fight dancing, while the latter uses more aerial and presentational strikes, often presuming an audience or show.

Despite the many laws that prohibited its practice after emancipation in 1888, Afro-Brazilians used *capoeira* techniques in defiance of a social order that did not liberate them from prejudice, oppression, or racism. Street-fighting forms died out during the mid-nineteenth century in Rio, but in Recife during Carnaval time, *capoeiristas* led neighborhood and district bands, and at times, *capoeiristas* worked as bodyguards and henchmen for powerful, elite families, politicians, and sometimes for the criminal element of Brazilian society.[39] Bahia has guarded the philosophy and martial skills through the men of Candomblé houses. Over time, *capoeira Angola* has spread beyond Bahia and Recife to Rio again, and across the Brazilian landscape to other parts of the Americas and Europe.[40]

Lessons of Combat Dance

The dance of life is the breath, which can be interrupted by surprises from nature, society, the body, or the emotional self. On these occasions, the human body shifts, stops, starts, and feints as it adjusts to and evades the surprise; the body dances its adjustments to interruptions. So the martial arts are crafted techniques that provide a life support and account for the natural, social, as well as personal challenges of life interruptions. Body practices are learned as combat dances, physical performances that are later repeated as competitive game-like strategies, so as to sharpen whatever skills have been acquired. The dances become lethal when humor, wit, and logic are not heeded, when anger and frustration are exhausted, when the ego has triumphed, or when individual identities or cultural concerns are in jeopardy.

The Afrogenic comparisons above suggest that Diaspora martial-art traditions were embodied practices that stored both physical and cognitive knowledge. Under the conditions of plantation slavery, embodied combat dances simultaneously augmented self-respect, protected life and limb, sharpened defensive skills, maintained ancestral culture, and strengthened spirituality. Bodily martial practices were used vis à vis plantation owners prior to emancipation and also military and police organizations later, but they were retained over time as a special dance type that fostered protection, coolness, and strategy formation.

Body movement—as dance, games, fights, and martial arts—is part of a survival-skills repertoire that African-descended people used in the Diaspora until they were thwarted in all attempts. Some practices, such as Cuban *juego de maní* and Curaçaoan *kokomakaku,* have disappeared; others, such as Trinidadian *kalinda* and *Curaçaoan tambú,* went underground, resurfaced, and then appeared in controlled cultural presentations. Still others, such as Martinican *ladja/danmyé* and related Brazilian *capoeira* and *maculelê,* continue as living, resilient traditions (see photos 12 and 13). Amidst the beauty and health offerings of combat techniques, ferocious dance continues.

CHAPTER NINE

Tourism, Globalization, and Caribbean Dance

In light of increased economic pressures and cultural collisions that have resulted in the wake of political globalization in the twenty-first century, dance investigation now seeks to unravel artistic trends in the Diaspora and to clarify how dancers and dance forms are encouraged, developed, and protected, particularly in the Caribbean. Analyses of the interaction between tourism enterprises and dance genres, dance artists, and island governments raise issues concerning cultural and economic globalization.[1]

Caribbean Resources

Resources on the islands are scarce generally, with only moderate to minimal dependence on sugar, nickel, tobacco, coffee, and fish in the Spanish islands; bananas, pineapples, sisal, nickel, and rum products in the French/Creole islands; salt mining and oil refining in the Dutch islands; and bauxite, alumina, oil, gold, and natural gas mining in English/Creole islands. None of these, except oil and oil refining perhaps, amounts to significant global trade, but multiple products save the region from dependence on the fragile mono-commodity economy of its past and aide the survival of Caribbean peoples. Everywhere in the islands, however, there are ecological treasures and admired cultural practices that signal tourist interest and economic potential. For example, public festivals of all sorts frequent the culture calendars of most Caribbean islands, and Caribbeans themselves are known for their unabashed outbreaks into danced partying, all of which is enticing for inquisitive tourists.

Accordingly, the large and small islands, and the culturally related mainland territories have consciously developed their human and natural resources toward tourism, the primary economic activity of the entire region. As skilled, computer-chip technology has all but wiped out the islands' historical offerings of cheap agricultural and unskilled manufacturing labor, islanders have looked more deliberately than in the past to their beaches, tropical forests, fish and small game reserves, and often toward their cultural reserves. Tourism interests have recognized the place of dance in terms of revenue and have integrated dancers, musicians, visual artists, and theatrical or spectacle specialists into national programs. Despite acknowledged downsides, tourism has been the main attraction and sometimes the sole income-generating domain for many islands, and it is within tourism enterprises that Caribbean dance has maintained an unheralded but active position.

Since the 1940s and 1950s, the islands have alternated as favored destination points for Europeans, Canadians, and U.S. Americans on vacation and in search of leisure. Recreational and educational cruise ships have etched out channels; airline agents have underscored air routes to packaged "exotic" and manicured Caribbean resorts. With the Cuban Revolution of 1959, the rise of ecotourism and health tourism seemed to blanket earlier decades of commercial, entertainment tourism.[2] As always, however, from the colonial period to the present, sex has been a constant (although unofficial) commodity within regional tourism.[3]

By the 1980s, "sun, sand, and sex tourism" yielded HIV and AIDS with substantial stigma and discrimination, eventually causing a decline in the tourist trade. Protestant, Catholic, and Caribbean cultural values struggled *against* sex education, programs to dispense condoms and needles, and adequate community health care, except in Cuba.[4] With the development of banking interests and yuppie and "buppie" (black yuppie) finance in the 1980s, Caribbean islands resumed the roles they had had historically as colonial outposts and commercial marketplaces, this time supplying European and American centers with global finance, offshore banking, drugs and drug trafficking, and a more pronounced sex industry—often with a visual illustration of a Caribbean dancer as the essence of island seduction.[5] The 1990s and early part of the twenty-first century have brought sharp increases in historical and ecological tourism, both of which foster a fresh look at tourism with sustainable and principled use of natural and human resources.[6] For dance performance, this has meant continued interest in and influence on Caribbean performance and maximum opportunities for Caribbean dance artists.

Global Markets and Caribbean Tourism

Caribbean islands have pressed toward tourism development as the most immediate source of revenue for nations with precarious economic conditions brought on by one or a combination of severe encumbrances, such as natural disasters like hurricanes, droughts, flooding, and earthquakes, as well as national unemployment, violence or crime, and constantly changing international priorities. Within the current global tourism market, there is dire need to maintain or increase the Caribbean share. The Caribbean tourist rate is only 2 percent of that of the Americas, which is 16 percent of global tourism; but tourism accounts for 20–70 percent of the Caribbean Gross Domestic Product (GDP).[7] For example, tourism in the U.S. Virgin Islands accounts for 70 percent of island jobs as well as 70 percent of the GDP, while Trinidad and Tobago does not have to rely on tourism because of its lucrative oil and oil refining industries. Local and regional associations develop tourism in desperate attempts to hinder marginalization of Caribbean islands within economic globalization; however, as one tourism study finds, the global market of free and limited preferential trade often places " too much profit from the tourist industry . . . in the hands of foreign investors. . . . [Critics] point out that . . . the growth of tourism in the Caribbean has created a new mono-commodity system. . . . In fact, currently, the Caribbean is four times more dependent on tourism than any other region in the world."[8]

Between the advantages and disadvantages of tourism and in step with present efforts for more local control and benefits, Caribbean dance and music making have been consistently integrated into regional development as aids to differing types of tourist planning.[9] The Greater Antilles islands have marketed and alternated among ecological, historical, cultural, health, and recreational tourism. The Lesser Antilles islands have been more dependent on either ecological or recreational tourism, emphasizing coral reefs, tropical rainforests and tropical deserts, or beach resorts and cruise activities. Most islands invest heavily in hotels, personnel training, and infrastructure development. To the extent that tourism enterprises attend to dance development, they include performance as an assumption within tried and successful programming. If there is doubt about this attention, imagine a Caribbean beach or hotel lobby *without* hearing "Yellow Bird" or "De-o," Bob Marley's "No Woman, No Cry," "*Guantanamera*," or "*Ba mwen un ti bo*," or imagine a Caribbean nightclub *without* dancing.

Chart 18. Tourist and Concert Dance Performance

Every type and form in the dance vocabulary of the island nation or entire region.

Globalization and Dance

Here, "global" means interrelated world cultures, and "globalization" involves a constant reconciling of cultural perspectives and economic interests, generally with widespread technological access. Globalization is not simply a political or superpower-centered world market of cultural and economic arrangements or monoculture shared globally; it is a cultural process, the result of mammoth, competing political and economic interests.

Globalization of dance performance most often refers to a wildly popular form or style that spreads across the globe in terms of familiarity and continuous performance, like nineteenth-century *ballet* and twentieth-century *hip-hop*. Dance globalism is a dynamic boost of local and regional to global performance; it can envelop local dance forms and change them in innovative ways. It can also facilitate the rapid spread and easy access to previously unfamiliar local forms.

Globalization in the Caribbean emerges as the processes of dynamic interactions between global economic pressures and local cultural trends. Globalization of Caribbean dance on an external journey assumes participation at an intercontinental level, which generates and/or greatly influences the dance product, dance artists, and heterogeneous audiences. Caribbean dance globalization on an internal journey assumes regional participation and generates local diversity and interisland creativity. Caribbean dance's internal path reveals performance wedged within crucial tourism enterprises.[10]

Classic Dance Globalization

Without much research and development or marketing strategies, U.S. American *hip-hop* was the most recent dance commodity that traveled externally via underground intercultural contagion, classic media, and cyberspace from the Bronx and Harlem in New York City across the globe.[11] It was *hip-hop* dancing or *breaking*, rhythmic DJ-ing (disc jockey-ing), and graffiti that initially triggered global attention.[12] Using the vernacular commentary of oppression—the upsetting lyrics that were not fully understood by older audiences—an underclass as well as an upper class of youths critiqued the status quo. The verbal attack was through rap lyrics; the nonverbal assault was through slick, ferocious dancing accompanied by incredible "scratching" DJ beats.

From the beginning, Caribbean influences shaped *hip-hop*. Latin American musical styles, Caribbean rhythms, and African Diaspora dance forms gained new elements from U.S. Puerto Rican and African American enclaves. Technology spread the dance across the states to the Caribbean, throughout North America, Europe, and eventually to Central and South America, Africa, South and East Asia, Australia, and the Pacific Islands. An evolved genre had emerged from U.S. *barrios* and ghettos that was in tandem with its related predecessors, especially Trinidadian *calypso* and Cuban *rumba*.

Technology fueled an artistic and social rebellion against corporate recording and international distributors. Young, entrepreneurial creators hoisted the artistic banner of a new model. Underground methods produced the speedy, independent, and gargantuan spread of artistic expression; unpolished artistic ensembles, minimal instrumentation, few written contracts, and "trunk-of-car-distribution" cut through corporate business models and augmented income incredibly—and in surprising locales. New business paradigms eventually provided a music distribution that was interdependent on dancing bodies, displaced and dispossessed youth, and contested space—first on flattened cardboard in urban streets, then on stage, and now in all the communication modes of stardom and celebrity. All dance elements exploded with tremendous influence on both native and nonnative audiences from Denmark and Germany to Japan, Hawaii, and England, as well as throughout the Caribbean and the Diaspora U.S.[13]

Caribbean Global Dances

As previous chapters have established, Caribbean dance creations have maintained public fascination and music industry attention for decades, particularly after waning interest in European classical music, U.S. jazz, and pop music. Dancers especially have been absorbed in Caribbean, Latin American, and African rhythms—called "world music" or "world beat."[14] Like hip-hop, other Caribbean dances have transcended all political and economic borders and tower over other dances across the globe. Merengue and salsa were among the very first dances to exhibit cultural globalization as part of every-night dancing.[15]

Merengue is the older dance and uses straight-back couple positioning and alternation of simple steps (RLRL). It became a comfortable alternate to *salsa* intricacies, with its natural alternating hip isolations beneath a relaxed and flexible upper body and above a relaxed knee and organic walking pattern. *Salsa* permeated the Americas and Europe in the 1970s, but more accurately, it represented the twentieth-century evolution of the 1830–60s Cuban *son*. In the hands of modern Puerto Rican and African American musicians and in the artistic hub of the world, New York City, traditional *son*-based rhythms, augmented with more and different instrumentation, energized the bodies of Caribbean, African American, Latin American, Italian, Jewish, and all sorts of peoples across the length of the Americas.

Previously in the 1950s inside New York's Palladium (a huge uptown dance hall), the *mambo* version of *son* had broken all records in terms of disrupting the prescribed class and "racial" boundaries that were in place within a segregated United States. It was the contagiousness of *son/mambo/ salsa*-related dancing, called Latin dance music also, that caused Puerto Ricans and Cubans to follow their musicians and dance wherever they were playing across New York's popular dance spots. That dancing and music also caused African Americans to frequent New York dance halls en masse and, consequently, caused promoters to shift the segregationist practices of the era so as to permit entry of all dance enthusiasts. Certain nights of the week were assigned to specific ethnic groups to minimize "racial" clashes and maximize financial profits.[16]

Mambo featured body-part isolations—hip shifts, elbow rotations, and shoulder shudders—and the *contratiempo* movements accentuated a repeated foot pattern for couples dancing in clasped-couple position or dancing together but apart. *Mambo* was lifted off the red wax or vinyl 78 RPM records of the 1950s that signified "Latin" music and was given a new name in the 1970s—"*salsa*," which represented a tasty sauce and the cultural mix of Latin origins. It became "world music" through its connection with African musics, and thereafter it enveloped the globe.

Salsa is symbolic of great dancing and great dance music, exemplifying the creative mixture of steady and syncopated rhythms. Its steady foundational patterns hold layers of syncopation together and permit both repetitive and innovative body movement. Its syncopation facilitates organic alternation or inversion of foot patterns (long, short, short [RLR], or short, short, long steps [RLR]) with creative torso, head, and arm accents. Contemporary couples execute splits, drops, hand gestures, leg flicks, and triple turns with intricate passes; the movements are full-bodied virtuosity.[17]

Jamaican *reggae* has also achieved world status, affecting Brazil and Cuba with *sambareggae* and *regetón* derivatives, England, and even penetrating Ghanaian borders to replace local *highlife*; it is now global and found in French-speaking Africa, France, Canada, and the English/Creole Caribbean, in addition to New York and Miami and other dance/music distribution centers. Martinican and Guadeloupean *zouk* has also challenged both the Spanish Caribbean world dances and Jamaican *reggae*. In fact, wherever recording technologies have transported Caribbean music and wherever Caribbean immigrant communities have carved out space, there, also, are Caribbean dances going global.

Foundational foot patterns of Caribbean dances are recognized world-wide and often favored over other national dances (such as *tango* or *rock*). Relatively simple in terms of execution, they are joyous dances that have transcended geopolitical borders to become examples of "the regional transformed as global." Their global journeys reveal the inclusive potential within dance. Nonnatives participate fully, demonstrate commitment to a "foreign" but popular dance form (and thereby to another or several other cultures), and share an appreciation of diverse values and forms. Commitment is not with regard to impersonation or an assumption of shared lifestyles (as in many cases of *hip-hop*), but to the dance, to a shared appreciation for cultures that value dancing and music making tremendously in London, Tokyo, Cali, Caracas, or New York.[18] For Caribbean dancers, *salsa* resonates with traditional dances, such as the syncopated Cuban *son* and *mambo* or the lilting Martinican *mazouk* and *biguine*. *Merengue* and *reggae* resonate with the steadied alternation of Trinidadian *chipping,* Cuban *conga* and *comparsa,* Jamaican *winin'* and *dancehall,* and Haitian *konpa*—plus Cuban *rueda de casino* and *timba,* Domínican *bachata,* Domínican *cadence-zouk,* Trinidadian *soca,* and Martinican and Guadeloupean *zouk*. All dances simultaneously complement each other and alternate as Caribbean world favorites.

Trends in Caribbean Dance

How do local Caribbean dances fare within cultural globalization or homogenizing trends, local market structures and tourism? And what or who controls twenty-first-century Caribbean dance production—-technology, the state, organizations of performance artists, or independent dance performers? Before answering these questions, a return to Caribbean history and culture is necessary.

Since Columbus's arrival, the Caribbean has been a mélange, a creole, a hybrid, or a microcosm of intermingling peoples and diverse cultures. Caribbean culture is itself a "constant cultural collision" in which much of the world is represented ethnically and musically; it is fundamentally "global" with African, European, Asian, and American ethnicities and their dances—especially in myriad variations across the islands themselves. Various dances are popular at different times and in disparate islands, but sharing and exchanging dances are routine activities within the region. Accordingly, the dance perspective accepts the fact of multiple cultures transcending borders as normal. It views current economic and cultural trends within Caribbean dance practices as the regular interchange of local and transnational dances.

Shifts over the past few decades from purely commercial to more principled tourism have affected dance on the tourist stage, minimizing exoticism and commercialism and equalizing dance genres. Caribbean dances have been enlisted for increased local benefits and decreased local exploitation. Dances have fared surprisingly well within the homogenizing forces of cultural globalization, and local markets and tourism have been boosted. Control over dance presentation is splintered, however. Sometimes control is found within island governments or with independent performers; control is found less frequently inside artist organizations.

Despite the organization of the Caribbean Alliance for Sustainable Tourism in 1997 and the World Conservation Congress in 2008, with their presumptions of historical and ecotourism, dance performance has routinely permeated Caribbean tourism. Dancing continues to be a requisite element in most Caribbean social spaces and in a packaged tourism experience. Caribbeans rely heavily on historical dances in tourist settings: Haitian *affranchi*, Cuban *tumba francesa*, St. Lucian *quadrille*, Martinican *haut-taille*, Guadeloupean *kadril*, the Dominican Republic's *sarandunga*, etc. Dances provide tourists with visual pleasure, as they also reflect history and present conditions, and educate audiences.

For example, Curaçaoan *kuadria* today points to danced colonial and contemporary identity as it is performed in public squares, near the ports and on restaurant patios where tourists cool in the desert heat with "blue rum" drinks. Similarly, *quadrille* danced to *scratch band* music in St. Thomas points to more than historical elite status; it reminds tourists that power was transferred from the Danish and that St. Thomians are represented in the U.S. Congress. What audiences see in historical dances of Curaçao and St. Thomas are elegance, dignity, and pride, but ultimately they witness regional authority in the hands of Caribbean people.[19] Similarly, *rumba* performances that feature a lower-class "black" dance publicize Cuba's reach toward social equality without explicit capitalism.[20] *Rumba* performance provides lively entertainment and simultaneously encapsulates the shift from postcolonial hierarchy to idealized socialist equality. When Martinican *bele*, Guadeloupean *lewoz*, Puerto Rican *bomba* and *plena*, Haitian and Dominican *merengue*, Trinidadian *calypso*, and other traditional social dances are included within tourist programming, Caribbean dance traditions are conserved, and the demise of local forms is forestalled.

Popular dance is also featured in planned cultural activities, tourist events, and open public dancing where Caribbean dances enthrall literally thousands of participating Caribbeans, as well as tourists. It promotes temporary fun in a worrisome world and encourages the display of diverse Caribbean identities and regional pride, as opposed to the superficial voyeurism, exoticism, and/or latent racism of past tourism programming. Also, Caribbean dances create a cordial ambiance of cultural interchange. That comfort supports political diplomacy and encourages economic negotiations for increased benefits to islanders.

Trends in Sacred Dance

Caribbean tourism enterprises customarily weave sacred dance into staged productions.[21] In response to tourist demands, exciting dance rituals have been condensed and altered for popular consumption.[22] Dancing from Haitian Vodou, Cuban Lukumí/Santería, Trinidadian Shouters, Jamaican Kumina, and other Caribbean religions has been recognized as an attractive magnet within the "must see" experiences of a Caribbean tour. Because tourist and global audiences (as well as school, festival, workshop, and tourist administrators who contract cultural performances) are mesmerized by the dynamics of ritual representations, sacred Caribbean dances are featured prominently (*Vodou dancing* is one example). This has temporarily placed Caribbean dancers and musicians in good economic positions, allowing them to support themselves and promote understanding of Caribbean culture, but also forcing them to contend with negative Caribbean images—especially "the master superstition" or Haitian "Voodoo" stereotype. Similarly, Cuban and Trinidadian dancers and musicians must confront exoticized notions of "wild possessions" and uninformed curiosity about "blood-letting animal rituals" when they bring native sacred performance to nonnative audiences.

The global legacies of Hollywood's movie industry and enduring colonial and postcolonial biases have often discredited the "dancing Caribbean religions." Despite a growing literature of informed documentaries, increases in the practice of Caribbean religions, and the unconventional ideas and activities of the younger generation, the unfortunate effects of perceived inferiority continue. Images of dark-hued, uniquely clothed, dancing male and female bodies feed into long-lasting puritanical notions against the body, against dancing as a viable human expression, and against those darker-skinned humans who delve so intimately within both dancing and the body. Contemporary tourist settings and new technologies have provided the curious, as well as the uninformed, with more than the unflattering and dishonest views of an "exoticized" Caribbean. Mushrooming information advances have engaged a substantially large audience, and although there are inherent problems in weeding out documented from unreliable information, more realistic images rather than unlovely stereotypes are circulating.

The trend of sacred performance within tourism enterprises is positive if and when tourism administrators are committed to principled programming and employ skilled and sensitive choreographers.

Trends in Concert Dance

The artistic thrust of Cuba's *Conjunto Nacional de Danza Contemporánea* and the National Dance Theatre of Jamaica began with a focus on national heritage and specifically brought local dance forms to the concert stage and, later, to global centers. In 1960 and 1962, respectively, Ramiro Guerra in Cuba and Rex Nettleford in Jamaica led dancers in the weaving together of local dance and "foreign" modern dance for Caribbean and global concert audiences.[23] They built on the work of many creative dance artists (Martha Graham, Doris Humphrey, José Limón, Alwin Nicolai, etc.), but certainly on the major Caribbean-influenced, Hollywood-recognized, and world-renowned choreographer Katherine Dunham, who had begun her craft in the 1930s by using local Haitian dance within a budding U.S. modern concert form.[24]

Diaspora artists and their communities have acknowledged Dunham's influence in the oral tradition, which, in the 1940s and 1950s, resulted in even more esteem than the national and international presses had attributed to her. She was received in the African-descended world as an artistic genius, a dance icon who fought consistently and publicly against segregation and racism, which was dangerous in that era of legal segregation. Dunham worked artistically and politically for equality and for peoples of African descent. During her intercontinental tours, she made a point to recruit Caribbean and Afro-Latin artists for her company. Her work was very well known within African-descended communities and was thereby a ready and automatic resource for Caribbean and even African concert dance development.[25]

Additionally, blending dance traditions is not difficult for Caribbean dancers, since they have a history of speaking both verbally and nonverbally in an array of languages and dance vocabularies. These include local dance vocabularies and other "foreign" dance languages that relate to former colonial connections, like Congo/Angola *soukouss,* Ghanaian *highlife,* Indian and Pakistani *film dancing,* or Javanese ritual dance. For example, many Trinidadian dance artists have facility in East Indian classical dance repertoires; just as Puerto Rican dancers use Spain's *zapateado* and *flamenco* dance, Cubans incorporate Yoruba dance traditions, and Surinamers allude to Javanese dance traditions within artistic productions.

Caribbean concert performers combine not only local dance, related foreign dance, modern dance, and ballet (the dominant languages of dance training), but also African Diaspora dance. They apply Diaspora dance to their work because of extensive connections to Caribbean enclaves in the Diaspora. With the fusion of complex combinations from the Caribbean, the Diaspora, and contemporary dance, including also deaf signing gestures and aerial movement, a dense Caribbean dance vocabulary resonates on the concert stage with many global overtones. Circum-Caribbean dancers are redefining island and regional dance mélanges.[26]

Concert dance is closely related to tourist performance; tourism directors and choreographers routinely condense several dance types for concert-like presentation on the tourist stage.[27] As a result, tourist audiences, like global concert audiences, have become increasingly conversant in diverse dance traditions and cultural understandings. Local Caribbean audiences view both concert fusions and tourist intermixtures as visual and visceral understandings of duple, triple, or quadruple dance types; very much like their daily encounters with automatic duple and triple translations (in English, French, Spanish, Dutch, Papiamento, Kreyol, Patois, Hindu, Chinese, Amerindian, Djuka, Saramaka, etc.). Most important is the model that concert forms provide. In large measure, concert presentations predict trends in tourist form, where choreographers condense social, sacred, concert, and popular dance types into short but impressive tourist repertory.

Trends in Popular Dance

Popular dance music groups (like *Los VanVan, NG La Banda,* or *La Charanga Habanera* in Cuba; *Gran Combo, Sonora Ponceña, Roberto Rohena and the Apollo Sound* in Puerto Rico; *Malavoi* of Martinique or *Mahogony* and *Kassav* of Guadeloupe) initiate dancing, congeniality, and creativity. When bands perform with or show the influence of traditional or historical popular dance (like *Los Muñequitos* and *Afro-Cuba* in Cuba; the *Ayala* and *Cepeda* families in Puerto Rico; *Nereyda* and *Senia Rodriguez* in the Dominican Republic; or *Wapa* in Martinique, etc.), they encourage dance movement interchange. When they incorporate fresh elements from *timba* or "spoken word," *rap,* internet, and other contemporary technologies, social dance grows. Intra-Caribbean dance mixtures are combinations that are distinct from concert fusions because they involve Caribbean/Diaspora meshing primarily and do not include modern concert dance or ballet vocabularies.

Creative mélanges occur in popular dance spaces as a result of joint interisland performance, shared histories, conscious collaboration, in addition to individual artistic influences and danced sociopolitico-economic conditions. What sometimes results from Caribbean genres in proximity is not simply a one-island creation that has emerged through creolization or hybridization, but reshaped, intra-Caribbean mixtures. These also evolve as a result of migration, intermarriage, and Pan-Caribbean dance music dialogue. Both historical and contemporary popular dancers have congregated in public patio spaces and community or tourist establishments in the ongoing creation of popular dance.

Intricate mixtures are danced as both couple-embrace and individual rapture, and they signal the joy of dance music and the pleasure of dancing. They have grown as island favorites of the young and have influenced immigrant Caribbean and non-Caribbean communities in the dance capitals of the world. Perhaps most important for global trends, Caribbean popular dance (French Caribbean *konpa* and *zouk,* English Caribbean *reggae* and *dancehall,* and Spanish Caribbean *merengue* and *salsa* especially) has resonated comfortably with international dancers. Dancers from heterogeneous backgrounds across the globe easily execute dance patterns and comfortably innovate bodily. The dances involve contagious sensations, which for natives and tourists alike generate fun-filled, engaging performance.

Yet, Caribbean popular dances often contain powerful political statements and reveal the hazards of body politics. Dancers reference their circumstances in lower- and working-class neighborhoods, their confrontation with unequal segments of island populations, and their opposition to privileged audiences in global centers and among texters, bloggers, and twitterers. Their movements are fierce, determined, and aggressive—upsetting and irritating for some, and wrenchingly honest for others. Anthropologist Umi Vaughan describes Cuban *timba,* for example, where "black" Caribbeans are at the center of public dance spaces, leading an untamed, raw, and hence "maroon" dance delirium. He states: "[I]n the public dance, the social order is inverted; those normally in power at the center are now marginalized on the periphery."[28]

In the controlled situation of tourist settings, Caribbean popular dances can also sear the excitement of performance to economic needs and political awareness within the dancing public. Dancing connects native performers to newfound foreign friends and provides both individual access to economic improvements and national access to potential tourist returnees and economic growth. Whether the native folkloric dance of a particular island or the beloved mixtures of Caribbean cultures, popular dance makes a memorable interlude or finale and can facilitate congenial attitudes and atmospheres. While arguments and fighting also occur within public dance settings, these are a consequence of socioeconomic conditions as well as of *macho* norms and behaviors. Consequently, trends in Caribbean popular dance reflect not only an exciting and unpredictable dance scene, but also a generalized anxiety surrounding the desperate politico-economic circumstances of the region and individual fears and pretenses within a precarious social environment.[29]

Globalization and Caribbean Dance Artists

Given the cultural centrality of dance performance in the Caribbean and the strategic centrality of dance in the tourist trade, Caribbean dancers should be well supported financially. This is only somewhat true for Cuba, but the vast majority of Caribbean dance artists and choreographers are saddled with severe economic hardships. In fact, many of the first generation of Caribbean superstar dancers (e.g., Katherine Dunham, Ivy Baxter, Beryl McBurnie, Pearl Primus, Lavinia Williams, Percival Borde, etc.) died in less than comfortable economic circumstances, despite international acclaim, regional adulation, or individual success.

Most contemporary Caribbean dancers need other (usually quite different) jobs that can support their artistic endeavors. Many compete for a position in their island's one national dance company or among two or three regional companies; and only the courageous few take on the demands of artistic directors with their own dance companies. Those who are involved in the tourism industry have fairly reliable support. When "the boats are in," there is abundant work; in tourist "off season," there is relatively little paid performance except in national companies and to some extent in schools, universities, or private studio teaching. In particular, solo artists live a grueling existence in pursuit of a dance career.

From time to time, Caribbean dancers have banded together in cooperative, intra-island support. For example, several years ago the Caribbean Arts Initiative (CAI) tried to unite dance artists Gabri Christa from Curaçao and Suriname, working in Puerto Rico and New York; Reggie Wilson from the United States and Trinidad, working in Zimbabwe and New York; and Nadine Moses and Rhetta Aleong from Trinidad, working in New York, for performance collaboration and joint productions. The organization fizzled due to the demands of earning a living, transnational opportunities away from the collective's New York center, and the resulting inconsistent support. Other groups in Trinidad, Martinique, and Aruba have surfaced and "drowned." As Christa states, " [F]olks do get frustrated and leave (or die)."[30]

Those who stay, perform, and teach manage sometimes in ballet; a notable example is Alicia Alonso, the wealthy ballet superstar, national hero, and dance elder of Cuba. More often, they struggle and thrive like Marlene Li Aling, a nationally acclaimed ballet dancer and teacher in Suriname. Most dancers work in the varied dance genres of their home islands—for example, Jacqueline Casimir and Jaqui Jaleme in Guadeloupe or Sonia Marc and Josy Michalon in Martinique. Many (Awilda Sterling-Duprey in Puerto Rico, Jean-Gui of Haiti, Josiane Antourel of Martinique and Canada, Sonja Dumas in Trinidad, Léna Blou in Guadeloupe, and Lucien Peter from Guadeloupe, French Guiana, and Martinique) fuse their specialties in Caribbean dance with modern concert technique and reveal top-notch artistry, but also the hierarchy and global dominance of ballet and modern concert dance over other stylistic forms. The struggles of Caribbean dance artists reveal the economic advantages of dominant dance practices and the resulting access to employment on the concert stage, in education, or in tourist settings.

University dance departments have yet to reflect the amount or range of twenty-first-century dance, or to develop sufficient rapport with global-dance-form dancers. What is sorely needed is a more democratic dance structure within academic settings that supports a core study of equally valued dance techniques, theoretical dance culture courses, and full-time faculty in both dance and music (for example, a dance teacher and a musician for representative dance forms). With a more representative structure of global dances in place, thousands of eager dance students could learn to dance eloquently and persuasively in twenty-first-century terms.

Surprisingly, in August 2007, a three-week conference sponsored by France convened in Haiti (and not on Martinique, Guadeloupe, or French Guiana, the legally connected island departments of France). The conference featured a dance component that sought sustainable Caribbean dance expression. Trinidadian dancer Sonja Dumas wrote during attendance: "One of the main objectives is to harness contemporary dance expression in the Caribbean and getting practitioners in the region to talk about the process and product. There is going to be a biennale in Cuba next year. . . . It is a three-year project initially, hopefully with developmental offshoots for dance in the region."[31]

The conference and especially contemporary fusions suggest that Caribbean dance artists are creating unique dance movement and challenging historical dance hierarchies; in the process, they are also acquainting global audiences with local Caribbean dance. For example, Trinidadian wedding and funeral customs appear in "For Better or Worse" and "Tribute to a King," by Astor Johnson; dancing from the Winti religion in Suriname is referenced in "Yeye," by Gabri Christa; old and new versions of *la bomba puertoriqueña* are abstracted in "*Oyo-oyo, Variaciones en Un Tema Africano,*" by Awilda Sterling-Duprey; and annual street dances that develop spontaneously in Bahia's *Carnaval* are performed within "Street Façade," by

Augusto Soledade. Through the fluidity of "dance languages" that Diaspora dance artists use in concert as well as in tourist performance, previously unfamiliar local dances are given a public platform on the global stage.

Additionally, Caribbean dance artists are adept in technological aids to choreography: they often combine movement with technology, such as backdrop and interactive film within choreography; they can execute simultaneous productions in two or three technologically connected and interactive sites across the world; and they commonly film their ephemeral art for computerized reproduction and extensive distribution. Caribbean dance artists willingly and proudly cooperate with island governments and regional associations (e.g., CARIFESTA) in the promotion of traditional and concert forms and also in the conservation of local genres.

Local and Global Tensions

The intensity of politico-economic pressure in the Caribbean is not so different from the overwhelming struggles against colonialism and imperialism of previous eras. Both large and small Caribbean islands participate in powerful global markets as small, industrially developing nations, hoping for economic benefits while trying to keep their own cultures intact. Analysis of Caribbean dance and tourism points to an equilibrium between the global and local tensions brought on by globalization. Privileged first-world-centered culture, in which hierarchy and dominance still reign, fades somewhat in tourism enterprises, and equality among differing local forms increases. As more democratic practices are consciously and routinely applied to Caribbean tourism, dance artists will be able to participate more fully and strategically in tourism, the lifeblood activity of the Caribbean. With a strong local situation, more benefits will flow to islanders rather than only to foreign investors. With a weak local situation, tremendous damage takes place, as can be seen in a brief note on the Haitian case.

As a result of persistent insecurities—especially since the 1990s, Haitian tourism has dropped sharply. With recent decades of political turmoil, increased emigration—and now utter havoc due to the devastating earthquake—tourism to Haiti has been severely reduced, and Haitian dance has been curtailed dramatically. In fact, the picture of dance performance in Haiti at the start of the second decade of the twenty-first century is blurred. What is seen clearly is grim—with basic infrastructure problems, lingering curfews that inhibit evening performances, a struggling and unreliable tourist operation, unsafe travel conditions within the capital and the countryside, and depleted finances for lighting, costumes, to say nothing of the paucity of available dance spaces. Although Haitian cultural centers were beginning to develop and regional dance employment was percolating before the 2010 earthquake, many dancers have had to emigrate.

Politicized Suggestions

How Caribbean and other Diaspora dance artists are treated in light of their struggle to keep dancing and teaching African-derived practices brings the issue of democratic processes to the fore. How dance performance is acknowledged among other relevant twenty-first-century perspectives and disciplines brings into stark review the tyranny of the powerful and the economically advantaged. Reflection on these two issues has pointed to a few reconsiderations.

In the line of Harvard law professor Lani Guinier's critique of "the tyrannical majority," my comments aim for the yearnings of Caribbean islands to bolster tourism enterprises as their lifelines to economic security. Accordingly, a direct focus is on the implementation of fair representation and more democratic processes within tourism enterprises. Professor Guinier guides my conclusions with her reminder about democratic principles as they apply to minority rights. She warns the political majority of its tendencies toward tyranny in pursuit of democracy, while she provides strategies for the minority to guard and exercise its rights: "In an ideal democracy, the people would rule, but the minorities would also be protected against the power of majorities . . . the majority cooperates with, or at least does not tyrannize, the minority . . . [and] those in the majority do not lose; they simply learn to take turns."[32]

I now apply her legal position to dance in the Caribbean, where Caribbean islands are global minorities with little power but with rights to fair representation on the economic as well as the cultural stage. I urge economic and political powers within the region to attend consciously to dance practices and attend conscientiously to dance artists. Like the political minority, Caribbean dance deserves its turn and Caribbean dancers have rights to an improved state of Caribbean dance.

Confronting the Tyrannies of Globalization

The recent actions of France (described above) demonstrate some of the activities that a twenty-first-century perspective entails when confronting pressures from cultural and economic globalization and avoiding weak politico-economic situations as exist in present-day Haiti. The French, as part of the global majority, supported Haiti as an impoverished minority rather than—or, more exactly, in addition to—Martinique and Guadeloupe, its own department islands. France's economic support of a Pan-Caribbean conference provided sorely needed economic assistance and a measure of stability for secured tourism in the Caribbean—even more so for Haiti. All islands could have benefited from a three-week conference in terms of tourism profits, but to have one in Haiti at that particular time was an example of the huge sacrifices that are sometimes involved in proper cultural behavior and thoughtful economic action within a democratic process. France's behavior in this instance exemplifies a twenty-first-century democratic practice by looking at apparent local, national, and regional needs and then giving the most needy economic support through cultural representation and economic advantage. In this manner, Haiti had fair representation and its economic turn.

Even if Caribbean artists, island governments, or the entire region have not "won first place" as Guinier would say—that is, have not made overwhelming contributions to global trade arrangements—global powers must learn to look for opportunities, as France did, that support and satisfy all participants, not just majority "first place winners." Like Haiti, all Caribbean nations are in the game of economics and deserve their turn within mammoth globalization processes. Further, the summoning of a conference on the arts also showcases the need for twenty-first-century attention to human and artistic resources in addition to agricultural, industrial, technological, ecological, and military resources. This noteworthy cultural gesture and its accompanying economic action are emblematic of a twenty-first-century perspective in which majority entities (the sciences, economics, visual art, and even music) learn to give fair representation to minority entities (such as dance). In that conference, France and other Caribbean governments pointedly staked out a turn for dance.

A twenty-first-century democratic perspective involves shifting centers, assessing global and local views, and consciously alternating support and advantage. In the Caribbean case, a twenty-first-century democratic perspective permits every island to have its concerns at the center and encourages transcendence over past conflicts in order for each nation to have an economic turn or advantage from time to time. This principle is asserted by Caricom (the English/Creole islands, Jamaica, Barbados, Belize, Suriname and Haiti) in its efforts toward collaboration on a single vision for Caribbean economic development. It is also shared by the Association of Caribbean States (including Cuba and all sovereign islands, Colombia, Venezuela, Guatemala, Nicaragua, Belize, Honduras, Mexico, Costa Rico, El

Salvador, Panama, with France for Martinique and Guadeloupe, and the former Netherlands Antilles,[33] and the British Turks and Caicos as associate members), which collaborates for better cooperation and sustainable development in the region. The region "healthily" profits when these general economic guidelines are followed; however, tourism enterprises need to expand cooperative efforts in the Caribbean and unleash dance activity from its wedged position in the tourist setting. Caribbean distinctions in dance performance should be promoted, especially in light of the global successes of Caribbean favorites, and Caribbean dance artists are the specialists who know how to build and use the transcendence of dance performance; they should be involved in tourism planning.

Support of dance performance by the Jamaican and Cuban governments, long-term governmental support of village festivals in Jamaica, and Trinidad and Tobago, widespread governmental support of regional *carnavales* in the Dominican Republic, added to the recent French government's investment in Pan-Caribbean dance artists and dance development, all confirm a serious but only intermittent interest in Caribbean dance development. That interest is argued here as economically based efforts to nurture the precarious situation of Caribbean islands with their dependency on global tourism. Without the economic base of tourism, continued development of Caribbean dance and the well-being of island cultures are tenuous. Without dance (and music) performance, Caribbean tourism is only remotely possible. What matters most are active and sustainable tourism enterprises if dance forms, artists, and islands are to thrive. Therefore, dance artists deserve acknowledgment for their part in successful enterprises thus far and also deserve a voice within strategic regional planning.

The case of Haitian dance serves to alert tourism enterprises to the devastating consequences of a weak local context within the global market. Cuban dance demonstrates what is possible with concerted, although limited, economic support for dancers and musicians in local tourism. The more common case throughout the Caribbean demonstrates the pivotal but unheralded positions of dance and dance artists within economic strategies that propose to increase global trade and tourism opportunities for the region. Most island governments rely tenaciously on the ongoing display of Caribbean dance and, thereby, on dance and music artists within tourism enterprises. Performances foster amicable social relations and generally facilitate local economic exchange; however, tourism administrators seldom review their use of Caribbean dance consciously and rarely involve the dance artists who have guarded it with fierce persistence. Professional Caribbean dancers, choreographers, artistic ensembles, and community dance leaders deserve their turns as reliable actors within the primary currency-gathering activity of the region.

Caribbean dance artists, musicians, and production specialists have been performing in local Caribbean tourist enterprises as well as in U.S., European, and Canadian centers in efforts to maintain a living and to grow their companies and their arts. For example, Haitians such as Jean-Leon Destiné, Louinés Louinis, Frisner Augustin, and younger dancer/choreographers such as Nadia Dieudonné, Colette Eloi, Perniel Guerrier, Julio Jean, Michelle Martin, and Mikerline Pierre, as well as drummer Damas Fanfan Louis, singer Erol Josue, and others have worked internationally and domestically simultaneously; some have done so for decades. The situation is "shaky" at best, not only for dance and dancers, but also for tourism and, therefore, for the entire region. The promise of principled tourism is one hope for dance performance, dance artists, and tourism growth in the Caribbean; what revolutionary dance artists and popular dance performers do independently is another.

Igniting Diaspora Citizenship

As previous chapters have indicated, there is an enormous amount of information within Caribbean and Atlantic Diaspora dance—beyond the physical articulation and expression of the body. These dances share with many other dance practices the splendor of the human body moving in space and time and creating aesthetic awe, but Diaspora dance also contains the major concerns of Diaspora dancers. This volume's review of dance genres across six Caribbean and Atlantic linguistic areas has ultimately revealed core corporeal, cultural, and sociological meanings of African Diaspora dance—namely, transcendence, resilience, and citizenship. Please note, however, that the focus has been on historical, national, popular, *Carnival*, sacred, and combat genres and not simply concert genres; in other words, dance "practices" in addition to "performances" have strong properties and piercing issues that communicate to dancers while dancing and to witnessing and participating others. Not only artistic, concert, or theatrical performances have this capacity, but so-called folkloric, traditional, and vernacular dances have these propensities also. The very aesthetic center of dance itself, as well as of Diaspora dance, has been the concern of this volume.

Transcendent Performance

Diaspora dance is uniquely contagious and well recognized for its transcendent tendencies. Its several genres have spread first across Caribbean locales and then, by means of migration, transnational connections, and communication technologies, to Caribbean niches in New York, Montreal, London, Paris, Dakar, Cali, Caracas, Rio de Janeiro, Montevideo, and other locales. Its contagion is initiated within the dancing body through the pure pleasure of Afro-Caribbean–based rhythms or through marketing of specific dances, televised performances, and the likes of YouTube entries, which bring particular dance genres and styles to distant sites as well. Still, translocal and transnational Diaspora dances become "world dance" performance when they travel beyond their niche communities to more distant cultures in Lagos, Kinshasa, Tokyo, Helsinki, Melbourne, etc. What else are Diaspora dances but contagious phenomena!

As Diaspora dance travels in translocal and transnational performances, transcendent experiences are shared. Among the varied genres that have been examined throughout this book, transcendence has been the repeated objective, effect, and meaning at the movement level of analysis. So many of the dances encourage performers to become totally at one with the movement such that the corporeal becomes the ecstatic, so that the ancestral world joins the present and transformational states of being preside, or so that dancers reach heightened levels of excitation where aesthetic response overflows. As Caribbean and other Diaspora dancers reach for the extraordinary, the overwhelming sensation of awe attains and their bodies (and those of some would-be "viewers") experience transcendence—even for a few moments. Performers and observers feel glimpses of the human/spirit connection and are inevitably affected; they are consequently transported to a realm of extreme fascination, engagement, and rapture. In that realm, everyday workers and community members transcend their routine roles to become "performers"; then dancing performers transcend to become creative artists, committed dance scene participants, or believing worshipers; interested observers become enthralled participants; the dance becomes music as the music becomes dance; and a dance community comes into being. Repeated transcendent experiences over time give the dancing community form and solidarity, and dancing itself encourages a virtual journey that makes the ephemeral moments of the dance usual, normal, the ideal.

Resilience

The resilience that has surfaced with transcendence throughout this volume is the underpinning cultural meaning of Diaspora dance. Despite the ease with which Diaspora dances transcend geographical borders, local Caribbean and Atlantic dances remain—a great many, for centuries. Local dances are practiced, revived when necessary, enjoyed in their own right, or employed as fertile contribution to intra-Caribbean and inter-Diaspora creations. While Caribbean dances, especially, are fundamentally "global," (because of both diverse foundational elements and worldwide popularity), they still retain island distinctions (for example, diverse *quadrilles*) and advertise many local dance genres and styles (Carnival, combat, sacred, and social dances, to name a few). They are also admired and practiced over time as intra-island, Pan-Caribbean, and Afro-Latin popular dances (*merengue, salsa, reggae, konpa, dancehall, zouk, timba*). Thus, the widespread repetition of one particular dance, such as *merengue* or *dancehall*, has not yielded mono-dance culture, nor is there much erasure of local dances.

Diaspora dance genres have longevity, and their undercurrent determinant derives from their resilience—in other words, the ability to bounce back from change, resume shape, and energetically proceed. The transcendent propensity of Diaspora dances inculcates profound and determined resilience in their performers, and dance community members are not passively resilient. They actively celebrate what is and who is with them in the dancing, and in so doing, they identify what is *not* there and who is *not* with them. Their cultural stronghold over would-be feelings of disillusionment, depression, or defeat has historically been a deep resilience that accepts and simultaneously persists and embraces agency.

Contemporary Diaspora dance practices welcome and include the materials of every dance genre, as they also rely heavily on exclusive dance development in Circum-Caribbean sites. There is clear and energizing growth within separate community-developed dance genres, and there is confident sharing when differing dance communities gather together without aesthetic boundaries. These occurrences have resulted such that the former "have-not" dancers of vernacular movement have carved out a position at the center of public dancing and also on the concert and tourist stages. The former "have nots" have almost convinced their young peers, who are part of twenty-first-century "haves" culture and who dance dominant styles and forms or more "traditionally-accepted" movement, to join them in the most potentially creative, sustaining, and rewarding dance movement possible. All dancers have become empowered by the pull toward a center where inter-Diaspora dance practice reigns, where it is seducing the political will of older, and yet still powerful, dance gatekeepers toward genuine dance (and human) equality.

The study of Caribbean and Atlantic Diaspora dance genres shows that they are resilient forms and their active steadfastness is increasingly blurring, erasing, and ambushing the structural borders and contextual boundaries of previously dominant dance practices. Both Diaspora dance and Diaspora dancers progress onward in response to change, springing back or reaching forward with formidable strength. Recovering spirit and energy in a quick but cool fashion, they manage all challenges.

Perceived Citizenship

Beyond both core physical and cultural meanings (transcendence and resilience), the social meaning of Diaspora dance continuously invokes citizenship amidst recreational or theatrical display. As sociologist Ángel Quintero-Rivera has independently posited for dance music in the Americas, and as cultural theorist Lucía Suarez has also previously concluded for one of the functions of Brazilian dance in urban modernity, citizenship is hard to separate out from culminating analyses of Caribbean and Atlantic dance.[1]

In this study, historical drum/dances, *quadrilles*, and *contredanses* have signaled entertainment and diversion—but also agency. Performers remembered and elaborated drum/dances and, in acts of contestation, refashioned African dance heritage; they repeated colonial set dances that camouflaged their opposition to how they were being treated and yet affirmed their sovereignty when leadership changed. The language of power relations was danced in the heyday and beyond of drum/dances or *quadrilles*, and performances continuously stated nonverbally that performers were free in a humane sense, recognizably confident and deserving of citizenship.

Likewise, the study of national dances has signaled social diversion, but also select membership has surfaced. Working-class Caribbean and Afro-Latin performers displayed local solidarity as they also searched for the tight bonds of community that elite and bourgeois classes proclaimed within revered national dance choices.

Popular dance has usually been the essence of social diversion, and Diaspora performers have routinely performed individual and group joy/pleasure/fun. Within their displays, however, a challenge to the status quo has been included. Today, timba couples, winin' Kings and Queens, and other popular dancers highlight body freedom with incredulous moves and "overkill or overboard" personas as they dance both their pleasures and their insecurities confidently, claiming defiant individual and brazen community identities. Their performances reveal indignities over their eligibility for broader citizenship and genuine representation.

Carnaval and parading dances have also signaled not-so-subtle political demands in the midst of theatrics and entertainment displays. Revelers mask religious rituals and social concerns behind outrageous, sexually oriented insults; they critique the powers that be with overt obscenities. Insistent demands for unfettered acceptance lurk in the background of carnivalesque spotlights—a desire for equal social recognition.

Sacred Diaspora dance generates bonds of acceptance; it provides spiritual well-being, ritualized protection, and worldly and spiritual integration. It creates and encourages a reliable but separate community through daily and periodic deepening into the dance practices that support its faith. This contained community remains strong, but a wider citizenship also evades its performers.

Combat dance creates recreational games and defensive play that provide a built-in defense for individuals and a solidified community. While dancing, Diaspora warriors are guaranteed membership in a special ritual community, but they display their larger sense of citizenship—again, not actualized, as they stand ready to protect kinsmen and neighbors.

Within each genre of Diaspora dance, there are slices of differing dimensions of life: social and recreational first, but also religious or ideological, historical, economic, and political, and the political dimension is usually packed. Each Diaspora genre shows concerns about authority and power; each dance type has "housed" a need to fight, struggle, and unveil what is missing. Most reveal a persistent, embodied challenge to domination and tyranny. Each genre displays and satisfies a desire for community but also contains the social need to belong with others on equal standing. Each dance practice attempts to seal the bonds of community membership and stimulate active citizenship, albeit in a community of participating dancers and musicians.

While dancing cannot confer legal citizenship, it does ignite feelings surrounding commitment to the group, bonds of solidarity, and communal connections within the dancing community. When genuine political actors attach specific goals to the sense of citizenship that accrues within Diaspora dance practices, the possibility of legal citizenship is great. Viable political action can then confer the citizenship that is inferred within Diaspora dance practices.

Caribbean and Atlantic Diaspora performers dance freedom, creativity, and spontaneity regularly, but also—routinely—contestation and opposition, because their freedom has rarely been guaranteed. They have usually been thwarted at the level of social citizenship. As the enslaved on plantations, as free workers in segregated nation states, and as official citizens living with prejudice and unofficial restrictions on civil and other rights, their circumstances have rarely satisfied their yearnings for genuine equality. Through dance, they have regularly challenged those in power to relax, share, and spread the well-being of the dance, and in return they have presumed reciprocity, a mutual exchange of well-being for a sense of citizenship. In the moments of the dance, feelings of belonging are generated and solidarity is affirmed, even if temporarily; in the moments of the dance, feelings of fierce self-worth, strength, and rebellion are also activated.

Personal Conclusions

This book is the result of my investigations on varied Diaspora, but especially Caribbean, dance forms; however, this is primarily a tribute to Katherine Dunham. The book forms a contextual foundation for students of Caribbean and Afro-Latin dance and, simultaneously, is my dialogue with Diaspora scholars about both shallow and abundant findings; however, it is fundamentally a reexamination and summary of what has been learned since Dunham's groundbreaking trilogy on Caribbean dance forms.

It was Katherine Dunham who started teaching the dance form of citizenship in her studios and in the public at large, and a great many Diaspora dancers have followed in her footsteps. Dunham insisted on individual rights and group integrity; her classes exuded personal development for a larger purpose than the immediate dance. Her company welcomed Diaspora others within the segregated rules of her era, and her celebrity provided a soapbox for civil and human rights. The world press publicized her relentless political commitment.[2]

It was Dunham also who first envisioned a dance focus that could yield sociological meaning beyond the content of either physical or artistic performance. It was she who first fathomed Diaspora dance both experientially and analytically, she who inspired and influenced thousands of dancers, researchers, Caribbeanists and Diaspora scholars, and she, in her living room at l'habitation LeClerc in Haiti 1970 and 1974, who showed me the path of dance anthropology.

In May 2006, immediately after hearing that my second book, *Dancing Wisdom*, had won an award, I made a telephone call to Ms. Dunham in New York from St. Thomas where I was completing field research. I was told she was asleep, but that my message would be relayed later. I hope she knew, before she died that day, that her work had been extended yet once again. It is to her that I and many others have dedicated our professional efforts. Because of her, the dances that she loved and their related forms across the Circum-Caribbean culture sphere have been analyzed in this volume. What I have presented here is on her shoulders, yet at her feet.

In sum, Diaspora dances connote diversion and recreation; however, the dance practices of Caribbeans and Afro-Latins have also projected convictions about the power of dance, convictions that survival depended on guarding and re-presenting the dances of the ancestors, and convictions that, through dance practice and innovation, dancers gained individual self-worth, group solidarity, and spiritual protection. Diaspora dancers have challenged the dominance and tyranny that they have experienced through the subterfuge of their dancing bodies, and they are convinced that the transcendence they experience within the elaboration of parading, historical, national, combat, sacred, folkloric, popular, or concert dance was and is a vehicle for creative and contagious well-being. (The resilience of my Diaspora people has been inspirational.) Again, Caribbean and Afro-Latin dancers do not just believe this, they are convinced of such potential within dance practices, and their dancing lifestyles prove it.

May Diaspora dance continue to teach and reveal the corporeal and cognitive lessons of transcendence, continue to finesse the world's inequalities with determined resilience, and continue to inject the delight and strength of human citizenship into dancing bodies for centuries to come.

NOTES

PREFACE

1. For varied geographical, anthropological, and historical views of the Circum-Caribbean region and its characteristics, see Michael Horowitz (*Peoples and Cultures of the Caribbean*), Sidney Mintz and Richard Price (*An Anthropological Approach to the Afro-American Past: A Caribbean Perspective*); Sidney Mintz and Sally Price et al. in *Caribbean Contours*; Franklin Knight and Colin Palmer (*The Modern Caribbean*); Alan Karras and J. R. McNeill (*Atlantic American Societies: From Columbus through Abolition 1492–1888*); and Percy Hintzen, "Cultural Politics of Development—Nationalism and the Invention of Development: Modernity and the Cultural Politics of Resistance." In these references, the terms "Circum-Caribbean," "Caribbean Basin," or "Greater Caribbean" are regarded equally, depending on the purpose and perspective of the study.

2. My application of "Circum-Caribbean" terminology may challenge Latin Americanists whose work has not included the African segment of Latin American culture, or at least, not until recently. The works of historian George Reid Andrews and that of anthropologists Kevin A. Yelvington and Herbert Klein, following the authors in Manuel Moreno-Fraginal's work and those in Ann Pescatello's edited volume have shown important connections but also undisputable erasures or omissions regarding which ethnicities are included in the term "Latin American culture." These views have generally neglected the ongoing culture niches within Latin America that echo Caribbean culture—in other words, the mixture of African and European heritages.

3. Alleyne, "Methodology and Historiography of the Caribbean."

4. Sheila Walker, *African Roots/American Cultures*, 7.

CHAPTER 1. DIASPORA DANCE: COURAGEOUS PERFORMERS

1. Readers should be mindful that even though this book is limited to the African Diaspora in the Americas or the "Atlantic Diaspora," the African Diaspora extended north to Europe, east to Russia, and throughout Asia, as well as west to the Americas.

See Harris, *African Presence*; DeBrunner; B. Lewis; Thornton; Gomez, *Diasporic Africa*; see also ASWAD (Association for the Study of World African Diaspora): www.aswadiaspora.org. From here on, the term "Diaspora" will presume the Atlantic African Diaspora.

2. As in any other region also, representative and contrasting dances draw from a dance vocabulary that is indigenous to the people who come to reside there. Thus, chart 1 indicates only one way to organize Caribbean dance culture. It is fleshed out in subsequent charts, but this particular chart serves as a representative structure for the vast variety of dances that can exist in any society. There may be other Diaspora dances beyond those listed, but I do not anticipate contrasts to the assessments of major types given here.

3. See Guerra, "My Experience."

4. In this section in particular, I have relied on the research of Nia Love; I have revised and augmented our original joint venture in documenting Diaspora dance and its protagonists.

5. This history is told insightfully in Foulkes, 130–56.

6. An exemplary account is in Gottschild, *Waltzing*.

7. See Daniel, "Company."

8. Compare biographical histories of African American dancers in the United States between Long, *Black Tradition*, and Myers, *Genius*.

9. Ethnologist Fernando Ortiz coined "transculturation" as the process in which European and African values and behaviors interrelated over time in Cuba (see Ortiz, *Contrapunteo*). Current dance scholarship has dealt with the meshing and interactions of cultures in a variety of ways: see, for example, Gonzalez, "Caught," 149–56; Scott, "What's it Worth," 2–18; and Thomas, *Modern Blackness*.

10. Rogelio Martinez Furé (founding member and ethnologist of Conjunto folklórico nacional de Cuba) was my first contact with the term "living library" in Cuba 1986; however, Malian historian and diplomat Amadou Hampâté Bâ is cited for the same concept in a speech made in Paris in 1960 (see Walker, *African Roots*, 36–37). Here, my term "experiential librarians" is not aimed at elders but more so at knowledgeable musicians and dancers, which I fully discuss in *Dancing Wisdom*, chapter 2. See also forthcoming reports from Harvard University Symposium on Embodied Knowledge, March 2011.

11. Welsh-Asante, "Commonalities," 71–82.

12. See Ephrim-Donkor; Fisher; MacGaffey, *Religion*.

13. Soledade, "Afro-Fusion"; see Gabri Christa's fusion of dance, theater, and film performance at www.danzaisa.org.

14. See dance critic Jennifer Dunning's review of Nia Love's work in "Sidewalk Cracks"; see also Love, "Deconstructing."

15. See Lamut; Tomko; also, see Desmond.

16. See Mackrell; *Dance Magazine*, "Young Choreographers."

17. This chapter was written in memory of Emmika, a Surinamese dancer who committed suicide in part under the stresses of Diaspora dance practices. For per-

haps more encouraging "black" dancer stories, see remaining chapters here, but also Gottschild, *Black Dancing Body.*

18. In this chapter and the next, I have relied heavily on two previously published encyclopedia entries: *Encyclopedia of Diasporas*, 347–55, and *Encyclopedia of the African Diaspora*, 356–66. I co-authored the latter entry with Nia Love, and I am grateful for her support in presenting our material within this chapter.

CHAPTER 2. DIASPORA DANCE
IN THE HISTORY OF DANCE STUDIES

1. There is also a vast folklore literature that features Zora Hurston in the U.S. and includes dance in Hungarian, German, Italian, and other European and a few Asian languages, like Hindi and Chinese (see Wilifred Bonner, *Bibliography of Folklore*). There is also a large and earlier Asian literature that describes dances and connects dance to religion, history, and ancient cultures in India, China, Korea, Japan, etc. The British and American schools of sociology/anthropology developed a cultural approach in the late nineteenth and early twentieth centuries, and Evans-Pritchard and Mead thrust dance into new theoretical territory and started a formidable dance bibliography in the English language. See Kraut for Hurston's important contributions to Caribbean (*Fire Dance* staging) and Diaspora U.S. (*Polk County* musical) dance history.

2. Evans-Pritchard, 446–52.

3. Mead, 110–21.

4. While Kurath published earlier articles on dance in 1931 and 1932, these did not constitute an interest in dance from a cultural or anthropological perspective. Her first publication from an anthropological perspective was "Los Concheros" in 1946. Katherine Dunham's first publication with an anthropological perspective was on her fieldwork in Jamaica in 1936–37: *Journey to Accompong,* published also in 1946.

5. Herskovits, *Myth of the Negro Past.*

6. I interviewed both Ms. Dunham and Ms. Kurath in extended interviews in January and February 1992 as part of a Ford Foundation fellowship based at the Smithsonian Institution. Taped portions of these interviews are in the film archives of the American History Museum of the Smithsonian.

7. See Kurath, *Dance Research.*

8. For example, see Fenton and Kurath; Martí and Kurath.

9. See Kurath, "Syncopated Therapy," "Rhapsodies of Salvation," and "Jazz Choreology" in Kurath, *Dance Research,* 207–13, 214–18, 372–81.

10. See detailed history in Aschenbrenner and summary history in Clark and Johnson, 3–15.

11. See Clark, 5–8.

12. There is not yet a thorough examination or comprehensive evaluation of the Dunham Technique; however, see slices within: Yarborough; Beckford, 49–52; Rose; compare with Emery, 256–60; Gottschild, *Digging*, 69–70; Long, 100–101.

13. Personal communication with author, July 24, 2010.

14. Personal communication from Ruby Streat, master teacher of Dunham Technique and holder of Dunham Repertory, East St. Louis, July 27, 2010.

15. McDonald, "Jack Cole: Jazz," a film by Annette MacDonald and Timeline Films, Los Angeles.

16. Personal communication via email, July 4, 2010.

17. Personal communication via telephone and email, July 23, 2010.

18. See complete bibliography of Dunham's publications in Clark and Johnson.

19. See video, *"Africa,"* in which Les Ballets Africains presents the history and culture of Guinea in dance on the occasion of the United Nations' anniversary of the adoption of the Human Rights Declaration and the welcome of the Republic of Guinea to the U.N. While Dunham obviously influenced African and Diaspora touring companies like this one, I would not be surprised if she were influential also with other national folkloric companies. After all, she was a prime movie star throughout the 1930s and 1940s, and the U.S. film industry permeated national capitals of Europe, Canada, Mexico, and Latin America. See also Senegal and Dunham in E. Diouf.

20. Compare with Clifford; Harrison; Schechner.

21. Primus, "African Dance" and "Life Crises"; see complete bibliography in Wenig.

22. For example, see Hanna, "African Dance," "Traditional Dance," "'Women's War,'" and "Highlife." See also Williams, "Sokodae" and "Bedu Moon."

23. See Kealiinohomoku, *Theory*; Kaeppler, *Structure*; Williams, *Role*; Hanna, *To Dance*; Royce.

24. See Kealiinohomoku, "Comparative Study"; also see taped 1992 interview with Kealiinohomoku, Allegra Synder, Anya Royce, Elsie Dunin, Judith Hanna, and other pioneering researchers in the American History Museum Film Archives of the Smithsonian.

25. See Nketia, *African Music*, "Interrelations," and *Music of Africa*.

26. See Wilson, "Association" and "Significance."

27. See Blum.

28. See Labat, *Nouveaux* and *Voyage*.

29. See Moreau de Saint-Méry.

30. Ahye, *Golden Heritage, Cradle*; compare with Alladin.

31. See Ortiz, *La africanía* and *Los bailes*.

32. John Turpin and Blanca Martinez were responsible for editing sections from Ortiz's work and sharing translated copies with a few drum apprentices who then shared these on the east and west coasts of the United States (Turpin, personal communication, 1997).

33. See Carbonero, *Bailes*; Carbonero and Lamerán; Carbonero, "Africanness," 62–65.

34. See Cashion.

35. See John; also see Guerra, "My Experience," 49–61.

36. Chasteen, 1–15, 19–21, 71–88.

37. See Daniel, *Rumba*, "Cuban Dance," and *Dancing Wisdom*.

38. See Quintero Rivera, *Salsa*; Flores; and Barton, "Challenges."

39. Pacini, *Bachata*; Austerlitz; Tejeda; Garrido de Boggs, 112–35; Lizardo, *Danzas* and *Metodología*; Davis, *Afro-Dominican* and "Dominican."

40. See Honorat; Yarborough, *Haiti: Dance*; Paul.

41. See Burroughs; Wilckens, *Drums* and "Spirit Unbounded"; Daniel, "Potency" and *Dancing Wisdom*, 105–19.

42. Gerstin, "Interaction," "Musical Revivals," and "Tangled Roots"; Cyrille, "Sa Ki Ta Nou" and "Politics"; Daniel, "Critical Analysis" and "Ethnographic Comparison." See also the works of Monique Desroches.

43. See Nettleford, *Dance Jamaica* and *Roots and Rhythms*.

44. Thomas, "Democratizing Dance" and *Modern Blackness*.

45. Compare Macdonald; David; and McDaniel.

46. See Andrade and Canton; compare with Perrone, Dunn, and Biancardi (includes specific dance data).

47. See Carneiro, *Candomblés* and "Structure."

48. For Rio de Janeiro, see Guillermoprieto; for Bahia, see Browning.

49. Scott, *"Falaque"*; also "Dance."

50. See Almeida; John L. Lewis; de Tavares, "Dança."

51. de Tavares, "Atitude."

52. See Walker, "Choreography."

53. See Andrews; Olivera Chirimini; Daniel, "Dancing Down River"; for Chile, see Salgado Henríquez, Marta.

54. See García; Rodriguez.

55. See Gonzalez, *Jarocho's Soul*.

56. See Greene.

57. Aguirre Beltrán, 222, 231; Waxer, *Situating Saba*; see also Satizábal.

58. See Chasteen; Garcia; Rodriguez. For Dutch Caribbean examples, see Rosalia; Christa. For Danish Caribbean, see Oldendorp.

59. See Spencer, *Society*.

60. See Middleton; Spencer, "Dance"; Blacking, "Movement."

61. See Williams, "Sokodae" and "Bedu Moon"; Hanna, "'Women's War'"; D. Green; Begho; Kubik; Welsh-Asante, "Zimbabwean."

62. See Drewal, "Symbols" and *Yoruba Ritual*; H. and M. Drewal; Ajayi; Chernoff; Blacking, *How Musical*; Waterman.

63. See also Foulkes; Adamczyk.

64. See R. Green; C. V. Hill.

CHAPTER 3. CONTREDANSE AND CARIBBEAN BODIES

1. "Fad" dancing refers to popular dance that is either the rage on a particular island or group of islands for a relatively short period or dances whose length of popularity has not been determined fully.

2. Dance historians routinely note such exchanges: see Quirey; Kraus, Hilsend-

ager, and Dixon; Téten video, *Dancetime! 500 years*. A Caribbean example is from Cuban dance historian Lester Tomé, who cites the influence of Basque dance on ballet (bridging the rural/urban and folk/nobility divides), the connection between *escuela bolera* and *ballet*, the presence of *commedia dell'arte* performers in early ballet spectacles of the seventeenth century where the nobility collaborated with popular entertainers, etc.

3. This chapter is augmented and taken from Daniel, "Ethnographic" and "Critical." Coloniality is explained further below; however, its references are in Quijano, and Lao. See Bilby and Neely, 238–43 for examples of nineteenth-century normal flow of exchange in dance music.

4. The word "Creole" here refers to the new languages of the non-Hispanic Caribbean islands; however, its more common usage refers to the mixed heritage—European and African—that became part of identity formation in the post-eighteenth-century Americas. Before the eighteenth century, however, the word was understood across the Caribbean as a person "born in the Americas," usually European descendants or "whites." The meaning that is especially important in this chapter refers to a new or truly original creation that results from the mixture of two or more historical and/ or ethnic sources: in other words, a unique creation as opposed to a variation.

5. See children's *quadrille* on Daniel Research DVD #10. Daniel Research DVDs include examples of Caribbean *quadrilles* that were examined on each representative island and are available at the Center for Black Music Research (CBMR) in Colombia College, Chicago.

6. I aim for clear and appropriate terminology, but dance names were not stable for each country and became further complicated as dances reached the Caribbean. See Hilton, *Dance of Court*, 14; Cyrille, "Politics," 48; Manuel, *Creolizing*, 9.

7. Compare with Rameau; Sharp; Hilton, *Dance of Court*, 3–21; Hilton, "Dance and Music," 35–54, 65–84.

8. Bilby and Neely report on "motley assemblages" over time and not solely the fifth or last set for local couple dancing (p. 243).

9. See detailed nomenclatures and separate area studies of Caribbean *quadrilles* from the music perspective through the authors in Manuel, *Creolizing*.

10. Moreau de Saint-Méry, 40.

11. Chasteen, 118.

12. Labat, *Nouveaux*, 401–4.

13. See Labat quoted in Cyrille, "Politics," 47.

14. See top picture in León, 253; see also Lewin, 131.

15. For limited discussions of West and Central African dance heritages, see Hazzard-Gordon, 3–48; Crowell, 11–22; also see authors in Welch-Asante, *African Dance*. Compare with descriptions of artist/priest in seventeenth-century Central Africa, Cavazzi da Montecuccolo, 166–69.

16. Thompson, *African Art*, 1–46; Gottschild, *Digging*, 11–19, and "Crossroads," 3–10; compare with Floyd; and Wilson, "Association."

17. Welsh-Asante, "Commonalities," 71–82.

18. This chart is a significant revision of an earlier one in Daniel, "Ethnographic."

19. After reading Bilby and Neely in Manuel, *Creolizing*, for the English/Creole islands (248–52), I was reminded of *contredanse*-related material in Haitian Vodou. *L'été*, the *quadrille's* second set, is referenced in the fourth variation of *mayi*, called *d'été* in Vodou rites. It marks a dynamic shift from 4/4 to 6/8 rhythm and promotes a festive ambiance, rather than the previous "serious" *mayi* undertaking. Also, the preceding *ciye* variation of *mayi* involves a distinct pirouette turn on the tip of the toes as the drum makes an ascending tone or *ciye* sound, unlike other *mayi* movement that references agriculture. I insert these *contredanse*-related movements now to include the different findings of Bilby and Neely (231–70), and Swed and Marks (29–36) for English-speaking islands and Diaspora U.S., respectively. These data are for *quadrilles* in religious contexts, which I discuss later.

20. See Cyrille, "Politics"; Gerstin, "Musical Revivals."

21. See authors in Manuel, *Creolizing*.

22. Recorded examples at CBMR in Columbia College, Chicago, easily show contemporary *contredanse*-derived movement across the region.

23. Demorizi, 49–50.

24. See Allende-Goitía; Chasteen. Allende-Goitía analyzes *villancicos*, or the songs performed inside and outside of the Church within official seventeenth- and eighteenth-century festivities, both in Spain and the Spanish Americas. Chasteen's work is mainly on nineteenth-century dances, which he prepares with well-documented summaries of even earlier Cuban, Brazilian, and Argentine dance history.

25. See Abbad y Lasierra, 188–90; author's translation.

26. Ledru, 47; author's translation.

27. M. Taylor, 94; Deitering, 40–45.

28. In addition, see Abbad y Lasierra, chapters 30 and 31; Walton, 133–37; de Utrera, 129–30; de Molina in de Nolasco, 50; and Rubio, 22–24.

29. See Labat, *Voyage*; Sainton et al.

30. Debien, 39–68; Saiton et al., 190–94; compare with Stein; Gisler; Vanony-Frisch.

31. For Trinidad, see Herskovits and Herskovits; also Besson and Brereton. For the West Indies, see Hart.

32. Millette, 9–14, 190–91; see also Besson and Brereton.

33. Patterson, 113–44; see charts on 139, 141, and 142. Compare with Millette for Trinidad's colored population, 225–66.

34. Patterson, 41–42.

35. Patterson 15–51, 231–49; Knight, *Caribbean*, 68–73; Lowenthal, 26–56; Price.

36. Patterson, 37.

37. Knight, *Caribbean*, 124–26.

38. Patterson, 207–15.

39. Knight, *Caribbean*, 218.

40. Willocks, 47–98.

41. *Ibid.*, 63; see also Oldendorp, 137–38, 161–70.

42. Willocks, 119–21, 141–44.

43. Hartog, 159–90.

44. *Ibid.*, 168–69.

45. *Ibid.*, 33–39, 91–96, 120–58; also Sainton et al., 188–90.

46. Hartog, 178, 182.

47. *Ibid.*, 129–31, 148–59.

48. See Vanony-Frisch, 5.

49. From the extensive descriptions and informative data left by Brother Olden-dorp (*History of the Mission*) for the Danish Caribbean, it seems that the history of brotherhoods in the Caribbean may reveal additional data on both African and European dance practices or even data on dance instruction for Africans. I am grate-ful to Vincent Cooper for recommending this work.

50. See Mintz and Price for separate anthropological studies of each linguistic area and more detailed historical comparisons of the region than this summary can give.

51. Here the differentiation is between "white" colonists and enslaved "blacks," both migrating from Haiti and both called "French-Haitians." This nomenclature continues today; see Gordo.

52. Alén, 9–13; Pérez, *Cuba*; Pérez, *On Becoming Cuban*; compare with Knight, *Caribbean*, 10–12, 22–24.

53. Linares, 25, 26–86; Alén, 27.

54. Chasteen, 122–23.

55. For history details and a genuine sense of how scandalous dancing was for early Caribbean colonies, see Cuban "transgressive" dance in Chasteen, 25–31, 189–97; also Linares, 25–32, 43–45; Manuel, *Creolizing*, 51–112.

56. Manuel, *Creolizing*, 14–17.

57. See Carpentier, 101–4; León, 282–83; Diaz Diaz, "Merengue," 183–84; com-pare with Manuel, *Creolizing*, 20, 100–101, 159.

58. For *tumba francesa*, see Alén, 26–41; compare dance description with videos of *tumba francesa* in Daniel, *Cuban Dance Examples* and Daniel Research DVD #2.

59. Manuel, *Creolizing*, 59, 101.

60. See Urfé; León, 250–51, 264, 274–76, 281–88; Daniel, *Rumba*, 26–44; Quintero Rivera, *Cuerpo*, 205–9; Manuel, *Creolizing*, 51–112.

61. For scattered descriptions of Spanish Caribbean dance in colonial times, see Chasteen, 117–25 (1512–1887); Carpentier, 20–21 (c.1519–21); Padilla in Allende-Goitía, 137–38 (1691); Abbad y Lasierra, 188–90 (1782); Moreau de Saint-Méry, 20, 27–37 (1803/1789); André Pierre Ledru, 47 (1797); Bremer, 37–39, 64–65, 72–74 (1851); Alonso, 100–108 (1882/83).

62. Jonas, 45; see also M. Taylor; Deitering.

63. Padilla in Allende-Goitía, 137–38.

64. Alonso, 100–108.

65. Personal communication with García Sánchez in February 2006 at the Center for Advanced Studies in San Juan, Puerto Rico.

66. Diaz Diaz and Manuel, 116, 113–54.

67. *Ibid.*, 113–18.

68. Compare with Concepción, 167–71.

69. For *bomba*, see Hector Vega-Drouet; López-Cantos; Barton, "Challenges," 183–98. For colonial dance in Puerto Rico, however, the literature is most often generalized; therefore, I am particularly indebted to the performance expertise and unpublished graduate research of performer/researcher Mágdalis García Sánchez (personal interviews, February 2006, Center for Advanced Study of Puerto Rican and Caribbean Culture).

70. Personal communication with Jesús Cepeda Brenes in February 2006 at the Center for Advanced Studies in San Juan, Puerto Rico.

71. For the Spanish interpretation, see Álvarez-Nazario, 222–23, 308–9. For another interpretation of *bele*, see Warner-Lewis, *Central Africa*, 237—namely a dance that features hip movement. This is discussed further under French Caribbean *bele*.

72. In Álvarez-Nazario, 308–9.

73. Personal interview with Gilda Hernández San Miguel, Center for Advanced Study, San Juan on February 9, 2006.

74. Curiously, Jesús Cepeda Brenes mentioned that his father, the famous *bomba* clan leader of northeastern Puerto Rico, was originally from Mayagüez in the west and that his father confirmed that the performance style of western Puerto Rico spread slowly across the island to Loiza Aldea and Santurce in the northeast, the more well-known centers of *bomba* performance today.

75. There is a wave of Puerto Rican dance research going on, mainly on *bomba* (see Cartagena, "Las Bomberas de la Bahia); see also Quintero Rivera, *Cuerpo y cultura*, 69–121.

76. *Danza* became the rhythm for Puerto Rico's national anthem; see Quintero Rivera, "Ponce."

77. See Davis, *Afro-Dominican* and "Dominican"; Garrido de Boggs; Lizardo, *Metodología* and *Danzas*.

78. See Pacini, *Bachata*; Austerlitz; Tejeda.

79. Tejeda, 54–55; Diaz Diaz, "Meringue," 179–210.

80. Lizardo, *Metodología*, 62–64; Manuel, *Creolizing*, 182–83.

81. Unfortunately, none of my informants or consultants could tell me what this word means.

82. See Dominican *sarandunga* performed by Grupo de San Juan Bautista La Vereda on Daniel Research DVD #3, courtesy of Martha Davis.

83. See dance floor patterns in Lizardo, *Danzas*; Garrido de Boggs. Also compare Davis, "Dominican," 142–43; Tejeda, 36–37, 40–41, 76–77; and Diaz Diaz, "Meringue."

84. For Haitian dance descriptions, see Dunham, *Dances of Haiti*; Honorat, 1–155; Yarborough, *Haiti: Dance*; Paul.

85. Affranchi with a capital "A" refers to the people; *affranchi* in lowercase italics refers to the dance.

86. Largey, *Haiti: Tracing the Steps of Méringue and Contredanse*, 210–18; Averill, *Day for the Hunter*, 32–36; Daniel, fieldwork 1974, 1991.

87. Largey, *"Tracing,"* 211.

88. New, recurring syncopated rhythms of the day; see also León, 282–83; Manuel, *Creolizing*, 20, 100–101, 159.

89. All information on Haitian *affranchi* choreographies and historical performance was confirmed in a telephone interview with Jean Léon Destiné, November 9, 2007.

90. See Dunham, *Dances of Haiti*, 33, 35, 38 and Daniel, *Dancing Wisdom*, 116–18.

91. Cyrille, "Politics," 48.

92. In the main language of the Congo kingdom, KiKongo, *bele* is derived from *"velele"* and *"vele,"* which means "undulation of the hips," or from *"mbele,"* which means "knife"; see Warner-Lewis, *Central Africa,* 237–39, and also Baker. Cyrille states that *bele* is an African corruption of a dance name, one that summons the spirits; see "Sa Ka Ta Nou," 241.

93. Interestingly, my informants' definition comes close to connotations in a lingua franca of Central Africa (see Akowuah); it was gathered over many conversations with teachers, dancers, and culture workers during four fieldwork periods.

94. See also Martinican *bele* on Daniel Research DVD #1, courtesy of Dominique Cyrille; also Cyrille, "Sa Ka Ta Nou," 230–36; compare with Sully-Cally, 117–29.

95. See Gerstin, "Musical Revivals." Gerstin has also examined what he and John Storm Roberts (*Black Music*) call "Neo-African" and "New World African" dances, which, with *bele*, comprise the dance vocabulary of Martinique's African heritage (see Gerstin, "Tangled Roots").

96. I am particularly indebted to my *bele* partner Georges Defrel and all members of Wapa ensemble.

97. See Gerstin, "Interaction."

98. See Eloidin.

99. See Martinican *haut-taille* on Daniel Research DVD #11, courtesy of Julian Gerstin.

100. See Raffe and Purdon, *Dictionary of the Dance*, 75.

101. Unfortunately, I have no comparative data for related French Guiana, but compare data in Cyrille, "Sa Ka Ta Nou" and "Creolizing."

102. On Guadeloupe's several islands, most agree that *bele guadeloupéenne* is sung music that exists with or without drumming, but it is *not* danced. People have varied notions about the absence of dancing in Guadeloupean *bele*. Guadeloupean dance history remains enigmatic.

103. For dance analyses of Trinidad, see McBurnie, *Dance Trinidad*; Ahye, *Golden Heritage*; Franco; Maharaj. For St. Lucia, see Issac. For Carriacou *Nation Dances*, see McDaniel; also see Macdonald, 570–76 and update in Sloat, 285–93. For music

studies with dance data, see Guilbault, "Strategies"; Warner-Lewis, *Trinidad Yoruba*; and Bilby and Neely, 231–70.

104. This distinct skirt is a sign of camouflage that I discuss below under Queen's *bele*.

105. See Daniel Research Photographs #1 and #2 at CBMR, Chicago: *belair* and *bele* costumes; also illustrations in McDaniel, 26, 29, and 83.

106. Ahye, *Golden Heritage*, 44–46.

107. Guilbault, "Strategies," 97–115.

108. See St. Lucian *kwadril* performance on Daniel Research DVD #4 and in Isaacs, 255–57; compare with excellent analyses of related Dominica and its *quadrille* practices in Wason, 237–44.

109. For overviews and dance descriptions of the English-speaking Caribbean, see rare attention to Barbados in Harewood and Hunte, 265–82; see also Nettleford, *Dance Jamaica* and *Roots and Rhythms*; Thomas, "Democratizing Dance," 512–50; Bilby and Neely, 231–70; Ryman; Stanley Niaah.

110. Dunham, *Journey*, 22–27, 125–37; Bilby, 143–72; Evleshin; Lewin; Patterson, 236, 242.

111. Abrahams and Szwed, 301, and also see 229–32, 313–14.

112. Dunham, *Journey*, 135; Evleshin, 12; see quotes in chapter 7 herewith.

113. Bilby, 153–54; Bilby and Neely, "English Caribbean," 232, 234, 236.

114. Ryman, 117–18.

115. Bilby and Neely, 243–52.

116. There is no equal substitute for ethnographic fieldwork. Therefore, I am cautious with conclusions for areas in which I have not had extended or repeated fieldwork, and, unfortunately, the fieldwork for this survey could not include Jamaica.

117. See French-style Virgin Island *quadrille* on Daniel Research DVD #7, courtesy of the St. Thomas Humanities Council; see German-style Virgin Island *kuadria* on Daniel Research DVD #8, courtesy of Heywood and Laurel Samuels. My apprenticeship was with Doreen Freeman, Rubina Leonard, and Laurel Samuels.

118. See *lancers* on Daniel Research DVD #9b, courtesy of Senator Shawn-Michael Malone, but also full performance of all *quadrille* sets on #9a.

119. According to Rene Rosalia in an interview April 8, 2006, *kuadria* music involves a big drum, iron bell or gong, bowed fiddle, and flute, and it is associated with *kaha di orgel* (an organ-grinder) in the nineteenth and twentieth centuries, as well as with *müzik di zumbi* (music of the dead spirits).

120. Suriel, 30–31.

121. See *kuadria* on Daniel Research DVD #5, courtesy of the Curaçao Public Library. Information given here was verified in personal communications with Renee Rosalia, Cesario Jean Louis, Astrid Duran, and community members in April 2006. Additionally, over the course of fieldwork in 2004 and 2006, I discovered that Rene Rosalia's mother, although too sick for an interview in 2006, is an avid *kuadria* dancer and caller; Astrid Duran is a *kuadria* dancer, and her mother is a caller; and

Ricardo, my taxi driver over two fieldwork experiences, and his family dance and call *kuadrias* also. These contacts refute the absence of written data on Curaçaoan *contredanse*, which would suggest no continuity of Dutch Caribbean quadrilles.

122. Cesario Jean Louis added critical information to my interpretations of Curaçaoan dance data in an interview on April 6, 2006. See *Curaçaoan danza* performance on Daniel Research DVD #6, courtesy of the Curaçao National Library.

123. Compare with analyses by Caribbean music specialists in Manuel, *Creolizing*.

124. There are many forms of *bele* in the Caribbean, and they are significantly different; see Gerstin, "Tangled Roots," 19–20, 30, and Cyrille, "Creolizing"; for Dominica, see Wason 231–36; for Trinidad and Tobago, see Franco 315–17; and for Carriacou, see MacDonald, 292.

125. Alén, 14–21, 28–41; Guilbault, "Strategies"; McAlister, 29, 33, 45, 137–38; Stanley Niaah, 132–48. Compare with, for the United States, Courlander, *Drum*, 105–9; Hazzard-Gordon, 42–43; for Latin America, Olivera-Chirimini.

126. James Smith of St. Croix in Abrahams and Szwed, 312–13. See many titles used throughout Cuba in Ortiz's discussion of *Dia de los reyes* celebrations, translated by Jean Stubbs in Bettelheim, *Cuban Festivals*, 1–40.

127. Thornton, *Africa and Africans*, 8, 76 (emphasis added).

128. Bettelheim, "Ethnicity," 177; see also Nunley, Bettelheim, and Bridges, 39–83.

129. Thornton, *Africa and Africans*, xxix, 93–94, 104; J. Miller, 40–43.

130. Thornton, *Africa and Africans*: in Africa, 83; in the Americas, 202–3.

131. Eltis, Behrendt, Richardson, and Klein; also see Heywood and Thornton, 49–52, 56–60; J. Miller, 21–69; Thompson and Cornet, 27, 34–37.

132. Thornton, *Africa and Africans*, 183–205, 253–62; J. H. Sweet, 106–15.

133. Walker, "Angola Royalty," 1–2.

134. See Cuban *tumba francesa/cabildo* Kings and Queens in Bettelheim, *Cuban Festivals*, 101–3, 144; and the coronation of Trinidadian Carnival King and other Kings and Queens in Nunley, Bettelheim, and Bridges, 59, 84, 95; see Antiguan royalty in Bettelheim, "Ethnicity," 184+; King and Queen dancing in Carriacou in Macdonald, 292–93. For Haitian *Rara* Kings and Queens, see McAlister, xx, 24, 53, 58, 84, 134, 197. Carnival Kings and Queens and *bele/belair* Queen of Trinidad and Tobago are found in Ahye, 19, 45, 47–49, 72. Staged characterizations of Jamaican aristocracy, Maroon leader Nanny, and Kumina Kings and Queens are in Nettleford, *Dance Jamaica*, 104, 129, 135, 147. See Brazilian Congo Kings and Queens in Kiddy, 165, 167, 174, 179.

135. I am sincerely grateful for access to the findings of Sheila Walker ("Congo Royalty," "Angolan Royalty," and personal communications 2004, 2006, 2007, 2008) and those of Lois Wilckens ("Swirl"), which confirm my own observations of Congo/Angola influence in the Americas and underscore my collected dance data on this point. I am also hugely indebted to John Thornton for providing one of the few and perhaps oldest references to Central African or Congo kingdom dance (see 1687 account by Cavazzi de Montecuccolo, 166–69). See also Gerstin, "Tangled Roots," 25–30, and Kiddy, 153–59.

136. I am indebted to the emic analyses of Trinidadian dance specialist Hazel Franco on Trinidadian *bele/belair*, presented at World Dance Alliance Summit, Brisbane, Australia, July 16, 2008.

137. See comparisons in Gerstin, "Tangled Roots," 2–18, and Warner-Lewis, *Trinidad Yoruba*, 232–43.

138. See Kiddy, 153–82.

139. McDaniel, 2–4, 20–28, 113.

140. Warner-Lewis, *Central Africa*, 237, 151, 354n6; emphases added.

141. McBurnie, *Outlines*, 26.

142. Ibid., 26. Performance analysis may have application to other female solos, especially Queen performances elsewhere in the region.

143. Quijano, 139–55; see also Lao.

144. Entioppe, 250–58; Cyrille, "Politics"; Gisler, 51; Maurer, "Caribbean Dance," 1–26.

145. Burton, 6–8; Vaughan, *Rebel Dance*, 19; both rely on de Certeau.

146. See Moreau de St. Méry; Labat, *Nouveaux*, 403–4.

147. Entioppe, 250–58.

148. Compare Ajayi, Welsh-Asante (*African Dance*), and Chernoff with Hilton (*Dance of Court*), Rameau, Sharp, and Kraus, Hilsendager, and Dixon.

149. See "aesthetic of the cool" in Gottschild, "Crossroads," 7–8, and *Digging*, 16–18; and Thompson, *African Art*, 43–45.

150. Thompson, *African Art*, 28–43; Gottschild, "Crossroads," 10.

151. Mrs. S., personal communication March 2006 in St. Thomas; also, Cyrille reports similarly, "because their parents and grandparents used to do so" ("Sa Ka Ta Nou," 227).

CHAPTER 4. CREOLE DANCES IN NATIONAL RHYTHMS

1. Several authors have clarified the nonaesthetic contributions these dances have made: Pacini, *Bachata*; Flores; Austerlitz; Chasteen; Tejeda; see also Hazzard-Gordon.

2. Chasteen, 194, 249.

3. Dunham, 46, 69; Fouchard, 34, 41, 84–86, 93, 105–11.

4. See comparative discussion of Jean Fouchard, Paul Austerlitch, and Darío Tejada about *méringue/mereng/merengue* origins in Tejeda, 10–11, 36–37, 40–41, 76–77; see also Austerlitz, 1–4, who disputes the probability of supportive statistics for Mozambican slavery in Haiti.

5. Largey, "Haiti," 209–30; Austerlitz, 15–51.

6. Averill, 20; McAlister, 48.

7. Personal communication, August 1982. Del Villard and I had several conversations during the Black Arts Festival in Paramaribo, Suriname. One was regarding the experience of a visit up-river in Saramaka territory that we both had enjoyed; and another was on *bomba*.

8. Diaz Diaz, 179–90; Diaz Diaz and Manuel, 113–54; Quintero Rivera, *Cuerpo y cultura*.

9. Quintero Rivera, *Cuerpo y cultura*, 164–66.

10. See Vega-Drouet; see also Barton, "Challenges," 183–98, and *Drum-Dance Challenge*.

11. While I attribute these characteristics to broad Central African dance heritage, I have not found a great deal of information on Congo/Angola dance; in fact, because of continuing wars in Central Africa over decades, it has been nearly impossible to verify on the continent what we find comparatively in the Diaspora. In September 2005, Puerto Rican scholar Marta Vega, founder and former director of the Caribbean Cultural Center in New York City, organized a conference in Loiza Aldea, Puerto Rico, in order to search out and examine Central African influences on the island. I have not seen the results of this research.

12. Quintero Rivera, "Ponce," 49–65.

13. Diaz Diaz, 188–90.

14. See Gerstin, "French West Indies"; see also Desroches.

15. Interchange of Spanish Caribbean in mid- to late 1800s, see Chasteen, 191; see also Diaz Diaz, 183–209, and Quintero Rivera, *Cuerpo*, 104–23.

16. León, 282–83; Manuel, *Creolizing Contradance*, 20, 100–101, 159; Diaz Diaz, 183.

17. The following is an augmented rendering of chapter two in Daniel, *Rumba*, 26–44.

18. Quintero Rivera, *Cuerpo* , 104–24, 142–48; Diaz Diaz, "Introducción," 1–26; compare with S. Hall.

19. Matteo and Goya, 84, 225.

20. Rogozinski, 51–52; Marx, 88–90; Knight, *Caribbean*, 32, 35, 60.

21. In Carpentier, 48 (author's translation).

22. Knight, *Caribbean*, 15–22, 33–37, 41–45; Eric Williams, 34–37.

23. See, for example, Rogozinski, 13–22; Knight, *Caribbean*, 3–22; E. Williams, 30–37; Lowenthal, 31–32.

24. Dirección Política de las FAR, 24.

25. Knight, *Caribbean*, 23–50, 213–14.

26. See Ortiz, *Contrapunteo*; Guerra y Sanchez; Knight, *Caribbean*, 93–120; Mintz, "Foreword" in Guerra y Sanchez, xi–xliv; Mintz, *Worker*; Klein.

27. Knight, *Caribbean*, 24, 45; Gomez, *Black Crescent*, 3–46.

28. See Martinez-Alier; Slater, 48–53; Knight, *Caribbean*, 105–9, and *Slave Society*, 61–63; and Bush.

29. Eric Williams, 46–57, 111–35; Mintz, "Foreword," xv–xvi, xxiii; Knight, *Slave Society*, 3–46.

30. See Moreno.

31. There are many scattered references to dance and related performance in the colonial period starting around 1519–1521 (see Chasteen, 117–18) or at the end

of the seventeenth century, around 1691 (see Allende-Goitía); for later references, see Labat, *Nouveaux*; Abbad y Lasierra, chapters 30 and 31; Moreau de St. Méry, 20–37; Walton, 133–37; Bremer, 30–31, 64–65, 72–73; Demorizi, 49–50.

32. Carpentier, 49–50; Chasteen, 192–93. See also Armstrong; Matteo and Goya.

33. Elósegui and Chao, 138–40; Hernández, 18–19; Carpentier, 56–57.

34. See Moreno-Fraginals, 5–22; Knight and Palmer, 6–10; Knight, *Caribbean*, 46–49, 63–66.

35. See Moreno-Fraginals; Deschamps Chapeaux; Duarte Jiménez; compare with James.

36. Current Diaspora research has pointed out the extent of African legacies within American cultures; see authors in Walker, *African Roots/American Cultures*.

37. Moreno, 3–18.

38. See León, 7–32; Alén Rodríguez, *De lo afrocubano*. For *cabildo* dance descriptions, see Daniel, *Dancing Wisdom* and *Rumba*; and Millet and Brea, 7–11.

39. Ortiz, *Los bailes*, 431.

40. Ortiz, *Los bailes*, 396–429; León, *Del canto*, 71–73.

41. In Cuba these terms are equivalent names for the African roots of Cuban culture; in Africa the names are not. Some refer to cultural groups (Congo/Angola, Congó, or Angola), ancient kingdoms (Arará), territories (Carabalí), and linguistically related groups (Yoruba and Bantú); however, all four branches are now found throughout Cuba. See Ortiz, *Los bailes*, 167–266; León, *Del canto*, 13; Cabrera, *El monte*, *La Sociedad*, and *Reglas*; Thompson, *Flash*. Note also that I now use Congo/Angola, in place of Kongo/Angola for one African legacy in Cuba; I attempt to be in sync with current historical research and usage rather than consistent with my earlier publications.

42. This chart is offered to clarify dance development, but also as an example of a detailed typology of all known dance legacies in one site.

43. Compare with the history of *mulata* dance music in Quintero Rivera, *Cuerpo y cultura*, 69–204, and "Ponce," 49–65. See also Diaz Diaz, 179–210, and "Introducción"; Tejeda, 54–60, 72–79; Austerlitz, 15–82; Diaz Diaz and Manuel, 114–24.

44. Chasteen, 226n.

45. Manolo Vazquez Robaina and Margarita Ugarte, Stanford Cuban Dance Program, 1991; verified in personal communication with Susan Cashion, October 2009.

46. Castillo Faílde, 145–46, 153 (author's translation).

47. Urfé, 170–88; Carpentier, 186–94.

48. Moore, 16–26; Elósegui and Chao, 190–94; Carpentier, 106–18, 231–42; Urfé, 185–88.

49. Quintero Rivera, *Cuerpo*, 49–51, 55–58, 70–202.

50. See chapters 5 and 9.

51. Alén Rodríguez, *De lo afrocubano*, 47–60; Ortiz, *Los bailes*, 426, 432–33; Hernández, 49–53; Carbonero and Lamerán, 113–22; Elósegui and Chao, 195–200; Daniel, *Rumba*.

52. The next chapter examines the effects of *rumba* in and out of Cuba.

53. See *comparsa* in chapter 6.

54. See Harewood and Hunte, 269–78, Ryman, 130–31; and Thomas, "Democratizing Dance," 512–50.

Chapter 5. Caribbean Popular Dance Transformations

1. Among others for the French Caribbean, see Largey, "Haiti and the French Caribbean," 117–42, and Cyrille, "Sa Ka Ta Nou," 221–46; see Bilby, 143–72 for development of *reggae, ska,* and *ragga*; see Roberts, *Latin Tinge*; Boggs; Waxer; see also Quintero Rivera, *Cuerpo*, for Spanish Caribbean dance music.

2. Waxer, 222–23, 231–32; Chasteen, 22–23; Quintero Rivera, *Cuerpo*, 119–21.

3. Guilbault et al.

4. *Ibid.,* 11–14.

5. Vaughan, "Visión."

6. See Perna; compare with Jamaica in Thomas, *Modern Blackness*.

7. See Vaughan, *Rebel Dance*.

8. See also chapter 9.

9. The following is revised and augmented from my chapter, "Rumba Now and Then: *Quindembo*," in Malnig.

10. Traditional *rumba* resurfaced amid the height of *hip-hop, rap,* and *dancehall* popularity; for *guarapachangueo*, see Bodenheimer.

11. Leymarie, 29; Alén Rodríguez, *De lo afrocubano*, 47–48.

12. I refer to original or traditional *rumba*'s displacement over decades in terms of a so-called "pretender" called "*rhumba*," which I explain later in this chapter.

13. Alén Rodríguez, *De lo afrocubano*, 47–54.

14. Chasteen, 115–16.

15. Alén Rodríguez, *De lo afrocubano*, 27–35; Orozco, 363–89; Roberts, *Latin Tinge*, 6–9.

16. Compare with liner notes in *Cuba, I am Time*, 19–22.

17. Moreau de Saint-Méry, 41–42, 54, 61. See also Bremer; Labat, *Voyage*; Carpentier; compare with the drawings of Miguel Covarrubias and the poetry of Nicolás Guillén and Langston Hughes.

18. Compare with *músicas mulatas* in Quintero Rivera, *Cuerpo*, 49–58, 80–85.

19. Chasteen, 199–203.

20. Ortiz, *Bailes*, 329–30.

21. Pérez, *On Becoming Cuban*, 202.

22. *Ibid.,* 198–218, for a historical discussion of this complex contradiction.

23. See Moore for a sociological and music history analysis.

24. *Ibid.,* 49–52.

25. *Ibid.,* 174.

26. Although Leymarie cites a switch of armies that brought musicians to opposite

ends of the island in 1906 (33), historian Louis A. Pérez contends that this line of thinking stems from conventional thought regarding the spread of musical culture. Pérez cannot account for a recorded move of the army from either side of the island to the other at that time or any other time in Cuban history. Rather, he suggests the spread of *son* occurred during the actual presidency of José Miguel Gomez around 1911 or 1912 (personal communication with Louis Pérez, summer 2003).

27. *Quindembo* is of Bantu linguistic origin, *ki n'dembo*, and means "mixture."

28. Bodenheimer, 188–92.

29. See Daniel, *Rumba*; see also Roy.

30. Roberts, *Latin Tinge*, 76–99; Moore, 166–91; Pérez, *On Becoming Cuban*, 165–218; Leymarie, 44–107; Sublette, 362–91.

31. A primary reason to keep two spellings is to have identifiable contrasts in form; "*rhumba*" differentiates "*rumba*," commercial and traditional styles respectively. Unfortunately, the ballroom dance community has dropped the "h" in "*rhumba*" and now uses "*rumba*" quite often as its performance name. This misleads students and the public into thinking that *rumba* is similar to its variants. In Spanish, there are many terms to specify which *rumba* is referenced over another (for example, *rumba traditional, rumba de cajón, rumba del campo, rumba de salon, rumba commercial, rumba internacional, rumba brava, rumba chancleta, rumba tahona*, or *yambú, guaguancó, columbia, giribilla, batarumba, mañunga*, etc.).

32. Moore, 173–82.

33. *Ibid.*, 158 and 160 (photographs), 11–12, 173, 180. See also Jahn, *Muntu*, 84.

34. León, 119–27, 139–45,151–65; Alén Rodríguez, *De lo afrocubano*, 27–35, 47–54; Linares, 13–16. Also, personal communications with both León at the Casa de las Américas (August 1986) and with Alén Rodríguez at Centro de la música cubana (1986–87) in Havana, Cuba.

35. Roberts, *Latin Tinge*, 231.

36. Leymarie, 31.

37. See Pérez, *On Becoming Cuban*, 187–98, and Moore, 49–52.

38. Moore, 186; also Leymarie, 61.

39. Jahn, 84. I agree with Robin Moore that the data on dancers who brought *rumba* outside of Cuba are exceedingly limited. Moore gives good biographical summaries of a few who popularized the dance in Cuba—Carmita Ortiz, Rita Montaner, and Alicia Perlá, for example—and he underscores the importance of René Ribero and Ramona Ajón (173–75, 186, 264–65). I have gathered other names and partial names in the process of my research: Pepe (José Benito), Garabato, Evaristo Benda, Juan Olimpo Lastre, Carmen Cuerbelo, Yolanda and Pablito, Delita, Killer Joe Piro, El Pidio and Margot, Paulito and Lilón, Rodney (Roderico Neyra), Rolando Espinosa and Anisia, Rolando Lima and Estela, and Carlos Yera and Pascualino. None of my Cuban informants could name the Cuban dancers with whom either U.S. Americans or Britons took classes in the 1930s to 1950s.

40. Leymarie, 49.

41. Daniel, *Rumba*, 20.

42. Email communication with Alfredo O'Farrill, February 11, 2007, author's translation.

43. Sublette, 272.

44. See historical clips of Cuban performances in Oscar Valdés and Hector Vitria, Rumba (n.d.), a film produced in Havana by Cuban investigators and distributed in New York, Center of Cuban Studies; also see 1935 Hollywood rendition in the movie *Rumba* with George Raft. For a full discussion of Cuban music and dance within the grip of tourist and market forces, see Moore, 223–25; Pérez, "Representation of Rhythm" in *On Becoming Cuban*, 198–218; Roberts, *Latin Tinge*, 127–59.

45. Popular dance teachers from Conjunto Folklórico Nacional in Cuba (Lourdes Tamayo in 1986, Moraima in 1998, and Ivan in 2001) have taught these steps as standard movements from the past. Also, teachers from Danza Nacional (such as Margarita Criegh and Manolo Vasquez Robaina) taught the same *mambo* step series to students in the Stanford University Cuban Dance workshop, summer 1990. Although these may be formalized patterns that Cuban dance teachers use to demonstrate *mambo*, they would be close, if not genuine, representations of what the dance looked like in the 1950s in Cuba.

46. See *Machito, A Latin Jazz Legacy,* for the dance and ethnic history of the New York dance music scene in relation to Cuba; compare with Katherine Dunham's choreographies for "*Mambo*" (1954). See also Pryor, O'Neil, and Gomes, *Cuba, I am Time* recording notes, including an overview of Cuban dance history by Linares, 59–70.

47. Entioppe, 250–58.

CHAPTER 6. PARADING THE CARNIVALESQUE: MASKING CIRCUM-CARIBBEAN DEMANDS

1. Cuban *carnaval* is the exception, which we discuss later in this chapter.

2. The related concept of *malicia*, "malice" or "evil intention," is found in Brazilian fight-dancing or *capoeira* (which does not figure significantly in Brazilian *Carnaval*); see J. Lewis, 32–33, 77–78.

3. The dance of the Moors and Christians is performed in many Latin American cultures, often with blackened masks or blackened faces, and only since about 1992 have many Latin countries officially recognized an African history within their cultures; see Mexican Fine Arts Center Museum. For Moor and Christian dances, see Cashion, *Dance Ritual,* 145–47, 241–43; also Pieper, 138–71, 230–55. Also, despite the Cuban government's suppression of Christianity and fighting forms, Cubans still call their ubiquitous rice-and-black-bean recipe "*moros y cristianos*"—"Moors and Christians."

4. See Guitar, www.domibachata.com/carnival/Carnaval%20Origins_w%20photos.pdf.

5. D. Hill, 25, 27.

6. Alleyne-Dettmers, 262.

7. See Burton, 172–74; Hill, 30–32.

8. For named costumes, see St. Coeur.

9. Hill, 20–21.

10. Shuffling suggests the shuffle step, which is a forward and a backward brush on the ball of the toe before taking a weighted step; I doubt seriously if that is what the nondance specialist authors who use this terminology mean.

11. Ahye, *Golden Heritage*, 18–43; Hill, 12–63.

12. Hill, 4, 24, 64–76, 203–9.

13. See pictures of Minshall's and other Trinidadians' fantastic Carnival art in Nunley, Bettelheim, and Bridges, 31, 99, 107.

14. Hill, 3–6; Liverpool, 185–210.

15. León, 35–37.

16. Here, we allude to a wide range of personal Carnival experiences, from provincial Camagüey (Florida) and Matanzas *Carnavales* to national Havana and Santiago *Carnavales* in the late 1980s.

17. Ortiz, *Los bailes*, 273–90.

18. Rogelio Martinez Furé, lecture, Havana, Cuba, January 1987; Carbonero and Lamerán, 55–56.

19. *Cabildos* are African guild-like associations in Cuba (details in chapter 7).

20. Personal communication between Fernando Ortiz's secretary, Sara Rivera, and Catherine Evleshin, 1990, Portland, Oregon.

21. Bettelheim, *Cuban Festivals*, 100.

22. *Comparsa* and *conga* are also the interchangeable names for the musical rhythms played in Havana and Santiago *Carnavales*.

23. Both the San Francisco and the Brooklyn Carnivals developed after 1950.

24. Compare with Haitian *Rara* in this chapter.

25. See Ortiz in Bettelheim, *Cuban Festivals*, 25–26.

26. *Ibid.*, 21–26.

27. Personal communication with sculptor Gabino Delmonte and Catherine Evleshin, Havana, July 1988; data corroborated by dancer/musician Roberto Borrell in Oakland, California, 1995.

28. See Sarduy, "These Things," 169–71.

29. Bettelheim, "Tumba Francesa," *Cuban Festivals*, 151.

30. Burton, 65–83.

31. Nunley, Bettelheim, and Bridges, 48.

32. Evleshin, elaborating on "Dances of Autonomy" draft, 2009.

33. Burton, 75–76.

34. Nunley, Bettelheim, and Bridges, *Caribbean Festival Arts*, 51.

35. Thompson, *African Art*, 219.

36. Burton, 73–74.

37. Nunley, Bettelheim, and Bridges, 41.

38. See also Brazil in this chapter and chapter 5.

39. See Bilby and Fu-Kiau; see also Bilby, 162–63.

40. Olive Lewin, lecture at the Culture Train Center, Kingston, Jamaica, 1993.

41. Bethel, 90–93.

42. See also chapter 9.

43. McAlister, 43–45.

44. *Ibid.*, 91.

45. *Ibid.*, 44.

46. *Ibid.*, 36–37.

47. Scott, 165.

48. See for example, Averill, 89–94, 154–60; McAlister, 78–83; and Laguerre, *Voodoo and Politics*.

49. Averill, 16–17, 163; McAlister, 167–77. See chapter 8, *acheté un pwen*.

50. *Betiz* is a form of Kreyol speech involving sexual innuendo that is prevalent among all Haitian classes.

51. McAlister, 60–61.

52. Averill, 13, 89–94.

53. *Ibid.*, 154.

54. *Ibid.*, 14.

55. McAlister, 50.

56. "Bahia" and "Salvador" are interchangeable, shortened forms for both (Salvador da) Bahia State and Salvador (da Bahia), the capital city.

57. See also chapters 5 and 9.

58. Biancardi, 272–82.

59. Crowley, 28–32.

60. See *Filhos de Gandhy*.

61. Personal communication with the author in Oakland, California, July 12, 2009. See also Boyce-Davies, 49–67.

62. *Calunga* is similar to *Kalunga*, the home of the Congo/Angola ancestors; see chapter 8.

63. Personal communication with Catherine Evleshin, July 1985, in Bahia.

CHAPTER 7. RESILIENT DIASPORA RITUALS

1. Walker, *African Roots*, 45–80; see also Drake.

2. This chapter was originally written in 2005 for Sam Floyd; his work has been an inspiration.

3. Daniel, *Dancing Wisdom*, 59, 61.

4. I discuss these in chapter 8.

5. Thompson uses the notion of instantaneous imaging in his comparative African and African American opus, *Flash of the Spirit*.

6. D. Stewart, 24.

7. Compare D. Stewart, 24–33, with Bastide, 126–32; Brandon, 9–31, 74–78.

8. Métraux, 25–57; Desmangles, 17–59.

9. Bascom, "Focus," 64–68, and also *Sixteen Cowries*; Brandon, 37–103; Ortiz, *Los bailes*; Cabrera, *El monte, La sociedad*, and *Reglas*; Bolívar.

10. Bastide; Verger, *Notes*; Harding, 38–77. For sacred regional folklore and dance, see Hurston, and Daniel, *Dancing Wisdom*, 148–62.

11. In this chapter, the religion will be called Lukumí or Santería; however, the dances will always be called Yoruba, as they are called in Cuba.

12. Throughout this chapter, I use "nation" with the African understanding of belonging to more than one community, society, culture, or people, and recognizing each as one's own family "nation." Thus, enslaved Africans had multiple nation identities in their origin sites before assuming other simultaneous Diaspora identities. See McDaniel, 36–43; Yai, 244–55.

13. *Cabildos* functioned as Catholic brotherhoods did previously in Spain. For Spanish antecedents, see Moreno; for Cuba, see Brandon, 70–74.

14. Bastide, 53–54, 60.

15. Compare with Matory, *Black Atlantic Religion*.

16. See Métraux; Deren; Laguerre, *Voodoo and Politics*, "Voodoo," 23–28, and *Voodoo Heritage*; Brown, *Mama Lola* and "Systematic Remembering," 65–89; Desmangles. This literature points repeatedly to the importance of dance and music, and to what happens when there is a lack thereof (see Deren and Brown, respectively). For Vodou dances, see Daniel, *Dancing Wisdom*, 94–104, 150–53.

17. Fleurant; Wilckens, *Drums*.

18. See Hurston; for videos and filmed examples, among many, see *Divine Horsemen* by Maya Deren, *To Serve the Gods* by Karen Kramer (a ceremony that is only performed every thirty years), and the author's *Public Vodun Ceremonies in Haiti*.

19. The dance, *congo*, is differentiated in Haiti from the capitalized dances, which are also ethnic and cultural groupings; otherwise, hip-circling *congo*, the mainstay movement of Congo/Angola heritage, would be Congo.

20. For Haitian dance and music perspectives, respectively, see Daniel, "Potency," and Wilckens, "Swirl."

21. Goldberg, "Play," 24–29; Burroughs; Daniel, "Dance Performance," 780–97; Hagedorn,107–35; Wilckens, "Spirit," 114–23.

22. Cyrille, "Sa Ka Ta Nou," 236.

23. Compare with Cyrille, "Sa Ka Ta Nou," 237, 223–44; Uri and Uri, 52.

24. See Heywood and Thornton, 49–108; Thornton, "Religious," 83–90; J. Miller, 35–60; and J. H. Sweet, 106–15).

25. See chronology in Knight, *Caribbean*, 218–19.

26. Ahye, *Golden Heritage*, 73–91, 100.

27. Bilby and Neely, 244–54.

28. McDaniel, 2–4, 15, 56–59, 168–69.

29. Allende-Goitía; Chasteen, 117–18; Deitering; M. Taylor.

30. McDaniel, 101–2; Emery, 122; Hazzard-Gordon, 79; Jonas, 167.

31. McDaniel, 18–19, 38–39.

32. McDaniel, 20–25; Macdonald, 570–76; Ahye, *Golden Heritage*, 105–9.

33. See winged skirts in chapter 3; see chapter 4 for winin'.

34. I refer to the chart of social life that shows the aesthetic dimension crosscutting social, economic, religious, and political dimensions in Daniel, *Dancing Wisdom*, 54.

35. See Thompson and Cornet, 43–46, 146, 183; also see discussion of *Kalunga*, the mirrored world of Angola ancestor spirits in Desch-Obi, 138–51.

36. For Jamaica, see D. Stewart; Lewin, 171–88; Ryman.

37. Dunham, *Journey to Accompong*, 135.

38. Evleshin, 12.

39. Ryman, 125.

40. For an anthropological perspective, see Bilby and Fukiau; for dance, Ryman, 118–20, and Evleshin, 21–23; for music/dance, Lewin, 33–34, 234–39; and Desch-Obi, 27.

41. For Dominican Republic, see Davis, *Afro-Dominican*; for Cuba, see Brandon, 70–74.

42. See Cabrera, *Reglas*; Vinueza; Lachatánere; Bolívar; and Sosa.

43. Note that Abakuá operates as a religious order that adheres to the constructs of other sacred dance practices.

44. See details in Daniel, *Dancing Wisdom*, 122–42.

45. For visual documentation of Cuban Lukumí religion and Yoruba dance and music practices, see videos: *Ache Moyuba Oricha*, *When the Spirits Dance Mambo*, and *Sacred Choreographies of Cuba and Haiti*. For Cuban Palo, see *Nganga Kiyangala: Congo Religion in Cuba*; *Cuban Dance Examples*. See Abakuá example *Cuban Dance Examples*.

46. *McCall*; compare with Miller.

47. See chapter 8.

48. Knight, *Caribbean*, 238–41.

49. Concepción, 170.

50. Daniel, *Rumba*, 6.

51. Moreau de Saint-Méry, 41–42, 47–49.

52. See contemporary evaluation of John Dewey in Paul C. Taylor, 1–28.

53. *Ibid.*, 23.

54. For Puerto Rican religious case studies, see La Ruffa; Vega. For Puerto Rico/U.S. relations history, see Knight, *Caribbean*, 121–45.

55. Compare both Haitian and Dominican versions of Vodú and Gaga, as well as other African-derived dances, in Davis, "Dominican Folk Dance," 134–41; McAllister; Daniel, *Dancing Wisdom*, 116–18, 122–23, 135.

56. J. C. Miller, 35–60; Thornton, "Religious," 83–90; compare with J. H. Sweet, 106–15, 191–96.

57. Davis, "Dominican Folk Dance," 136–37, and *Afro-Dominican Religious Brotherhoods*.

58. I have not seen a great deal of sacred Dominican dance, but what I have seen has reiterated the intriguing observations noted here.

59. See Rosalia.

60. *Ibid.*, 74; see chapter 8 for what happens when *trankamentu* fails.

61. Christa, 291–302.

62. See chapter 8 for *tambú* as stick-fighting dance.

63. Walker, *Conocimiento*, vols. I and II; Andrews; Yelvington, 227–60; Klein and Vinson; Moreno-Fraginal; Pescatello.

64. Daniel, *Dancing Wisdom*, 94–103, 143–46, 156–59; see also Fryer; Biancardi, 298–353.

65. See visuals *Bahia: Africa in the Americas* and *Tambor de Mina*.

66. Matory, *Black*, 38–72.

67. Carneiro, *Candomblés* and "Structure"; Landes; Verger, *Notes*; Leacock and Leacock; Bastide; Wafer; Harding; Matory, *Black*.

68. See Price; Goslinga; Brana-Shute.

69. Some Surinamese Maroon dances look like Ghanaian court dances seen on film and on tour in the United States. Similar dances were also found during fieldwork in the surrounding areas of Abomey, Benin, in 2001.

70. See Platvoet; Hoogbergen.

71. See Price and Price; Daniel, "Dancing Down River"; Agerkopf; Martinus-Guda. Also, I am grateful for the kind collegiality of Corinna Campbell, one of the very few dance researchers who has explored Surinamese dance and who made helpful comments on this brief overview; see her presentation paper "Personalizing Tradition in Surinamese Maroon Folkloric Dance," Harvard University Symposium on Embodied Knowledge, March 26, 2011.

72. See Olivera Chirimini; Rodriguez; Molina and Lopez; Garcia; Salgado Henríquez, I:243–47.

73. See same dance form throughout chapter 3.

74. Chapter 3 reveals similar results for secular dance formations.

75. See Foulkes; Gottschild, *Black*.

76. See Gottschild, *Digging*.

77. Jonas, 50.

78. Labat, *Nouveaux*, 403–4; Moreau de Saint-Méry, 37–43; Bremer, 37–39, 64–65, 72–74; see also Emery.

79. Gerstin, "Tangled Roots"; Chasteen, 17–32.

80. Emery, 120–26; Stuckey, 60, 67; Raboteau.

81. Allen, Ware, and Garrison, eds., xiii–xiv.

82. Hazzard-Gordon, 69–70, 77–79.

83. See M. Taylor; Deitering, 38–49.

CHAPTER 8. FEROCIOUS DANCE

1. Dunham, "L'Ag'ya," 86; Desch-Obi, 137.

2. Desch-Obi, 17–51; Heywood and Thornton, 95–96, 119–120; J. Miller, "Central Africa," 46–48; Sweet, *Recreating Africa*, 56.

3. Desch-Obi, 36–37; de Jong, 89; Almeida, 16.

4. Desch-Obi, 38–41.

5. Desch-Obi, 36; Sweet, 140–43; see also Sweet, 56–57.

6. Desch-Obi, 37–38; Congo scholar Bunseki FuKiau quoted in de Jong, 89; Danny Dawson, personal communication, October 9, 2009.

7. Desch-Obi, 77–121,142–43, 282–83.

8. Desch-Obi, 92, 256n75. Notice my conclusions for dance are in sync with Desch-Obi's analyses for martial arts, and these fit conclusions of de Tavares, "Dança de Guerra."

9. Desch-Obi, 20–22, 147, 284n186. Also, the Congo Queen Njinga is a stunning example of Central African women as formidable fighters.

10. Gerstin, "Tangled Roots," 11.

11. Courlander, *Drum*, 106, 133.

12. See Dunham's fieldwork compilations of "l'ag'ya": www.youtube.com/watch?v=pDDCNve_; also www.youtube.com/OYY&feature=relatedwatch?v=R 14CCEEse_fl.

13. *Ibid.*

14. Desch-Obi, 132–34, 137.

15. For a similar Guadeloupean practice called "*libo*," see Desch-Obi, 133+.

16. See Daniel, *Dancing Wisdom*, 59, 65–66, 91–93.

17. Cyrille, "Sa Ka Ta Nou," 239–40.

18. Desch-Obi, 49–51.

19. Desch-Obi, 122–27.

20. Desch-Obi, 6; Daniel, *Dancing Wisdom*, 91–93; see also de Tavares, "Dança de guerra."

21. Ortiz, *Los bailes*, 396–429.

22. León, 71–73.

23. Ortiz, *Los bailes*, 429. Although I had heard that one of my Cuban colleagues/consultants was a knowledgeable *manisero*, I never witnessed *juego de mani* in Cuba during the years I either lived there or visited frequently (between 1985 and 2000).

24. Hill, 17, 25–32; Desch-Obi, 7, 13, 30–36.

25. I use the term *kalinda* for combat practices with sticks; I reserve *kalenda* and other spellings for unarmed dance practices.

26. Hill, 25–32; Burton, 173–77; and chapter 6 herewith.

27. For costuming, see St. Coeur; for dance, see Ahye, 116–18.

28. See Rosalia, *Tambu*.

29. See Christa, "Tambu."

30. See de Jong, "*Kokomakaku*"; see also Rosalia, *Tambu*, 75–76.

31. See Juliana, *Origen*.

32. Again, I reference usage in Burton, 6–8; Vaughan, *Rebel Dance*, 19.

33. Rosalia, 35, 56, 75–76; de Jong, 92–95.

34. Rosalia, 102–3; de Jong, 93; compare with Daniel, "Dancing Downriver," and Ryman, 122, 126–27.

35. Rosalia, 74.

36. Christa, 298.

37. de Tavares, "Dança de guerra"; see also Desch-Obi, 159–66.

38. See Almeida, 6, 1–29.

39. Capoeira, 131–33.

40. See J. L. Lewis; Dawson and Atwood.

CHAPTER 9. TOURISM, GLOBALIZATION,
AND CARIBBEAN DANCE

1. This is a revised chapter from a World Dance Association's publication, *Dance Transcending Borders*, 155–81.

2. See Tamayo Torres; Feinsilver, "Cuba," and "Cuban Biotechnology."

3. See Chasteen, 17–88; also Tchak.

4. See Ngunjiri; Alleyne Downer; UK Coalition of People Living with HIV and AIDS Limited, 121.

5. See Silver; Giordano, Lanzafame, and Meyer-Stamer; King, LeBlanc, and Van Lowe; McKay.

6. See Scarpaci; Bayer and Deutsch Lynch; also compare with Reid.

7. U.N. World Tourism Organization (UNWTO), 2004.

8. King, LeBlanc, and Van Lowe, 1.

9. For other studies of dance and tourism, see Kaeppler, "Polynesian"; Sweet, "Burlesquing"; Daniel, "Dance Performance"; Gonzalez, "Mambo."

10. See Maurer, "Fish Story"; Guilbault et al.

11. See Flores; Dyson.

12. See Huntington; Miller, *Aerosol Kingdom*.

13. Torp, 6–7. See also Hesmondhalgh and Melville; Condry; Kato; Osumare, 105–48.

14. See ethnomusicologists Deborah Pacini, "Amalgamating Musics," 19–21, and Timothy Brennan, *Secular Devotion*, who provides a provocative definition of world music in which Latin popular music usurps other popular musics as "a world music" and where European classical music reigns as the other genuine "world music."

15. See Cashion and Porter.

16. In *Machito, A Latin Jazz Legacy*, segregationist practices are documented visually, and my background perspective is prominent, growing up in Harlem with *mambo* as my teenage dance craze. For another perspective on the same period, see D. Garcia, 165–81.

17. See Moore; Leymarie; Sublette; also chapters 4 and 5 herewith.

18. Román-Velázquez, 259–88; Hosokawa, 289–312; Satizábal, 247–58; Ulloa. See also Largey, "Haiti and the French Caribbean"; Guilbault et al.; chapters 5 and 6 herewith.

19. Referencing chapter 3.

20. Daniel, "Economic Vitamins," 126–53, "Dance Performance," 780–97, *Rumba*, 124–32, and video, *Cuban Rumba*.

21. Goldberg, "Play," 24–29; Burroughs; Wilckens, "Spirit Unbounded," 114–23; Hagedorn.

22. Compare with transposed *hula* in Kaeppler, "Polynesian Dance as 'Airplane Art.'"

23. Mousouris; *Thomas*, "Democratizing," 515–18, 522–33; John, 73–78.

24. See Aschenbrenner.

25. See E. Diout.

26. Soledade, "Afro-Fusion Dance," 68–70; Dunning; Daniel and Love, 362–63; Blou. Also, Brazilian Rosangela Sylvestre has unpublished writings on a dance technique in the professional descension of Katherine Dunham, using local Brazilian dance.

27. Daniel, "Dance Performance."

28. Vaughan, "Visión," 18.

29. For case examinations, see Guilbault, *Governing Sound,* on Trinidadian *calypso*; Vaughan, *Rebel Dance,* on Cuban *timba*.

30. Email communication with Gabri Christa, August 6, 2007.

31. Email communication with Sonja Dumas, August 7, 2007.

32. Guinier, 4, 5, 7.

33. Huge political changes in October 2010 made unclear the exact membership of the former Netherlands Antilles.

Conclusion. Igniting Diaspora Citizenship

1. See Quintero Rivera, *Cuerpo,* 39–68; Suarez, 95–120.

2. See Aschenberger, 173–202; also see Dunham in chapter 1 and in Daniel, "Company."

SELECTED BIBLIOGRAPHY

Abbad y Lasierra, Fray Iñigo. *Historia geográfica, civil, y natural de la isla de San Juan Bautista de Puerto Rico.* 1782. San Juan: Ediciones de la Universidad de Puerto Rico, 1969.

ABC. *Good Morning America,* special on Cuba, 1992.

Abrahams, Roger, and John Szwed. *After Africa: Extracts from British Travel Accounts and Journals of the Seventeenth, Eighteenth, and Nineteenth Centuries concerning Slaves, Their Manners, and Customs in the British West Indies.* New Haven: Yale University Press, 1983.

Acogny, Germaine. *Danse Africaine.* Dakar, Senegal: Les Nouvelles Editions Africaines, 1980.

Adamczyk, Alice. *Black Dance: An Annotated Bibliography.* New York: Garland, 1989.

Agerkopf, Terry. "La música en Surinam." *Del Caribe,* 26 (1997): 21–29.

Aguirre Beltran, Gonzalo. *La población negra de México, 1519–1810: Estudio etnohistórico.* Mexico, D.F., Ediciones Fuente cultural, 1946.

Ahmed, Tara. "African Culture as a Commodity: Commercialized Dance in Dakar," unpublished paper. Amherst: University of Massachusetts, 1992.

Ahye, Molly. *Cradle of Caribbean Dance: Beryl McBurnie and the Little Carib Theatre.* Petit Valley, Trinidad: Heritage Cultures, 1982.

———. *Golden Heritage: The Dances of Trinidad and Tobago.* Petit Valley, Trinidad: Heritage Cultures, 1978.

Ajayi, Omofolabo. *Yoruba Dance: The Semiotics of Movement and Body Attitude in a Nigerian Culture.* Trenton, N. J.: Africa World Press, 1998.

Akowuah, Thomas A. *Lingala-English-Lingala: Hippocrene Dictionary and Phrase Book.* New York: Hippocrene, 1996.

Alén Rodríguez, Olavo. *De lo afrocubano a la salsa: Géneros musicales de Cuba.* Havana: Edición ARTEX, 1994.

———. *La música de las sociedades de Tumba Francesa.* Havana: Casa de Las Américas, 1987.

Alladin, M. P. *Folk Dances of Trinidad and Tobago*. Maraval, Trinidad: M. P. Alladin, 1970.

Allen, William Francis, Charles Pickard Ware, and Lucy McKim Garrison, comp. *Slave Songs of the United States*. 1867/1971 (45 [#59]). New York: A. Simpson, 1971.

Allende-Goitía, Noel. "The Mulatta, the Bishop, and Dances in the Cathedral: Race, Music, and Power Relations in Seventeenth Century Puerto Rico." *Black Music Research Journal* 26.2 (2006): 137–64.

Alleyne, Mervyn C. "Methodology and Historiography of the Caribbean." In *General History of the Caribbean*, ed. B. W. Higman, I:19–45. London: UNESCO Publishing/MacMillan Education, 1999.

Alleyne, Oluatoyin. "U.N. Met Promises: HIV/AIDS Related Stigma Still a Major Problem in Guyana." In *Panoscope,* before UNGASS+5: Keeping the Promise: A Five Country Survey, May 2006.

Alleyne-Dettmers, Patricia T. "The Moko Jumbi: Elevating the Children." In Sloat, *Caribbean Dance from Abakuá to Zouk*, 262–90.

Almeida, Bira. *Capoeira, a Brazilian Art Form*. Richmond, Calif.: North Atlantic, 1986.

Alonso, Manuel. *El Jíbaro* (Félix Córdoba Iturregui edición). 1882/83. Rio Piedras: Ediciones Huracán, 2001.

Álvarez Nazario, Manuel. *El elemento Afronegroide en el Español de Puerto Rico*. San Juan: Instituto de Cultura de Puerto Rico, 1974.

Amira, John, and Stephen Cornelius. *The Music of Santería: Traditional Rhythms of the Batá*. Crown Point, Ind.: West Cliffs, 1992.

Andrade, Marilia, and Katia Canton. "Overview of Dance Research and Publications in Brazil." *Dance Research Journal*, 28.2 (1996): 114–22.

Andrews, George Reid. *Afro-Latin America, 1800–2000*. New York: Oxford University Press, 2004.

Appleby, T. "Ghost of Capitalist Future Haunts Cuba." *Washington Times*, September 25, 1994.

Armstrong, Lucile. *Dances of Spain*, Vol. I. New York: Chanticleer, 1950.

Arslanian, Sharon. "The History of Tap Dance in Education: 1920–1950," Ed.D. diss.thesis, Temple University, 1997. Ann Arbor: UMI Diss. Services, 1998.

Aschenbrenner, Joyce. *Katherine Dunham: Reflections on the Social and Political Contexts of Afro-American Dance*." Special edition of *Dance Research Annual (1980)*, New York: CORD, 12:3–118.

Austerlitz, Paul. *Merengue: Dominican Music and Dominican Identity*. Philadelphia: Temple University Press, 1997.

Averill, Gage. *A Day for the Hunter, a Day for the Prey: Popular Music and Power in Haiti*. Chicago: University of Chicago Press, 1997.

Baker, Philip. "Assessing the African Contribution to French-based Creoles." In *Africanisms in Afro-American Language Varieties*, ed. Salikoko S. Mufwene, 123–55. Athens: University of Georgia Press, 1993.

Barnes, Sandra T., ed. *Africa's Ogun: Old World and New.* Bloomington: Indiana University Press, 1989.

Barton, Hal. "The Challenges of Puerto Rican Bomba." In Sloat, *Caribbean Dance from Abakuá to Zouk,* 183–98.

———. "The Drum-Dance Challenge: An Anthropological Study of Gender, Race and Class Marginalization of Bomba in Puerto Rico." PhD diss., Cornell University, 1995. Ann Arbor: UMI Diss. Services, 1995.

Bascom, William. "The Focus of Cuban Santeria." *Southwest Journal of Anthropology,* Spring 6.1 (1950): 64–68.

———. *Sixteen Cowries: Yoruba Divination from Africa to the New World.* Bloomington: Indiana University Press, 1980.

Bastide, Roger. *The African Religions of Brazil.* Baltimore: Johns Hopkins University Press, 1978.

Bayer, Sherrie, and Barbara Deutsch Lynch, eds. *Beyond Sun and Sand: Caribbean Environmentalism.* New Brunswick: Rutgers University Press, 2006.

Beckford, Ruth. *Katherine Dunham: A Biography.* New York: Marcel Dekker, 1979.

Begho, Felix. "Traditional African Dance in Context." In *African Dance: An Artistic, Historical, and Philosophical Inquiry,* ed. K. Welsh-Asante, 163–81. Trenton, N.J.: Africa World Press, 1998.

Besson, Gerard, and Bridget Brereton. *The Book of Trinidad.* Port of Spain, Trinidad and Tobago: Paria, 1992.

Bethel, E. Clement, with Nicolette Bethel. *Junkanoo: Festival of the Bahamas.* London: Macmillan Caribbean, 1992.

Bettelheim, Judith, ed. *Cuban Festivals: A Century of Afro-Cuban Culture.* Kingston: Ian Randle/Princeton: Markus Wiener. 2001.

———. "Carnival in Santiago de Cuba." In Bettelheim, *Cuban Festivals,* 94–126.

——— "Ethnicity, Gender and Power in Carnaval in Santiago de Cuba." In *Negotiating Performance in Latin/o America,* ed. Diana Taylor and Juan Villegas, 176–212. Durham: Duke University Press, 1994.

———. "Jonkonnu and Other Christmas Masquerades." In Nunley, Bettelheim, and Bridges, *Caribbean Festival Arts,* 39–84.

———. "The Tumba Francesa and Tajona of Santiago de Cuba," in Bettelheim, *Cuban Festivals,* 141–53.

Biancardi, Emília. *Raízes musicais da Bahia; Musical Roots of Bahia.* Salvador, Bahia: Omar G., 2006.

Bilby, Kenneth. "Jamaica." In *Caribbean Currents: Caribbean Music from Rumba to Reggae,* ed. P. Manuel, 143–72. Philadelphia: Temple University Press, 1995.

Bilby, Kenneth, and Bunseki Fu-Kiau. *Kumina: A Kongo-based Tradition in the New World.* Brussels: Centre d'Études et de Documentation Africaines, 1983.

Bilby, Kenneth, and Daniel T. Neely, "English-Speaking Caribbean: Re-embodying the Colonial Ballroom." In Manuel, *Creolizing,* 231–70.

Blacking, John. *How Musical Is Man?* Seattle: University of Washington Press, 1973.

———. "Movement, Dance, Music and the Venda Girls' Initiation Cycle." In *So-*

ciety and the Dance, ed. P. Spencer, 64–91. Cambridge: Cambridge University Press, 1985.

Bloch, Maurice. "Symbols, Song, Dance, and Features of Articulation: Is Religion an Extreme Form of Traditional Authority?" *Archives Européennes de Sociologie*, 15 (1974): 52–81.

Blou, Léna. *Techni'Ka: Researches sur l'émergence d'une méthode d'enseignement á partir des danses Gwo-ka*. Pointe-à-Pitre, Guadeloupe: Èditions Jasor, 2005.

Blum, Odette. *Dance in Ghana*. New York: Dance Perspective, 1973.

Bodenheimer, Rebecca. *Localizing Hybridity: The Politics of Place in Contemporary Cuban Rumba Performance*. PhD diss., University of California, Berkeley, 2010.

Boggs, Vernon, ed. *Salsiology*. New York: Glenwood, 1992.

Bolívar, Natalia. *Los orichas en Cuba*. Havana: Ediciones Union, 1990.

Bonner, Wilifred. *Bibliography of Folklore* (Dance). London: Folklore Society, 1972.

Bordieu, Pierre. *Distinctions*. Cambridge: Cambridge University Press. 1984.

Bourguignon, Erica. *Possession*. Prospect Heights, Ill.: Waveland, 1991.

———. *Trance Dance*. New York: Dance Perspectives, 1968.

Boyce Davies, Carole. "Re-/Presenting Black Female Identity." In Rahier, 49–67.

Brandon, George. *Santería from Africa to the New World*. Bloomington: Indiana University Press, 1993.

Brana-Shute, Gary, ed. *Resistance and Rebellion in Suriname: Old and New*. Williamsburg, Va.: College of William and Mary, Department of Anthropology, 1990.

Bremer, Fredrika. *Cartas de Cuba*. 1851. Havana: Editorial Arte y Literatura, 1980.

Brennan, Timothy. *Secular Devotion: Afro-Latin Music and Imperialist Jazz*. New York: Verso, 2008.

Brickel, C. "You'd Hardly Know Cuba's Open for Business." *New York Times*, editorial, November 15, 1994.

Brown, Karen McCarthy. *Mama Lola: A Voodoo Priestess in Brooklyn*. Berkeley: University of California Press, 1991.

———. "Systematic Remembering, Systematic Forgetting: Ogou in Haiti." In Barnes, 65–89.

Browning, Barbara. *Samba: Resistance in Motion*. Bloomington: Indiana University Press, 1995.

Buonaventura, Wendy. *The Serpent and the Nile: Women and Dance in the Arab World*. New York: Interlink, 1990.

Burroughs, Joan. "Haitian Ceremonial Dance on the Stage: The Contextual Transference and Transformation of Yanvalou." PhD diss., New York University, 1995. Ann Arbor: UMI Diss. Services, 1995.

Burton, Richard D. E. *Afro-Creole: Power, Opposition, and Play in the Caribbean*. Ithaca, N.Y.: Cornell University Press, 1997.

Bush, Barbara. *Slave Women in Caribbean Society 1650–1838*. Bloomington: Indiana University Press, 1990.

Cabrera, Lydia. *El monte*. 1954. Miami: Colección del Chichereku.

———. *La Sociedad secreta Abakuá*. 1958. Miami: Ediciones C.R., 1970.

————. *Reglas de congo, Palo Monte Mayombe*. 1979. Miami: Ediciones Universal, 1986.

Campbell, Corinna. "Personalizing Tradition in Surinamese Maroon Folkloric Dance." Presentation at Harvard University Symposium on Embodied Knowledge, March 26, 2011.

Capoeira, Nestor. *Capoeira: Roots of the Dance-Fight-Game*. Berkeley: North Atlantic, 2002.

————. *The Little Capoeira Book*. Berkeley: North Atlantic, 1995.

Carbonero, Graciela Chao. *Bailes Yorubas de Cuba*. Havana: Editorial Pueblo y Educación, 1980.

————. "Africanness of Dance in Cuba." In Sloat, *Making Caribbean Dance*, 62–66.

Carbonero, Graciela Chao, and Sara Lamerán. *Folklore Cubano I, II, III, IV*. Havana: Editorial Pueblo y Educación, 1982.

Carneiro, Edison. *Candomblés da Bahia con Ilustrações Carybé e Cantor*. 1967. Rio de Janeiro: Edições de Ouro, 1978.

————. "Structure of African Cults in Bahia." *Journal of American Folklore*, 53 (1940): 271–78.

Carpentier, Alejo. *La música en Cuba*. 1946. Mexico City: Fondo de Cultura Económica, 1979.

Cartagena, Juan. "Las Bomberas de la Bahia: Expanding the Space for Women in Bomba." *Güiro y Maraca*, 11.3(2007): 2–7.

Carty, Linda. "Caribbean Women: Economics of Prostitution." Proceedings of the Fifth Conference of North American Philosophers, Havana, 1993.

Cashion, Susan. "Dance Ritual and Cultural Values in a Mexican Village: Festival of Santo Santiago." PhD diss., Stanford University. Ann Arbor: University Microfilms, 1983.

————. "Educating the Dancer in Cuba." In *Dance, Current Selected Research*, ed. Lynnette Y. Overby and James H. Humphrey, 1:165–85. New York: AMS, 1986.

Cashion, Susan, and Ron Porter. "Latin American Dance." In Encyclopedia Britannica Online: http://www.search.eb.com.offcampus.lib.washington.edu/eb/article-9439495. 2008.

Castillo Faílde, Oswaldo. *Miguel Faílde, creador musical del danzón*. Havana: Editorial del Consejo Nacional de cultura, 1964.

Cavazzi da Montecuccolo, Giovanni Antonio. *Istorica Descrizione de tre regni Congo, Matamba ed Angola*. Bologna: Giacomo Monti, 1687.

Chartrand, René, and Donato Spedaliere. *The Spanish Main, 1493–1800*. Oxford: Oxprey, 2006.

Chasteen, John C. *National Rhythms, African Roots: The Deep History of Latin American Popular Dance*. Albuquerque: University of New Mexico Press, 2004.

Chernoff, John Miller. *African Rhythm and African Sensibility: Aesthetics and Social Action in African Musical Idioms*. Chicago: University of Chicago Press, 1979.

Christa, Gabri. "Tambu: Afro-Curaçao's Music and Dance of Resistance." In Sloat, *Caribbean Dance from Abakuá to Zouk*, 291–304.

Clark, Veve. "Katherine Dunham: Method Dancing or the Memory of Difference." In Myers, 5–8.

Clark, Veve, and Sarah Johnson, eds. *Kaiso!: Writings by and about Katherine Dunham*. Madison: University of Wisconsin Press, 2005.

Clark, Veve, and Margaret Wilkerson, eds. *Kaiso! An Anthology of Writings*. Berkeley: University of California Press, 1978.

Clifford, James. *The Predicament of Culture: Twentieth Century Ethnography, Literature, and Art*. Cambridge: Harvard University Press, 1988.

Cohen, Erik. "Authenticity and Commoditization in Tourism." *Annals of Tourism Research* 15 (1988): 371–86.

Concepcion, Alma. "Dance in Puerto Rico: Embodied Meanings." In Sloat, *Caribbean Dance from Abakuá to Zouk*, 165–75.

Condry, Ian. *Hip-hop Japan: Rap and the Paths of Cultural Globalization*. Durham: Duke University Press, 2006.

Cooper, Carolyn. "Erotic Play in the Dancehall: Slackness Hiding from Culture," Paper presented at the Women in Dancehall Conference, Kingston, Jamaica, University of West Indies, Mona Campus, 1990.

Copeland, Roger. "Why Cuba Champions Ballet." *New York Times*, June 11, 1978.

Courlander, Harold. *Haiti Singing*. Chapel Hill: University of North Carolina Press, 1939.

———. *The Drum and the Hoe*. Berkeley: University of California Press, 1973.

Crowell, Nathaniel Hamilton Jr. "What is Congolese in Caribbean Dance?" In Sloat, *Caribbean Dance from Abakuá to Zouk*, 11–22.

Crowley, Daniel J. *African Myth and Black Reality in Bahian Carnaval*. Los Angeles: Museum of Cultural History/University of California, Los Angeles, 1984.

Cyrille, Dominique. "Creolizing Quadrilles of Guadeloupe, Dominica, Martinique, and St. Lucia." In Manuel, *Creolizing*, 188–208.

———. "Recherche sur la musique rurale de la Martinique." PhD diss., Université de Paris, Sorbonne, 1996.

——— "Sa Ka Ta Nou (This belongs to us): Creole Dances of the French Caribbean." In Sloat, *Caribbean Dance from Abakuá to Zouk*, 221–46.

——— "The Politics of Quadrille Performance in Nineteenth-Century Martinique." *Dance Research Journal*, 38.1/2 (2006): 43–60.

Dance Magazine. "'Young Choreographers Defining Dance' Program by African American Male Choreographers," Aaron Davis Hall, New York City, October 2–3, 1998.

Dance Research Journal. New York: Congress on Research in Dance (CORD), 1974–.

Daniel, Yvonne. "A Critical Analysis of Caribbean *Contredanse*." *Transforming Anthropology*, October, 17(2) (2009): 146–53.

———. "An Analysis of Sacred Diaspora Dance/Music." In *Black Music Scholarship and the Bridging of Diasporal Sacred Worlds*, ed. S. Floyd. Berkeley: University of California Press, n.d.

———. "An Ethnographic Comparison of Caribbean Quadrilles." *Black Music Research Journal* 30.1 (2010): 1–31.

———. "Caribbean Performance and Cultural and Economic Globalization." In *Dance Transcending Borders*, ed. D. Urmimala Sarkar Munsi, 155–81. New Delhi: Tulika, 2008.

———. "Changing Values in Cuban Rumba, a Lower Class Black Dance Appropriated by the Cuban Revolution." *Dance Research Journal* 23.2 (Fall 1991): 1-10.

———. "Come with Me and Let's Talk about Caribbean Quadrilles." In *Cariso* 6 (2006): 6–12.

———. "Cuban Dance: An Orchard of Caribbean Creativity." In Sloat, *Caribbean Dance From Abakuá to Zouk*, 23–55.

———. "Dance Performance in Tourist Settings: Authenticity and Creativity." *Annals of Tourism Research*, 23.4 (1996): 780–97.

———. "Dancing Down River: A Presentation on the Dance of Suriname." *Dance Ethnologists* (University of California, Los Angeles), 7 (1983): 24–39.

———. *Dancing Wisdom: Embodied Knowledge in Haitian Vodou, Cuban Yoruba, and Bahian Candomblé*. Urbana: University of Illinois Press, 2005.

———. "Economic Vitamins from the Cuban Aesthetic System or Commoditization and Cultural Conservation in Cuban Tourism." In *The World of Music*, ed. Tomoaki Fujii, trans. Nobukiyo Eguchi, vol.10, 126–53. Osaka, Japan: Museum of Ethnology/Tokyo Shoseki Press, 1990.

———. "Economic Vitamins of Cuba: Sacred and Other Dance Performance." In *Rhythms of the Afro-Atlantic World*, ed. M. Diouf and I. Nwankwo, 19–40. Madison: University of Michigan Press, 2010.

———. "Embodied Knowledge in African American Dance Performance." In Walker, *African Roots*, 352–61.

———. "In the Company of African American Women Artists." In *Dance Women: Living Legends*, 6–9. New York: 651, An Arts Center, 1997.

———. "Peniel Guerrier." *Bomb: Art and Cultural Interviews: A Tribute to Haiti* 90 (Winter 2004–05): 62–67.

———. *Rumba: Dance and Social Change in Contemporary Cuba*. Bloomington: Indiana University Press, 1995.

———. "Rumba Now and Then: *Quindembo*." In *Ballroom, Boogie, Shimmy Sham, Shake: Social and Popular Dance Reader*, ed. J. Malnig, 146–64. Urbana: University of Illinois Press, 2009.

———. "The Potency of Dance: A Haitian Examination." *Black Scholar*, 11.8 (1980): 61-73.

Daniel, Yvonne, and Nia Love. "Dance in the African Diaspora." In *Encyclopedia of the African Diaspora*, ed. C. Boyce Davies, 2:356–66. New York: ABC/CLIO, 2008.

David, Christine. *Folklore of Carriacou*. St. Michael, Barbados: Coles, 1985.

Davis, Martha Ellen. "Afro-Dominican Religious Brotherhoods: Structure, Ritual and Music." PhD diss., University of Illinois, Urbana. Ann Arbor: UMI Diss. Services, 1976.

———. "Dominican Folk Dance and the Shaping of National Identity." In Sloat, *Caribbean Dance from Abakuá to Zouk*, 127–51.

Dawson, C. Daniel, and Jane Atwood. *Capoeira: A Martial Art and a Cultural Tradition*. New York: Rosen, 1999.

de Andrade, Marilia, and Katia Canton. "Overview of Dance Research and Publications in Brazil." *Dance Research Journal* 28.2 (1996): 114–22.

Debien, Gabriel. *Les esclaves aux Antilles francaises, XVIIe-XVIIIe siècles*. Basse-Terre, Guadeloupe: Société d'histoire de la Guadeloupe, 1974.

DeBrunner, Hans Warner. *Presence and Prestige: Africans in Europe*. Basel: Basler Afrika Bibliographien, 1979.

DeFrantz, Thomas, ed. *Dancing Many Drums: Excavations in African American Dance*. Madison: University of Wisconsin Press, 2002.

Deitering, Carolyn. *The Liturgy as Dance and the Liturgical Dancer*. New York: Crossroad, 1984.

de Jong, Nanette. "*Kokomakaku* and the (Re-) Writing of History." *Afro-Hispanic Review* 2 (2007): 87–101.

Delgado, Celeste Fraser, and José Estevan Muñoz. *Everynight Life: Culture and Dance in Latin/o America*. Durham: Duke University Press, 1997.

Demorizi, Emilio Rodriguez. *Música y baile en Santo Domingo*. Santo Domingo: La Herencia Hispañiola, 1971.

de Nolasco, Flerida. *Vibraciones en el tiempo*. Ciudad Trujillo, Dominicana: Editora Montalvo, 1948.

de Pool, John. *Del Curacao que se va*. Santiago de Chile: Ercilia, 1935.

Deren, Maya. *Divine Horsemen: The Living Gods of Haiti*. 1953. New Paltz, N.Y.: McPherson, 1983.

Deschamps Chapeaux, Pedro. *El negro en la economía habanera del siglo XIX*. Havana: Premio Unión de Escritores Y Artísticas de Cuba, 1971.

Desch-Obi, M. Thomas J. *Fighting for Honor: A History of African Martial Art Traditions*. Columbia: South Carolina Press, 2008.

Desmangles, Leslie. *The Faces of the Gods: Vodou and Roman Catholicism in Haiti*. Chapel Hill: University of North Carolina Press, 1991.

Desmond, Jane, ed. *Dancing Desires: Choreographing Sexualities On and Off the Stage*. Madison: University of Wisconsin Press, 2001.

Desroches, Monique. "Musical Tradition in Martinique: Between the Local and the Global." Trans. Sharon Berman and Catherine Potter. In *Revista Transcultural de Música Transcultural Music Review* 2, 1976. Available at http://www.sibetrans.com/trans/trans2/desroches.htm. (accessed March 25, 2011).

de Tavares, Julio Caesar. "Atitude, Crítica Social e Cultura Hip-Hop: A face Afro-descendente dos Intelectuais Publico Brasileiros." *Revista Espaço Acadêmico* 36 (2004). Available at http://espacoacademico.com.br (Electronic Journal, ISSN 1519.6186, ano III. 2004).

———. "Dança de Guerra, Arquivo e Arma: Elementos para uma Teoria da Capoeiragem e da Comunicação Corporal Afro-Brasileira." Master's thesis, University of Brasilia, 1984–85.

de Utrera, Fray Cipriano. *Nuestra Señora de Altagracia.* Santo Domingo: Padres Franciscanos Capuchinos, 1933.

Diaz Diaz, Edgardo. "Merengue dominicana: una prehistoria musical en diez pasos." In *Merengue en la cultura dominicana y del Caribe,* ed. Darío Tejeda and Rafael Emilio Yunén, 179–210. Santo Domingo: Centro León/Instituto de estudios caribeños, 2006.

———. "Introducción." *Revista sciencias sociales: Nueva Epoca,* 4 (1998):11–26.

Diaz Diaz, Edgardo, and Peter Manuel. "Puerto Rico: The Rise and Fall of Danza as National Music." In Manuel, *Creolizing,* 113–54.

Diouf, Esailama. "Staging the African." PhD diss., Northwestern University, 2011 (manuscript copy).

Diouf, Mamadou, and Ifeoma Kiddoe Nwankwo, eds. *Rhythms of the Afro-Atlantic World: Rituals and Remembrances.* Ann Arbor: Michigan University Press, 2010.

Dirección Política de las FAR, *Historia de Cuba* 1 (1971): 24.

Downer, Andrea. "HIV/AIDS-related Discrimination: A Blot on Jamaica's Record." *Panoscope,* Before UNGASS+5: Keeping the Promise—A Five Country Survey, May 2006.

Drake, St. Clair. *Black Folk Here and There: An Essay in History and Anthropology.* Los Angeles: Center for Afro-American Studies, University of California, 1987.

Drewal, Henry, and Margaret Thompson Drewal. *Gelede: Art and Female Power Among the Yoruba.* Bloomington: Indiana University Press, 1990.

Drewal, Margaret Thompson. "Symbols of Possession: A Study of Movement and Regalia in an Anago-Yoruba Ceremony." *Dance Research Journal,* 7.2 (1975): 15-24.

———. *Yoruba Ritual and Thought: Play, Performance, Agency.* Bloomington: Indiana University Press, 1991.

Duarte Jiménez, Rafael. *El negro en la sociedad colonial.* Santiago de Cuba: Editorial Oriente, 1988.

Dudley, Shannon. *Carnival Music in Trinidad: Experiencing Music, Expressing Culture.* New York: Oxford University Press, 2004.

Dunham, Katherine. *Dances of Haiti.* Los Angeles: Center for Afro-American Studies, University of California, 1985. Originally published in *Acta Antropologica,* 2.4 (1947): 1-64.

———. *Island Possessed.* Garden City, N.Y.: Doubleday, 1969.

———. *Journey to Accompong.* New York: Holt, 1946.

———. "L'Ag'ya of Martinique." *Esquire* 12.5: 84–85, 126.

———. Personal communications, 1992.

Dunning, Jennifer. "Through Sidewalk Cracks, Hardy Cultural Flowers Leap toward the Sun." *New York Times,* June 7, 2001.

Dyson, Michael Eric. *Between God and Gansta Rap: Bearing Witness to Black Culture.* New York: Oxford University Press, 1996.

Elder, Jacob D. *From Congo Drum to Steelband: A Socio-historical Account of the*

Emergence of the Trinidad Steel Orchestra. St. Augustine: University of the West Indies, 1969.

Eloidin, Ester. "La Haut-Taille: Tradition musicale du milieu rural du sud de la Martinique," Diplôme universitaire d' "Ethnorythmes," Nice Sophia Antipolis, France, 2003.

Elósegui, Josefina, and Graciela Chao. *Apreciación de la danza*. Havana: Editorial Pueblo y Educación, 1982.

Eltis, David, Stephen D. Behrendt, David Richardson, Herbert S. Klein. *The Trans-Atlantic Slave Trade: A Database on CD-ROM*, 1999. Available at http://www.slavevoyages.org/tast/index.faces.

Emery, Lynne. *Black Dance in the United States from 1619 to 1970*. 1972. Hightstown, N.J.: Dance Horizon, 1988.

Entioppe, Gabriel. *Nègres, Danse et Résistance—la Caraïbe du 17ᵉ et 18ᵉ siècle*. Paris: Editions L'Harmattan, 1996.

Ephirim-Donkor, Anthony. *African Spirituality: On Becoming Ancestors*. Trenton, N.J.: Africa World Press, 1997.

Espino, Maria Dolores. "Tourism in Cuba: A Development Strategy for the 1990s." In Perez-Lopez, *Cuba at a Crossroad*, 147–66.

Evans-Pritchard, E. E. "Dance." *Africa*, 4 (1928): 446-62.

Evleshin, Catherine. *Dance In Jamaica: Celebrating Autonomy*, unpublished manuscript, n.d., 1–53.

Fernández, Armando. Public lecture on *La historia de los haitianos en Cuba* at La Casa de las Américas, October 16–20, 1986.

Feinsilver, Julie. "Cuba as a 'World Medical Power.'" *Latin American Research Review*, 24.2 (1989): 1–34.

———. "Cuban Biotechnology: A First World Approach to Development." In Perez-Lopez, *Cuba at a Crossroad*, 167–89.

Fenton, William N., and Gertrude P. Kurath. *The Iroquois Eagle Dance: An Offshoot of the Calumet Dance with an Analysis of the Eagle Dance and Songs by Gertrude Kurath*. Washington, D. C.: U.S. Government Print, 1953.

Fisher, Robert B. *West African Religious Traditions: Focus on the Akan of Ghana*. Maryknoll, New York: Orbis, 1998.

Fleurant, Gerdès. *Dancing Spirits: Rhythms and Rituals of Haitian Vodun, the Rada Rite*. Westport, Conn.: Greenwood, 1996.

Flores, Juan. *From Bomba to Hip-hop: Puerto Rican Culture and Latino Identity*. New York: Columbia University Press, 2000.

Floyd, Sam. "Black Music in the Circum-Caribbean." *American Music* 17.1 (Spring 1999): 1–37.

Fouchard, Jean. *La méringue: danse nationale d'haïti*. Ottawa, Canada: Editions Leméac, 1973.

Foulkes, Julia. *Modern Bodies: Dance and American Modernism from Martha Graham to Alvin Ailey*. Chapel Hill: University of North Carolina Press, 2002.

Fraleigh, Sondra, and Penelope Hanstein, eds. *Researching Dance: Evolving Modes of Inquiry*. Pittsburgh: University of Pittsburgh Press, 1999.

Franco, Hazel. "Tradition Reaffirming Itself in New Forms: An Overview of Trinidad and Tobago Folk Dances." In Sloat, *Making Caribbean Dance*, 297–320.

Franqui, Carlos. *Family Portrait with Fidel: A Memoir*. Trans. Alfred MacAdam. New York: Vintage, 1985.

Fryer, Peter. *Rhythms of Resistance: African Musical Heritage in Brazil*. Hanover, New Hampshire: University of New England Press, 2000.

García, David. "Embodying Music/Disciplining Dance: The Mambo Body in Havana and New York City." In *Ballroom, Boogie, Shimmy Sham, Shake: A Social and Popular Dance Reader*," ed. Julie Malnig, 165–81. Urbana: University of Illinois Press, 2009.

García, Jesús (Chucho). "Demystifying African Absence in Venezuelan History and Culture." In Walker, *African Roots*, 284–90.

Garrido de Boggs, Edna. "Baile." In *Reseña histórica del folklore dominicano*, 149–78. Santo Domingo: Dirección Nacional de Folklore, Secretaría de Estado de Cultura, 2006.

Gerstin, Julian. "French West Indies." In *New Grove Dictionary of Music*, 2nd ed., ed. Stanley Sadie. London: Macmillan, 2000. Available at http://www.colorquilts .com/julian/NewGrove.html (accessed March 25, 2011).

———. "Interaction and Improvisation between Dancers and Drummers in Martinican *Bélè*." *Black Music Research Journal*, 18.1/2 (1998): 121–65.

———. "Musical Revivals and Social Movements in Contemporary Martinique: Ideology, Identity, and Ambiguity." In *The African Diaspora: A Musical Perspective*, ed. Ingrid Monson, 295–328. New York: Garland, 2000.

———. "Tangled Roots: Kalenda and Other Neo-African Dances in the Circum-Caribbean." In *New West Indies Guide*, 78.1/2 (2004): 5–41; updated reprint. In Sloat, *Making Caribbean Dance*, 11–34.

Gilroy, Paul. *The Black Atlantic: Modernity and Double Consciousness*. Cambridge: Harvard University Press, 1993.

Giordano, Paolo, Francesco Lanzafame, and Jörg Meyer-Stamer, eds. "Asymmetries in Regional Integration and Local Development," Washington, D.C.: Inter-American Development Bank, 2005.

Gisler, Antoine. *L'esclaves aux Antilles français, 17e -siècle*. Paris: Éditions Karthala, 1981.

Goldberg, Alan. "Commercial Folklore and Voodoo in Haiti: International Tourism and the Sale of Culture." PhD diss., Indiana University, Bloomington, 1981.

———. "Play and Ritual in Haitian Voodoo Shows for Tourists." In *The Paradoxes of Play*, ed. John Loy, 24–29. West Point, N.Y.: Leisure, 1982.

Gomez, Michael. *Black Cresent: Experience and Legacy of African Muslims in the Americas*. Cambridge: Cambridge University Press, 2005.

Gomez, Michael, ed. *Diasporic Africa: A Reader*. New York: New York University, 2006.

Gonzalez, Anita. "Caught between Expectations: Producing, Performing and Writing Black/Afro-Latin and American Aesthetics." *Journal of Dramatic Theory and Criticism*, Spring 1999, 149–56.

———. *Jarocho's Soul: Cultural Identity and Afro-Mexican Dance*. Lanham, Md.: University Press of America, 2004.

———. "Mambo and the Maya." *Dance Research Journal*, 35.2/36.1 (2003–04): 131–45.

Gordo, Isabel. "Configuraciones de los Haitiano-Cubanos en la cultura cubana." Manuscript, Havana: Instituto de Ciencias, 1985.

Goslinga, Cornelius. *A Short History of the Netherlands Antilles and Surinam*. The Hague: M. Nijhoff, 1979.

Gottschild, Brenda Dixon. "Crossroads, Continuities, and Contradictions: The Afro-Euro-Caribbean Triangle." In Sloat, *Caribbean Dance: From Abakuá to Zouk*, 3–10.

———. *Digging the Africanist Presence in American Performance: Dance and Other Contexts*. Westport, Conn.: Greenwood, 1996.

———. *The Black Dancing Body: A Geography from Coon to Cool*. New York: Palgrave MacMillan, 2003.

———. *Waltzing in the Dark: African American Vaudeville and Racer Politics in the Swing Era*. New York: St. Martin's, 2000.

Graburn, Nelson. "Tourism: The Sacred Journey." In *Hosts and Guests*, Verene Smith, ed., 21–36. Philadelphia: University of Pennsylvania Press, 1989.

Green, Doris. "Traditional Dance in Africa." In *African Dance: An Artistic, Historical, and Philosophical Inquiry*, ed. K. Welsh-Asante, 13–28. Trenton, N.J.: Africa World Press, 1998.

Green, Richard. "(Up)Staging the Primitive: Pearl Primus and 'The Negro Problem' in American Dance." In *Dancing Many Drums*, T. DeFrantz, ed., 105–39. Madison: University of Wisconsin Press, 2002.

Greenberg, Kim. "The Dance Studio as Dance Culture." Unpublished master's thesis, Columbia University, Teachers' College, New York, 1996.

———. "Questions of Authenticity in African Tourist Art," unpublished paper, University of Massachusetts, Amherst, 1993.

Greene, Oliver N. "Ethnicity, Modernity, and Retention in the Garifuna Punta." *Center for Black Music Research Journal*, 22 (Fall 2004): 189–216.

Guerra y Sanchez, Ramiro. *Azúcar y población en las Antillas*. Havana: Editorial de ciencias sociales, 1970.

Guerra, Ramiro. *Eros Baile: Danza y Sexualidad*. Havana: Editorial Letras Cubanas, 2000.

———. "My Experience and Experiments in Caribbean Dance." In Sloat, *Making Caribbean Dance*, 49–61.

———. *Teatralización del folklore y otros ensayos*. Havana: Editorial Letras Cubanas, 1989.

Guilbault, Jocelyn. *Governing Sound: The Cultural Politics of Trinidad's Carnival Musics*. Chicago: University of Chicago Press, 2007.

———. "Oral and Literate Strategies in Performance: La Rose and La Marguerite Organizations in St. Lucia." *Yearbook of Traditional Music* 19 (1987): 97–115.

Guilbault, Jocelyne, Gage Averill, Edouard Benoit, and Gregory Rabess. *Zouk: World Music in the West Indies*. Chicago: University of Chicago Press, 1993.

Guillermoprieto, Alma. *Samba*. New York: Knopf, 1990.

Guinier, Lani. *Tyranny of the Majority: Fundamental Fairness in Representative Democracy*. New York: Free Press, 1994.

Guitar, Lynne. "The Origins of Carnival and the Special Traditions of Dominican Carnaval." Available at http://www.domibachata.com/carnival/Carnaval%20 Origins_w%20photos.pdf .

Gutierrez, Ramon A., and Genevieve Fabre. *Feasts and Celebrations in North American Ethnic Communities*. Albuquerque: University of New Mexico Press, 1995.

Hagedorn, Katherine. *Divine Utterances: The Performance of Afro-Cuban Santería*. Washington, D.C.: Smithsonian Institution Press, 2001.

Hall, Stuart. "Introduction: Who Needs 'Identity'?" In *Questions of Cultural Identity*, ed. S. Hall and Paul du Gay, 1–17. London: Sage, 1996.

Hanna, Judith. "African Dance and the Warrior Tradition." In *The Warrior Tradition in Modern Africa*, special issue of *Journal of Asian and African Studies*, ed. Ali Mazuri, 12.1–2 (1977): 111–33.

———. "Africa's New Traditional Dance." *Ethnomusicology* 9 (1965): 13–21.

———. "Dance and the 'Women's War.'" *Dance Research Journal* 14.1–2 (1981–82): 25–28.

———. "The Anthropology of Dance-Ritual: Nigeria's Ubakala Nkwa di Iche Iche." PhD diss., Ann Arbor: UMI Diss. Services, 1976.

———. "The Highlife: A West African Urban Dance." In *Dance Research Monograph One*, ed. Patricia A. Rowe and Ernestine Stodelle, 138–52. New York: CORD, 1973.

———. *To Dance is Human: A Theory of Nonverbal Communication*. Austin: University of Texas Press, 1979.

Harding, Rachel. *A Refuge in Thunder: Candomblé and Alternative Spaces of Blackness*. Bloomington: Indiana University Press, 2000.

Harewood, Susan, and John Hunte. "Dance in Barbados: Reclaiming, Preserving, and Creating National Identities." In Sloat, *Making Caribbean Dance*, 265–84.

Harris, Joseph. "The African Diaspora in World History and Politics." In Walker, *African Roots*, 104–17.

———. *The African Presence in Asia: Consequences of the East African Slave Trade*, Evanston, Ill.: Northwestern University Press, 1971.

Harrison, Fay V., ed. *Decolonizing Anthropology*. Washington, D.C.: Association of Black Anthropologists, American Association of Anthropology, 1991.

Hart, Daniel. *Trinidad and the Other West Indian Islands and Colonies*. 2nd ed. Port of Spain, Trinidad and Tobago: Chronicle Publishing Office, 1866.

Hartog, Johan. *Curaçao: From Colonial Dependence to Autonomy*. Aruba, Netherlands Antilles: De Wit, 1968.

Hazzard-Gordon, Katrina. *Jookin': The Rise of Social Dance Formations in African-American Culture*. Philadelphia: Temple University Press, 1990.

Hernández, María del Carmen. *Historia de la danza en Cuba*. Havana: Editorial Pueblo y Educación, 1980.

Herskovits, Melville. *The Myth of the Negro Past*. New York: Harpers, 1941.

Herskovits, Melville, and Francis Herskovits. *Trinidad Village*. New York: Knopf, 1947.

Hesmondhalgh, David, and Casper Melville. "Urban Breakfast Culture: Repercussions of Hip-Hop in the United Kingdom." In *Global Noise: Rap and Hip-Hop Outside the USA,* Tony Mitchell, ed., 86–110. Middletown, Conn.: Wesleyan University Press, 2002.

Heywood, Linda, ed. *Central Africans and Cultural Transformations in the American Diaspora*. Cambridge: Cambridge University Press, 2002.

Heywood, Linda, and John Thornton. *Central Africans, Atlantic Creoles, and the Foundation of the Americas 1585–1660*. Cambridge: Cambridge University Press, 2007.

Hill, Constance Vallis. "Katherine Dunham's Southland: Protest in the Face of Repression." In *Dancing Many Drums*, ed. T. DeFrantz, 289–316. Madison: University of Wisconsin Press, 2002.

Hill, Donald R. *Calypso Calaloo: Early Carnival Music in Trinidad*. Gainesville: University Press of Florida, 1993.

Hilton, Wendy. *Dance of Court and Theater: French Noble Style, 1690–1725*. Ed. by Caroline Gaynor. Labanotation by Mereille Backer. Princeton, N.J.: Princeton University Press, 1981.

———. "Dance and Music of Court and Theater: Selected Writings of Wendy Hilton." In *Dance and Music Series* 10. Hillsdale, N.Y.: Pendragon, 1997.

———. "Dances to the Music of Jean-Baptiste Lully." In *Early Music* 14.1: 51–63.

Hintzen, Percy C. "Cultural Politics of Development—Nationalism and the Invention of Development: Modernity and the Cultural Politics of Resistance." *Social and Economic Studies* (Mona, Jamaica: Institute of Social and Economic Research) 54.3 (2005): 66–96.

———. *The Costs of Regime Survival: Racial Mobilization, Elite Domination, and Control of the State in Guyana and Trinidad*. Cambridge: Cambridge University Press, 1989.

Honorat, M. Lamartinière. "Les danses folkloriques haitiennes." In *Bureau de Ethnologie*, special edition, 2.11 (1955): 1–155.

Hosokawa, Shuhei. "Salsa no tiene fronteras; Orquestra de la luz and the Gobalization of Popular Music." In Waxer, 289–311.

Huntington, Carla Stalling. *Hip-hop Dance: Meanings and Message*. Jefferson, North Carolina: McFarland, 2007.

Hurston, Zora Neale. *Tell My Horse*. Philadelphia: Lippincott, 1938.

Isaac, Tania. "Helen, Heaven, and I: In Search of a Dialogue." In Sloat, *Making Caribbean Dance*, 247–64.

Jahnheinz Jahn, *Muntu: African Culture and the Western World*. New York: Grove Press, 1961.

James, C. L. R. (Cyril Lionel Robert). 1938. *The Black Jacobins: Touissaint L'Ouverture and the San Domingo Revolution*, New York: Vintage, 1968.

John, Suki. "Técnica Cubana." In Sloat, *Caribbean Dance*, 73–78.

Jonas, Gerald. *Dancing: The Pleasure, Power and Art of Movement*. New York: Harry N. Abrams with Thirteen/WNET, 1992.

Juliana, Elis. *Origen di balia di tambú na Korsou*. Curaçao: Kristóf, 1983.

Kaeppler, Adrienne. "Polynesian Dance as 'Airplane Art.'" *Dance Research Journal* 8 (1973): 71–85.

———. "The Structure of Tongan Dance." PhD diss., University of Hawaii, 1967. Ann Arbor: UMI Diss. Services.

Kasfir, Sidney L. "African Art and Authenticity: A Text with a Shadow." *African Arts* 25.2 (1992): 40–53.

Kato, M. T. *From Kung Fu to Hip-hop: Globalization, Revolution, and Popular Culture*. Albany: State University of New York Press, 2007.

Kealiinohomoku, Joann. "A Comparative Study of Dance as a Constellation of Motor Behaviors among African and United States Negroes." *Dance Research Annual*, 7 (1975[1965]): 1–181.

———. "An Anthropologist Looks at Ballet as an Ethnic Dance." *Impulse* (1969/1970), 24–33.

———. "Theory and Methods for an Anthropological Study of Dance." PhD diss., Indiana University, 1976. Ann Arbor: UMI Diss. Services.

Kiddy, Elizabeth. "Who is the King of Congo? A New Look at African and Afro-Brazilian Kings in Brazil." In Heywood, *Central Africans*, 153–82.

King, Dana, Danielle LeBlanc, and Carlton R. Van Lowe. "The Impact of Tourism in the Caribbean." *TransAfrica Forum Issue Brief*, July 2000.

Klein, Debra. *Yorùbá Bàtá Goes Global: Artists, Culture Brokers, and Fans*. Chicago: University of Chicago Press, 2007.

Klein, Herbert. *Slavery in the Americas: A Comparative Study of Virginia and Cuba*. Chicago: University of Chicago Press, 1967.

Klein, Herbert, and Ben Vinson III. *African Slavery in Latin America and the Caribbean*. 2nd edition. New York: Oxford University Press, 2007.

Knight, Franklin. *Slave Society in Cuba during the 19th Century*. Madison: University of Wisconsin Press, 1970.

———. *The Caribbean: The Genesis of a Fragmented Nationalism*. 1987. New York: Oxford University Press, 1990.

Knight, Franklin, and Colin Palmer, eds. *The Modern Caribbean*. Chapel Hill: University of North Carolina Press, 1989.

Kraus, Richard, Sarah Chapman Hilsendager, and Brenda Dixon. *History of the Dance in Art and Education*. 3rd edition. Englewood Cliffs, N.J.: Prentice-Hall, 1991.

Kraut, Anthea. "Everybody's Fire Dance: Zora Neale Hurston and American Dance History." *Scholar and Feminist Online* 3.2 (2005): 1–5.

Kubik, Gerhard. *Angolan Traits in Black Music, Games and Dances of Brazil: A Study of African Cultural Extensions Overseas*. Lisbon: Junta de Investigações Científicas de Ultramar, 1990.

Kurath, Gertrude. *Half a Century of Dance Research*. Ann Arbor, Michigan: Cushing-Malloy, 1986.

———. "Los Concheros." *Journal of American Folklore*, 59.234 (1946): 387–99.

———. Personal communication, Ann Arbor, Michigan, 1992.

Labat, Père Jean Baptiste. *Nouveaux voyages aux îles de l'Amérique*, Vol. 2. 1724. Fort-de-France, Martinique: Éditions des Horizons Caraïbes, 1972.

———. *Voyage aux Iles: Chronique aventureuse des Caraïbes 1693–1705*. 1722. Paris: Édition Phébus, 1993.

Lachatánere, Rómulus. *Manuel de Santería*. Havana: Editorial Caribe, 1942.

Laguerre, Michel. *Voodoo and Politics in Haiti*. New York: St. Martin's, 1989.

———. "Voodoo as Religious and Political Ideology." *Freeing the Spirit* 3.1 (1974): 23–28.

———. *Voodoo Heritage*. Beverly Hills, Calif.: Sage, 1980.

Lamur, Humphrey E. "Slave Religion in Suriname." In *Resistance and Rebellion in Suriname: Old and New*, ed. Gary Brauna-Shute, 103–17. Williamsburg, Va.: College of William and Mary, Department of Anthropology, 1990.

Lamut, Phyllis. "Through the Looking Glass: A Dancer and a Choreographer Writes, Dealing with Downtown." *New Dance Review*, January-March 1991, 18–20.

Landes, Ruth. *City of Women*. 1947. Albuquerque: University of New Mexico Press, 1994.

Lao, Agustín. "Puerto Rico, Puerto Ricans, and the New Politics of Decolonization." Unpublished paper, University of Massachusetts, Department of Anthropology. n.d.

Largey, Michael. "Haiti and the French Caribbean." In Manuel, *Caribbean Currents*, 117–42.

———. "Haiti: Tracing the Steps of the Méringue and Contredanse." In Manuel, *Creolizing*, 209–30.

LaRuffa, Anthony. *San Cipriano: Life in a Puerto Rican Community*. New York: Gordon and Breach, 1971.

Leacock, Seth and Ruth. *Spirits of the Deep: A Study of an Afro-Brazilian Cult*. Garden City, New York: Anchor Press, 1975.

Ledru, André Pierre. *Viaje a la isla de Puerto Rico*. 1797. San Juan: Ediciones del Instituto de Literatura Puertorriqueña, Universidad de Puerto Rico, 1957.

León, Argeliers. *Del canto y el tiempo*. Havana: Editorial Letras Cubanas, 1984.

Levine, Barry, ed. *The New Cuban Presence in the Caribbean*. Boulder, Colo.: Westview, 1983.

Lewin, Olive. *Rock It Come Over: The Folk Music of Jamaica*. Mona: University of the West Indies, 2000.

Lewis, Bernard. *Race and Slavery in the Middle East*. New York: Oxford University Press, 1990.

Lewis, John L. *Ring of Liberation*. Chicago: University of Chicago Press, 1992.

Leymarie, Isabelle. *Cuban Fire: The Story of Salsa and Latin Jazz*. 1997. London: Continuum, 2002.

Linares, Maria Teresa. *La música y el pueblo*. 1974. Havana: Editorial Pueblo y Educación, 1989.

Liverpool, Hollis. "Chalkdust." *Rituals of Power and Rebellion: The Carnival Tradition in Trinidad & Tobago, 1763–1962*. Chicago: Research Associates School Times Publication, 2001.

Lizardo, Fradique. *Danzas y bailes folklóricos dominicanos*. Santo Domingo: Editora Taller, 1975.

———. *Metodología de la danza*. Santo Domingo: Ediciones Fundación García-Arevalo, 1975.

Long, Richard A. *The Black Tradition in American Dance*. New York: Rizzoli, 1989.

López Cantos, Angel. *Fiestas y juegos en Puerto Rico (siglo xviii)*. San Juan: Centro de Estudios Avanzados de Puerto Rico y el Caribe, 1990.

Love, Nia. "Deconstructing Body Poses in the Diaspora," Unpublished paper, Contemporary Issues Panel of Association for the Study of Worldwide African Diaspora Conference, Oct. 3, 2003.

Lowenthal, David. *West Indian Societies*. New York: Oxford University Press, 1972.

MacCannell, Dean. "Staged Authenticity: Arrangements of Social Space in Tourist Settings." *American Journal of Sociology* 79 (1973): 589–603.

Macdonald, Annette. "The Big Drum of Carriacou." *Revista/Review Interamericana*, 8.4 (1978/79): 570–76. Updated reprint in Sloat, *Making Caribbean Dance*, 285–96.

MacGaffey, Wyatt. *Kongo Political Culture: The Conceptual Challenge of the Particular*. Bloomington: Indiana University Press, 2000.

———. *Religion and Society in Central Africa*. Chicago: University of Chicago Press, 1986.

Mackrell, Judith. "Vanishing Pointe: Where Are All the Great Female Choreographers?" U.K. *Guardian*, October 27, 2009.

Maharaj, Ravindra Nath "Raviji." "A Narrative on the Framework of the Presence, Change, and Continuity of Indian Dance in Trinidad. In Sloat, *Making Caribbean Dance*, 321–36.

Mahler, Elfrida, Ramiro Guerra, and José Limón. *Fundamentos de la danza*. Havana: Editorial Orbre, 1978.

Manuel, Peter, with Kenneth Bilby and Michael Largey. *Caribbean Currents: Caribbean Music From Rumba to Reggae*. Philadelphia: Temple University Press, 1995.

Manuel, Peter, ed. *Creolizing Contradance in the Caribbean*. Philadelphia: Temple University Press, 2009.

Marks, Morton. "Exploring *El monte*: Ethnobotany and the Afro-Cuban Science of the Concrete." In *En Torno a Lydia Cabrera*, ed. Isabel Castellano and J. Inclán, 227–45. Miami: Universal, 1987.

Martí, Samuel, and Gertrude Kurath. *Dances of Anáhuac: The Choreography and Music of Precortesian Dances*. Chicago: Aldine, 1964.

Martinez-Alier, Verena. *Marriage, Class and Colour in 19th Century Cuba: A Study of Racial Attitudes and Sexual Values in a Slave Society*. Cambridge: Cambridge University Press, 1974.

Martinez Furé, Rogelio. Personal communications, August and October 1986, and January and March 1987 at *Conjunto nacional de Cuba*, Havana.

Martinus-Guda, Trudi. *Drie eeuwen Banya: De geschiedenis van een Surinaamse slavendans*. Paramaribo, Suriname: Minov-Directoraat Cultuur, 2005.

Marx, Robert. *Treasure Fleets of the Spanish Main*. New York: World, 1968.

Mason, John. *Orin Orisa: Songs for Selected Heads*. Brooklyn, N.Y.: Yoruba Theological Archministry, 1992.

Matory, J. Lorand. *Black Atlantic Religion: Tradition, Transnationalism, and Matriarchy in the Afro-Brazilian Candomblé*. Cambridge: Cambridge University Press, 2005.

———. "'The Cult of Nations' and the Ritualization of Their Purity." *South Atlantic Quarterly* 100.1 (2001):171–214.

———. "The English Professors of Brazil." *Comparative Studies* 41.1 (1999): 72–103.

Matteo (Matteo Marcellus Vittucci), and Carola Goya, et al. *Language of Spanish Dance*. Norman: University of Oklahoma Press, 1990.

Maurer, Bill. "A Fish Story: Rethinking Globalization on Virgin Gorda British Virgin Islands." *American Ethnologist*, 27.3 (2000): 670–701.

———. "Caribbean Dance: Resistance, Colonial Discourse, and Subjugated Knowledges." In *Nieuwe Est Indische Gids/West Indies Guide*, 65.1/2 (1991–92): 1–26.

McAlister, Elizabeth. *Rara! Vodou, Power, and Performance in Haiti and Its Diaspora*. Berkeley: University of California Press, 2002.

McBurnie, Beryl. *Dance Trinidad Dance*. Port of Spain: Little Carib Theater/Beryl McBurnie, 1953.

———. *Outlines of the Dances of Trinidad*. Port of Spain: Guardian Commercial Printery, n.d.

———. Personal communication, Port of Spain, Trinidad, 1999.

McCall, John. *Dancing Histories: Heuristic Ethnography of the Ohafia Igbo*. Ann Arbor: University of Michigan Press, 2000.

McDaniel, Lorna. *The Big Drum Ritual of Carriacou: Praisesongs in Rememory of Flight*. Gainesville: University Press of Florida, 1998.

McKay, Leslie. "Women's Contribution to Tourism in Negril, Jamaica." In *Women and Change in the Caribbean*, ed. J. Momsen, 278–86. Kingston: Ian Randle/Bloomington: Indiana University Press/London: James Currey, 1993.

Mead, Margaret. *Coming of Age in Samoa*. New York: Morrow, 1928.

Métraux, Alfred. *Voodoo in Haiti*. 1959. New York: Knopf, 1972.

Mexican Fine Arts Center Museum. *The African Presence in México*, coordinated by Claudia Herrera, Angelina Villanueva, and Elisa Saeta. Chicago: Mexican Fine Arts Center Museum, 2006.

Middleton, John. "Dance Among the Lugbara of Uganda." In *Society and the Dance*, ed. P. Spencer, 165–82. Cambridge: Cambridge University Press, 1985.

Miller, Ivor. *Aerosol Kingdom: Subway Painters of New York City*. Jackson: University Press of Mississippi, 2002.

———. *Voice of the Leopard: African Secret Societies and Cuba*. Jackson: University of Mississippi Press, 2009.

Miller, Joseph C. "Central Africa During the Era of the Slave Trade, c. 1490s-1850s." L. Heywood, *Central Africans*, 21–70.

Millet, José, and Rafael Brea. *Grupos folklóricos de Santiago de Cuba*. Santiago de Cuba: Editorial Oriente, 1989.

Millette, James. *Genesis of Crown Colony Government*. Trinidad: Moko Enterprises, 1970.

Mintz, Sidney. "Foreword." 1964. In Guerra, *Azúcar*, xi–xliv. Havana: Editorial de Ciencias Sociales, 1970.

———. *Worker in the Cane: A Puerto Rican Life History*. New York: Norton, 1974.

Mintz, Sidney, and Sally Price, eds. *Caribbean Contours*. Baltimore: Johns Hopkins University Press, 1985.

Mitchell, Tony, ed. *Global Noise: Rap and Hip-hop Outside the U.S.A.* Middletown, Conn.: Wesleyan University Press, 2001.

Molina, Lucia Dominga, and Mario Luis López. "Afro-Argentineans: 'Forgotten' and 'Disappeared'—Yet Still Present." In Walker, *African Roots*, 332–47.

Moore, Robin. *Nationalizing Blackness: Afrocubanismo and Artistic Revolution in Havana, 1920–1940*. Pittsburgh: University of Pittsburgh Press, 1997.

Moreau de Saint-Méry, Médéric Louis Elie. *de la Danse*. 1789. Parma: Bodoni, 1803.

Moreno, Isidoro. "Festive Rituals, Religious Associations, and Ethnic Reaffirmation of Black Andalusians: Antecedents of the Black Confraternities and Cabildos in the Americas." In Rahier, *Representations*, 3–18.

Moreno-Fraginals, Manuel, ed. *Africa in Latin America: Essays on History, Culture, and Socialization*. 1977. Trans. by Leonor Blum. New York: Holmes & Meier/ UNESCO, 1984.

Mousouris, Melinda. "The Dance World of Ramiro Guerra: Solemnity, Voluptuousness, Humor, and Chance." In Sloat, *Caribbean Dance from Abakuá to Zouk*, 56–72.

Murphy, Joseph M., and Mei-Mei Sanford, eds. *Ọ̀ṣun Across the Waters: A Yoruba Goddess in Africa and the Americas*. Bloomington: Indiana University Press, 2001.

Myers, Gerald, et al. *African American Genius in Modern Dance*. Durham, N.C.: American Dance Festival, 1993.

Nettleford, Rex. *Dance Jamaica: Cultural Definition and Artistic Discovery; National Dance Theater Company of Jamaica, 1962–1983.* New York: Grove, 1985.

———. *Roots and Rhythms; Jamaica's National Dance Theatre.* New York: Hill and Wang, 1970.

Ngunjiri, Pauline. "Civil Society Still in Denial About HIV/AIDS." In *Panoscope, Before UNGASS+5: Keeping the Promise—A Five Country Survey,* May 2006.

Nketia, J. H. K. *African Music in Ghana: A Survey of Traditional Forms.* Accra: Longmans, 1962.

———. "The Interrelations of African Music and Dance." *Studia Musicologica,* 7 (1965): 91-101.

———. *Music of Africa.* New York: Norton, 1974.

Nunley, John W., Judith Bettelheim, and Barbara Bridges. *Caribbean Festival Arts: Each and Every Bit of Difference.* Seattle: University of Washington Press, 1988.

Nwankwo, Ifeoma, and Mamadou Diouf, eds. *Rhythms of the Atlantic World: Rituals, Remembrances, and Revisions.* Ann Arbor: University of Michigan Press, 2010.

Oldendorp, Christian Georg Andreas. *History of the Mission of the Evangelical Brethren on the Caribbean Islands of St. Thomas, St. Croix, and St. John.* 1777. Abridged version of 2 vols. Ed. by Johann Jakob Bossard, English trans. by Arnold R. Highfield and Vladimir Barac. Ann Arbor: Karoma Publishers, 1987.

Olivera Chirimini, Tomás. "Candombe, African Nations, and the Africanity of Uruguay." In Walker, *African Roots,* 256–74.

Opoku, Alfred M. "Choreography and the African Dance." *Institution of African Studies Research Review* (University of Ghana), 3.1 (1965): 53–59.

Orozco, Danilo. "El son: ¿Ritmo, baile o reflejo de la personalidad cultural cubana?" In *Musicología de Latina America,* ed. Zoila Gomez García, 363–89. Havana: Editora Arte y Literatura, 1984.

Ortiz, Fernando. "Afro-Cuban Festival 'Day of the Kings.'" In Bettelheim, *Cuban Festivals,* 1–40.

———. *Contrapunteo cubano del tabaco y el azúcar.* 1940. Havana: Consejo nacional de Cultura, 1963.

———. *La africanía de la música folklórica de Cuba.* Havana: Educaciones Cárdenas y Cia. 1950.

———. *Los bailes y el teatro de los negros en el folklore de Cuba.* Havana: Editorial Letras Cubanas, 1951.

Osumare, Halifu. *The Africanist Aesthetic in Global Hip-Hop: Power Moves.* New York: Palgrave McMillan, 2007.

Pacini, Deborah. *Bachata: A Social History of a Dominican Popular Music.* Philadelphia: Temple University Press, 1995.

———. "Amalgamating Musics: Popular Music and Cultural Hybridity in the Americas." In *Musical Migrations: Transnationalism and Cultural Hybridity in Latin/o America, Vol. I,* ed. Frances Aparicio and Candida Jáquez, 13–32. New York: Palgrave Macmillan, 2003.

Patterson, Orlando. *The Sociology of Slavery*. Rutherford, N. J.: Fairleigh Dickinson University Press/London: Associated University Presses, 1969.

Paul, Emmanuel. *Panorama du folklore Haïtien*. 1962. Port-au-Prince: Edition Fardin, 1978.

Pedro, Alberto. "La semana santa haitiano-cubano." *Etnología y Folklore* 4 (1967).

———. Public lectures on Haitian-Cuban culture at La Casa de Las Américas, October 16–20, 1986.

Pérez, Louis A. *Cuba: Between Reform and Revolution*. New York: Oxford University Press, 1988.

———. *On Becoming Cuban: Identity, Nationality, and Culture*. Chapel Hill: University of North Carolina Press, 1999.

Pérez-López, Jorge. "Islands of Capitalism in an Ocean of Socialism: Joint Ventures in Cuba's Development Strategy." In *Cuba at the Crossroads: Politics and Economics after the Fourth Party Congress*, ed. Jorge Pérez-López, 190–219. Gainesville: University Press of Florida, 1994.

Perna, Vincenzo. *Timba: The Sound of the Cuban Crisis*. Burlington, Vt.: Ashgate, 2005.

Perrone, Charles A., and Christopher Dunn, eds. *Brazilian Popular Music and Globalization*. Gainesville: University Press of Florida, 2001.

Pescatello, Ann, ed., *The African in Latin America*. New York: Knopf, 1975.

Pieper, Jim. *Guatemala's Masks and Drama*. Torrance, Calif.: Pieper, 2006.

Platvoet, Johannes Gerhardus. *Comparing Religions: A Limitative Approach; An Analysis of Akan, Para-Creole, and IFO-Sananda Rites and Prayers*. The Hague: Mouton, 1981.

Price, Richard. *Maroon Societies: Rebel Slave Communities in the Americas*. Baltimore: Johns Hopkins University Press, 1979.

Price, Sally, and Richard Price. *Afro-American Arts of the Suriname Rain Forest*. Los Angeles: Museum of Cultural History, University of California/Berkeley: University of California Press, 1980.

Primus, Pearl. "African Dance: Eternity Captured." *Caribe* 7.1/2 (1983): 10–13.

———. "Life Crises: Dance from Birth to Death." *American Therapy Association: Proceedings from the Fourth Annual Conference*. (Philadelphia, 1969), 1–13.

Pryor, Al, Jack O'Neil, and Nina Gomes, comps. and eds. *Cuba, I am Time*. (Liner notebook). Bethpage, N.Y.: Blue Jacket Entertainment, 1987.

Quijano, Anibal. "Coloniality of Power, Eurocentrism, and Latin America." *Nepantla* 1.3 (2000): 139–55.

Quintero Rivera, Ángel. "Ponce, the Danza and the National Question: Notes toward a Sociology of Puerto Rican Music." *Cimarrón, New Perspectives on the Caribbean* 1.2 (1976): 49–65.

———. *Salsa, sabor y control: Sociología de la música 'tropical'*. Mexico: Siglo Veintiuno Editores. 1998.

———. *Cuerpo y cultura: Las músicas "mulatas" y la subversión del baile*. Madrid: Iberoamericana, 2009.

Quirey, Belinda. *May I Have the Pleasure? The Story of Popular Dance.* London: BBC/Princeton: Dance Books, 1987.

Raboteau, Albert. *Slave Religion.* New York: Oxford University Press, 1978.

Raffe, W. G., and M. E. Purdon, comp. *Dictionary of the Dance.* 1964. New York: A.S. Barnes, 1975.

Rahier, Jean, ed. *Representations of Blackness and the Performance of Identity.* Westport, Conn.: Bergin and Garvey, 1999.

Rameau, Pierre. *The Dancing Master 1725.* Original trans., 1931, by Cyril Beaumont. Brooklyn: Dance Horizons, 1970.

Reid, Basil, ed. *Archaeology and Geoinformatics: Case Studies from the Caribbean.* Tuscaloosa: University of Alabama Press, 2008.

Rice, J. "Cuba Talks Business with Americans, Europeans." *Washington Times,* June 11, 1992.

Rivera, Rachel. *New York Ricans from the Hip-hop Zone.* New York: Palgrave Macmillan, 2003.

Roberts, John Storm. *Black Music of Two Worlds.* New York: Morrow, 1972.

———. *The Latin Tinge: The Impact of Latin American Music on the United States.* Tivoli, N.Y.: Original Music, 1979.

Rodriguez, Romero Jorge. "The Afro Populations of America's Southern Cone: Organization, Development, and Culture in Argentina, Bolivia, Paraguay, and Uruguay." In Walker, *African Roots,* 314–31.

Rogozinski, Jan. *A Brief History of the Caribbean: from the Arawak and the Carib to the Present.* New York: Meridian/Penguin, 1994.

Román-Velázquez, Patria. "The Making of a Salsa Music Scene in London." In Waxer, *Situating Salsa,* 259–88.

Römer, Renee. *Cultureel mozaïek van de Nederlandse Antillen: constanten en varianten.* Zutphen, Netherlands: De Walburg Pers, 1977.

Rosalia, Rene. *Tambu: De legale en kerkelijke repressie van Afro-Curaçaose volksuitingen.* Zutphen, Netherlands: Uitgeversmaatschappij Walburg Pers, 1997.

Rose, Albirda. *Dunham Technique: "A Way of Life."* Dubuque, Iowa: Kendall/Hunt, 1990.

Roy, Maya. *Cuban Music: From Son and Rumba to the Buena Vista Social Club and Timba Cubana.* Princeton: Markus Weiner Publishers, 2002.

Royce, Anya. *The Anthropology of Dance.* Bloomington: Indiana University Press, 1977.

Rubio, Fray Vicente. *Las casas moradas del Secretario Diego Caballero.* Santo Domingo: Ediciones fundación García Arévalo, 1979.

Ryman, Cheryl. "When Jamaica Dances." In Sloat, *Making Caribbean Dance,* 97–131.

Sainton, Jean-Pierre, et al. *Histoire et Civilisation de la Caraïbe (Guadeloupe, Martinique, Petites Antilles), Tome I: Le temps des Genèses; des origines á 1685.* Paris: Maisonneuve and Larose, 2004.

Salgado Henríquez, Marta. "El legado africano en Chile." In *Conocimiento desde Adentro,* ed. S. Walker, 223–70. La Paz, Chile: Fundación PIEB, 2010.

Sarduy, Pédro Perez. "Flashback on Carnival: A Personal Memoir." In Bettelheim, *Cuban Festivals*, 154–65.

———. "These Things Happen in My Country: Carnival in Havana during the 'Periodo Especial.'" In Bettelheim, *Cuban Festivals*, 166–72.

Satizábal, Medardo Arias. "Se Prohibe Escuchar 'Salsa y Control': When Salsa Arrived in Buenaventura, Colombia." In Waxer, *Situating Salsa*, 247–58.

Scarpaci, Joseph L. *Barrios and Plazas: Heritage Tourism and Globalization in the Latin American Centro Histórico*. Tucson: University of Arizona Press, 2005.

Schechner, Richard. *Between Theater and Anthropology*. Philadelphia: University of Pennsylvania Press, 1985.

Scott, Anna. "'A Falaque Fav/Words That Work': Performance of Black Power Ideologies in Bloco Afro Carnaval in Salvador, Bahia, Brazil, 1968–Present." PhD diss., Northwestern University, 2001. Ann Arbor: UMI Diss. Services.

———. "Dance." In *Culture Works*, ed. Richard Maxwell, 107–30. Minneapolis: University of Minnesota Press, 2001.

———. "What's It Worth to Ya? Adaptation and Anachronism: Remy Harris's Pure Movement and Shakespeare." *Discourses in Dance*, 3 (2003): 2–18.

Scott, James C. *Domination and the Arts of Resistance: Hidden Transcripts*. New Haven: Yale University, 1990.

Sharp, Cecil. *The Dance: An Historical Survey of Dancing in Europe*. London: Halton & Truscott Smith, 1924.

Silver, Ira. "Marketing Authenticity in Third World Countries." *Annals of Tourism Research*, 20 (1993): 302–18.

Slater, Mariam K. *The Caribbean Family: Legitimacy in Martinique*. New York: St. Martin's Press, 1977.

Sloat, Susanna, ed. *Caribbean Dance from Abakuá to Zouk: How Movement Shapes Identity*. Gainesville: University Press of Florida, 2002.

———. *Making Caribbean Dance: Continuity and Creativity in Island Cultures*. Gainesville: University Press of Florida, 2010.

Snyder, Allegra Fuller. "The Dance Symbol." *Dance Research Annual*, 6 (1974): 213–24.

Society of Dance History Scholars' Journal. Riverside, Calif.: Society of Dance History Scholars, 1983–.

Soledade, Augusto. "Afro-Fusion Dance: A Perspective from the Diaspora." In *Encyclopedia of the African Diaspora*, ed. C. Boyce Davies, 1:68–70. New York:ABC/ CLIO, 2008.

———. "Moving Poetics of the Sweet and Sour: A Phenomenology of African Diaspora Fusion Aesthetics." Unpublished paper, Contemporary Issues Panel of ASWAD Conference, Oct. 3, 2003.

Sosa, Enrique. *El Carabalí*. Havana: Editorial Letras Cubanas, 1984.

Southern, Eileen. *The Music of Black Americans: A History*. New York: Norton, 1971.

Spencer, Paul. "Dance as Antithesis in the Samburu Discourse." In *Society and the Dance*, ed. P. Spencer, 140–64. Cambridge: Cambridge University Press, 1985.

————, ed. *Society and the Dance: The Anthropology of Performance*. Cambridge: Cambridge University Press. 1985.

Stanley Niaah, Sonjah. "Dance Divas, Queens, and Kings." In Sloat, *Making Caribbean Dance*, 132–48.

St. Coeur, Jill. "Jonkonnu: Cultural Perpetuation of a Caribbean tradition." Master's thesis, Department of Consumer Studies, University of Massachusetts, Amherst, 1997.

Stein, Robert Louis. *The French Slave Trade in the Eighteenth Century: An Old Regime Business*. Madison: University of Wisconsin Press, 1979.

Stephens, Henri J. M. *Wintiliederen (Winti songs)*. Amsterdam: Karnac, 2003.

Stewart, Diane. *Three Eyes for the Journey: African Dimensions of the Jamaican Religious Experience*. London: Oxford University Press, 2005.

Stewart, John O. "Cultural Passages in the African Diaspora: The West Indian Carnival." In Walker, *African Roots*, 206–21.

Stuckey, Sterling. *Going through the Storm: The Influence of African American Art on History*. New York: Oxford University Press, 1994.

Suarez, Lucía. "Citizenship and Dance in Urban Brazil: Grupo Corpo: A Case Study." In *Rhythms of the Afro-Atlantic World*, ed. M. Diouf and I. Kiddoe Nwankwo, 95–120. Ann Arbor: University of Michigan Press, 2010.

Sublette, Ned. *Cuba and Its Music: From the First Drums to the Mambo*. Chicago: Chicago Review Press, 2004.

Sully-Cally, Lézin. *Musiques et danses Afro-Caraïbes: Martinique*. Gros Morne, Martinique: Sully-Cally/Lézin, 1990.

Summers, Bill, Michael Spiro, Duraldo Devar, and Vanessa Lindu. *Bata Rhythms from Matanzas*. San Francisco: Cabiosile, 2007.

Suriel, S. Miguel. *Boeki di quadrilla: La renaissance, un ensaye chiquitu di educadora social*. [c. 1914–1940] (Reliable publishing information not available.)

Swed, John F., and Morton Marks. "Afro-American Transformation of European Set Dances and Dance Suites." *Dance Research Journal* 20.1 (1988): 29–36.

Sweet, James Hoke. *Recreating Africa: Culture, Kinship, and Religion in the African-Portuguese World, 1441–1770*. Chapel Hill: University of North Carolina Press, 2003.

Sweet, Jill. "Burlesquing 'The Other' in Pueblo Performance." *Annals of Tourism Research*, 16 (1989): 62–75.

Tamayo Torres, Guillermo. *Pinar del Río: Turismo verde*. Havana: Edición José Martí, 1999.

Taylor, Margaret Fisk. *A Time to Dance: Symbolic Movement in Worship*. Philadelphia: United Church Press, 1967.

Taylor, Patrick, ed. *Nation Dance: Religion, Identity, and Cultural Difference in the Caribbean*. Bloomington: Indiana University Press, 2001.

Taylor, Paul C. "Harmonize in the Mission: John Dewey and Black Religious Music." In *Black Music Scholarship and the Bridging of Diasporal Sacred Worlds*, ed. Samuel Floyd, 1–28. Berkeley: University of California Press, in press, n.d.

Tchak, Sami. *La prostitution á Cuba: Communisme ruses et débrouille*. Paris: L'Harmattan, 1999.

Tejeda, Dario. *La pasión danzaria*. Santo Domingo: Academia de Ciencias de República dominicana, 2002.

Thomas, Deborah. "Democratizing Dance: Institutional Transformation and Hegemonic Re-ordering in Post-colonial Jamaica." *Cultural Anthropology*, 17.4 (2002): 512–50.

———. *Modern Blackness: Nationalism, Globalization, and the Politics of Culture in Jamaica*. Durham, N.C.: Duke University Press, 2004.

Thompson, Robert Farris. *African Art in Motion*. Berkeley: University of California Press, 1974.

———. *Flash of the Spirit*. New York: Random House, 1983.

Thompson, Robert Farris, and Joseph Cornet. *Four Moments of the Sun: Kongo Art in Two Worlds*. Washington, D.C.: National Gallery of Art, 1981.

Thornton, John K. *Africa and Africans in the Making of the Atlantic World, 1400–1800*. 1992. Cambridge: Cambridge University Press, 1998.

———. "Religious and Ceremonial Life in the Kongo and Mbundu Areas, 1500–1700." In Heywood, *Central Africans*, 71–90, 2002.

Tomé, Lester. "The Cuban Ballet: Its Rationale, Aesthetics and Artistic Identity as Formulated by Alicia Alonso." PhD diss., Temple University, 2011.

Tomko, Linda. *Dancing Class: Gender, Ethnicity, and Social Divides in American Dance, 1890–1920*. Bloomington: Indiana University Press, 1999.

Torp, Lisbet. "Hip-Hop Dances: Their Adoption and Function Among Boys in Denmark from 1983–1984 (1986)." In Anca Giuchescu and Lisbet Torp, "Theory and Methods in Dance Research: A European Approach to the Holistic Study of Dance," *Yearbook for Traditional Music* 23 (1991): 6–7. New York: International Council for Traditional Music.

Turner, Victor. *Celebration: Studies in Festivity and Ritual*. Washington, D.C.: Smithsonian Institution Press, 1982.

Turner, Victor, and Edith Turner. *Image and Pilgrimages in Christian Culture: Anthropological Perspectives*. New York: Columbia University Press, 1978.

Turner, Victor, and Edward M. Bruner. *The Anthropology of Experience*. Urbana: University of Illinois Press, 1986.

Turpin, John. Personal communication, Oakland, California, 1997.

Ulloa S., Alejandro. "El baile: Un lenguaje del cuerpo: el baile sabe mas del mundo que consiencia" (manuscript, 1–20). 2nd ed. *El baile*. Cali, Colombia:Modalidad Ensayo, 2002/2005.

U.K. Coalition of People Living with HIV and AIDS Limited. "Closet of the Caribbean," 121. Available at http://www.ukcoalition.org (2006).

U.N. World Tourism Organization (UNWTO). Available at http://www.worldtourism.org (2004).

Urfé, Ordillio. "Music and Dance in Cuba." 1977. In *Africa in Latin America: Essays on History, Culture and Socialization*, ed. M. Moreno Fraginals, trans. Leonor Blum, 170–88. New York: Holmes and Meier, 1984.

Uri, Alex, and Francoise Uri. *Musiques et Musiciens de la Guadeloupe*. Paris: Con Brio, 1991.

Vanony-Frisch, Nicole. *Les esclaves de la Guadeloupe á la fin de l'ancien régime d'après les sources notariales (1770–1789)*. Paris: Lienhart et Cie, 1985.

Vaughan, Umi. *Rebel Dance, Renegade Stance: Timba Music and Black Identity in Cuba*. Ann Arbor: University of Michigan Press, 2012 [forthcoming].

———. "Visión de los bailes públicos en La Habana." *Catauro, revista cubana de antropología*, 6.10 (2007): 109–20.

Vaughan, Umi, and Carlos Aldama. *The Life of Carlos Aldama: The Drums, Cuba, and the African Diaspora*. Bloomington: Indiana University Press, 2012 [forthcoming].

Vega, Marta Moreno. *The Altar of My Soul: The Living Traditions of Santería*. New York: Ballentine Publishing Group, 2000.

Vega-Drouet, Hector. "Historical and Ethnological Survey on Probable African Origins of the Puerto Rican Bomba, Including a Description of Santiago Apostol." PhD diss., Wesleyan University, 1979.

Verger, Pierre Fatumbi. *Ewé: O uso das plantas na sociedade iorubá*. Sao Paulo: Editora Scharcz, 1995.

———. *Notes sur le culte des Orisa et Vodun a Bahia*. Dakar: Ifan, 1957.

Vinueza, Maria Elena. *Presencia Arará en la música folclórica de Matanzas*. Havana: Casa de las Américas, 1988.

Voeks, Robert A. *Sacred Leaves of Candomblé: African Magic, Medicine, and Religion in Brazil*. Austin: University of Texas Press, 1997.

Wafer, James William. *The Taste of Blood: Spirit Possession in Brazilian Candomblé*. Philadelphia: University of Pennsylvania Press, 1991.

Walker, Sheila S. "A Choreography of the Universe: The Afro-Brazilian Candomblé as a Microcosm of Yoruba Spiritual Geography." *Anthropology and Humanism Quarterly* 16.2 (1991): 42–50.

———, ed. *African Roots/American Cultures: Africa in the Creation of the Americas*. Lanham, Md.: Rowman & Littlefield, 2001.

———. "Angola Royalty Traditions in the Americas." Unpublished presentation from the 4th Conference on the History of Angola, Luanda, September 2010, 1–21.

———. *Ceremonial Spirit Possession in Africa and Afro-America*. Leiden, Holland: Brill, 1972.

———. "Congo Kings, Queen Nzinga, Dancing Devils, and Catholic Saints: African/ African Syncretism in the Americas." In *Héritage de la Musique Africaine dans les Amériques et les Caraïbes*, ed. Alpha Noël Malonga & Mukala Kadima-Nzuji, 125–32. Brazzaville, Congo: Festival Pan-Africain de la Musique (FESPAM) and Paris: l'Harmattan, 2007.

———, ed. *Conocimiento desde adentro: Los afrosudamericanos hablan de su historia y sus pueblos*. La Paz, Bolivia: PIEB (Programa de Investigación Estratégica en Boivia), 2010.

Walton, William. *El estado actual de las colonias españolas*. 1808. Tomo I. Santo Domingo: Editora de Santo Domingo, 1976.

Warner-Lewis, Maureen. *Central Africa in the Caribbean: Transcending Time, Transforming Cultures*. Mona, Jamaica: University of the West Indies, 2003.

———. *Trinidad Yoruba: From Mother Tongue to Memory*. Tuscaloosa: University of Alabama Press, 1996.

Wason, Janet. "Bele and Quadrille: African and European Dimensions in the Traditional Dances of Dominica, West Indies." In Sloat, *Making Caribbean Dance*, 227–46.

Waterman, Charles. *Juju: A Social History and Ethnography of an African Popular Music*. Chicago: University of Chicago Press, 1990.

Waxer, Lise, ed. *Situating Salsa: Global Markets and Local Meaning in Latin Popular Music*. New York: Routledge, 2002.

Welsh-Asante, Kariamu, ed. *African Dance: An Artistic, Historical, and Philosophical Inquiry*. Trenton, N.J.: Africa World Press, 1994.

———. "Commonalities in African Dance: An Aesthetic Foundation." In *African Culture: Rhythms of Unity*, ed. Molefi and Kariamu Welsh Asante, 71–82. Westport, Conn.: Greenwood, 1985.

———. "The Zimbabwean Dance Aesthetic: Senses, Canons and Characteristics." In Welsh-Asante, *African Dance* 203–20.

Wenig, Adele. *Pearl Primus: An Annotated Bibliography of Sources from 1943–1975*. Oakland, Calif.: Wenadance Unlimited, 1983.

Wilckens, Lois. "Spirit Unbounded: New Approaches to the Performances of Haitian Folklore." In Sloat, *Caribbean Dance from Abakuá to Zouk*, 114–23.

———. *The Drums of Vodou, featuring Frisner Augustin*. Tempe, Arizona: White Cliffs Media, 1992.

———. "We Swirl Our Kongo Skirts," unpublished manuscript, n.d.

Williams, Drid. "Dance of the Bedu Moon." *African Arts*, 2 (1968): 18–21.

———. "The Role of Movement in Selected Symbolic Systems." PhD diss., Oxford University, 1976. Ann Arbor: UMI Diss. Services.

———. "Sokodae: Come and Dance." *African Arts*, 3.3 (1970): 36–39.

———. "Traditional Danced Spaces: Concepts of *Deixis* and the Staging of Traditional Dance." *International Journal of African Dance*, 1.2 (1994): 8–20.

Williams, Eric. *From Columbus to Castro: The History of the Caribbean*. 1970. New York: Vintage Books, 1978.

Willocks, Harold W. L. *The Umbilical Cord: History of the U.S. Virgin Islands from the Pre-Columbian Era to the Present*. Christiansted, St. Croix: H. Willocks, 1995.

Wilson, Olly. "Association of Movement and Music as a Manifestation of a Black Conceptual Approach to Music Making." In *Essays on Afro-American Music and Musicians*, ed. Irene V. Jackson, 1–23. Westport, Conn.: Greenwood, 1981.

———. "Black Music as an Art Form." *Black Music Research Journal*, 1983: 1-22.

———. "The Significance of the Relationship between Afro-American and West African Music." In *Black Perspective in Music II* 1 (1974): 3-22.

Yai, Olabiyi. "African Diasporan Concepts and Practice of the Nation and their Implications in the Modern World." In Walker, African Roots, 244–55.

Yarborough, Lavinia Williams. *Haiti: Dance*. Frankfurt am Main, Germany: Bronners Druckeri, c.1958.

———. "Katherine Dunham Method and Technique: 1940–1945 Notations." In J. Aschenbrenner, "Katherine Dunham: Reflections on the Social and Political Contexts of Afro-American Dance," *Dance Research Annual*, 12 (1980): 121–59.

Yearbook for Traditional Music. 1982–. New York: International Council for Traditional Music.

Yelvington, Kevin A. "The Anthropology of Afro-Latin America and the Caribbean: Diasporic Dimension." *Annual Review of Anthropology* 30 (2001): 227–60.

Zimbalist, Andrew, ed. *Cuba's Socialist Economy towards the 1990s*. London: Lynne Rienner, 1987.

———. "Reforming Cuba's Economic System from Within." In Perez-Lopez, *Cuba at a Crossroad*, 220–38.

Cited Films and Recordings on Dance

Ache Moyuba Oricha. Video recording. Antonio Martin Gonzalez and Christina Gallardo, R. Francis Entertainment, 1990.

Africa. 16mm film with introduction and commentary. Translated by Alistair Cooke. 28 min. Contemporary Films/McGraw Hill, 1967.

Ag'ya. Compilation of Katherine Dunham's original field recordings (1936–37), some with sound imposed and reconstructed versions (1988), with Alvin Ailey Company on YouTube.

Bahia: Africa in the Americas. Video recording. Geovanni and Michael Brewer. 58 min. University of California Media Extension, Berkeley, 1988.

Black Orpheus. Janus Films/Connoisseur Video Collection, Los Angeles.

Conflicto rumba: Persistence of Memory. Documentary DVD recording. Berta Jotar, 2002.

Cuba, I am Time. Recordings with notes. Al Pryor, Jack O'Neil, and Nina Gomes, eds. Bethpage, New York: Blue Jacket Entertainment, 1997.

Cuban Dance Examples: A Glimpse of Cuba through Dance. Documentary video. Yvonne Daniel and Marian Judd. 40 min. New York: Insight Media, 1992.

Cuban Rumba. Documentary video. Yvonne Daniel, Karen Donaldson, and Joel Sax. 50 min. New York: Insight Media, 1992.

Dance in America, Great Performances: Katherine Dunham, JVC Anthology of World Music and Dance. Multicultural Media, Barre, Vermont.

Dancetime! 500 Years. Vol. 1: 15th to 19th centuries. Video recording. Carol Téten. 45 min. Dallas: Dancetime Publications.

Dancing (PBS specials). Rhoda Grauer, Vols. 1–8.

Divine Horsemen. Video recording. Filmed by Maya Deren, 1947–1953; edited and produced by Cherel and Teiji Ito, 1985. Mystic Fire, New York.

Filhos de Gandhy. DVD recording. Lino de Almeida, 2005.

Free to Dance. Madison Davis Lacey, N.Y.

Jack Cole: Jazz. Annette MacDonald and Timeline Films.

JVC/Smithsonian Video Anthology of the Americas. Multicultural Media, Montpelier.

Machito, A Latin Jazz Legacy. Video recording. Carlos Ortiz. 57 min. First Run/ Icarus Films, 1987.

Mambo. 16mm film. Carlo Ponti, Dino de Laurentiis, Robert Rossen, Katherine Dunham. 1954.

Nganga Kiyangala: Congo Religion in Cuba. Video recording. Tato Quiñones and Louis Soto. 1991.

Public Vodun Ceremonies in Haiti. Documentary video. Yvonne Daniel, Sharon Arslanian, Marian Judd, and Glen Kwasny. 55 min. 1997.

Rumba. Film. Oscar Valdés and Hector Vitria. Havana and New York: Center of Cuban Studies, n.d.

Rumba. Marion Gering, William LeBaron. International Movie Database, 1935.

Sacred Choreographies of Cuba and Haiti. Documentary video. Sharon Arslanian and Yvonne Daniel. 20 min. Insight Media, New York, 2005.

Tambor de Mina. Video footage from Maranhão, Brazil. Daniel Halperin. 50 hours. Film Archives of the Smithsonian Institution's American History Museum, 1991.

To Serve the Gods. 16mm film. Karen Kramer. Karen Kramer/Ezurlie Films, New York, 1981.

When the Spirits Dance Mambo. DVD/video recording. Marta Vega and Bobby Shepard, 2003.

Daniel Research DVDs at CBMR in Columbia College, Chicago

#1- Martinican *bele*, courtesy of Dominique Cyrille.

#2- Cuban *tumba francesa*, from Daniel, *Cuban Dance Examples.*

#3- Dominican *sarandunga*, performed by Grupo de San Juan Bautista La Vereda, Familia Juan Pablo Gonzalez, and directed by Confesor Gonzalez, courtesy of Martha Ellen Davis.

#4- St. Lucian *kwadril*, courtesy of the St. Thomas Humanities Council.

#5- Curaçaoan *quadrilla/kuadria*, courtesy of Curaçao National Public Library.

#6- *Curaçaoan danza*, courtesy of Curaçao National Public Library.

#7- French-style Virgin Island *quadrille*, performed by St. Croix *Contredanse* Dancers, courtesy of the St. Thomas Humanities Council.

#8- German-style Virgin Island *quadrille,* performed by St. Thomas and St. John dancers, courtesy of Heywood and Laurel Samuels.

#9a- *quadrille*, performed by St. Thomas Heritage dancers, courtesy of Senator Shawn-Michael Malone.

#9b- *lancers,* performed by St. Thomas Heritage Dancers, courtesy of Senator Shawn-Michael Malone.

#10- Children's *quadrille*, St. Thomas Heritage Dancers, courtesy of Senator Shawn-Michael Malone.

#11- Martinican *haut-taille*, courtesy of Julian Gerstin.

Daniel Research Photographs:
belair and *bele* costumes at CBMB

#1- copy of original lithograph drawn by Agostino Brurias, reprinted by Peter Shim around the time of the Cedulla of Population and published in Besson and Brereton, *The Book of Trinidad*.

#2- Contemporary costume, courtesy of Tobagonian cultural worker Dayne Job.

INDEX

YVONNE DANIEL is a professor emerita of dance and Afro-American studies at Smith College and the author of *Dancing Wisdom: Embodied Knowledge in Haitian Vodou, Cuban Yoruba, and Bahian Candomble* and *Rumba: Dance and Social Change in Contemporary Cuba.*

The University of Illinois Press
is a founding member of the
Association of American University Presses.

———————————————

Composed in 10/13 Sabon LT Std
at the University of Illinois Press
Manufactured by Sheridan Books, Inc.

University of Illinois Press
1325 South Oak Street
Champaign, IL 61820-6903
www.press.uillinois.edu